D1627138

# · MYTHIC WORLDS, MODERN WORDS ·

OTHER TITLES IN THE
COLLECTED WORKS OF JOSEPH CAMPBELL

*Thou Art That:*
*Transforming Religious Metaphor*

*The Inner Reaches of Outer Space:*
*Metaphor As Myth and As Religion*

*Flight of the Wild Gander:*
*Explorations in the Mythological Dimension (Selected Essays 1944–1968)*

*Sake & Satori:*
*Asian Journals — Japan*

*Baksheesh & Brahman:*
*Asian Journals — India*

*The Hero's Journey:*
*Joseph Campbell on His Life and Work*

*Myths of Light:*
*Eastern Metaphors of the Eternal*

More titles forthcoming

# JOSEPH CAMPBELL

• MYTHIC WORLDS,
MODERN WORDS •

ON THE ART OF JAMES JOYCE

Edited and with a foreword by Edmund L. Epstein, Ph.D.

JOSEPH CAMPBELL FOUNDATION

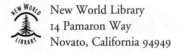 New World Library
14 Pamaron Way
Novato, California 94949

Cover design by Mary Ann Casler
Text design and typography by Tona Pearce Myers

Managing Editor for the first edition of this work was Antony Van Couvering.
Permissions acknowledgments on p. 339 are an extension of the copyright page.

Library of Congress Cataloging-in-Publication Data
Campbell, Joseph,
  Mythic worlds, modern words : on the art of James Joyce / by Joseph Campbell ; edited by E.L. Epstein.
      p.   cm.
Includes bibliographical references and index.
  ISBN 1-57731-406-9 (Hard Cover : alk. paper)
  1. Joyce, James, 1882–1941—Literary style. 2. Joyce, James, 1882–1941—Knowledge—Psychology. 3. Joyce, James, 1882–1941—Knowledge—Mythology.
4. Archetype (Psychology) in literature. 5. Mythology in literature. 6. Myth in literature. 7. Figures of speech. I. Epstein, Edmund L. II. Title.
  PR6019.O9Z526373 2004
  823'.912—dc22                                                   2003024620


First printing, February 2004
ISBN 1-57731-406-9
Printed in Canada on acid-free, partially recycled paper
Distributed to the trade by Publishers Group West

10  9  8  7  6  5  4  3  2  1

# CONTENTS

CHAPTER IV
-

# FINNEGANS WAKE 193

## Introduction

# THE WILDER AFFAIR

## CHAPTER V

## THE SKIN OF WHOSE TEETH? 257

# DIALOGUES

## CHAPTER VI

## DIALOGUES 271

# ABOUT THE COLLECTED WORKS OF
# JOSEPH CAMPBELL

At his death in 1987, Joseph Campbell left a significant body of published work that explored his lifelong passion, the complex of universal myths and symbols that he called "Mankind's one great story." He also left, however, a large volume of unreleased work: uncollected articles, notes, letters, and diaries, as well as audio- and videotape recorded lectures.

The Joseph Campbell Foundation was founded in 1991 to preserve, protect, and perpetuate Campbell's work. The Foundation has undertaken to archive his papers and recordings in digital format, and to publish previously unavailable material and out-of-print works as *The Collected Works of Joseph Campbell*.

THE COLLECTED WORKS OF JOSEPH CAMPBELL
Robert Walter, Executive Editor
David Kudler, Managing Editor

# EDITOR'S FOREWORD

Classically, it was with an enigma that Joseph Campbell entered the labyrinth of James Joyce.

I had gone over to Paris in 1927 to study medieval philology and Old French and Provençal, and here's this *Ulysses, Ulysses, Ulysses.* So I buy the book and take it home, and when I get to chapter three, it starts out: "Ineluctable modality of the visible: at least that if no more, thought through my eyes. Signatures of all things I am here to read . . ." It had been published by Sylvia Beach, at Shakespeare & Co., at 12 rue de l'Odéon in Paris, so I went around there—you know, in high academic indignation: "What do you think of this!" And Sylvia Beach—I didn't know who she was—just took me on and sold me the books that would sell me on Joyce. I took them back to my little room, and that was almost the end of my interest in medieval philology.

So Sylvia Beach gave me the clues about how to read *Ulysses,* and then she sold me this journal called *transition,* published by Eugène Jolas, in which sketches of the early chapters of *Finnegans Wake* were appearing under the title "Work in Progress." That's what taught me. And there you have it. It's funny how it changed my career.[1]

For the next sixty years, until his death in 1987, Campbell moved through the labyrinth of Joyce's creation; using the methods of depth psychology, comparative religion, anthropology, art history, discovering a great many things as he excavated that would form parts of his work in comparative mythology and religion. In the course of his study, he became one of the great students of Joyce. The book he wrote with Henry Morton Robinson, *A Skeleton Key to Finnegans Wake,* has been since 1944 one of the basic texts in Joyce criticism of the *Wake.* However, all the time he was evolving a total explanation of the works of Joyce, and all deriving from the passage in *Ulysses* that provided his initial puzzle.

The passage that puzzled Campbell begins the "Proteus" chapter in *Ulysses.* In this chapter, Stephen Dedalus is walking on Sandymount strand, attempting to make his life cohere. Stephen is very much like Hamlet, in his knowledge that the world is out of joint, both the outer world and his own inner world. Stephen feels that his country is ruled by usurpers, just as Hamlet does, and declares to himself that he, as poet, should be the "ruler" of Ireland. However, in the first chapter we have seen that Ireland respects science, in the person of Buck Mulligan, and England, in the person of Haines. Stephen's inner life is, if anything, more in turmoil than his outer life. His inner life swirls around his constant feeling of guilt for his refusal to pray at his mother's bedside; in fact, his Pyrrhic victory is threatening to paralyze his poetic gift, making the whole sacrifice useless.

Stephen attempts to give form to his inner and outer life by philosophical meditation, again just as Hamlet does. The "Proteus" monologue is the equivalent in Joyce of the "To be or not to be" soliloquy in Hamlet, and just as in that soliloquy, Stephen's meditations on the world as presented to the senses covers a growing despair. When Stephen experiments with visual perception by closing his eyes and walking onward, he says, "Has all vanished since? If I open and am for ever in the black adiaphane." (U31) It is possible to detect a yearning for annihilation, as there is in Hamlet's soliloquy.

"Ineluctable modality of the visible: at least that if no more, thought through my eyes." At least that if no more; the desperation is palpable. Stephen is attempting to find in the phenomenal world what has vanished from his moral universe: a center for the soul. However, according to Schopenhauer, a philosopher who plays a central role in Campbell's analyses, to embrace the phenomenal is to abandon the possibility of moral insight, of a feeling for others. As Campbell explains it:

> The notion of separateness is simply a function of the way our senses experience us here in time and space. We're separate in this room because of space. We're separate from the group that were here last night because of time. These are the separating factors, what Nietzsche calls the *Principium Individuationis,* the individuating factors. And Schopenhauer says this is secondary. The notion of you and the other is a secondary one, and every now and then, this other realization comes up.... [C]ompassion releas[es] you from the ego orientation.[2]

Immersion in sense perception, in the phenomenal world, simply emphasizes your own individuality, an individuality indistinguishable from sterile isolation. Feeling for others, compassion (Schopenhauer's term is *Mitleid*), love, is found only in the noumenal world. A poet must not reject the world of moral sympathy. However, in his attempt to get "thought through my eyes," this is just what Stephen in his despair and pain is attempting.

It is from this root that Campbell's description of the major work of Joyce stems. In the same chapter Stephen thinks of a man who had been drowned a few days before in Dublin Bay and whose body is due to be recovered. For Campbell the sea in which the man has drowned is the sea of phenomena. Stephen asks himself if he would save such a man if he could, and answers,

> I would want to. I would try. I am not a strong swimmer. Water cold soft. When I put my face into it in the basin at Clongowes. Can't see. Who's behind me? Out quickly, quickly! Do you see the tide flowing quickly in on all sides, sheeting the lows of sand quickly, shellcocoa-coloured? If I had land under my feet. I want his life still to be his, mine to be mine. (U38)

"I want his life still to be his, mine to be mine." In this sentence, Stephen affirms the isolation of the individual in the phenomenal world.

*Ulysses,* devoted to the reproduction of the isolated souls in the phenomenal world, is the equivalent for Campbell of Dante's *Inferno,* the realm of hopelessness, where all motion is circular without rising. Hidden within the paralyzed world of *Ulysses,* however, Campbell perceives a purgatorial process, in which the isolated Stephen is released from his circular swamp of guilt by compassion for another sufferer. Campbell sees the breakthrough occurring in the "Circe" chapter. The whores in Nighttown somehow sense that Leopold Bloom is a cuckold and begin to mock him (U463). In the "Oxen of the Sun" chapter, when Stephen was frightened by thunder (U323–324), Bloom had attempted to comfort him. Now Stephen, moved by Bloom's plight, tries to make a diversion and starts babbling about the sexual customs of Paris, which stratagem succeeds in diverting the attention of the whores from Bloom.

If *Ulysses* is *Inferno,* where is the rest of the Dante universe? It is here that Campbell achieves an interpretation of all of the major works of Joyce. *A Portrait* is the equivalent of the *Vita Nuova; Ulysses* is *Inferno,* and *Finnegans Wake* is the journey up the mountain of Purgatory to the Earthly Paradise. The images in *Ulysses,* Campbell argues, are perceived by the "waking consciousness" of Buddhist analysis and represent "gross objects"; *Finnegans Wake,* by contrast, represents the "dream consciousness" of Buddhism, and its objects are "subtle matter," luminous with the *claritas* of complete esthetic apprehension.

*Finnegans Wake* is Purgatory because there is no release from the cycle of the book if the reader chooses not to exit on the final page. In Buddhist terms, rebirth as a return to the world of suffering is what is symbolized by the connection between the final "a way a lone a last a love a long the" and the first word of the *Wake,* "rivverrun." Where, then, is *Paradiso?* For Campbell, Joyce's *Paradiso* is the Fourth Book, the book that Joyce did not live to write. In this book, Campbell hypothesizes, Joyce completes the Dantean journey begun in *Ulysses.* In the Fourth Book, Joyce would have described the indescribable, the state of *nirvāṇa* or *mokṣa,* the state of release from rebirth, which Joyce would have symbolized by the sea.

> …one of the great Hindu images of the World Dream is of Viṣṇu dreaming the universe; we are all part of Viṣṇu's dream. I'm almost certain that he was going to give us the dream of Viṣṇu floating on the ocean. In one of the Indian Purāṇas—one of the Indian Bibles you might call them—in the Mārkandeya Purāṇa, a sage who didn't die when the world dissolved sees Viṣṇu couched on a serpent named Ananta ("unending"), floating on the cosmic ocean out of which all

energy comes. So you have the oceanic level, and you have the animal level of the serpent that forms the couch on which Viṣṇu reclines. Now in the Indian pictures we see the world dream coming from Viṣṇu in the form of a lotus growing from his navel. This lotus unfolds then in history. Joyce says at one time:

"...Now day, slow day, from delicate to divine divases. Padma, brighter and sweetster, this flower that bells, it is our hour or risings. Tickle, tickle. Lotus spray. Till herenext. Adya." (598.11–14)

*Lotus spray:* ["let us pray"] the history of the unfolding of the lotus. And then at the end of the world, the lotus closes and goes back to Viṣṇu's body, and then comes forth again.[3]

——— ∽∿∾ ———

From his first encounter with Joyce's writings in Paris in 1927, Campbell remained deeply involved with the works of Joyce. He gave many lectures on Joyce, frequently read from his works, and published a number of articles on Joyce's works. This book provides a survey of Campbell's Joycean studies by conflating his articles and representative lectures, from his obituary notice on the death of Joyce in 1941 to lectures delivered within a few years of Campbell's death. Also included, in the "Dialogues" section, is a selection of Campbell's responses to questions from members of the audience at some of his lectures. Questions from listeners seemed to fire Campbell, and some of these exchanges provide a deeper insight into the material presented in the formal lectures. This book contains both elementary material and advanced analysis of the work of Joyce; it is, therefore, both an introduction to Joyce's major works and a major contribution to Joyce criticism. The whole provides a representative portrait of Joseph Campbell as a critic of Joyce.

It is an impressive intellectual achievement to go from an enigma to a schema which includes all the major works of a great writer. Whether or not one agrees with all the conclusions of Campbell (I have put some of my reservations in the "Notes"), it is possible to see the magnitude of his achievement for what it is—the fruit of a lifetime's meditation on the works of James Joyce.

This material has been edited to avoid repetition and arranged as a running commentary on *A Portrait, Ulysses,* and *Finnegans Wake.* There has also been some transposition of material to provide smooth transitions, as well as silent editing of the lectures to eliminate hesitations, incomplete comments, and irrelevancies. Where it has been necessary to add more than an individual word or a short phrase to bridge a gap in the conflated texts, I have enclosed such interpolated passages in square brackets. In the "Notes," I have distinguished my notes from Campbell's by putting mine in square brackets. For those students of Campbell who wish to see the original texts from which this conflation was made, transcripts of the lectures and texts of the articles are on file at the Joseph Campbell Archive & Library at Pacifica Graduate Institute in Carpenteria, California.

## Texts of James Joyce

Campbell used a number of different texts of Joyce's works, some of them not readily available to the modern reader, such as his Shakespeare and Company edition of *Ulysses.* For the convenience of the reader, I have used modern standard editions of these works and have checked Campbell's quotations by these editions. No point of Campbell's has been affected by this choice of texts.

A. The edition of *A Portrait of the Artist as a Young Man* that has been used is the "definitive text, corrected from the Dublin holograph by Chester G. Anderson and edited by Richard Ellmann," and published by the Viking Press in 1964.

Quotations from this text appear in this form: (p27); that is, the quote is on page 27 of this edition of *A Portrait.*

B. The text of *Ulysses* is still the subject of intense and bitter debate. Every edition of *Ulysses* contains errors. I have used the edition that is most widely available in the United States, the Random House edition of 1986, the "corrected text" edited by Hans Walter Gabler with Wolfhard Steppe and Claus Melchior. In my opinion, there are still errors in this edition, and in the "Notes" I have also departed from the Gabler edition in two respects: the asterisk at the head of each chapter in the Gabler has been omitted, and the dashes with which Joyce introduced direct discourse, in the French style of citation, have been indented in the French fashion, rather than being allowed to remain flush left as Gabler has printed them. Nothing material is affected in Campbell's text, either by the choice of this edition or by errors in the editions that Campbell used.

Quotations from *Ulysses* appear in this form: (u41–42); that is, the quote is on pages 41 and 42 of the 1986 edition. Present *Ulysses* scholarship is beginning to use the number of the chapter and the number of the lines quoted, as for example (3:461–505), a quotation from the end of the "Proteus" chapter. However, I think my style is simpler for the reader.

C. There is essentially only one text of *Finnegans Wake* at the moment, that of the Viking Press edition of 1958, incorporating Joyce's corrections from the first edition. There are, or seem to be (every statement about the *Wake* requires qualification), errors in this text, and where necessary I have indicated where a modification may be necessary. There are very few such places, and none of them affect Campbell's commentaries.

Quotations from *Finnegans Wake* conform to the usage of present *Wake* scholarship; that is, the page number and the line number of the quotation is given in a parenthesis: (628.8–16) means that the quotation is on page 628, and includes lines 8 to 16. The abbreviation *FW* is not necessary for such a citation form, and has been omitted here.

## ACKNOWLEDGMENTS

I would like to dedicate this book to my wife, Tegwen, who impelled me to complete my first book on Joyce more than twenty years ago.

I would like to acknowledge the active and constant support of Robert Walter, Executive Editor of the *Collected Works of Joseph Campbell,* in the editing and production of this book, and the delightful encounters with Campbell's wife, Jean Erdman. I would like to acknowledge thirty years of consultation with the late Frances Steloff, and the deep debt I owe to William York Tindall, the director of my doctoral studies in Joyce at Columbia. I would also like to thank an old friend, Lois Wallace, who introduced me to Robert Walter, for this and many other favors. Then there are all the rest, some present, some absent.

Edmund L. Epstein, Ph.D.

# James Joyce (1882–1941):
## An Obituary Notice[4]

James Joyce is dead. He died in Zurich. That is the city in which, during the last world war, he devoted himself to the writing of *Ulysses*. When the book appeared people in Scandinavia, Germany, Italy and France attempted to read it. Many succeeded. In the United States and the British Isles the book was burned and banned. That was because it was obscene. Eleven years later an American judge actually studied the book and discovered it to be no more obscene than many another. Whereupon it was legally introduced to the citizens of the United States. It became officially a work of art. It is now available in the Modern Library, 768 pages for $1.25.

James Joyce died of an unsuccessful abdominal operation eight months after the German occupation of Paris. James Joyce between world wars had been a resident of that city. There he had labored on the sequel to *Ulysses, Finnegans Wake*. He had labored seventeen years on this volume, and when it was completed it was permitted publication in the United States and the British Isles. The morning after publication the newspapers declared that it was impossible to discover what the volume was about. The language was obscure. People who purchased copies, intending to read the book between *Gone with the Wind* and *The Grapes of Wrath*, discovered that the language was obscure. Professors in universities indicated that the language was obscure. The book was set aside. Wise Time would decide whether it was enduring art or mere maze and artifice. Then another world war came along and there were published many interesting books about Hitlerism and the meaning of Democracy.

James Joyce died January 13, 1941, at the age of 58, in Zurich, where he had gone to spend the second world war and to compose the book that would culminate his trilogy. It was found difficult to evaluate his death, because Wise Time had not yet brought in a decision about his books. A learned editor of *The New York Times* tentatively declared that the work was ambiguous, enigmatic, pedantic, unintelligible, tiresome, eccentric, spoofing. "Wise Time," said he, "will decide whether it is enduring art or mere maze and artifice." James Joyce had been psychologically queer: naturalist, symbolist, and fantasist, all at once. Furthermore, his language was obscure.

So the Western World, the other day, lost one of its few magnificent men. And he was buried under a heap of newspaper rubbish.

James Joyce, who, as a young man, went heroically forth from his native Dublin to forge in the smithy of his soul the uncreated conscience of his race, and toiled then thirty-seven years to effect a divinely comical transmutation of the entire spectacle of modern life; of the God with Two Arms, not alone in the rock of Peter's church but in every stone in the street, not alone in the Sacrifice of the Altar but in every utterance of man, beast, fowl, or fish—in every sound whatsoever, from the music of the supernal spheres to the splash of a sewer or the crack of a stick; James Joyce, who in one continuous present tense integument slowly unfolded all cycle-wheeling history, is dead.

Lord, heap miseries upon us yet entwine our arts with laughters low.[5]

## · THE NOVELS OF JAMES JOYCE ·

CHAPTER I

# INTRODUCTION[6]

## AFFECT IMAGES

I recently read some articles by Dr. John Weir Perry on the phenomenology of schizophrenia, and I was simply stunned to find that the imagery he observed was exactly that which I had written about in *The Hero with a Thousand Faces*. By speaking of mythological images as *affect images,* images that immediately evoke in the observer equivalent sentiments and emotional impulses, Perry made what to me was an important statement, for my own definition of an effective mythological symbol has been "an energy-releasing and directing sign." As I understand it, Perry has observed that affect images become dissociated in the schizophrenic state: a separation takes place between affect and image; that is to say, one's emotional life is not supplied with images through which it can communicate, not only to others, but to one's own consciousness as well. And in our tradition, of course, mythological images have lost their relationships to affects and are interpreted in terms of rational devaluations or (as in the Hebrew and Christian traditions) in terms of historical events which may or may not have taken place and, in either case, are of little importance to a person's psyche today.

One of the things I hope to do in these talks is make some connection between what I have learned from Perry about the imagery of schizophrenia and the imagery in Joyce's visionary writing. Looking at the work of James Joyce in the light of Perry's observations, I realize that ever since I first encountered *Ulysses* and the *Portrait* in Paris in 1927, Joyce has been a kind of guide for my own interpretation of mythological material. The big thing Joyce did for me, and might also do for others, is bring the vast heritage of mythological images that we have from many many sources and strains of thought into relationship with my own affect system. The work of Joyce is a bringing together of the personal experience of affect with the general heritage of affect images. I think this is the impact. What I am going to try to do here is point out how it seems to me Joyce built these images.

It's my feeling that our imagery has been deprived of its affect by our strongly rational tendency in the interpretation of images and by our religious traditions concretizing symbols, so that they refer, not past themselves to symbolic themes, but to historical events—when, for example, we interpret the resurrection of Christ as having been an historical event instead of seeing the resurrection as a psychologically crucial moment of crisis, this deprives the imagery of its affect. And when you have a priesthood that is simply repeating what has been taught in theological seminaries and not, as in the world of art, rendering individual personal experiences, then you have a group of teachers who are not teaching us, so to say, how to relate our experiences to the imagery.

I distinguish between traditional and creative mythologies in this way: the traditions present systems of images to which one is supposed to have certain responses, and one either will or won't have those responses; the artist has an experience first and then seeks the imagery through which to render it. And these are reverse processes. The priest is a communicator of inherited images. Unless he is a superb pedagogue, he is not watching to see whether the person to whom he is communicating the image is ready for that image yet; and there's nothing more stultifying than receiving all the significant images at a time too early for you to experience them. They're all dead then when you come to them.

I have learned from Perry's discussion of the schizophrenic problem that there are a number of types of experience that can dissociate the individual from his environment, and we are going to find all of them in *A*

*Portrait of the Artist as a Young Man.* First, there is the experience of being an outsider for one reason or another. In the *Portrait,* the little boy goes to a school where athletics play a big role, and he is no good at them. He falls down. He is chilly. He is anxious. To compensate for this experience of being outside, Perry says, inner fantasies arise that put the individual at the heart of belongingness. One of the principal images, or tendencies toward imaging, in the schizoid situation is that of seeking to find a center. There is a psychic shift to an unknown place which will be the center, and the imagery associated with that centering is very important in the person's thinking. You have the cross and the center.

A second situation Perry identifies as a damaged self-image. This can happen when parents continually scold a child or tell him he is doing things the wrong way, rather than thanking him and complimenting him for his little positive achievements. Or if a person comes into an environment where his character is not appreciated, where his cultural heritage or the social milieu from which he comes is not respected (where, for example, his race is not respected) then his self-image can be damaged. Perry says that to compensate for a damaged self-image there comes this urge for power, this quest for the feeling that one has the power to bring one's own psychological field into order. And this again we are going to get in Stephen very strongly. There are a number of reasons for his damaged self-image, and we see in him the notion of his power to bring order into his life. That is what lies behind his strong estheticism: an esthetic urge to organize a field—the field, first, of the work of art, but then the field, also, of his whole life.

A third type of experience involves a negative mother-fixation, which entangles the person in a rather tawdry and inadequate sort of family network, so that he doesn't grow out of his infantile context. The mother then becomes a kind of threatening figure (a strongly disciplining mother perhaps plays a role of this kind) and to compensate for that, one has an urge to find and become related to the great father image. Now this runs through—in fact, this is—*Ulysses.* Stephen's family is a rather disheveled one. They have dropped considerably in their economic status. His father is an Irish chap about town, rollicking around and kidding with his friends and so on, and young Stephen feels alienated from him and seeks then the great father. His search for this great father, in contrast to the father whom his mother married, is the big motif. And Stephen wants to bypass, not only the father whom his mother married, but also his mother's God—that is to say, his mother's idea of God as taught to him in childhood, the God that the priests represent. Stephen wants to go past all of that to another father-image entirely.

A fourth situation that leads to schizophrenia is an experience of life as something that is fiercely controlled rather than something that can be genially lived. And we certainly get that in the *Portrait,* with those Jesuits and their extremely severe discipline. The Irish Jesuits, some of whom I myself experienced in my youth, are extremely formidable in this way. They tolerate no nonsense, and they'll take the strap to you if you are not on the line. No juvenile delinquency allowed here. Stephen experiences this fierce rigidity of Irish Catholicism quite intensely, and to compensate for that—and now we come to the main theme of the process—his psyche drifts toward the quest for the principle of *eros,* as opposed to the principle of *thanatos:* the will in the way of erotic and loving experiences—pleasure, rather than the fierce disciplines.

As a result of these types of experiences, the person's self-image is lost. And the characteristic result is a split self-image, which is the beginning of schizophrenia. The individual imagines himself to be the outcast, the clown, the fool; and at the same time (on another level, more secretly) he imagines himself to be the desired hero, the one who is going to set right not only his own life, but the whole world. Prominent in the mind of the schizophrenic in this context are images of world kingship, the divine king at the center of the world, and also savior images. These are precisely the two images in the Buddha history and in Christ's history also: Christ the King and Christ the Savior; the Buddha, the *Cakravartin,* the Lord of the World, and at the same time the Savior. Every schizophrenic could say with Christ (so to speak), "My kingdom is not of this world." He is king, yet the world that he is to bring about is the new world. These are all images in the mind of the schizophrenic, but he hasn't the power to coordinate the flow of images that come upon him.

Perry analyzed the imagery of the schizophrenic crisis and found ten motifs, all of which appear in the hero's journey as I described it years and years ago.[7] The difference between the hero's journey and the schizophrenic's plight is that the schizophrenic falls into a swamp of disorganized impacts from these images, but the hero, the one with the energy to master the situation, goes through in a progressive sequence.

The first of these motifs is the tendency to try to find a new world center. There is a shift of center from the world in which the individual finds himself to one that he intends to establish. We will see Stephen Dedalus do this. In the early chapters of *A Portrait,* he is becoming disillusioned with his world, and then comes the moment when he experiences the vision of the girl in the stream (P171–173), and his own new center begins. In the *Vita Nuova,* Dante starts in the new center with the beholding of Beatrice, and with that vision, the world drops off. In Stephen's case, however, the world drops off first, then he finds his center.

The second motif, that of death or sacrifice, dismembering of the hero, is what we get throughout *Ulysses.* In the lectures on *Ulysses* I will accent some of the sections where Joyce brings out this motif.

Proceeding directly from this motif is the third, the return to the beginning: the imagery of descent from the light world into the abyss. In *Ulysses* this culminates in the *Walpurgisnacht* scene in the brothel, where everything splits to pieces and goes flying apart. This certainly is a schizoid situation: a pellmell of disconnected images rush forward, which Joyce the artist connects by simply indicating echoes from one to the other, but the hero is not connecting.

Now associated with these first three motifs are two more. The fourth motif is that of cosmic conflict: the conflict between light and dark, good and evil, god and devil. Joyce renders this in *Ulysses* by a Black Mass. The whole of *Ulysses* is a Black Mass, which comes to its fulfillment in the *Walpurgisnacht* scene of the "Circe" chapter, where the Black Mass becomes equivalent to the White Mass—as when you hold up a mirror, and everything that was reversed is then seen the right way. So when the angels cry out "Alleluia!"—Praise the Lord! Praise God!—"God" is simply the word "dog" reversed (U489–490): God is present in the dog. Further, the Adonai's cry of "Dooooooooooog!" also evokes the important theme in *Ulysses* of the dog, the symbol of "beastly" death: in the third chapter (U37–39), for example, a dog stops roaming on the beach to sniff at the body of a drowned dog, which brings yet again to Stephen's mind the theme of death.

The fifth motif is fear of the opposite sex—and fear of being turned into the opposite sex. Now, Bloom has no such fear. "O, I so want to be a mother,"[8] he says, and then he gives birth to eight wonderful children, gold and silver, who immediately assume high offices of state. (U403) But Stephen's problem from the beginning of the book is that the female principle is catching up with him and threatening to engulf him; and in the *Walpurgisnacht,* it is the appearance of his dead mother, dripping with gore and with a crab (cancer) eating her, that drives him beyond his senses.(U473-475)

These five motifs are all of negative, shattering images. Now come five positive ones, two of which Perry names. The first is apotheosis, when the hero finally puts himself in the position of, or imagines himself to be, the universal king or savior. We will see Stephen doing this. The other motif Perry mentions is that of the sacred marriage, where the hero (if it's a male hero) marries the divine goddess, or if the hero is a woman, she marries the divine progenitor and then gives birth to the hero child.

The eighth, ninth, and tenth motifs are the fulfillment images: new birth (that's the eighth), an idealized society (the ninth), and tenth, images of a quadrated world: the garden of paradise where rivers flow to all four points of the compass. *Finnegans Wake,* in four books, is a quadrated world, not only spatially, but also in terms of temporal cycles (the ages of gold, silver, bronze, and iron).

Now the difference between the schizophrenic's situation and that of the true hero is that the hero has the courage and energy to integrate all these images. When the hero lives out of his own nature and center, there is an integrity in his life that guides him through these images; but if he is unable to assimilate them, he disintegrates.

## WINGS OF ART

When you open *A Portrait of the Artist as a Young Man,* the first thing you come on is a little statement in Latin, *"et ignotas animum dimittit in artes"*: "and he turns his mind to unknown arts." This line is from Ovid's *Metamorphoses* (Book 8, line 188), where it refers to Daedalus, the great master craftsman who fashioned the labyrinth in Crete. The mystery of the labyrinth is the work of this artist, who is regarded in the classical tradition as the patron of the arts. You will recall that King Minos, the tyrant of Crete, tried to keep Daedalus as a kind of serf, but he determined to fly from Crete with his son Icarus. So Daedalus *turns his mind to unknown arts,* makes two sets of waxen wings, and they do fly. The opening motto, then, refers to Joyce's decision to make wings of art. Now this motif of flight and the bird of art is a dominant one throughout Joyce's work. It even appears right at the end of *Finnegans Wake,* written years and years and years after the writing of this little line in the *Portrait.* I don't know why it is that people talking about the flight of the artist always refer to Icarus and not to Daedalus. Icarus flew too high, the wax on his wings melted, and he fell into the ocean. The sentiment on most people's part seems to be that artists can't make it. Well, Daedalus did. Joyce was an optimist with respect to the capacity of a competent artist to achieve release.

Now what is the sense of this motto? The first allegory that comes to mind is: Daedalus escaped from Crete to the mainland, Joyce escaped from the provincial culture of Ireland to its great mainland source. But Joyce is also making another flight: from the symbolism of the Roman Catholic Church to the universals that Jung calls the "archetypes," of which Christian imagery is an inflection. He escapes (so to speak) from his own spiritual provincialism into the total humanity which is our deep shared heritage.

As a Catholic, Joyce was brought up surrounded by Catholic inflections of Jung's archetypes. When you go into a Catholic home, what pictures do you see? You see the Madonna, you see crucifixes, you see the Christ with (as Leopold Bloom puts it) his heart on his sleeve. The Catholic child is brought up in the presence of these mythological images. He is an expert in archetypal images. His mother and father, for example, are simply local inflections of the great archetypes of the Virgin Mother and God the Father. The Catholic youngster growing up, however, has the problem of relating the actual world to the images he's been brought up with that somehow don't fit. What Joyce does is start with those images behind him and the world out there, and then he opens the imagery out and hands it back with changes of associations all over the place.

In my own case, I too had been brought up a Roman Catholic, and long before reading Joyce I had lost all conviction in the force of the images. With Joyce, I learned how one can open out the local symbols into larger ones, and what the psychological aspect of this journey might be. I think the work of Joyce will do this for others as well, not only with respect to Christian imagery, but with respect to whatever heritage one has.

In relation to the art of the novel, there is here a further point to be made: James Joyce inherited the late-nineteenth-century tradition of the naturalistic novel, and the motto at the opening of *A Portrait*—"and he turns his mind to unknown arts"—suggests that his flight is to be, not only from provincial Ireland to the mainland and from Roman Catholicism to the great archetypes of myth, but also from the naturalistic novel to the archetypes of mythology as well. The details of a life are themselves to be opened out so we can feel the archetypes playing under them.

Joyce wasn't the only person who was working that way at that time. One of the things I found most interesting about the literature of the first half of the twentieth century is that a number of authors, starting out from that naturalistic tradition, then went by stages into the sphere of mythological thought. In this regard, the one whom I think of always in relation to James Joyce is Thomas Mann: Joyce was a Catholic who left Catholicism behind, Mann was a Protestant who left his Protestant heritage behind, and their first works came out within a few years of each other. The first work of each was naturalistic, but with an esthetic echoing device that began to point the emotions past the naturalistic level.

After the First World War, each man (ignorant of what the other was doing) turned out a major work, apparently naturalistic in form, that went into the mythological realm. Mann's *Magic Mountain* appeared in 1924, Joyce's *Ulysses* in 1922, and in both works there's a deliberate calling-in of myth, using intentionally and with direct references the mythology of the hero's voyage into the world of darkness, the abyss, and the return. When we come to *Ulysses,* I'll show how Joyce handled this. Then in their last works—Joyce's *Finnegans Wake,* which appeared in 1939, and Thomas Mann's *Joseph* novels (1934–44)—both abandoned the upper world and plunged into the myth world entirely. It was Joyce's intention to write still another work, which would have completed his journey, you might say, but he died before doing so.

## Consubstantial Metamorphoses

Ovid's *Metamorphoses,* from which Joyce drew his opening motto, gives us another clue. There is a wonderful scene in the fifteenth book of *Metamorphoses,* where Ovid is talking to Pythagoras, a sage living in isolation who gives the theme of the book: namely, that the one animating power is moving from one form to another, showing itself in the animal world, the plant world, the human world, the divine world. Nothing dies. The spirit simply appears in various forms—these metamorphoses take place. Ovid, furthermore, gathers his myths in categories. He gives many examples of the god and nymph in play, for instance, or of the son seeking the father, so that again we see that these great themes appear in many metamorphoses.

Now a theme throughout Joyce's work, and central to *Ulysses,* is consubstantiality, which is a theological concept. God the Father, God the Son, and God the Holy Ghost are said to be consubstantial: three distinct personalities in one divine substance. What is that substance? What is its psychological validity? Are the father and son consubstantial? Questions such as these are moving in Stephen's mind throughout the work. So in a sense, Ovid has given Joyce, not only the start from Ireland to the mainland, but also this theme of consubstantiality, the one form showing through all things.

Furthermore, any good edition of Ovid's *Metamorphoses* is as fine a handbook of the classical mythological tradition as you can get. You have only to look up in the index what you are interested in, and there it is. But what you notice as soon as you open Ovid is that the main lines of the stories are duplicated also in the Bible, so that you can jump from the classical tradition to the Semitic tradition. Antecedent to both, of course, is the Sumero-Babylonian tradition, from which both the Greek and the Hebrew have come. So we are moving back to sources again, moving from the provincial worlds of the classical and the biblical to the earlier worlds from which they stem. We are beginning to find that there is, as it were, a general human tradition that shows itself in all these myths.

Ovid's time, you may recall, was the period of the great Hellenistic coming together of Oriental and Occidental materials. And Joyce follows that through. Early in *Ulysses,* he moves into the Oriental sphere, talking about the Upaniṣads and the theosophical movement in Dublin and London in those days, and in all of his narrative climaxes he makes use of Hindu mythological images: Śiva, Śakti, and so on. What he is doing is not mere eclecticism. He is compounding all these myths in a valid syncretism, pointing out that they are all metamorphoses of a basic material. And when Joyce writes *Finnegans Wake,* the two main characters shine through everything in the book, just as the one animating spirit, the light of God, shines through all things. Their names keep resounding in one change after another: Humphrey Chimpden Earwicker, HCE, the hero in his mythological aspect whose initials stand for Here Comes Everybody; and his spouse Anna Livia Plurabelle, ALP, whose initials spell *Alp,* the German word for a demon that causes a nightmare,[9] but she is the *śakti* of her spouse. They are one, and they shine through everything.

## Joyce and the Jungian Unconscious

Now while Joyce and Mann were descending into the mythological realm, in exactly those same years, Frazer was undertaking the same exploration in anthropology, and Freud and Jung in psychology, and all of them were interpreting mythology in psychological terms.

Frazer's rational, associational approach was pre-Freudian, and he was frustrated when he tried to find the ultimate interpretations of these symbolic forms. He interpreted them in a late-nineteenth-century way as being mistakes. Magic, for instance, he interpreted in terms of what he called a "sympathetic system": because ideas are associated in the person's mind, the person thinks they are associated in fact. For instance, you shake a rattle and make a sound like rain falling, and you think it is going to bring rain. That's an example of association by imitation, or what he called the "Law of Similarity." Or a nail pierces your foot, so to heal yourself you clean the nail and take care of it. That's an example of association of contiguity, of things that have touched, which he termed the "Law of Contagion." Frazer did not realize, however, that there are associations on the unconscious level which are not susceptible to rational interpretation.

Frazer was Freud's anthropologist. Freud began with Frazer and simply followed the same route, but he dropped in the dimension of the unconscious. Freud's unconscious is the repressed recollections of one's infancy. The contents of the unconscious, for Freud, once were conscious and can be made conscious again through analysis, and that is the cure. In other words, they stem from biography, from your own life. And in *Totem and Taboo,* he interpreted the great mythological motifs of the totemic and taboo systems in terms of remembered and repressed historical events. So the Freudian unconscious is essentially an unconscious of a biographical and historical order. It is as though you had written something badly on a memo pad, and when you come back, you can't recall what it was you wrote down. And it's annoying: you know it means something, but you can't read what it is. Then, perhaps, you think back—"Oh, I remember!"—and you can read what you wrote.

Jung accepted Freud's unconscious—that is, the unconscious containing images from personal experience, which Jung called the "personal unconscious." But Jung went a step further. When someone came to him with dreams to be interpreted, in order to discover that person's associations out of his biographical experiences, Jung would ask: "What does this make you think of? What does that make you think of?" Every now and then, however, an image appeared in one of his patients' dreams that the person had never experienced, a mythological image. The person had dropped out of the realm of personal recollection and into another realm.

So Jung theorized that the contents of the unconscious were not only the residuum of personal experiences, but also functions of the dynamics of the human body which the person didn't invent. The unconscious for Jung, then, came first. It was primary. Consciousness was something that arose out of unconsciousness. Biologically, this is a fact, both in terms of the history of the race and in terms of the history of the individual. The child's body and its functioning and all the implications of that body are fashioned in the mother's womb. The child isn't rationalizing about this; it is born with a lot of impulses that it never decided to have. When these are pushed back or frustrated or thrown off the line, discombobulations occur which then have to be corrected. And from where does the correction come? It comes from the body impulse. So Jung postulated the existence of what he called a "collective unconscious," and he interpreted the mythological imagery in a patient's dreams, not by asking, "What does this remind you of?" but by looking around to see what that symbol has meant forever in myths: a technique he called "amplification through comparative mythological studies."

Jung's thesis was that the unconscious compensates for consciousness: it has a positive, corrective value. For Freud, the imagery of the unconscious is trying to disguise wishes that are taboo. For Jung, the imagery of the unconscious is not trying to disguise, rather it is trying to tell you the correction of your conscious attitude, but you can't read it because you have forgotten the language. Jung says, "It is like a text in a script that you haven't deciphered. And so," he says, "let's decipher it." How does one decipher a script? He takes what he calls the "philological attitude." You get a letter from a friend who doesn't write very clearly, and there is a word you can't make out at all; you look at the first letter to see if there is another one like it in a word that you can read—"Now, yes, she's making her A's this way this year"—and then the next letter, and so on, and thus you put the word together. So it is with a dream. When there is a moment that you can't interpret, you look to see how it has been interpreted in other manifestations of the unconscious.

Joyce takes Jung's attitude toward the unconscious. It is interesting to read Joyce's novels in relation to what one knows of Jung and see there exactly the themes that Jung has already explicated. When we move from the *Portrait* through *Ulysses* to *Finnegans Wake,* we find the same motifs coming up, the same themes being amplified. But in the *Portrait,* we are dealing with biography, with waking life; in *Ulysses,* we are moving through the dream realm of the biographical unconscious, with archetypal echoes beginning to come up; and when we get to *Finnegans Wake,* about the time when we were "yung and easily freudened" (115.22–23), the power of the archetypes takes right over, and the characters mix right into each other.

## Joyce's Dantean Model

Now the next point. Joyce's master and model was Dante. I think it is fair to say that Dante, in his wonderful *Vita Nuova* and *The Divine Comedy,* brings to experiential statement the implications of the medieval gothic dogmas, for he renders the motifs, not as dogma, but as experienced affect. Dante's first work, the *Vita Nuova,* is a collection of poems with commentary that he wrote as a youth in praise of a girl named Beatrice Portinari. At the conclusion of the *Vita Nuova,* Dante says, "I now stop writing and go to prepare myself to write of her such a book as has never before written of woman." The book he wrote, recounting how the aspect of Beatrice wakened his inner eye and carried him finally to the very throne of God, was the *Commedia,* composed in three parts: *Inferno, Purgatorio,* and *Paradiso.* Joyce imitates Dante. Joyce's first work, *A Portrait of the Artist as a Young Man,* is the equivalent of the *Vita Nuova* and imitates it in all of its basic themes. Then Joyce moves on to his own "Divine Comedy," which was also to have been in three parts: *Ulysses,* as the *Inferno; Finnegans Wake,* as the *Purgatorio;* and the book Joyce didn't live to write, as the *Paradiso.*

Why is *Ulysses* the *Inferno?* What is hell? Hell is the state of a soul that is absolutely committed to its earthly experiences, fixed (as it were) in their time-space aspects, without recognizing through these experiences the radiance of the divine dimension. Hell is simply the experience of your limitations, to which you are so firmly committed that nothing can break them. No one can show you the divine dimension of life that transcends your experiences. That is the state of the characters in *Ulysses:* they are bound, locked in the hard ring of their ego systems, devaluing the mystical dimension. As Dante and Virgil wander through hell looking at souls bound to their little circles, so too do Stephen and Bloom wander through Dublin. Dante takes us to hell and shows us the people of Florence there; it is impossible to understand Dante without footnotes that tell you who these different characters were, what their lives were like, and why they are there. So, Dante depicts Florence as hell. Joyce reverses this idea: he depicts hell as Dublin. Dante pitches us out of this world and into the mythological dimension. Joyce brings the mythological dimension into the world and shows us this dimension through the world.

Why is *Finnegans Wake* the *Purgatorio?* Purgatory is a kind of graduate school into which go souls who have learned the lessons of life well, but not well enough to graduate into heaven. Their spirit has been somewhat opened, but not to the extent of being able to apprehend the Beatific Vision. So their occluding commitments, what are called venial sins, sins that can be cleared away, must be purged away in Purgatory so that their eyes can open to the Beatific Vision. This is the equivalent of the reincarnation motif in Oriental systems: from one life to another you become cleansed of your occluding limitations until finally you are utterly released. Joyce has made a complete analogy between the motifs of purgatory and reincarnation. What is being reincarnated is, not only the individual, but also the universe. It goes around and around and around—that's the motif of the circle that the Buddha holds up when he assumes the teaching posture: round and round and round. How do you get out? *Finnegans Wake* is written in a circle with a break: There is an out. It is exactly the purgatory;

exactly the reincarnation. [But if one avoids the circle of rebirth,] one goes out into the void—which would have been [the setting of] Joyce's *Paradiso,* the book of heaven.[10]

One more point on this part of my story. Joyce, in his theory of art, divides writing into three categories: the lyric, the epic, and the dramatic.[11] The lyric mode presents the statement in immediate relation to the subject: "Oh, I feel great! Oh my, I feel wonderful!" The dramatic presents the objects in immediate relation. When you see a stage presentation, the author (properly, at any rate) isn't sticking his head out from the wings saying, "Isn't she wonderful? Now watch here, this is the way." The objects are simply presented, and all their implications must come from them. The epic mode is intermediate between the two: the objects are presented, and the author's comment is present as well. Joyce definitely decided to use the dramatic mode, and he renders his material in the style of the person he is writing about. *A Portrait of the Artist as a Young Man,* for instance, opens with a little boy, just a tiny tot. And it begins with this sentence:

> Once upon a time and a very good time it was there was a moocow coming down along the road and this moocow that was coming down along the road met a nicens little boy named baby tuckoo.... (P7)

Now that's not how Joyce at the age of twenty-one was talking. That's the little boy talking, and the style grows up with him. By page twelve it's like the style Hemingway used for his first writing. When Stephen becomes a college student, suffering all the religious agonies of a college student, the style is that of Cardinal Newman. Later, in *Ulysses,* the style for each chapter is a sheer invention meant to render by its form the affect of the time of day and intention of the scene. And when Joyce moves to the dream world of *Finnegans Wake,* the psychological interior world of churning archetypes with the light shining through, Joyce writes in dream language, so that the words carry multiple meanings:

> Sir Tristram, violer d'amores, fr'over the short sea, had passencore rearrived from North Armorica on this side the scraggy isthmus of Europe Minor to wielderfight his penisolate war: nor had topsawyer's rocks by the stream Oconee exaggerated themselse to Laurens County's gorgios while they went doublin their mumper all the time: nor avoice from afire bellowsed mishe mishe to tauftauf

thuartpeatrick: not yet, though venissoon after, had a kidscad buttended a bland old isaac: not yet, though all's fair in vanessy, were
sosie sesthers wroth with twoone nathandjoe. (3.4–12)

Now that's really different. What the heavenly language was to have
been for Joyce's unwritten fourth book, we do not know, but Joyce is re-
ported to have said that it was going to be lucid, simple, and clear. Which
is as it should have been for Paradise.

———~/\/\/~———

With that little prelude, then, we have the concept of affect images, oper-
ating both in the schizoid situation and in the hero's journey; we have the
classical Ovid behind us in the beginning, with the image of Joyce's
Daedalus flight and the suggestion that all mythologies are metamorphoses
of form of a single great mythological system—the theme of consubstantiality; we have an understanding of Jung's conception of the unconscious,
which Joyce embraced; and we have Dante as our guide to the gothic
inflection of themes echoed through Joyce, who will read the whole of
modern life, all the paraphernalia of the modern world (little of which ex-
isted in Dante's time), re-seen and re-cooked (so to say) in this brew of
mythological themes.

What I propose to do is, first, go through *A Portrait;* then explore
*Ulysses;* and finally, as a kind of "Let's all have fun," read and comment on
sections of *Finnegans Wake,* which is something I enjoy doing very much.
But the real question we will be addressing throughout is how you get your
own life-imagery to link to the great archetypes; that is to say, how to re-
join affect and image (which I think Joyce has done), so that you experience in terms of your own affects, not only the imagery of your own life,
but the imagery of the whole heritage of human culture.

## CHAPTER II

# A PORTRAIT OF THE ARTIST AS A YOUNG MAN

## ESTHETIC ARREST

Since Dante was Joyce's model, let me preface our examination of *A Portrait* with the *Vita Nuova*. In the very beginning, Dante beholds Beatrice. She is nine years old, and so is he is. When he next sees her, they are both eighteen (twice 9; 1 + 8 = 9), so there is a human apparition at the root, and the dimension of mystery leads to God. Dante's entire work is going to follow that line to the root. When Dante sees Beatrice, he experiences what we may call "esthetic arrest." It is an eternal moment. He says, "At this moment, the lord of my heart recognizes that I have found my master. The lord of my senses recognizes that I have found my bliss. The lord of my body recognizes that I have found my agony." What he sees is not simply a lovely girl, but a ray of the light of eternity. It opens his third eye (his inward eye); the world drops back a dimension; his life is now committed to this seizure. He writes a poem about the experience, and he analyzes the poem, telling us all about the circumstances surrounding its composition. Then, exactly in the middle of the book, Beatrice dies, and his sentiments are pitched further out of the world, into another reach of that dimension. At the end, he promises to write of her such a book as has been never written. In *A Portrait* this same principle is followed.

About this miracle of esthetic arrest: Dante comes out of the trouba-
dour tradition, and the troubadours achieve a definition of love in their
discussions. Now usually when people talk of love, particularly in ecclesi-
astical circles, they contrast *agapē* with *eros,* as though these two were the
only possibilities. Both *agapē* (spiritual love, Christian love) and *eros* (mere
biological, physical love) are indiscriminate: *agapē* ("love thy neighbor as
thyself") means that no matter who your neighbor is you love that person,
which is a fine sentiment of course; as for *eros,* it's really the lure and
appeal of the organs to organs—in the dark anyone will do. In the early or-
giastic cults, indiscriminate love was the rule; and one doesn't have to go
back that far to encounter love of that kind. However, love as defined by
the troubadours is different. Guiraut de Borneilh, one of the great twelfth-
century poets of Provençe, describes love as being born of the eyes and the
heart—which is exactly what Dante said. De Borneilh says:

> ... the eyes are the scouts of the heart,
> And the eyes go reconnoitering
> For what it would please the heart to possess.[12]

And when the eyes have found an object that fascinates them, they recom-
mend this object to the heart. If it is a "gentle heart"—that is to say, a heart
capable not simply of lust, but of love—that heart is wakened, and love
is born. This is specific. This is *amor.* It's not for everybody; it's for the
gentle heart, whose scouts are the eyes.

In Dante also, the beginning of this journey, this personal call, comes
into being through distinctly personal experience of love, not through an
undifferentiated experience. I have called this experience of personal love
"esthetic arrest."

Dante, in the *Vita Nuova,* elucidates his esthetic theory in a sophisti-
cated way. Joyce, in *A Portrait,* also states his esthetic theory directly and
openly. This theory, which he formulated very clearly, is a classic and completely well-understood and realized theory of esthetics. One studies esthetics and reads this author, that author, the other, and it all seems so
complicated. Joyce puts his knife through all that complication and comes,
as he came in every aspect of his work, to a very clean, precise definition.

Joyce distinguishes between proper and improper art. Proper art is art
in the service of what is properly the function of art. Improper art is art in

the service of something else. And, Joyce says, proper art is static and improper art is kinetic. Static art produces esthetic arrest. What, then, is the opposite of static art? What does Joyce mean by kinetic art? He tells us:

> Desire is the feeling which urges us to go to something and loathing is the feeling which urges us to go from something and that art is improper which aims at exciting these feelings in us whether by comedy or by tragedy.[13]

Pornographic art is art that excites desire. It is not proper art. If you see a picture of a dear old lady, for example, and you think, "What a lovely old soul! I'd love to have a cup of tea with her"—that is pornography. You are exciting desire for a relationship to the object. Or you open a magazine and see a picture of a refrigerator and a beautiful girl standing beside it and smiling, and you think, "I would love to have a refrigerator like that." This is not art, Joyce says, it is pornography. Or you go into the home of people who like to ski in the wintertime, and you see pictures of Alpine peaks and wonderful ski slopes; all that is pornography. It excites desire for the object depicted; it is not a reaction to the artwork itself.

Another type of improper art is art critical of society, art in the service of sociology. Such art excites loathing, and Joyce calls it "didactic art." Those who produce such art I call "didactic pornographers."Almost all of our novels since Zola's time are didactic pornography. The formula was established by Zola, and it has endured down to our day: you have wonderful moral lessons, and then people take their clothes off all over the place. The esthetic experience has nothing to do with biology or sociology. It has to do with that "waking" which Dante spoke of.

Now how does Joyce describe Dante's waking? Since neither desire nor loathing is to be excited, what is to be excited? Joyce then goes to Aquinas for his next set of definitions. Aquinas says, in short, that beauty is what pleases[14]—which is not of much help. But then he defines the key aspects of the esthetic experience in terms of three Latin words: *integritas, consonantia,* and *claritas.* Stephen translates them as "wholeness," "harmony," and "radiance."

*Wholeness:* The thing rendered is to be seen as one object set off from everything else in the world. We can, for example, draw a frame around part of this shelf, let us say, and the elements within that frame—two candles, a section of shelf, a fraction of a picture, a bit of a bottle—are one object. The rest of the shelf is totally other. We are to concentrate only on what is within that frame. It is to be seen as one object.

*Harmony:* When you have seen whatever is within the frame as one object, what matters is the arrangement of forms in relationship to each other: part to part, each part to the whole, and the whole to each of its parts: That rhythmical organization, what Joyce calls "the rhythm of beauty," is the magical thing. These parts include colors, relationship of colors, forms, intensities of light.

The instrument of art is rhythm. This is also true in writing—in prose and in poetry. If you are writing simply to communicate information, your concerns are only the length of your sentences (they shouldn't be too long) and organizational clarity: that within each paragraph you're saying what you intend to say and presenting a clean, neat statement. However, if an esthetic effect is to be achieved, then the rhythm of the prose counts. The precise selection of words, the way the consonants follow each other along, and so on: all of that counts. Poets are also interested in the sounds of the words, which is why you have rhyme and rhythm. This is art.

*Radiance:* When the artwork is well achieved, when the object is fortunately rendered, it fascinates. It is satisfactory, adequate in itself. That is the radiance. If it's a radiance that doesn't overwhelm you, we call it beauty. But if the radiance so diminishes your ego that you are in an almost transcendent rapture, this is the sublime. What renders the sublime is immense space or immense power. Very little art handles the sublime. I don't know of any. One can, however, experience the sublime. For instance, one of the intentions of Buddhist monuments and Japanese gardens is to bring you up, up, up, so that the space that you behold becomes vaster and vaster and vaster. The breaking open of a vast space is a curious experience: with the diminishing of ego, you get a sense of release, and your own inner space opens out. I have talked with people who were in middle-European cities during American and British saturation bombing—that horrible business. They said that they were blown away by the immensity of the power, that the experience of ecstasy can come in these situations.

Now this *radiance* is a mysterious psychological problem: why is it that one arrangement pleases and another does not? The whole function of the artwork, says Joyce, is to hold you to that rhythmical arrangement. Then you see it is that thing which it is and no other thing. You are not moved with desire or with fear or with loathing. You are simply held in esthetic arrest by the beautiful accord, Joyce's "rhythm of beauty," the "enchantment of the heart." This is a breakthrough. You have gone through the object and felt the transcendence that manifests through it, the transcendence of which you are yourself a manifestation. Pure object turns you into pure subject. You are simply the eye, the world eye, regarding beyond desire and loathing, just as God beholds the world on the seventh day. Nothing to do. This is it.

This brings us to a deep mystical realization: there is no *meaning* there. In the absolute sense, the universe and all the things in the universe are absolutely without meaning. Meanings are rational associations to thought systems and relationships. No sooner do we hear this than we recall that the Buddha is known as the one "thus come" (*tathāgata*), and that Buddha consciousness is simply the consciousness of what is. What is; ethics, morality, biology, and so on, all are relationships on this side of that realization. When one realizes in the esthetic impact that it is the radiant object which is acting and no other thing, one is pushed beyond the meaning sphere (so to say) and is thrown into one's own being. The subject proper to that radiant object is experienced as yourself. This is a great moment, and it is exactly the Buddha's illumination. You'll recall the story of the Buddha at the Bodhi-tree: the Immovable Spot, esthetic arrest, stasis. When the Lord of Life, whose name is Lust and Death, came to him, the Buddha simply touched the earth, Nature, which has the depth rooted in the trinity, you might say. The Buddha dispelled the Lord of Desire and Loathing and was himself in the middle spot. This point is supremely important: in our world, the secular arts (insofar as they are proper arts and not in the service of this, that, or the other cause or lust) are the doors that open to the infinite dimension.

What happens when you have human beings in your work who are desirable or loathsome, or when you're depicting adventures that in life excite fear and desire and loathing? Joyce begins by saying that the proper emotions [evoked by a work of art] are the tragic and the comic. In the *Portrait* Stephen says that Aristotle names the tragic emotions: pity and terror. "And," says Stephen arrogantly (he is an arrogant youth!), "Aristotle has not defined pity and terror. I have." As follows—and here is the great secret:

> Terror is the feeling which arrests the mind in the presence of what-
> soever is grave and constant in human sufferings and unites it with
> the secret cause. (P204)

Every single word of that is important. "Terror is the feeling which arrests
the mind in the presence of whatsoever is grave and constant in human
sufferings and unites it with the secret cause."

> Pity is the feeling which arrests the mind in the presence of whatso-
> ever is grave and constant in human sufferings and unites it with the
> human sufferer. (P204)

What is meant by "the secret cause?" What is meant by "grave and
constant?" If Mr. A. shoots and kills Mr. B., what is the cause of Mr. B.'s
death? Obviously the bullet. Perhaps political differences between Mr. A.
and Mr. B. But those are *instrumental* causes. What is the *secret* cause of
Mr. B.'s death? What is grave and constant?

If in depicting this event you stress the fact that Mr. A. is black and
Mr. B. is white (or vice versa), or Mr. A. is a communist and Mr. B. something else (or vice versa), then you are talking about things that are not
grave and constant. In Mr. B's death, what is grave and constant is mortality, the passage of time, the fact that all must die. If you are stressing that
a man who is a fascist shot someone, you are not telling us that *death* has
come in this way. That grave and constant thing is what lifts the hair on
your head and lets you know that this is a human sufferer. The sufferer becomes a hero insofar as he is without any fear or desire and is in movement
towards his destiny, which inevitably brings his death. We are not in a
work of art if we say, "Oh, this should not have happened." We are in
a work of art if we say, "This should happen! I, too, should die this way."
Then you have a tragic work of art, for you are talking about mortality—
the big, general, secret cause. We are all going to die. How we die is indifferent; what we are talking about is the mystery of dying.

The terror is a positive experience of mystical awe before the *mysterium
tremendum* of being. The pity is a positive experience of compassion for the
*human* sufferer—not the sufferer of this, that or another category. And
when you have experienced both as positive, not as negative, then you have
a tragedy. In that light, you can look at *The Death of a Salesman* and see if
it is a tragedy—and it isn't. When you feel these tragic emotions open

through the work that static vista—so you don't want to go out and burn down the town or, indeed, do anything—you are rendered at that moment aware of the deep dimension. Here you have art as a revelation.

The other proper emotion, Joyce says, is the comic. The comic emotion, he tells us (not in *A Portrait,* but in some notes that didn't get into that book), is joy.[15] But joy isn't *desire.* Joy is *possession.* You are there. [You do not desire happiness; the joy of comedy has already given you happiness.] In Joyce's work what we get is tragic comedy; that is to say, both tragedy and comedy together. We find the same combination also in Oriental works, where the peace of repose must be felt beneath all the activity. So it is in Joyce's work: he holds you in a sense of joyous realization even while depicting the poignancies of the tragic and the sorrowful.

To conclude, let us return to the image of the Buddha under the Bodhi-tree. That tree is the same tree that we know from the Garden of Paradise, where it is traditionally depicted as two trees because it actually has two aspects. That tree is at the mid-point where One breaks into Two, where the divine Bindu, or "drop" [that is, the Absolute[16]], the impact of eternity on the sphere of time, breaks into the pairs of opposites. In the temple cave at Elephanta, there is a wonderful image of Śiva Maheśvara, Śiva the Great Lord, depicted with a single great head. On the right side of the head is a masculine profile, and on the left, a female profile; one aggressive, the other reposeful and dreamy; this one the power, that one erotic; masculine and feminine. The visage in the middle is that eternal one out of which the two have come. Or when you look at the image of the Bodhisattva Avalokiteśvara in the cave at Ajanta—a beautiful, graceful, princely youth holding a lotus in his hand—the right earring is masculine, and the left is feminine. It is the same image of this One that comes into Two. So, the tree in Paradise is that Bindu, and the fruit of that tree was eaten by Adam and Eve, who were ignorant of the play of time, for there was no time then: there was no death, there was no birth, there was nothing of that kind in the mythological age. So, they ate of the Tree of the Knowledge of Good and Evil, the tree of the Two. And if they then had eaten of the other tree, the Tree of Immortal Life, which takes you back to the One again, they would have been as gods. But after they ate of the tree of the Two, God the Father said, "Let's get rid of these two, lest they eat of the other tree and be as gods." He expelled them from the Garden, and he stationed at the gate two cherubim with a flaming sword between to keep them out.

During the war with Japan, I saw in a New York newspaper a most curious picture. It was of one of the two, great, fierce-looking, door-guardians at Nara. And under the picture was this legend: "The Japanese worship gods like this." Well, I knew enough to know that the idea was not to stop and worship those figures, but to walk between them. Then you would come to the Tōdaiji Temple, and there would be the Great Sun Buddha, seated under the Tree of Immortal Life, with his hand saying, "Don't be afraid." And it suddenly occurred to me that it was we, not the Japanese, who worship a fierce god, because our god is the one who stationed the cherubim at the Garden gate so that we shouldn't pass. Then I looked more closely at these two door-guardians to learn more about them; this is the way one amplifies a mythological image. I noticed that one of them had his mouth closed, and the other had his mouth open. And what do those two expressions mean? I read around to find out what they meant, and I discovered that the closed mouth is aggression, and the open mouth, desire. Those are exactly the two sentiments of the kinetic experience. They keep us out of the Garden of Paradise, and they keep us out of the garden of art. If we can kill them in ourselves, we will walk right through the gate.

Now in the Christian version of this whole affair, Christ's tree, Christ's cross, is identified with the Tree of Immortal Life in the Garden from which men have been excluded. And Christ was celebrated in the Middle Ages as that hero who, like Prometheus, stole from the negative god the good that he was hoarding to himself: fire in one case, eternal life in the other. So, the Cross is that tree, and Christ on the Cross is the fruit of that tree who guides us to it: he is exactly the Buddha, who is under that tree. Christ is hanging on the tree, the Buddha is seated beneath it. The Lord of Death and Lust approached the Buddha. The Buddha, absolutely immobile, dispelled him by touching the earth. The god, earth herself, said to the Lord of Death and Lust, "This is my beloved son, who through many lifetimes has so given of himself that there is no one here. Go away, you bad man!" Illumination was achieved.

The Buddha touching the earth is the exact equivalent of the crucified Christ. With that act the Buddha crucifies (as it were, "cuts out") the nature impulses. Christ gives his body with its nature impulses and goes through the central point of the Cross to the Father. The Buddha, likewise, goes to, but is not, the Father: in the Buddhist tradition, he goes to eternal consciousness. Now in the Christian tradition, the expulsion from the Garden and the return to the Cross is interpreted in terms of guilt and atonement. But the word "atonement" (in English, at any rate) can be read as "*at-one-ment.*" If you presuppose that you and God are separate from each other, if you interpret atonement as meaning "I have offended God and am now atoned with Him," then you are reading this motif as a kind of pedagogical nursery-story, and those two cherubim are actual angels put there to keep you out. But if you interpret those angels as simply aspects of your own sentiments, as desire and loathing, then you realize you are being kept out of the Garden by your own sentiments. Then the whole mythology can be interpreted, not as a nursery-story, but in psychological terms, which is exactly what Joyce does with all of these themes. He takes the Christian symbology, which describes a God who is supposed to exist and our relationship to that God, and he rereads it in terms of gnostic principles—principles of psychology, instead of pedagogy—and the whole story opens up with a new life.

What I hope to be able to show through Joyce, then, is not only what he has done, but also what happens to the symbologies when one approaches them this way. Every symbology worth even thinking about is in Joyce. I don't know how he did it. His eyes were so bad he could hardly read, yet he seems to have read every book, and it is all there in his art.

## A Portrait

Right from the beginning Joyce shows affect images. Our little boy is encountering images and always recognizing the affect value for himself. As I mentioned earlier, Joyce writes in the style of the character about whom he is writing. When the boy is an infant it is the infant style; the style grows up with the youth.

> Once upon a time and a very good time it was there was a moocow coming down along the road and this moocow that was coming down along the road met a nicens little boy named baby tuckoo....
> His father told him that story: his father looked at him through a glass: he had a hairy face.

The motif of the mirror glass is associated here with the father; the infant experiences the father through the glass: "He had a hairy face"[17]—which will distinguish him from the mother in a minute.

> He was baby tuckoo. The moocow came down the road where Betty Byrne lived: she sold lemon platt.

And then a little verse:

> O, the wild rose blossoms
> On the little green place.

Already we have mythological images: the little green place and the wild rose blooming. The rose is the mandala, the symbol of the center towards which we are going to move, and it's already connected in the youngster's mind to the little green place: a little plot of land, but also Ireland. By centering this Ireland image in the cosmic image, Joyce addresses the problem I spoke of earlier: the transition from a provincial, limited experience of religion, race, and loyalties to a larger archetypal understanding.

So Joyce has already introduced two sets of images: the father and the woman down the road who sold lemon platt, and the little green place and the wild rose. Now comes another set, the warm-cold motif that will run all through *Finnegans Wake*.

> When you wet the bed first it is warm then it gets cold.

Now the mother enters; she is attending, being gentle and kind.

> His mother put on the oilsheet. That had the queer smell.

Smells, deceptive sensations that when recognized are always related to something, are now being related to mother and father and the little crises of the child's early life.

> His mother had a nicer smell than his father. She played on the piano the sailor's hornpipe for him to dance.

The music theme is here being associated with the mother; the rhythm will go on and on this way, so that finally in *Finnegans Wake* Anna Livia Plurabelle is the rhythm of the world in flow. Stephen will go dancing and jigging all the way through. Whenever he's in a buoyant spontaneous mood, a dance comes along. And I'm told that Joyce had a kind of crazy, stiff-legged jig that he liked to do.[18] Joyce also played the piano, and he made a great point of being a singer—his great disappointment was that he couldn't sing as well as, or wasn't thought to sing as well as, John McCormack.

He danced:

> *Tralala lala*
> *Tralala tralaladdy*
> *Tralala lala*
> *Tralala lala.*

"Rhythm begins, you see," he says later in *Ulysses* (U31); and as I have said, rhythm is the basic esthetic principle. Now we have one more motif.

Uncle Charles and Dante clapped.

"Dante" is only the child's way of saying "Auntie," yet the name of Dante comes in on the first page.

> They were older than his father and mother but uncle Charles was older than Dante.

Stephen is figuring out age and the relation of age to people.

> Dante had two brushes in her press. The brush with the maroon velvet back was for Michael Davitt and the brush with the green velvet back was for Parnell. (P7)

Here is a tremendously important theme in Joyce: the story of Parnell, the leader of the Irish Parliamentary party in Westminster, who was doing very well until he got into a jam with Kitty O'Shea, when the adultery scandal led the Church to betray him. Little Stephen's father is for Parnell, and Dante will later side with the Church, so immediately, in the conflict between the father and the religiously-oriented aunt, we have the world conflict between church and state. Michael Davitt was another Irish patriarch, the founder of the Land League who turned against Parnell, so in the maroon brush and the green brush we get the motif of conflict between these two traditions.

> The Vances lived in number seven. They had a different father and mother. They were Eileen's father and mother.

Eileen is the first girl image in the book. There will be many more. This is the Beatrice motif; Dante first beheld Beatrice at the age of nine.

When they were grown up he was going to marry Eileen. He hid under the table....

Immediately the boy-girl relationship brings a sense of guilt and shame: He hides under the table. And what goes on?

His mother said:
—O, Stephen will apologize.
Dante said:
—O, if not, the eagles will come and pull out his eyes.

Here we have a fierce image introduced. Then comes a little poem that resolves this terrible conflict.

> *Pull out his eyes,*
> *Apologise,*
> *Apologise,*
> *Pull out his eyes.*
>
> *Apologise,*
> *Pull out his eyes,*
> *Pull out his eyes,*
> *Apologise.*(P8)

Stephen is beginning to get these affects tied up with images.

Then he goes to school, where he is confronted with new images to evaluate: experiences in the playground, the different boys, the roughing up he gets from some of them—a chap named Wells, for instance, shoulders him into a latrine runoff.

Then Stephen goes home for the holidays, and Christmas dinner is smashed up by a quarrel between his father and his aunt about Parnell and the priests. It's one of those awful family meals that go to pieces because everybody loses his temper. Stephen's home disintegrates before his eyes.

When Stephen returns to school, a terrible event occurs: the strict disciplinarian motif enters again. Stephen falls, breaks his glasses, and is excused from studying by his teacher, Father Arnall; but when the prefect of studies comes in and sees this little boy not studying, and Father Arnall tells him, "He broke his glasses...and I exempted him from work," the prefect says, "I know that trick.... Out with your hand this moment!"[19] And he gives him a couple of wallops with this pandybat, which hurts the boy terribly, both inside and outside. Cruel things are happening: Stephen respects the priests, yet they are not dependable and do not really warrant his respect; the boys are nasty, though some are nice; and his image of the school disintegrates. Here images are beginning to be associated with affects, but the affects are not the kind the little boy can take, so he is rejecting, rejecting, rejecting.

Then comes a period when the family's fortune goes to pieces. Among other incidents, Stephen's father meets the rector of the school to whom Stephen had complained about his treatment, and then he tells Stephen how they talked in a joking way about what happened—what a brave boy he was—which cruelly devalues his son's brave rebellion against injustice.

Some time later, Stephen goes to Cork with his father and sees him joshing with his old friends. By this point, Stephen feels quite dissociated from his father. He is beginning to know something; he is growing up; he's learning. He is studying the literature of the English heritage, the classical heritage, the biblical heritage. He is beginning to wrap these images together and associate them with his experiences. Now comes a very strong mythological image. The men are drinking and the boy is watching.

> Stephen watched the three glasses being raised from the counter as his father and his two cronies drank to the memory of their past. An abyss of fortune or of temperament sundered him from them. His mind seemed older than theirs: it shone coldly on their strifes and happiness and regrets like a moon upon a younger earth. (p95)

Here we have a whole train of fundamental images. The main motif is the moon, a worldwide mythological image. The moon dies and is resurrected every month. It carries its own shadow in itself, in contrast to the sun, which is luminous and radiant and scatters shadows before it. So the shadow and the sun, darkness and the sun, are separate from each other. The moon hero is the tragic hero in whom darkness rests, he has his own death in him, and he sheds his death as a serpent sheds its skin. The moon is therefore associated with the serpent, lord of the energies of the earth, who sheds his skin to be reborn: the reborn serpent, the reborn moon.

Now the creature that pounces on the serpent is the high-flying eagle, and the bird-and-serpent conflict is a basic mythological motif. In certain mythologies they stand as enemies—as they do, for example, in biblical mythology, where the serpent is cursed by the winged powers, the powers of the upper atmosphere. The bird represents the free-flying spirit (it is released from the earth) and flight: the flight motif of Daedalus. The serpent, however, represents the bound-to-the-earth spirit. Later, Stephen feels that he will fall, that he will experience the abyss; this knowledge is knowledge of the serpent power.

> The snares of the world were its ways of sin. He would fall. He had not yet fallen but he would fall silently, in an instant. Not to fall was too hard, too hard: and he felt the silent lapse of his soul, as it would be at some instant to come, falling, falling but not yet fallen, still unfallen but about to fall. (P162)

In certain mythologies where the bird and serpent symbols are synthesized, you have the image of the dragon as a winged serpent. The winged lizard is the synthesis of the two. You can have either the attack and the separation, or the synthesis; but to arrive at the synthesis, one has to go through the separation. We will see Joyce working out this symbolism— actually alchemical symbolism. Stephen himself will synthesize the serpent image with that of the bird—[the fall with the rise]—when he experiences the girl on the beach as a dove, her eyes calling him "to live, to err, to fall, to triumph, to recreate life out of life!"(P171)

But now, returning to our story, images of the moon accompany Stephen's feelings of separation from his father and his father's cronies. He is a dead satellite: a wasteland theme is beginning.

> His mind seemed older than theirs: it shone coldly on their strifes and happiness and regrets like a moon upon a younger earth. No life or youth stirred in him as it had stirred in them. He had known neither the pleasure of companionship with others nor the vigour of rude male health nor filial piety.

He has not experienced the orthodox sentiments of childhood and young manhood. What do you do when you don't experience orthodox sentiments? Can you go on accepting the world that lives by them? He is already in exile. Remember: Stephen's still just a boy in school.

> Nothing stirred within his soul but a cold and cruel and loveless lust. His childhood was dead or lost and with it his soul capable of simple joys, and he was drifting amid life like the barren shell of the moon.

> *Art thou pale for weariness*
> *Of climbing heaven and gazing on the earth,*
> *Wandering companionless...?*

He repeated to himself the lines of Shelley's fragment. Its alternation of sad human ineffectualness with vast inhuman cycles of activity chilled him, and he forgot his own human and ineffectual grieving. (P95–96)

It *is* a chilling experience. Two pages later, he is overwhelmed.

> How foolish his aim had been! He had tried to build a breakwater of order and elegance against the sordid tide of life without him and to dam up, by rules of conduct and active interests and new filial relations, the powerful recurrence of the tides within him. Useless.

Here is the deluge motif: annihilation of the ego system. His conscious programs are breaking up. He is being overwhelmed by the surges of his own nature, which does not run in the channels designated by his strongly disciplinary society.

> From without as from within the water had flowed over his barriers: their tides began once more to jostle fiercely above the crumbled mole.

His barriers have broken already.

> He saw clearly too his own futile isolation. He had not gone one step nearer the lives he had sought to approach nor bridged the restless shame and rancour that had divided him from mother and brother and sister.

This sense of no consubstantiality, no accord, is very strong in him. This is hell: separateness, each soul separate from the other in its own little iron-bound world.

> He felt that he was hardly of the one blood with them but stood to them rather in the mystical kinship of fosterage, fosterchild and fosterbrother. (P98)

In *The Myth of the Birth of the Hero*, Otto Rank discusses the feeling children have that they are so superior to, or different from, their parents that they must have been adopted and that their real parents are somewhere else. This is, of course, the Moses motif: Moses was a Jew who was adopted by the Egyptian house, and his whole life was given to recovering his original source; Freud speaks of this. Countless stories tell of the one who is exposed—Oedipus is exposed on Mount Cithaeron and then taken up by a shepherd and adopted by King Polybus. In many traditional tales, the hero is adopted by animals, as in the story of Romulus and Remus. So, this feeling of having been adopted is an automatic thought that children have, but it is one that leads right into the big myths.

Now as I have said, Joyce's model for this book was Dante's *La Vita Nuova, The New Life*. What is the New Life? The New Life is the awakening in a person's life of a spiritual (as opposed to an economic, political, or social) trajectory or aim or dynamic. This birth of the spiritual life in a human animal is what is called the virgin birth. We share with the animals certain zeals: we hang on to life to beget future lives, we fight to gain and to win. But another life goal can be awakened.

When Dante first saw Beatrice, she was nine years old and so was he. She was wearing a scarlet dress. In the Middle Ages, scarlet was the color of the Christ. Dante said, "Beatrice is a nine because her root is in the Trinity." She was transparent to transcendence; and he looked at her, not with the eye of lust—that is, not with desire—but with awe at her beauty as a manifestation of the radiance of God's love for the world. By hanging onto that awe and remaining in that meditation, which was the meditation of his entire life, he was carried to the throne of God. That was Dante's meditation.

In *Portrait* there are several women, and the female plays the decisive part in Stephen's awakening spiritual life, as it did in Dante's. At first, when Stephen is a little boy, there are little girls; but he is a very precocious boy, and as he gets older he begins to follow what is called in tantric yoga the left-hand path.

> He burned to appease the fierce longings of his heart before which everything else was idle and alien. He cared little that he was in mortal sin, that his life had grown to be a tissue of subterfuge and falsehood. Beside the savage desire within him to realize the enormities which he brooded on nothing was sacred. (P98–99)

In Dublin in those days there was a big brothel section, and there Stephen, while still a boy in prep school, has found, you might say, the female aspect in its dark side.

In the very middle of the *Vita Nuova,* there is a radical shift from the earthly to the transcendent sphere: Beatrice dies, and since Dante no longer has the delight of her physical presence, his meditation is translated to the invisible. And right in the middle of every one of Joyce's books is a similar crisis where the perspective shifts. You can almost find the crisis in one of his books just by opening it to the last page, writing down the page number, dividing it by two, and then turning to that page. This happens in *Ulysses* and in *Finnegans Wake,* and it happens here, at the end of the second section of the *Portrait.*

The New Life is the life of the awakened spiritual, poetic (rather than practical) relationship to the world through the physical realm and the experiences informing it. Here is the emergence of the New Life for Stephen, the crisis in *A Portrait.* If you open the book exactly in the middle, at the beginning of the third section, you find Stephen, this boy who has got himself into this terrible condition, listening to a hell-sermon by a priest named Father Arnall.

Recall what has brought us to this crisis: Joyce begins with this little boy with his family—you recall, his mother had a nicer smell than his father and so on—and then the boy goes to school, and as he grows, every one of his experiences is translated into its subjective aspect. He internalizes everything, and since he has been trained in Roman Catholic theology, his experiences very soon become linked to that theology. We begin to get the inward sense of Stephen's experiences, and from that understanding, we move into a wonderful expansion of those experiences by way of a mythological interpretation. This dynamic carries right through the whole work.

Now in Catholic schools, there is usually an annual retreat, where you stop studying and just hear about the spiritual life and think about these things. I can remember that the big number in every retreat was always the sermon on hell. You are sitting there, the priest comes in and describes hell, and then you are a good boy for about the next two weeks. I've heard about six of those sermons in the course of my life. We would always say, "Here comes the hell-sermon." And some boy would always get sick in the course of it. So, this is the sermon that Stephen hears:

> —*Hell has enlarged its soul and opened its mouth without any limits*—
> words taken, my dear little brothers in Christ Jesus, from the book

of Isaias, fifth chapter, fourteenth verse. In the name of the Father
and of the Son and of the Holy Ghost. Amen.

The preacher took a chainless watch from a pocket within his
soutane and, having considered its dial for a moment in silence,
placed it silently before him on the table.

He began to speak in a quiet tone.

—Adam and Eve, my dear boys, were, as you know, our first
parents and you will remember that they were created by God in
order that the seats in heaven left vacant by the fall of Lucifer and his
rebellious angels might be filled again. Lucifer, we are told, was a son
of the morning, a radiant and mighty angel; yet he fell: he fell and
there fell with him a third part of the host of heaven: he fell and was
hurled with his rebellious angels into hell. What his sin was we cannot say. Theologians consider that it was the sin of pride, the sinful
thought conceived in an instant: *non serviam: I will not serve.*

*Non Serviam: I will not serve.* That is Joyce's motto.

That instant was his ruin. He offended the majesty of God by the
sinful thought of one instant and God cast him out of heaven into
hell for ever. (P117)

Father Arnall tells the story of the creation of Adam and Eve, their fall
from the garden. Then he describes hell:

Every sense of the flesh is tortured and every faculty of the soul
therewith: the eyes with impenetrable utter darkness, the nose with
noisome odours, the ears with yells and howls and execrations, the
taste with foul matter, leprous corruption, nameless suffocating filth,
the touch with redhot goads and spikes, with cruel tongues of flame.
And through the several torments of the senses the immortal soul is
tortured eternally in its very essence amid the leagues upon leagues
of glowing fires kindled in the abyss by the offended majesty of the
Ominipotent God and fanned into everlasting, and ever increasing
fury by the breath of the anger of the Godhead.

—Consider finally that the torment of this infernal prison is in-
creased by the company of the damned themselves. (P122)

Father Arnall describes hell as a place where all of the senses are fiercely
tortured. The fire that burns is a dark fire, a horrendous fire that does not
consume what it burns. He says: "Place your finger for a moment in the

flame of a candle," and then imagine this pain for eternity over your whole body. Then there is the unbearable stench: "All the filth of the world, all the offal and scum of the world...shall run there as to a vast reeking sewer..."—that's like the latrine outflow Stephen was shouldered into. The unbreathable air, thick with pestilential odors, suffocates, but you don't die. Your sight is assaulted with horrific visual images. Furthermore, there's the permanent separation from God, whom you have seen for a moment—the moment of personal judgment when He condemns you to hell and says, "Go to the fires of eternal death!" And the contrast between the life you have lived—the things that you have sought, what you thought was beauty and pleasure, and so on—and this momentary experience of what you should have been intending fills you with a dreadful sense of loss.

The aspect of hell is pain. People in hell are people fixed in their temporal interests, people trapped in their ego systems, people for whom the practical world has not become transparent. That is what hell is: a place for people who are fixed forever. And being fixed for eternity is very painful. Every sense is tormented—sound, smell, taste—and a black fire burns but does not consume.

Again, the *Portrait* follows *La Vita Nuova*. When Beatrice dies in the middle of Dante's book, he is transformed by the experience of death and the relationship of the temporal life that he has led to the totality of human potentialities for experience. Similarly, in the middle of the *Portrait,* Stephen is transformed: the hell-fire sermon works. Poor Stephen, who has been a sinner, is suddenly struck with the realization of the degradation of the life he has been leading. His life is amplified into a hell image, the one image the Church has to give that really does something to Stephen, and that image is so fierce, it transforms his character.

Now most kids haven't committed any real sins at all. I mean, they go to confession and say, "Bless me Father, I didn't say my morning prayers three times and I said 'boo' to my mother once." Well, a hell-fire sermon is terrifying even if your only sins are not saying your prayers and disobeying your mother, but Stephen is a boy who has been way, way deep into sin. He is living in what the Church calls "mortal sin"—that is to say, the type of sin that puts a person in hell. And when Father Arnall's sermon is over, Stephen is filled with remorse for the life that he has been leading.

> Could it be that he, Stephen Dedalus, had done those things? His conscience sighed in answer. Yes, he had done them, secretly, filthily, time after time, and, hardened in sinful impenitence, he had dared to wear the mask of holiness before the tabernacle itself while his soul within was a living mass of corruption. How came it that God had not struck him dead? (P137)

So Stephen decides to go to confession and repair his life. He goes sneaking around to find another church, where he can confess to a priest whom he does not know. Well, he makes his confession, and the priest, though appalled that this youngster is confessing such sins, gives him his penance. The boy really resolves not to sin this way again. He becomes devoutly religious and—like the schizophrenic who is filled with the impulse to become the king, the hero—he decides he is going to be a saint. He has always wanted to go to the extreme in everything. Now a good way to become a saint or prophet is to become a Jesuit, so he begins to watch the Jesuits. He becomes such a devoted and saintly boy that they begin to think of him as a potential priest. Eventually the director summons Stephen to his office and asks him if he has ever felt that he had a vocation. Then, observing that God calls only a chosen few to the religious life, the priest tells him:

> —To receive that call, Stephen, said the priest, is the greatest honour that the Almighty God can bestow upon a man. No king or emperor on this earth has the power of the priest of God. No angel or archangel in heaven, no saint, not even the Blessed Virgin herself has the power of a priest of God: the power of the keys, the power to bind and to loose from sin, the power of exorcism, the power to cast out from the creatures of God the evil spirits that have power over them, the power, the authority, to make the great God of Heaven come down upon the altar and take the form of bread and wine. What an awful power, Stephen! (P157–158)

But while listening to the director, Stephen thinks about priests who condemn books they haven't read and about how they talk in clichés. The images of the tradition are being communicated by people who have not had equivalent affect experiences; there is a dissociation of image from affect. Stephen, who takes the vow of vocation very seriously to his heart, is aware of this split, of the priests not being what they stand for, so he does not know what path to follow. He wants not just to fall into a job, but to determine what his life is going to be.

Later, at loose ends, he wanders one day on the beach north of Dublin where some of his friends are swimming. Now in *Ulysses,* Stephen declares that he "was hydrophobe" (U550), but I think Joyce also was hydrophobic; that is to say, both were afraid of water. The boys swimming call to Stephen— "Stephanos Dedalos! Bous Stephanoumenos! Bous Stephanoumenos!"— addressing him with Greek endings on the words. As they banter and call, Stephen starts to think of himself as lost, not knowing what direction his life is going take. And it is just after this moment, in this condition, that he encounters the girl in the stream, the experience which opens him to the call of life.

He comes to a little tidal inlet, takes off his sneakers and throws them over his shoulder, and starts wading in the little stream. And then comes this beautiful moment, the awakening:

> He was alone. He was unheeded, happy and near to the wild heart of life. He was alone and young and wilful and wildhearted, alone amid a waste of wild air and brackish waters and the seaharvest of shells and tangle and veiled grey sunlight and gayclad lightclad figures, of children and girls and voices childish and girlish in the air.
>
> A girl stood before him in midstream, alone and still, gazing out to sea. She seemed like one whom magic had changed into the likeness of a strange and beautiful seabird. Her long slender bare legs were delicate as a crane's and pure save where an emerald trail of seaweed had fashioned itself as a sign upon the flesh. Her thighs, fuller and softhued as ivory, were bared almost to the hips where the white fringes of her drawers were like featherings of soft white down. Her slateblue skirts were kilted boldly about her waist and dovetailed behind her. Her bosom was as a bird's soft and slight, slight and soft as the breast of some darkplumaged dove.

It is as though she were a bird, the dove-tailed spirit.

> But her long fair hair was girlish: and girlish, and touched with the wonder mortal beauty, her face.
>
> She was alone and still, gazing out to sea; and when she felt his presence and the worship of his eyes her eyes turned to him in quiet sufferance of his gaze, without shame or wantonness. Long, long she

suffered his gaze and then quietly withdrew her eyes from his and
bent them towards the stream, gently stirring the water with her foot
hither and thither. The first faint noise of gently moving water broke
the silence, low and faint and whispering, faint as the bells of sleep;
hither and thither, hither and thither: and a faint flame trembled on
her cheek.

Stephen doesn't know who she is, and it doesn't matter. Like Dante,
he views the girl, not with lust, but in rapture.

—Heavenly God! cried Stephen's soul, in an outburst of profane joy.

The Holy Spirit, in the shape of the dove, has spoken to him through
her. He's in movement now, but not psychologically.

He turned away from her suddenly and set off across the strand. His
cheeks were aflame; his body was aglow; his limbs were trembling.
On and on and on and on he strode, far out over the sands, singing
wildly to the sea, crying to greet the advent of the life that had cried
to him.

She has opened him. She has passed into his soul forever, as once
Beatrice passed into Dante's.

Her image had passed into his soul for ever and no word had broken
the holy silence of his ecstasy. Her eyes had called him and his soul
had leaped at the call. To live, to err, to fall, to triumph, to recreate
life out of life! A wild angel had appeared to him, the angel of mortal youth and beauty, an envoy from the fair courts of life, to throw
open before him in an instant of ecstasy the gates of all the ways of
error and glory. On and on and on and on!

She was, as it were, transparent to transcendence: a call, not to herself,
but to life.

He halted suddenly and heard his heart in the silence. How far had
he walked? What hour was it?

The world has dropped off. Time and space are gone in the enchantment of the heart.

There was no human figure near him nor any sound borne to him
over the air. But the tide was near the turn and already the day was
on the wane. He turned landward and ran towards the shore and,

running up the sloping beach, reckless of the sharp shingle, found a sandy nook amid a ring of tufted sandknolls and lay down there that the peace and silence of the evening might still the riot of his blood.

He felt above him the vast indifferent dome and the calm processes of the heavenly bodies; and the earth beneath him, the earth that had borne him, had taken him to her breast.

He closed his eyes in the languor of sleep. His eyelids trembled as if they felt the vast cyclic movement of the earth and her watchers, trembled as if they felt the strange light of some new world. His soul was swooning into some new world, fantastic, dim, uncertain as under sea, traversed by cloudy shapes and beings. A world, a glimmer, or a flower? Glimmering and trembling, trembling and unfolding, a breaking light, an opening flower, it spread in endless succession to itself, breaking in full crimson and unfolding and fading to palest rose, leaf by leaf and wave of light by wave of light, flooding all the heavens with its soft flushes, every flush deeper than other. Evening had fallen when he woke and the sand and arid grasses of his bed glowed no longer. He rose slowly and, recalling the rapture of his sleep, sighed at its joy.

He climbed to the crest of the sandhill and gazed about him. Evening had fallen. A rim of the young moon cleft the pale waste of sky like the rim of a silver hoop imbedded in grey sand; and the tide was flowing in fast to the land with a low whisper of her waves, islanding a few last figures in distant pools. (P171–173)

Here is an actual, physical, earthly, and spiritual experience, understood in terms of a mythological experience: the impregnation of his soul by the dove, the Holy Spirit, symbolized in this girl, who is the counterpart of Dante's Beatrice. This vision becomes the inspiration of Joyce's life and of all his heroines. The heroine of *Ulysses,* Molly Bloom (who is, so to speak, the gross aspect), is all through that book, although she's never out of bed. When we get to *Finnegans Wake,* the heroine running and flowing throughout that book is Anna Livia Plurabelle, a great female power. This vision of the girl in the stream becomes Stephen's inspiration. It opens him past all of the various conflicts: his family and its situation, his vocation, the clergy's experiences not matching the import of their imagery, and his own confusion. Here is a moment where the imagery suddenly speaks: he sees the girl as a dove, as the Holy Spirit announcing the incarnation.

There is another aspect to the evocation of the Holy Spirit. Joyce had read the prophecies of Joachim of Floris, who saw three transformations of the spirit of God in the world: the first, that of the Old Testament, the age of the Father and the law; the second, of the Son and the Church; and there is to come a third age, when the Holy Spirit will speak directly to each and the Church will no longer be necessary. The contemporaries of Joachim, who lived until 1200, associated Saint Francis of Assisi with the beginning of the third age, when the Church was going to dissolve. In Joachim's time the idea of embracing the hermit life and leaving the Church behind became strongly expressed in the imagery of medieval romance—in the *Quest de Saint Graal,* for example, this plays a big role. So, the idea that the secular mind will receive directly the inspiration of the Holy Ghost is the sense of the image of the girl as a dove, calling the individual to be his own redeemer, his own salvation.

It is also important to recall here the teachings of Pelagius, a fourth-century heretic (born, I think, in Britain). He said human nature is inherently good and each individual has the responsibility of saving himself. His disciple, Celestius, denied the doctrine of Original Sin—that we all inherited the sin of Adam and Eve. Since sin cannot be inherited, they argued, the Christ serves, not as a magical savior through whose grace we partake in the sacraments by which we are saved, but simply as a model for us. Our own effort saves us. And Stephen, like Daedalus, will "turn his mind to unknown arts" and fly his own flight—becoming himself, then, the bird in flight, the image of the Holy Ghost. This is the imagery assaulting Stephen at this point. Released from the Church, he is now on his way.

Dante precedes each of the poems in the *Vita Nuova* with a description of the circumstances that brought about the writing, and he also follows each of the poems with an analysis of his poetic structure and what he intended to render through that. Joyce does the same here. In the section after his vision on the beach, Stephen describes his esthetic theory to a friend and then we read about the circumstances surrounding his writing of a little villanelle: a girl had looked at him without shame or wantonness, and without revulsion or desire being invoked; it's an ecstatic moment. So he has translated his esthetic into precise imagery. He's going to be an artist, a celebrator of this image. He is ready to take flight from Ireland, for Ireland spreads nets, as all social orders do:

> When the soul of a man is born in this country there are nets flung at it to hold it back from flight. You talk to me of nationality, language, religion. I shall try to fly by those nets. (P203)

The nets are political, social, and religious traditions, and also the revolutionary traditions:

> MacCann began to speak with fluent energy of the Csar's rescript, of Stead, of general disarmament, arbitration in cases of international disputes, of the signs of the times, of the new humanity and the new gospel of life which would make it the business of the community to secure as cheaply as possible the greatest possible happiness of the greatest possible number. (P196)

Stephen is here being invited to "change the world," with the main image of change being, not Marx, but Tsar Nicholas II, who was a man (we don't hear about this so much now) of great progressive intentions and designs.[20] But Stephen says:

> —Keep your icon. If we must have a Jesus, let us have a legitimate Jesus.

Now Stephen's friends know that he is dropping the Church, but later, when his friend Cranly inquires, "Then . . . you do not intend to become a Protestant?" Stephen gives the classic answer which I think is in every Catholic's heart:

> —I said that I had lost the faith, Stephen answered, but not that I had lost selfrespect. What kind of liberation would that be to forsake an absurdity which is logical and coherent and to embrace one which is illogical and incoherent? (P243–244)

And when his friend presses, asking if Stephen fears Judgment Day and everlasting hell-fire, Stephen makes this terrific statement:

> I do not fear to be alone or to be spurned for another or to leave whatever I have to leave. And I am not afraid to make a mistake, even a great mistake, a lifelong mistake and perhaps as long as eternity too. (P247)

That is to say, I may burn in hell for this—and this is courage: the courage of facing complete shipwreck on the rocks, disaster, schizophrenic disintegration, hell, anything.

The tawdriness of Joyce's family life is almost inconceivable: His father was a hale-fellow-well-met and so on; his family was always in trouble with the rent and had to move about ninety-eight times; his mother had fifteen pregnancies, ten children that lived past babyhood, and was absolutely trapped into chores and an inelegant life. For James, who did not want to participate in all of that, the girl on the beach opened up the way to a life of adventure into the unseen and unknown. So, at the very end of *A Portrait,* Stephen resolves to leave Ireland. This shows that shift of center that Perry was talking about.

> *24 March:* Began with a discussion with my mother. Subject: B.V.M. Handicapped by my sex and youth. To escape held up relations between Jesus and Papa against those between Mary and her son. Said religion was not a lying-in hospital. Mother indulgent. Said I have a queer mind and have read too much. Not true. Have read little and understand less. Then she said I would come back to faith because I had a restless mind. This means to leave church by back door of sin and reenter through the skylight of repentance. Cannot repent. Told her so and asked for sixpence. Got threepence.

These are probably Joyce's actual diary entries, you know.

> Then went to college. Other wrangle with little roundhead rogue's-eye Ghezzi. This time about Bruno the Nolan....

Giordano Bruno of Nola, who had the privilege of being burned at the stake in 1600 for professing the same ideas as those that are the context of Joyce's books.

> Began in Italian and ended in pidgin English. He said Bruno was a terrible heretic. I said he was terribly burned. He agreed to this with some sorrow. Then gave me recipe for what he calls *risotto alla berga-masca.* When he pronounces a soft *o* he protrudes his full carnal lips as if he kissed the vowel. Has he? And could he repent? Yes, he could: and cry two round rogue's tears, one from each eye....
>
> *25 March, morning:* A troubled night of dreams. Want to get them off my chest.
>
> A long, curving gallery. From the floor ascend pillars of dark vapours. It is peopled by the images of fabulous kings, set in stone. Their hands are folded upon their knees in token of weariness and their eyes are darkened for the errors of men go up before them for ever as dark vapours.

Strange figures advance from a cave. They are not as tall as men. One does not seem to stand quite apart from another. Their faces are phosphorescent, with darker streaks. They peer at me and their eyes seem to ask me something. They do not speak. (P248–249)

We'll pass down to the last dates now.

*16 April:* Away! Away!

The spell of arms and voices: the white arms of roads, their promise of close embraces and the black arms of tall ships that stand against the moon, their tale of distant nations. They are held out to say: We are alone. Come. And the voices say with them: We are your kinsmen. And the air is thick with their company as they call to me, their kinsman, making ready to go, shaking the wings of their exultant and terrible youth.

*26 April:* Mother is putting my new secondhand clothes in order. She prays now, she says, that I may learn in my own life and away from home and friends what the heart is and what it feels. Amen. So be it. Welcome, O life! I go to encounter for the millionth time the reality of experience and to forge in the smithy of my soul the uncreated conscience of my race.

*27 April:* Old father, old artificer, stand me now and ever in good stead. (P252–253)

At the end of the *Vita Nuova*, Dante says, "I now go forth to prepare myself to write of her such a work as has never been written before." And he writes the *Commedia,* enlarging the inspiration that came through Beatrice into a vision of God's world. Stephen (Joyce) does the same. "Old father, old artificer" is Daedalus, the Greek master artist. Emulating him, Stephen flies, so to say, from Dublin; and Joyce undertakes to write *Ulysses,* wherein Stephen will observe:

Fabulous artificer, the hawklike man. You flew. Whereto? Newhaven-Dieppe, steerage passenger. Paris and back. Lapwing. Icarus. *Pater, ait.* Seabedabbled, fallen, weltering. Lapwing you are. Lapwing he. (U173)

*A Portrait* ends with:

Dublin 1904
Trieste 1914

Beginning in Dublin in 1904 and finishing in Trieste in 1914, this young man spent ten years writing this little book.

## CHAPTER III

# ULYSSES

## INTRODUCTION

### *The Waste Land*

In Paris, Stephen receives a telegram from his father that says, "Mother dying come home father."[21] So he returns to Dublin, and it is in Dublin, on June 16, 1904, that *Ulysses* opens. He has returned to the land of death, the wasteland. As I once wrote:

> *Ulysses* . . . is cast on the plane of waking consciousness, with citizens and characters aware of nothing else; and there Bloom and Stephen roam—both wearing the black of mourning—as it were through a hell. For in hell, they say, the souls are linked forever to their sins— that is, to the limitations by which their lives were bounded, and so, lost—which, in the reach of timeless time, prove, beyond endurance, dull; whereas in Purgatory, on the other hand, the protective molds are broken, dissolved, and there is process, change, motion: a purging away of those various states of pride in ignorance that on earth encumber the soul's realization of its own true and deepest yearning, which is to say, as we are told, for God.
>
> Through the dreaming micro-macrocosm in ferment of *Finnegans Wake,* the One that is in all things immanent ( *"iste"*) is felt

and perceived to be ubiquitous in its duality (*"isce et ille"*: 92.7–11), whereas in *Ulysses* there is no such fermentation, save in the minds of the counterpoised heroes, Stephen and Bloom. Its world is depicted, rather, as a wasteland, once fair, now sterile, dry and without rain. The cattle are dying of a plague. Women are unable to give birth. The government is of aliens: England's Crown and Redcoats, Rome's Priests and Papal hat. And the complacent, garrulous citizenry is largely an assortment of easy-going jokesters—singularities self-enclosed, stone-dry—rattling around and among each other without inward transformation, while maintaining by all means the general convenant of innocence of their own boredom and banality.[22]

T. S. Eliot's *The Waste Land* came out the same year as *Ulysses,* but Eliot had read *Ulysses* before he wrote *The Waste Land.* There are constant echoes in *The Waste Land* of themes and images from *Ulysses*—the drowned man, the voice of the thunder, and others.

*Ulysses* takes place mainly on Thursday—Thor's day, Jeudi, Jove's day; the Day of Thunder—and in the exact middle of the book, a thunderclap wakes Stephen's heart.[23] In Sanskrit, the word for "thunderbolt" (*vajra*), also signifies "diamond" and connotes transcendent illumination. As the lightning shatters phenomenal forms, so too does transcendent illumination; and as the diamond can be neither cut nor marred, so neither can Illumination by any cut of phenomenal experience. So, the thunder in the middle of *Ulysses* marks the instant of transition from Stephen's fixed and sterile, self-protective pose of spiritual pride to the commencement of a purgatorial process which is to culminate, "whirled without end to end" (582.20–21), in the consubstantial night-sea of *Finnegans Wake,* to which the last five chapters of *Ulysses* are the passage.

Eliot also uses the voice of thunder as the waking motif. It is the same thunderclap that resounds in "What the Thunder Said," Part V of *The Waste Land.* Eliot takes as his text the passage in the Bṛhadāranyaka Upaniṣad where the thunder voice speaks his ultimate word to gods, men, and demons; and what it says is "*Da.*" Now *da* is a Sanskrit root that lies behind three great words: *damyata, datta,* and *dayadhvam,* which mean "restrain yourself," "give," and "be compassionate." These are the sentiments that open one to the world and turn one into a beneficent bodhisattva.[24] These are also the sentiments that are coming to statement in Stephen's heart in *Ulysses.*

Eliot regards London as a wasteland in the same way that Joyce regards Dublin as a wasteland: both cities are filled with people doing what they are supposed to do instead of what their inner urgency moves them to do. These dead souls are all pretenders of one kind or another, ice-hard and stone-dry, self-enclosed, witty and self-protective, always verbally fencing, letting no one through—and Stephen, himself, is worst of all: "Kinch, the knifeblade," his stately pal Mulligan names him. [Yet Stephen and Bloom will both find purgation in the circular swamps of the Dublin hell.]

## Ulysses and the Odyssey

Joyce's model for *Ulysses* is the *Odyssey.* Some critics once said that his use of the *Odyssey* was just a device to give order to chaos. That's not true. [The two works are similarly structured and use the same mythic motifs, and the central concern of both is male initiation into a world different from that of brutal masculine assertion].

*Ulysses* is divided into three sections, which roughly correspond to the three divisions in Homer. In the *Odyssey,* Books I–IV recount the adventures of Telemachus, the son of Odysseus; Books V–XIV recount the adventures of Odysseus; and Books XV–XXIV recount the combined adventures of Telemachus and Odysseus. In *Ulysses,* the central figures are Stephen Dedalus and Leopold Bloom. In the first section, all three chapters have to do entirely with Stephen; in the second section, made up of twelve chapters, the center of gravity shifts from Stephen to Bloom (although Stephen has some chapters of his own) and in the later chapters of this section, the two of them come together; and the third section, then, which also contains three chapters, has to do with Stephen and Bloom together.

The central imperative of the *Odyssey* is twofold: one concerns Odysseus; the other, Telemachus. When Odysseus was drafted into the army to go to Troy, his son Telemachus had just been born. So Telemachus grows up for twenty years with no father, and his imperative is: "Young man, go find your father." What that means is: "Find your model. Find your life path." The boy's finding of the father is a very important part of the *Odyssey* [and of the life of every male human being].

The first three chapters of *Ulysses* show Stephen in the role of Telemachus, who has not found his father and is called to find him. Stephen, of course, has an actual father, Simon Dedalus, but Simon is not his spiritual father. Here we have the problem of spiritual fatherhood. It's not uncommon in our culture for the son, following in the father's footsteps, to find his own career eventually; and then he has to find his spiritual father (or as we now say, his guru), the one who will show him, not so much by pedagogical instruction as by example, what the aim and direction in his life is going to be. So Stephen is Telemachus, and in the beginning of *Ulysses*, he is living in a Martello tower with two other young men, one of whom, Buck Mulligan, calls the tower the "Omphalos," the world navel. These three young men, all intellectuals, are cut off by the thick fortress walls of the tower from Nature and the natural world. It's just the three of them—the Father, Son and Holy Ghost—living there.

The second section of *Ulysses* is largely about the adventures of Leopold Bloom as he moves around Dublin. Bloom, who is totally different from these three intellectuals, is a mature man with many rambling intellectual interests who knows how to assimilate and relate what he knows to living life. Bloom will be Stephen's spiritual father [the Odysseus to his tormented Telemachus]. Near the end of the middle twelve chapters, Stephen and Bloom meet in a maternity hospital (the place of rebirth), where they hear the thunderclap, after which Stephen, casting off his old ego, begins to be reborn as the new trans-Stephen character.

The next three chapters—the "Circe" chapter from the second part of the book, and *Eumaeus* and *Ithaca* from the third part—show Bloom and Stephen together. The chapter after they meet in the maternity hospital takes place in Nighttown, the brothel section of Dublin, which is, of course, the place of Circe with her death initiations. By this time Stephen is infinitely drunk and ends up in quite a mess. He's knocked down on the street by a couple of British soldiers, and Bloom [keeps him from being arrested, and] takes charge of him.

Then, in the third section of *Ulysses*, Bloom invites Stephen to his home for a cup of cocoa. They go there, and in a way refresh each other. Then Stephen leaves, and Bloom goes up to bed with Molly, and we have the last chapter, the *Penelope* chapter, Molly Bloom's soliloquy, for which everybody bought the book.

## The Odyssey of Initiation

Who was Odysseus? He was a much-traveled man who had had every kind of experience. For ten years, he has been in Troy, fighting a war in a he-man world, where no dialogue between men and women takes place, and women are simply booty—just argent goods to be possessed and used. Now the earlier religious tradition [of Greece and Asia Minor] was of the great goddess, but when the patriarchal Indo-Europeans came in, the goddess was put down, just as she is in the Bible, where she is called the Abomination, the goddess of the Canaanites, and so forth. She was put down in Greek literature also.

[The *Iliad* and the origin of the Trojan war] are based on masculine put-downs of the concept of the great goddess. You will recall that the Trojan War was caused by the Judgment of Paris—this languid lad, of a kind which in my own youth we used to call a "lounge lizard." Paris was called upon to award a golden apple to one of the three great goddesses of Greece: Aphrodite, the goddess in her literary aspect of lust, who represents (to use biblical terms) seduction and sin; Hera, who was the spouse of Zeus and represents woman as wife, mother, and matriarch; and Athena, the young virgin goddess born from the forehead of Zeus, her father. (Zeus had a pain in his head one day and sent for Hephaestus; he cracked Zeus's head open, and out jumped Athena in full armor—voilà!—Daddy's girl.) These same three aspects of the goddess are the aspects of the female that appear in *Ulysses* [to initiate the male characters]: woman as Hera, the wife, is Molly; woman as the temptress Aphrodite, we get in the brothels; and woman as Athena, the daughter-virgin, is Bloom's young daughter, Milly, whose name echoes that of her mother, Molly. The *Odyssey,* then, is [an account of the maturing of Odysseus and the story of his initiation into the mysteries of manhood.]

When the Trojan War is over, there come what are known as the *nos-toi,* the "returns," when the warriors return home. Menelaus returns home with Helen—Helen of Sparta: that must have been a happy mansion; Agamemnon goes home and gets killed in the bathtub; and Odysseus's adventures begin with his attempts to return home with twelve ships. They sail north to a little town called Ismarus, where he and a bunch of ruffians go ashore, plunder the town, and rape the women.[25] They are still in the warrior mode. Their psychological drives are those of the exploiter, the buccaneer, with no relationship to the female. The gods say, "This is no way for a man to go home to his wife." So they blow the ships around at sea for ten days, until Odysseus doesn't know where they are. Then the real story begins.

The *Odyssey* could be seen as a night sea journey, a dream trip. The first port that Odysseus and his men come to after being blown around is that of the Lotus-Eaters, probably a town in North Africa. Lotus-Eating: this is LSD. So, they are in Dreamland, and from this moment on, they don't meet human beings. They meet nymphs—little goddesses—and several monsters.

Their first monstrous encounter is with Polyphemus, the giant cannibal with one eye in the middle of his forehead. Polyphemus is the son of Poseidon, Lord of the Abyssal Waters, so he represents the threshold guardian, the foreground of the power that is going to be initiating Odysseus throughout his journey. Whenever one goes into a field of adventure, there is a threshold guardian, the foreground of the adventure that is to come. The Cyclops has one eye, and when Odysseus and his men pierce his eye, it represents their going over the threshold, through the narrow gate, and into the realm of dream.

So, Odysseus and twelve men go ashore to explore this strange land. They discover a cave, go in, and find pots of milk and curd and butter. They think, "Well, we're in the home of a shepherd." But when this shepherd comes in, he turns out to be a giant cannibal. This monster asks Odysseus, "Who are you?" and Odysseus has the wit to answer: "No-man"—which is to say, having moved into the dream realm, the realm of the gods, he has divested himself of his secular character. Well, everybody knows what happens. The Cyclops eats half a dozen of the men, and Odysseus concludes that he has a serious problem. So, with one of the meals, he offers Polyphemus some wine that the priest of Ismarus has given him. The Cyclops drinks the wine, goes to sleep, and the men then drive his eye out with a great big beam. Oh, he hollers then. But when the other Cyclopes ask, "What's the matter in there? Who's hurting you?" he says, "No-man." So they say, "Well, then, shut up and keep it to yourself."

Then Polyphemus sits outside the cave to get Odysseus and the six remaining men as they go out. Here we have a very important scene. How do they get out of the cave? Odysseus ties three sheep together with one of his men underneath them; when the sheep go out of the cave, the blind Cyclops touches them and, thinking they are only sheep, lets them pass. Odysseus repeats the ploy: three more sheep go out with another man, three more with another, and so on. Finally, Odysseus ties himself underneath the great ram, the leader of the flock, and the ram carries him out of the cave. Now at that time, in that part of the world, the ram was symbolic of the solar power. So Odysseus, divesting himself of his secular character, takes the name of "No-man," and identifies with the solar power. He establishes his consubstantiality with the sun, as it were, and his final adventure, you will recall, is to be in the Isle of the Sun.

Having passed over the threshold, having escaped from the Cyclops on the solar ram, going through the narrow gate past the dangerous door guardian, having done all of this, one could feel the type of spiritual exaltation known as inflation. It happens in every ashram: you can see inflation all over the place. And so Odysseus turns up next on the island of inflation, the volcanic isle of Aeolus, the God of the Winds, who gives Odysseus a wallet full of all the winds except the one that would send him home. Then, when the ships are in sight of home, Odysseus's men, thinking there is treasure in the wallet, open it, and all the contrary winds escape and blow the ships far away from Ithaca. Odysseus and his men are now deflated. Inflation, deflation, inflation, deflation: manic depression.

They come next to the isle of the Lestrygonians, who are also cannibals, and they smash eleven of Odysseus's twelve ships. So, now there is only one boat left, and this brings us, then, to the second great initiation, the initiation of Circe, the woman who turns men into swine. The one who was put down by the patriarchal judge is the one who now has to be faced, and she introduces the hero to the two other great initiations: the first, into the abyss, the biological force; the other, to the Isle of the Sun, the light, the illuminating source—and both come from the negative woman. These are also the initiations Bloom and Stephen will undergo in the Dublin brothel.

[The initiations are introduced by a dismemberment motif that is found in many myths.] The twelve ships having been reduced to one, which is dismemberment of a sort, the surviving ship arrives on Circe's Isle. The dismembered party goes ashore to see where they are. They come to a big swampy area,[26] in the midst of which is a great palace, and in it is Circe of the braided locks, weaving. Most of the men go inside and are turned into swine, but Odysseus, fortunately, does not go with them. Hermes comes to him and says, "Look, you're in trouble. This is a woman who cannot be pushed around. I'm going to give you a charm to protect yourself from her magic." And he gives him a little plant called a *moly*. We'll see that Bloom carries in his pocket a potato to protect himself against arthritis, rheumatism, or sciatica. This is his *moly*, and when it's taken from him, he stands in the midst of swine. Then Hermes says, "When you go, keep this with you. She will attempt to enchant you. But just pull out your dagger and threaten her and she'll quiet down and invite you to her bed. Well, go." The temptress, the seductress, the one who leads you into the realm of sin and turns you into a pig: she is the initiator. It is through that aspect of the female that the male comes to perceptions beyond the bounds of what one learns from school and from the pulpit.

There are two initiations in the Circe episode: one is Odysseus's initiation to the underworld, wherein he meets the Ancestral Powers that build our body; the other is his going to the land of her father, the Isle of the Sun, where he comes to illumination of consciousness. Circe gives Odysseus both of these initiations. First, she sends him to Hades, the underworld, where the energy of biological forces are encountered. Most of the figures he meets there are just shadowy spooks; but he has one important encounter with a diplastic presence, the main figure in the underworld: Tiresias, who represents the androgyne, of which each of us is a part.

The story of Tiresias is that he was out walking in the forest one day when he came upon a pair of copulating serpents, and he placed his staff between them and was transformed into a woman. He was a woman for seven years, and at the beginning of the eighth year, she/he was walking through the forest and came upon two copulating serpents. And she/he placed his/her staff between them and was turned back into a man.

[Then, one day, Zeus and Hera were discussing whether men or women had greater delight from sex. Tiresias, of course, would be the ideal one to consult on the matter, since he had been both man and woman. So, they sent for him, and he decided in Zeus's favor, that women had the greater joy in sex.] Well, for some reason, Hera took this badly and struck Tiresias blind.

I remember talking about this in a seminar one time, and in the interval between sessions, a woman came up to me and said, "I can tell you why Hera got angry." Well, it's good to learn from women, so I said, "All right, I'd love to hear it." She said, "Because from now on she cannot say to Zeus, 'I'm doing this for you, darling.'"

So Zeus, feeling a certain responsibility for Tiresias's plight, gave him the gift of prophetic sight. Having closed his eyes to the mere phenomenality of the world, Tiresias was on the inside and in touch with the great morphological powers that shape and terminate life courses. So, having been both man and woman, Tiresias knows both sides of the mystery: not just the he-man side, but the woman's side as well. Hence, Odysseus meets him in the underworld; for the hero's great problem is to acquiesce in a dialogue with the female, where the male is not dominant, but in interaction with an equivalent, but different, entity. That, we will see, is Stephen's problem: "Can I, like Tiresias, become one with the female power?" That's Bloom's problem also.

The second initiation Circe gives him is the solar initiation in the Isle of the Sun, the Lord of Light. [Here Odysseus's hungry men kill the sacred cattle of the Sun, and Zeus promises to destroy the sacrilegious killers of light. Odysseus himself is spared, because he did not eat the cattle, but his ship is struck by Zeus's lightning.] Here he undergoes complete self-divestiture: his ships and men are all smashed up, and he is pulled back from Penelope once again.

He stops then for seven years on the island with Calypso. She is [a nymph, a little goddess, the second magical female creature in his journey.] Again the female introduces the hero to that side of life which he had not taken into account. He is learning down in this realm of dream, of spiritual experiences, the dialogue (so to say) of the feminine principle, first through Circe, then through Calypso.

From Calypso's isle he goes to the Isle of Creations, where he learns other things from the lovely young Nausicaa, and it is here that he tells his story to her parents. The Phaeacians then put him on a ship, transport him back to his homeland, and leave him asleep on the shore. So on this whole voyage, he has been, as it were, in sleep, being introduced to the female powers of the psychological world to which he had paid no attention.

In his own land again, Odysseus meets his son. Where? In the swineherd's shelter: again the pig motif. The pig was an important sacrificial animal in the ancient world. It was the animal whose blood was poured downward into the underworld in sacrifice to the abyssal powers. It is with the swineherd then (as it was with Circe, who turns men into swine) that the great chthonic crises are to be experienced. And so in *Ulysses,* the meeting of father and son is in a brothel, and the mother superior of the brothel is depicted as a pig woman; and it's there that the whole underside of Bloom's character comes up, and he is turned into a shy little female piglet. But you must remember: although Circe turned Odysseus's men into swine, he compelled her to turn them back into men; and when she did, they were younger and fairer and stronger than they had been before they were turned into swine. That is the lesson to be learned here.

So that's the story of how Odysseus, his fixation on ego and self-interest having been cancelled, undergoes this induction of the male into the mystery of union with the female power. Having been opened up to compassion—not passion, but compassion—he is now ready to meet his wife in a proper way. And with that opening to compassion, one opens to the world, as well as to the female power.

Homer has presented in the *Odyssey,* which was created in the eighth century B.C., the three aspects of the female in relation to the male in the western world. However, these aspects are archetypes still operative in our own time, and Joyce uses these archetypes: they are the aspects of the female that Bloom has in his mind and will encounter. With these aspects of initiation in mind, then, we will now go through *Ulysses* in detail, chapter by chapter.

## THE TELEMACHUS CHAPTERS

### *Telemachus*

Stephen has come back to Dublin and is teaching school in Dalkey, south of Dublin, and he's living in a martello tower in Sandycove with two companions, Buck Mulligan, an Irish medical student, and Haines, an English invader who has come to Ireland to collect folklore. The English have taken everything else from Ireland, and now they are going to get the folklore and sell it.

Now, Martello towers are circular fortresses. They were built in the

British Isles at the time when Napoleon was threatening to attack, and they have walls about six feet thick that shut out the world and the kind of slot windows you can shoot through. I've been inside several of these towers. The eerie, cool gray light within makes the rooms seem a strange, artificial environment. On the top of Stephen's Martello tower (which stands near Dun Laoghaire, south of Dublin) there is a parapet, where the first chapter of *Ulysses* begins.

Stephen's Irish companion, Mulligan, who is going to be in the role of the Father, but the false Father, enters in the role of a priest.

> Stately, plump Buck Mulligan came from the stairhead, bearing a bowl of lather on which a mirror and a razor lay crossed. A yellow dressinggown, ungirdled, was sustained gently behind him on the mild morning air. He held the bowl aloft and intoned:
> —*Introibo ad altare Dei.* (u3)

"I will go unto the altar of God." Those are the first words of the Mass; this is a mock Mass. Mulligan enters like a priest—you've seen a priest come in to say Mass: carrying the chalice with the paten on top of it, his vestments sustained behind him on the morning air. That's what Mulligan is doing. He puts his shaving-bowl down on the parapet, looks out over Dublin Bay, and makes believe he is a priest saying Mass.

> Halted, he peered down the dark winding stairs and called out coarsely:
> —Come up, Kinch! Come up, you fearful jesuit!

He is calling Stephen. Then he continues his ritual.

> Solemnly he came forward and mounted the round gunrest. He faced about and blessed gravely thrice the tower, the surrounding land and the awakening mountains. Then, catching sight of Stephen Dedalus, he bent towards him and made rapid crosses in the air, gurgling in his throat and shaking his head. . . .
> He added in a preacher's tone:
> —For this, O dearly beloved, is the genuine christine: body and soul and blood and ouns. . . . One moment. A little trouble about those white corpuscles. Silence, all. (u3)

The mug contains shaving soap (white corpuscles) which is not the same color as the wine of the Mass, the red corpuscles. Then Mulligan turns around, just as the priest turns in the Mass, and he begins shaving. So we have this mockery of the Mass, a Black Mass, which runs all through the book. *Ulysses* is not only Dante's hell and the *Odyssey* of Homer, it is also a Black Mass.

After the Mass has been celebrated, Buck and Stephen go downstairs to have breakfast. Mulligan hacks three fried eggs out of a pan and puts them on the plates. Now, three fried eggs: this represents the mystery of the Trinity. The Trinity is three divine personalities—the Father, the Son, and the Holy Ghost—in one divine substance. Well, look at three fried eggs in a pan. That's what you've got: three separate, perfectly circular, sunny-side-up personalities in a single, consubstantial, circular, white ground—yellow and white, by the way, are the colors of the Roman Church's flag! As Buck flops the eggs on the plates, he specifically identifies what they symbolize:

> He hacked through the fry on the dish and slapped it out on three plates, saying:
> —*In nomine Patris et Filii et Spiritus Sancti.* (U11)

"In the name of the Father, the Son, and the Holy Ghost"—that's who they are: Mulligan is the Father, but the false Father; Stephen is the Son, the Christ, the incarnate king savior; and Haines, who has been having dreams about shooting a black panther, is an inverted, negative Holy Ghost. What lies behind this black panther theme? Around the time Joyce was writing this, Thomas Hardy published "Panthera," his poem about an accusation directed at Mary (in the Talmud or the Midrash, one or the other) that claimed she had conceived Jesus, not from the Holy Ghost, but from a Roman officer named Panthera, the false Holy Ghost.[27] So Haines is the false Holy Ghost, as Mulligan is the false Father. And as these young men are eating eggs, in comes a little Irishwoman, bringing the milk.

> He watched her pour into the measure and thence into the jug rich white milk, not hers. Old shrunken paps. She poured again a mea-sureful and a tilly. Old and secret she had entered from a morning world, maybe a messenger. She praised the goodness of the milk, pouring it out. Crouching by a patient cow at daybreak in the lush field, a witch on her toadstool, her wrinkled fingers quick at the squirting dugs. They lowed about her who they knew, dewsilky

cattle. Silk of the kine and poor old woman, names given her in old times.

*Silk of the kine and poor old woman...* These are Irish names for Ireland. This woman is the symbol of plundered Ireland itself. Her counterpart in Homer is Athena, the goddesss who tells Telemachus, "Go find your father." It is Athena–Mother Ireland who has come into this male domicile. Stephen is alerted by her to the problem of Ireland, the consciousness of his race.

A wandering crone, lowly form of an immortal serving her conqueror and her gay betrayer...

Haines is the conqueror; Mulligan, the betrayer invited him in.

their common cuckquean, a messenger from the secret morning. To serve or to upbraid, whether he could not tell: but scorned to beg her favour.
—It is indeed, ma'am, Buck Mulligan said, pouring milk into their cups.
—Taste it, sir, she said.
He drank at her bidding. (U12)

*He drank at her bidding.* Thus Stephen-Kinch is reminded of the exploitation of Ireland, that the Irish spirit is being exploited and wiped out. Remember that in *A Portrait* Stephen said: "I go... to forge in the smithy of my soul the uncreated conscience of my race." (P253) Stephen has been caught by the little old woman, and this moment is his call to restore, you might say, the Irish spirit to Ireland. The first three sections of *Ulysses,* then, will focus on the launching of his intention, and this theme will culminate in the "Proteus" chapter, as he walks on the same beach on which Joyce later would walk with Nora Barnacle. In the meantime, Buck addresses the milkwoman "somewhat loudly," as a master.

—If we could live on good food like that, he said to her somewhat loudly, we wouldn't have the country full of rotten teeth and rotten guts. Living in a bogswamp, eating cheap food and the streets paved with dust, horsedung and consumptives' spits.
—Are you a medical student, sir? the old woman asked.
—I am, ma'am, Buck Mulligan answered.
—Look at that now, she said.

> Stephen listened in scornful silence. She bows her old head to a voice that speaks to her loudly, her bonesetter, her medicineman: me she slights. To the voice that will shrive and oil for the grave all there is of her but her woman's unclean loins, of man's flesh made not in God's likeness, the serpent's prey. And to the loud voice that now bids her be silent with wondering unsteady eyes.
>
> —Do you understand what he says? Stephen asked her.
>
> —Is it French you are talking, sir? the old woman said to Haines.
>
> Haines spoke to her again a longer speech, confidently.
>
> —Irish, Buck Mulligan said. Is there Gaelic on you?
>
> —I thought it was Irish, she said, by the sound of it. Are you from the west, sir?
>
> —I am an Englishman, Haines answered.
>
> —He's English, Buck Mulligan said, and he thinks we ought to speak Irish in Ireland.
>
> —Sure we ought to, the old woman said, and I'm ashamed I don't speak the language myself, I'm told it's a grand language by them that knows.
>
> —Grand is no name for it, said Buck Mulligan. Wonderful entirely. (U12–13)

That is where poor little Ireland stands. It is a wasteland of lost causes, ruled politically by an English king, spiritually by an Italian pope, sentimentally by rhetoric, and socially by the pub. And this old woman, who comes to Stephen as Athena came to Telemachus, is the messenger saying, "Go find your father." So Stephen, who has been living with an Englishman and an anglicized Irishman, begins to think, "I've got to find my father elsewhere." He now knows that he will leave the usurped tower to go forth on a quest to find his father, to forge in the smithy of his soul the uncreated conscience of his race, to become the savior of Ireland.

### Nestor

The next chapter, "Nestor," takes place at the school south of the tower where Stephen is teaching. His schoolmaster-employer, an Irishman named Mr. Deasy, is an Anglophile, which Stephen finds repulsive. Deasy (a flower motif: "Deasy"[28] and "Bloom") is a collector of old coins and shells. Shells are crystallizations of life: life fixed and brought to a halt, life left behind. Coins are concretizations of life energy, but they are not life. If one collects money for money's sake, it's like collecting shells for the shell's sake, money being but a token for the possibility of spending it. Likewise, to hold on to one's ego, ego-sentiments, ego-ideals, and ego-principles—even, indeed, on occasion, to one's life—is to arrest the flow and to become a shell. Mr. Deasy pompously lectures Stephen on thrift:

> —Because you don't save, Mr Deasy said, pointing his finger. You don't yet know what money is. Money is power. When you have lived as long as I have. I know, I know. *If youth but knew.* But what does Shakespeare say? *Put but money in thy purse....*
>
> —He knew what money was, Mr Deasy said. He made money. A poet, yes, but an Englishman too. Do you know what is the pride of the English? Do you know what is the proudest word you will ever hear from an Englishman's mouth?...I will tell you.... *I paid my way.... I paid my way. I never borrowed a shilling in my life.* Can you feel that? *I owe nothing.* Can you? (U25)

Well, Stephen has never paid his way anywhere, and he is in debt right now. Money is not what he understands. It may be crystallized energy, but it doesn't become viable energy until it is released in life. The life in Mr. Deasy is gone. This academic man is simply dealing with shells. Stephen sees that in the schools, just as in the Church, it is all playing with hollow shells. Where, O where, is life?

Also, Deasy is anti-Jewish, which Stephen finds discomforting. Since his revelation this day is to come from a Jew, it is appropriate that this theme comes in here.

> —Mark my words, Mr Dedalus, he said. England is in the hands of the jews. In all the highest places: her finance, her press. And they are the signs of a nation's decay. Wherever they gather they eat up the nation's vital strength. I have seen it coming these years. As sure as we are standing here the jew merchants are already at their work of destruction....
>
> —A merchant, Stephen said, is one who buys cheap and sells dear, jew or gentile, is he not?
>
> —They sinned against the light, Mr Deasy said gravely....
>
> —Who has not? Stephen said.
>
> —What do you mean? Mr Deasy asked.

He came forward a pace and stood by the table. His underjaw fell sideways open uncertainly. Is this old wisdom? He waits to hear from me.

—History, Stephen said, is a nightmare from which I am trying to awake.

Outside, some boys are noisily playing hockey.

From the playfield the boys raised a shout. A whirring whistle: goal. What if the nightmare gave you a back kick?

—The ways of the Creator are not our ways, Mr Deasy said. All human history moves toward one great goal, the manifestation of God....

Stephen jerked his thumb toward the window saying:

—That is God.

Hooray! Ay! Whrrwhee!

—What? Mr Deasy asked.

—A shout in the street, Stephen answered, shrugging his shoulders. (u28)

*A shout in the street...* is God. Stephen's shift of emphasis is a very important theme: God isn't the transcendent one "out there"; God is the immanent principle right here in everything, in everybody. In the dog that is going to be walking about on the shore, God (dog in reverse) is right there in him. God is a shout in the street: God is immanent everywhere and in everything. Mr. Deasy speaks of the process of God in history. There is no process, Stephen says, God is present. This resembles the idea in the Gnostic *Gospel According to Thomas:* "The kingdom of the Father is spread upon the earth and men do not see it." (Thomas 99:16–18) That revelation of the Father's kingdom is also the radiance of esthetic arrest. Stephen says, "History is a nightmare from which I am trying to awake." His quest is for that eternal core, that essence of all things which moves through all history—the metamorphoses I spoke of—that one spirit that lives through all the metamorphoses of all things.

## Proteus

And now we come to the third chapter, "Proteus," and this is the one I've been moving towards. It's the last of the Telemachus chapters, and it presents the key to Stephen's problem, for it is here that he realizes his problem is not to escape from Ireland, but to escape from his own ego. This fantastic chapter is terribly compact, so let me begin by giving you a sense of what we will be encountering.

The chapter opens with Stephen, walking in a reflective mood by the waters of Dublin Bay, along Sandymount shore. He is trying to penetrate the fluctuant mirage of phenomenality and intuit the hidden substance (or, possibly, the void) behind, beyond, below, and within the modalities, the visible forms of time and space, which he names (using Schopenhauer's terms) the *Nacheinander* and *Nebeneinander,* the field of things "succeeding each other" (in time) and "beside each other" (in space). The rolling in of the waves—appearing, transforming themselves, breaking, and disappearing—Stephen identifies with these modalities, which are "ineluctable . . . at least that if no more": ineluctable and ever changing; so that, in trying to hold to any present shape, even to one's own, one is against life, which, passing on, leaves behind a shell that in the end must also disappear. Stephen hears the shells on the beach beneath his feet going "Crush, crack, crick, crick."

Out beyond the rising of the waves is a boat, in which some men are waiting to fish up the body of a drowned man, whom Stephen associates with the void or substance he is trying to apprehend. The theme of the man drowned in the sea evokes the alchemical motif of the king drowned in the ocean who asks for his son to come and rescue him.[29] It reflects the Gnostic idea of the spirit, descended into matter and now lost in matter, that must be rescued by the son of the spirit, the son of man. So who is the drowned man in the ocean? The waves represent modalities, and beneath the waves of modality is the mystery of the one who is drowned. Recall the idea of God being a noise in the street? The drowned man is a symbol for God, drowned in the world, in the ocean of street noises, in the ocean of our lives. The divine is there and can be personified as God. So when we look at forms all around us, what are we looking at? We're looking at God, but we don't see Him; we see only forms, modalities of the visible world. Stephen thinks of the old Irish sea-god Mananaan MacLir, hidden lord of the "Land Below Waves"; the curling breakers, row upon row, are the necks of his "whitemaned seahorses." But the god himself is invisible and, even now, taking to himself that invisible drowned man. Stephen thinks:

"A drowning man. His human eyes scream to me out of horror of his death. I . . . With him together down . . ."(u38)

Here the narrative question of the novel is announced: Will Telemachus dare to leave his fatherless house and go in quest of Ulysses? Is Stephen the true son? Will he have the courage to let go of the shell of himself and unite . . . *together down* . . . with that drowned man, entrusting himself to the invisible god, Mananaan, the Former of forms, below waves? Will he die to save that man?

There is an inspired passage in Schopenhauer's paper "On the Foundation of Morality," where he argues that the first law of nature is self-protection; and he asks: "By what inversion of that law does it become possible for an individual to respond to the suffering of another as though it were his own, even to the point of forgetting his own safety and, at the risk of life and limb, going to that other's aid?" His answer is that in such an apparently unnatural act one is responding to the signal of a deeper nature, the intuition of a deeper truth, namely, that one is actually, transcendentally, of one substance with that other. Such compassion (*Mitleid,* "shared suffering"), he says, is the only truly moral sentiment. It is the heart's perception of a truth transcending the *Nebeneinander* and *Nacheinander*—the apparent truths of space and time, where things appear to be separate from each other and self-protection is the law of life— namely, that you and the other, being of one substance, are, in fact, one.[30]

In Richard Ellmann's massive biography of James Joyce, there is a charming clue, from Joyce's own background, to the personal crisis commemorated in Stephen's meditation. For it was on the very day of the action of *Ulysses*—Thursday, June 16, 1904—that young James Joyce, twenty-two years old, strolled for the first time, of an evening, with the girl he later married, Nora Barnacle; and the scene of that fateful adventure was Sandymount shore. Correspondingly, the practical problem, the personal crisis, haunting Stephen and fueling his lofty cerebrations, simply and plainly is ultimately the threat of marriage, which is quite an agony for any young man.

Furthermore [the date, June 16, is also significant because it is less than a week before the summer solstice.] The sun at the summer solstice, the longest day of the year, reaches the climax of its curve and then begins its descent into winter. Stephen, the young bachelor, has reached the climax of his individual curve and is about to move into double harness. This haughtily independent, self-protecting, retaining youth is going to undergo a seachange. He is going to have to lose himself and open up. The question he is asking himself is: "How can I (this wonderfully luminous separate person with no responsibilities) acquiesce in this way in the will and being of another?" This theme is symbolized here in two aspects: one, giving oneself to a wife; the other, giving oneself to another in the character of one's father. So as Stephen walks along the beach, the thought hidden in his mind is not only, "Would I save a drowning man?" but "Can I open myself to marriage?" Can I open to the possibility of a life at least partly out of my control and in the control of somebody else? No longer am I the center of the shell.

Now let's take a detailed look at this real luster of a chapter. It begins with this paragraph:

> Ineluctable modality of the visible: at least that if no more, thought through my eyes. Signatures of all things I am here to read, seaspawn and seawrack, the nearing tide, that rusty boot. Snotgreen, bluesilver, rust; coloured signs. Limits of the diaphane. But he adds: in bodies. Then he was aware of them bodies before of them coloured. How? By knocking his sconce against them, sure. Go easy. Bald he was and a millionaire, *maestro di color che sanno.* Limit of the diaphane in. Why in? Diaphane, adiaphane. If you can put your five fingers through it it is a gate, if not a door. Shut your eyes and see.(U31)

*Ineluctable modality of the visible:...Ineluctable* means you can't get away from it; *modality* refers to the formal aspect of experience, to forms that are visible and mobile, not to the substantiality which cannot be penetrated by our eyes. The *ineluctable modality of the visible* is what we behold.

*...at least that if no more,...* Stephen is trying to identify the things that one can be sure of. This is the visible world. What's the substance behind this modality? Who knows? There may or may not be a metaphysical problem defining it. It's ineluctable. What Stephen knows about this *modality of the visible is:*

*...thought through my eyes.* The thought has come to Stephen through his eyes. They are open and see only these modalities. Stephen is walking near the waves of the sea. Now if once every five hundred years you were to take a picture of this seashore on movie film, and if you did this for several

million years and then viewed that film, you would see mountains rising and falling as waves. The whole world that we are in, viewed in a different time perspective, is seen to be throwing us out like bubbles that then sink down again.

*Signatures of all things I am here to read...* That phrase is Jakob Boehme's "signatures of all things." But who signed all these things? Who or what is the source responsible for all of this? Stephen sees everything as a life statement signed by something: a life has left it. The shells on the beach bear signatures of a snail, or an oyster, or a clam. Stephen is here to find who or what wrote these signatures. He is looking for the reality that is behind the ineluctable.

*...seaspawn and seawrack...:* thrown up by the tide, as we all are (as it were) tossed up from the sea of the infinite dark out of which all things come. That eternal sea is forever throwing up forms, throwing up forms. The world of waking consciousness is the world of experiencing what has become. The life pulse in us is always throwing forth the very next quarter-second of our being, but I get you a second late. All we see are the *seaspawn* and *seawrack* that has been tossed up by a process that we don't contact.

*...the nearing tide, that rusty boot. Snotgreen, bluesilver, rust: coloured signs.* These motifs are of the sea, mother ocean. *Snotgreen:* The ocean is snotgreen; the green of the sea is associated with the mother (U5); the mother is within you; the snot is the ocean within you. You can't get away. The fluid of vital substances, the life that is in the ocean: all this is in you, in Stephen; and it comes out there on the handkerchief. We are of the substance of the sea.

*Limits of the diaphane.* A diaphanous gown is one through which you can see: *the diaphane* is that through which you can see, and there is a limit to it. *But he adds: in bodies.* It is not something outside. It is inside. *Then he was aware of them bodies before of them coloured.* This refers to Locke's problem about what we are experiencing in colors.[31] There are no colors; there are only light waves that hit our eyes. The colors are in our heads. Bodies seem to be out there. *How?...* do we know there are bodies out there? *By knocking his sconce against them, sure.* You get it as a body without seeing it as a colored body; that is to say, sight moves now to touch.

*Go easy. Bald he was and a millionaire,...* This theme is about the father, Odysseus; and it also has to do with Aristotle:[32] *maestro di color che sanno,* the next phrase, is Dante's description of Aristotle.

*Limit of the diaphane in. Why in? Diaphane, adiaphane.* Stephen is raising this polarity now. The adiaphane is the non-diaphanous into which we do not penetrate: the world beyond the world of conscious experience, or within it.

*If you can put your five fingers through it it is a gate, if not a door.* The door shuts you off; the gate lets you see through. This is transparency to transcendence. Can we turn things that are doors into gates, so that we can see through the phenomenal world into the transcendent dimension? So much for space.

*Shut your eyes and see.* Stephen is trying to follow his inner eye. Can you turn these walls into a gate? Can you have them open, as it were, to reveal the dimension of the mystery?

> Stephen closed his eyes to hear his boots crunch crackling wrack and shells. You are walking through it howsomever. I am, a stride at a time. A very short space of time through very short times of space. Five, six: the *Nacheinander.*

Schopenhauer's word.[33] We've had the problem of space, now here we get the time motif. Kant said that space is the form of the outer sense, and time the form of the inner sense. Schopenhauer, following Kant, calls space the *Nebeneinander,* since things are beside each other in space. Time he calls the *Nacheinander,* because things follow each other in time. There would be no separateness were it not for space and time. So Stephen, his eyes closed, is inside of himself now, trying to go past space and time to that substance beyond separateness which is the consubstantial base of all beings.

Exactly: and that is the ineluctable modality of the audible.

We are shut out from our own interior self by the tick of time: one, two, three, four, beat. We experience that within. That is the inner form of sensibility which shuts us out from "*das Ding an sich.*"

Open your eyes. No. Jesus! . . .

The idea comes of the one incarnate in space and time, Jesus, the sacrifice. Before we saw the one outside: the father, the bald one, *Nebeneinander,* space. Now we see the one inside: the son, time.

> If I fell over a cliff that beetles o'er his base, fell through the *Nebeneinander* ineluctably!

He is associating himself with Jesus, with Hamlet, with the son seeking the father.

> I am getting on nicely in the dark. My ash sword hangs at my side.

He has a stick he always carries with him [an ashplant, a cane made of ashwood with the bark on it,] that he uses as a fencing sword, Hamlet's sword. Stephen is a great fencer. He is always dueling, verbally and in every other way, defending his ego against attack, holding off the world. Inside he's scared stiff about everything, but outside he is crusty and ego-defensive. But the ashplant is also a wand, the sign of the master magician.

> Tap with it: they do.

Blind people do. Stephen is the blind man here: he is walking with his eyes closed. Blind: symbolic of the dynamic of the will just in space, and not with eyes open. Bloom later will be leading a blind boy. A blind-boy motif runs through the book: tap-tap, tap-tap. The tap-tap is time, living in the field of time.

> My two feet in his boots are at the ends of his legs, *nebeneinander.*

He is wearing Buck Mulligan's shoes and second-hand trousers—"Secondleg, they should be," says Mulligan (U5)—and Stephen thinks of himself as mixed up with another person.[34] Without space, he might be Buck Mulligan.

> Sounds solid: made by the mallet of Los *demiurgos.*

*Demiurgos* is the demiurge, the creative power of God; *Los,* Blake's idea of the Creator, is the word "*sol*" ("sunlight") spelled backwards. *Los demiurgos:* that interior demonic principle that throws forth the forms of the world. Now Stephen asks:

> Am I walking into eternity along Sandymount strand? Crush, crack, crick, crick. Wild sea money. Dominie Deasy kens them a'. . . .

This is Deasy's world: shells—bodies cast up by life, but emptied of life. Many of us. And now comes a very amusing motif.

> Open your eyes now. I will. One moment. Has all vanished since? If I open and am for ever in the black adiaphane. *Basta!* I will see if I can see.

*Has all vanished since?* Not at all. Your eyes are not the ones that create the world. God's eyes create the world. In the Kabbala the *Makropro-sopos,* the great face of God, is shown in profile because the other side is un-known and unknowable; and the eye has no lid, because if God were to close his eye the world would dissolve.

> See now. There all the time without you: and ever shall be, world without end. (U31)

So, we've talked about space; we've talked about time; we've talked about modality. Schopenhauer reduces Kant's transcendental esthetic to those three terms—space, time, and modality—which shape and enclose our experience of the world. In India it's called *māyā*. Now here's an epis-temological problem: If I shut my eyes, has it all disappeared? You can't have an object without a subject. An object is not in the field of time and space unless through our sensory apparatus we put it in the field of time and space. If there's no one around to hear a tree falling in the wilderness, does it make a sound? The waves are there in the air, but is there a sound? Well, I suppose the mice are hearing it. You're not the only one that's hold-ing the world together. That's God's job.

There are two midwives walking on the beach.[35]

> They came down the steps from Leahy's terrace prudently, *Frauenzimmer:* and down the shelving shore flabbily, their splayed feet sinking in the silted sand. Like me, like Algy, coming down to our mighty mother. Number one swung lourdily her midwife's bag, the other's gamp poked in the beach. From the liberties, out for the day. Mrs Florence MacCabe, relict of the late Patk MacCabe, deeply lamented, of Bride Street. One of her sisterhood lugged me squeal-ing into life. Creation from nothing. What has she in the bag? A mis-birth with a trailing navelcord, hushed in ruddy wool.

This image is intriguing with respect to causality: Rudy is the name of Bloom's little boy, who died eleven years before, at the age of eleven days, and was buried in a wool jacket: *ruddy wool.* So here Stephen is having, as it were, a premonition of meeting Bloom. There are a number of things like this throughout the book, and I think Joyce has a feeling that you live this way if you are open enough inside. Somehow you have premonitions of what's to come, and events unfold in mysteriously appropriate ways, with what Jung called "synchronicity."

> The cords of all link back, strandentwining cable of all flesh. That is
> why mystic monks. Will you be as gods? Gaze in your *omphalos.*
> Hello! Kinch here. Put me on to Edenville. Aleph, alpha: nought,
> nought, one.
>
> Spouse and helpmate of Adam Kadmon: Heva, naked Eve. She
> had no navel.

Now Stephen is speaking of navel cords. [*Omphalos* is Greek for the
navel; Stephen sees the navelcords of all humanity as a long-distance telephone line linking us all to Eve:][36] She had no navel because she had no
mother. Here is the problem of the first cause:

> Gaze. Belly without blemish, bulging big, a buckler of taut vellum,
> no, whiteheaped corn, orient and immortal, standing from everlast-
> ing to everlasting. Womb of sin.

Stephen is quoting a seventeenth-century book about the Golden Age
of wheat, Mother Nature timeless: *standing from everlasting to everlasting.*
*Womb of sin.*[37] Joyous and immortal Eve: it is from her that we have fallen
into the world of sin. So Stephen is seeking the solution to the mystery of
the begetting that is behind the mother as the pristine virginal earth.

> Wombed in sin darkness I was too, made not begotten.

Here is that idea of double fatherhood, that you have two fathers: the
physical father, the instrumental cause, the one who begets you; and
the formal or secret cause, God the Father, the one who creates you, by
whom you are made. Stephen is now going to seek the creative, not the
begetting, father.[38] Stephen was made:

> By them, the man with my voice and my eyes and a ghostwoman
> with ashes on her breath.

His mother is the *ghostwoman with ashes on her breath,* who died in
front of his eyes. You'll recall that Stephen was called back to Ireland by
his father's telegram: "Nother [sic] dying come home father." Stephen returns home. His mother is dying of cancer—that is a recurring motif. She
asks him to kneel down and pray, and he refuses. There's ego: your dying
mother's asking you to pray, but, "No! I've rejected that whole system of
popular religion." And so she dies. For an Irish Catholic mother this is a
terrible way to die, with the thought that your son has condemned himself

to eternal hell. He wouldn't save her in that extinction, and so this is gnawing at him. Mulligan challenges him on this: You're so damn proud you wouldn't even yield to your mother's last request.

> They clasped and sundered, did the coupler's will. From before the ages He willed me...
>
> ...that's the Big He...
>
> ...and now may not will me away or ever. A *lex eterna*...
>
> ...an eternal law...
>
> ...stays about Him. Is that then the divine substance wherein Father and Son are consubstantial?

*Consubstantial* is a technical theological term meaning "of one substance." Stephen, strolling along the shore, is thinking of the relationship of visible things to their source—of a son to a father, of Hamlet to Shakespeare, of himself to the ground of his being—and he comes to the relationship of Jesus, the Son, to God the Father, which is a Christian problem. If Jesus is God, and his Father is God also, what then is the relationship? Jesus said, "I and my Father are one," and those words brought him to the cross. The Sufi mystic al-Hallaj said the same thing, "I and my Beloved are one," and he too was crucified. This is the mystic realization: you and that divine immortal being of beings of which you are a particle, are one. The classical statement of the idea is *tat tvam asi*, "you are that," the famous formula in the Chāndogya Upaniṣad: "you are yourself the divine mystery you wish to know." "I and my father are one." *Is that then the divine substance wherein Father and son are consubstantial?* This is what Stephen is worrying about now. And he asks:

> Where is poor dear Arius to try conclusions?

Arius, an early fourth-century Greek patriarch of Alexandria, was a formidable and highly influential challenger of the dogma of the incarnate Son as at once True God and True Man. He said that Jesus was not true God because he was created by the Father and substantially unlike Him; he was not true man, on the other hand, because he was "adopted" by God and did not have a human soul. So the relationship of father and son is a problem.

Warring his life long upon the contransmagnificandjewbangtantiality. Illstarred heresiarch! In a Greek watercloset he breathed his last:
*euthanasia.* With beaded mitre and with crozier, stalled upon his
throne, widower of a widowed see, with upstiffed *omophorion,* with
clotted hinderparts. (U31–32)

*Warring his life long upon the contransmagnificandjewbangtantiality.*
Now this long word, the first of Joyce's big long words, is the key to the
whole problem. Let's examine it in detail.

The first syllable (*con-*) with the last five (*-tantiality*) echoes the theological concept of "consubstantiality," which, as I've already mentioned,
refers to the well-known orthodox view that God the Father and Jesus, the
Son, are two persons of one substance. The Father is the final and perfect
object of knowledge; the Son, the only subject capable of perfect knowledge of that object—since to know God is to be equal to God in the measure of one's knowledge and, consequently, to know God perfectly is to be
God. Whereby the Holy Ghost, Third Person of the one Trinity, per-
sonifies the relationship between the Two, which finally is of identity.
Throughout Joyce's novels, the operation of this third power is represented
in the image of the bird as awakener of the spirit. You will recall that in *A
Portrait,* for example, that lovely girl whom Stephen saw wading in an inlet
of the sea and who was indeed the wakener of his spirit to its destiny is described as a bird: "She seemed like one whom magic had changed into the
likeness of a strange and beautiful seabird." (P171)

And so we come to the second syllable (*-trans-*), which joined to the
last five (*-tantiality*), suggests "transubstantiality," or better, "transubstantiation," the reference being to that central mystery of the Catholic Mass,
when the priest says, "This is my body" (*Hoc est enim corpus meum*),
whereby, as the Church describes it, the bread and wine of the sacrament
are transubstantiated, that is, changed (literally, according to Catholic doctrine) into the body and blood of Christ. The phenomenal, apparent aspects of the bread and wine remaining, their substance nevertheless
changes. The wafer and wine substance moves out, the God substance
moves in: transubstantiation. And this mystery-theme, like that of consubstantiality, resounds through the whole of this third chapter. For example, on the very next page, there is a passage where Stephen is thinking
of the possibility of two priests celebrating masses in two chapels of the

same cathedral not quite simultaneously: consecrating the host, setting it down and genuflecting, elevating it, again genuflecting:

> Dan Occam thought of that, invincible doctor. A misty English morning the imp hypostasis tickled his brain. Bringing his host down and kneeling he heard twine with his second bell the first bell in the transept (he is lifting his) and, rising, heard (now I am lifting) their two bells (he is kneeling) twang in diphthong.(U33–34)

The problem here is the relation of an *eternal* moment to *discrete* moments (*nacheinander* and *nebeneinander*) in the field of time and space; also, since the body and blood of Christ are declared to be wholly present in every wafer (indeed, in every particle of every wafer) of the consecrated host, the metaphysical problem arises of the miracle by which the One God becomes Many on the separate altars of this world; or, in more general, non-theological terms, how the All can be All in all of us.

Which brings me to what I conceive to have been Joyce's chief theological theme, not only here in *Ulysses* and (as we've already seen) in the *Portrait,* but also (as we will soon see) in *Finnegans Wake* as well: namely, Joyce's answer to the biblical representation of divinity as a kind of personage somewhere "out there," absolutely transcendent of nature, and thus in no sense immanent in all things. For, in the orthodox view, there is an ontological distinction between God and man, Creator and creature, even between God and nature. God created; but a creator and his creatures, it is argued, cannot be the same, since A is not Not-A. As though the logical categories of causality and plurality can be extended to apply to metaphysical questions beyond the fields of space and time! According to this orthodox view, no one but Jesus can pretend to an experience of *identity* with divinity.

In the Orient, on the other hand, as both Joyce and Schopenhauer knew, the aim of the religious life is to realize that one is indeed in substance identical (that is, consubstantial) with the immanent Being of beings, which, while transcending all categories of logical thought and temporal experience, is yet the inhabiting and supporting ground of all things: *tat tvam asi,* "you are that." However, the "you" (*tvam*) intended in this formula is not the *you* with which one would normally identify oneself: separate from others, a shape, a shell, phenomenal in space and time, due to fade one day and disappear. On the contrary, the "you" which is "that" (*tat*) is consubstantial with the Being of all being and transcendent of temporality, as well as of logic, duality, and relationship. And the function of art—or, at least of Joyce's art, as he told us in the *Portrait*—is to transubstantiate phenomenality so that everything is seen as an epiphany of that "thatness," radiant of its own *quidditas,* or "whatness." We normally think in Christian terms of the Incarnation as unique. No one can properly say with Jesus, "I and the Father are one." For the rest, our mode must be only of a *relationship* to the Father by grace of the Incarnation: I, through my humanity, relate to the manhood of Jesus; He, through His divinity, relates me then to God. But this, I believe, is not the attitude of Joyce in his art.

It is my thesis that Joyce, in both *Ulysses* and *Finnegans Wake,* has translated the imagery of the Incarnation into Oriental terms or, rather, into such unorthodox terms as those of the Gnostic *Gospel According to Thomas,* where Christ himself is said to have declared to his disciples: "Cleave a piece of wood. I am there; lift up the stone and you will find me there" (Thomas 94:26–28). There is actually a great strain of this mystical tradition in the Christian West. It is generally thought of as Oriental only because the West has generally suppressed it. From time to time, on the other hand, it has reappeared in strength, as it did in the Renaissance, in the writings, for instance, of Pico della Mirandola, to whom Stephen likens himself in this seaside meditation. [U34] It is evident, likewise, in the works of one of the leading names and figures of *Finnegans Wake,* Giordano Bruno, who has already made an appearance in the *Portrait.* [P249] The ninth-century Irishman Scotus Erigena was a philosopher of this kind; as were, also, one millennium later, the great Germans from Kant and Goethe on down to Nietzsche.

Schopenhauer, however, was the first of these to recognize in the Indian Upaniṣads an Eastern counterpart of the transcendentalism of Kant: the term *māyā* in the Indian system corresponding both to Kant's "*a priori* forms of sensibility" (space and time), and to his "categories of thought" (quantity, quality, relation, and modality); the terms *brahman, ātman,* and *brahman-ātman,* pointing to the same enigmatic "ground," meanwhile, as the Kantian term "Thing in itself." In the Indian view, it is because of *māyā* (the *a priori* forms of time and space and the categories of thought) that we are cut off from the realization of our identity in *brahman* (*tat*), the absolute, transcendent of categories. We are separate from each other in space; separate from each other in time. But if one thinks of space and time as simply "forms of sensibility," then the whole experience of the world in terms of separateness will be recognized as secondary and delusory; the primary, deeper truth being of the consubstantiality that *Mitleid,* "compassion," reveals.

Moreover, here and now, in this world today, just as it is, and in every particle of its broad display, the whole of the mystery is immanent; nor will it be more so in a hundred years, a thousand, or in any time to come. This fundamental principle of Joyce's art was announced only a few pages earlier, in the second chapter, when Stephen, talking with his schoolmaster employer, declares, "History is a nightmare from which I am trying to awake" (which, by the way, is Joyce's first statement of the main theme of *Finnegans Wake*); and Mr. Deasy answers, "All history moves toward one great goal, the manifestation of God": which puts the day of meaning in the future, as though the moment *now* were but the means to another and better moment, a fulfilling moment, to come at the end of time, a sort of apocalyptic "Day of God" or Marxian Revolution. And, you will recall, as they are talking, sounds from a playing field are coming in through the window—a referee's whistle and schoolboys shouting, "Goal! Hooray!"—to which Stephen refers when he says, "That is God." *Contransmagnificandjew*BANG—God is a noise in the street—*tantiality!*

But Stephen, as we will see, is going to experience this very day his own realization of the Presence through his meeting with Leopold Bloom, who will reveal compassion and transubstantiation. As Joyce tells, the two were "poles apart": Stephen, an introverted, self-defensive Aryan; and Bloom, an extroverted, generous-hearted Jew: *Contransmagnificand*JEW *bangtantiality!* Moreover, Christ the Savior came in love on the Cross, as a demonstration of love, to invoke our love: as Bloom is to give himself to Stephen.

So, finally, *magnificand:* it's a reference to the "Magnificat," a Catholic prayer celebrating the words that the Virgin Mother Mary addressed to her cousin Elizabeth: "My soul doth magnify the Lord" (Luke 1:46); signifying, namely, "God is within me"—which is to be read as referring not alone to the condition of the Mother of God, two thousand years ago in Judea, but to every one of us, here and now. *Contrans*MAGNIFICAND*jewbangtantiality!*

It's quite a word: *contransmagnificandjewbangtantiality.* Joyce has summed up the whole problem of the book in that word. Now, to learn the relevance of this great word to the crisis of Stephen's own impending transubstantiation, let's return to the youth, who has been strolling on Sandymount shore, listening to the crackling of shells beneath his feet, watching the boatmen out at sea fishing for the body of a drowned man, brooding on the fluency of water.

> Airs romped round him, nipping and eager airs. They are coming, waves. The whitemaned seahorses, champing, brightwindbridled, the steeds of Mananaan. (U32)

I'm now living by the beach, and I frequently think of this image when I look out and see the waves rolling in, the foam flying like the manes of the four seahorses pulling the chariot of Mananaan MacLir, the Irish Lord of the Sea. He is a hospitable host, with a great palace under the sea where he entertains the dead who drown in his waters.

And now Stephen, who has been thinking that life is fluent, as is death, retreats from the flood tide, sits in a Hamlet-like pose on a rock facing the sea. Full of melancholy thoughts, he is at a loss for the sense of his life.

> A bloated carcass of a dog lay lolled on bladderwrack. Before him the gunwale of a boat, sunk in sand. *Un coche ensablé* Louis Veuillot called Gautier's prose. These heavy sands are language tide and wind have silted here. And these, the stoneheaps of dead builders, a warren of weasel rats. Hide gold there. Try it. You have some. Sand and stones. Heavy of the past. Sir Lout's toys. Mind you don't get one bang on the ear. I'm the bloody well gigant rolls all them bloody well boulders, bones for my steppingstones. Feefawfum. I zmellz de bloodz odz an Iridzman.
>
> A point, live dog, grew into sight running across the sweep of sand. Lord, is he going to attack me? Respect his liberty. You will not be master of others or their slave. I have my stick. Sit tight. . . .
>
> The dog's bark ran towards him, stopped, ran back. Dog of my enemy. I just simply stood pale, silent, bayed about. *Terribilia meditans.* A primrose doublet, fortune's knave, smiled on my fear. For that are you pining, the bark of their applause? Pretenders: live their lives. (U37–38)

As he sits there, watching the dog, into his mind comes his great question: Would he have the courage to dive down and try to save that drowning man? Stephen says to himself:

The truth, spit it out. I would want to. I would try. I am not a strong swimmer. Water cold soft. When I put my face into it in the basin at Clongowes. Can't see! Who's behind me? Out quickly, quickly! Do you see the tide flowing quickly in on all sides, sheeting the lows of sand quickly, shellcocoacoloured? If I had land under my feet. I want his life still to be his, mine to be mine.

That's a subtle allusion to Schopenhauer's question about a person risking his own life to save another's.

A drowning man. His human eyes scream to me out of horror of his death. I . . . With him together down. . . . I could not save her.

His mother.

Waters: bitter death: lost.

Now, John Weir Perry brought up the point that in the schizoid situation, the process of resolution has to do with evoking and cultivating a sentiment of love, of *eros,* in contrast to one of self-protection, self-control, self-defense. That is Stephen's great problem, and while he is wrestling with this dilemna, he watches the "live dog" roam the beach. He sees in the dog's mercurially changing moods the forms of many other beasts. This sequence brings together the motifs of animality and "beastly death," which run throughout the book. The dog belongs to:

A woman and a man. I see her skirties. Pinned up, I bet.

Their dog ambled about a bank of dwindling sand, trotting, sniffing on all sides. Looking for something lost in a past life. Suddenly he made off like a bounding hare, ears flung back, chasing the shadow of a lowskimming gull. The man's shrieked whistle struck his limp ears. He turned, bounded back, came nearer, trotted on twinkling shanks. On a field tenney a buck, trippant, proper, unattired. At the lacefringe of the tide he halted with stiff forehoofs, seawardpointed ears. His snout lifted barked at the wavenoise, herds of seamorse. They serpented towards his feet, curling, unfurling many crests, every ninth, breaking, plashing, from far, from farther out, waves and waves.

Cocklepickers. They waded a little way in the water and, stooping, soused their bags and, lifting them again, waded out. The dog yelped running to them, reared up and pawed them, dropping on all

fours, again reared up at them with mute bearish fawning. Unheeded
he kept by them as they came towards the drier sand, a rag of wolf's
tongue redpanting from his jaws. His speckled body ambled ahead
of them and then loped off at a calf's gallop. The carcass lay on his
path. He stopped, sniffed, stalked round it, brother, nosing closer,
went round it, sniffling rapidly like a dog all over the dead dog's
bedraggled fell. Dogskull, dogsniff, eyes on the ground, moves to
one great goal. Ah, poor dogsbody! Here lies poor dogsbody's body.

*Poor dogsbody* is Stephen. Wearing secondhand clothes, his teeth already
in decay, he has picked up Mulligan's insult and been calling himself that.

—Tatters! Outofthat, you mongrel!
    The cry brought him skulking back to his master and a blunt
bootless kick sent him unscathed across a spit of sand, crouched in
flight. He slunk back in a curve. Doesn't see me. Along by the edge
of the mole he lolloped, dawdled, smelt a rock and from under a
cocked hindleg pissed against it. He trotted forward and, lifting again
his hindleg, pissed quick short at an unsmelt rock. The simple pleasures
of the poor. His hindpaws then scattered the sand: then his forepaws
dabbled and delved. Something he buried there, his grandmother. He
rooted in the sand, dabbling, delving and stoppped to listen to the air,
scraped up the sand again with a fury of his claws, soon ceasing, a pard,
a panther, got in spousebreach, vulturing the dead. (u37–39)

The dog makes off *like a bounding hare,* turns and comes back *on
twinkling shanks...a buck.* He rears up, his *rag of wolf's tongue redpanting.*
Loping *off at a calf's gallop,* he stops at the carcass of a dog that lies in his
path, sniffs, stalks round it, nosing closer, *sniffling rapidly like a dog all over
the dead dog's bedraggled fell....He rooted in the sand* (like a pig), then
*stopped to listen to the air, scraped up the sand again with a fury of his claws,
soon ceasing, a pard, a panther.*

Further examples of this animality motif: the two friends who have
been sharing Stephen's lodging are associated with beasts: Buck Mulligan
with a "buck,' a "horse," and a "dog"; and Haines, the Englishman who
dreams of black panthers, with a panther ["all-beast" in Greek].

Moreover, it is of significance to note that later, in the "Circe" chapter,
in a scene of hellish nightmare, the word "Dog" will be reversed and become
"God." (u489–490); and soon thereafter, Stephen will be struck down by

an "English dog," a Redcoat (u484); after which, sprawled in a gutter and completely smashed in his pride, he will be rescued by the fatherly Good Samaritan Leopold Bloom, whose name—from the Middle High German *liutbald,* meaning "bold (*bald*) for the people (*liut*)"—suggests the Latin *Leo,* "lion," added to our English *polled,* or "headed": the Lion-head.

It is all the same, a trick of mirrors: God above, Dog below. The Crucifixion regarded from below is seen as a death; from aloft, it is Life Eternal. The same body in the mirrors of the mind is a dogsbody, a man, a godsbody. And what would it be with all mirrors whatsoever gone?

At the end of the "Proteus" chapter, Stephen's conflict is presented again, in a passage that provides the key to Stephen's whole [dilemma]. He is at the edge of the water where he is going finally to drown, to disappear in darkness at the end of the book. He is gazing out to sea, and he thinks of Ariel's song in *The Tempest:*

> Full fathom five thy father lies;
> > Of his bones are coral made:
> Those are pearls that were his eyes,
> > Nothing of him that doth fade,
> But doth suffer a sea-change
> Into something rich and strange.
> Sea-nymphs hourly ring his knell:
> > > Ding–Dong!
> Hark! now I hear them,—ding-dong bell.[39]

The "father" of this song and the drowned man off-shore suggest to the melancholy Stephen the mystery of Father Ocean, the Father of Life, the Former of forms who is to be sought and found beyond or within the waves of the sea of being.[40]

> Five fathoms out there. Full fathom five thy father lies. At one, he said. Found drowned. High water at Dublin bar. Driving before it a loose drift of rubble, fanshoals of fishes, silly shells. A corpse rising saltwhite from the undertow, bobbing a pace a pace a porpoise landward. There he is. Hook it quick. Sunk though he be beneath the watery floor. We have him. Easy now.

And now Stephen imagines himself going down, down, into the watery abyss, where the drowned man is disintegrating and turning into other things.

> Bag of corpsegas sopping in foul brine. A quiver of minnows, fat of a spongy titbit, flash through the slits of his buttoned trouserfly. God becomes man becomes fish becomes barnacle goose becomes featherbed mountain. Dead breaths I living breathe, tread dead dust, devour a urinous offal from all dead. Hauled stark over the gunwale he breathes upward the stench of his green grave, his leprous nosehole snoring to the sun.
>
> A seachange this, brown eyes saltblue. Seadeath, mildest of all deaths known to man. Old Father Ocean. *Prix de Paris:* beware of imitations. Just you give it a fair trial. We enjoyed ourselves immensely. (U41–42)

Here we see the struggle of life against death. You will recall, however, that this day (Thursday, June 16, 1904) is the day that Joyce first walked on the same beach with the woman whom he married. That was the moment of Joyce's passage from self-insulation and protection to marriage, where two become one. Stephen, likewise, is today at the noon of his life, facing the same crisis, so in this last sequence we also see the struggle of the male against the female. That is another of those things in this schizoid situation: the fear of passing over into the power of the female principle or, for the woman, the fear of the male. Stephen has to give himself and yield and become a married man. This is the moment of his doing it.

> Come. I thirst. Clouding over. No black clouds anywhere, are there? Thunderstorm. Allbright he falls, proud lightning of the intellect, *Lucifer, dico, qui nescit occasum.* No. My cockle hat and staff and hismy sandal shoon. Where? To evening lands. Evening will find itself.
>
> He took the hilt of his ashplant, lunging with it softly, dallying still. Yes, evening will find itself in me, without me. All days make their end. By the way next when is it Tuesday will be the longest day. Of all the glad new year, mother, the run tum tiddledy tum. Lawn Tennyson, gentleman poet. *Già.* For the old hag with the yellow teeth. And Monsieur Drumont, gentleman journalist. *Già.* My teeth are very bad. Why, I wonder. Feel. That one is going too. Shells. Ought I go to a dentist, I wonder, with that money? That one. This. Toothless Kinch, the superman. Why is that, I wonder, or does it mean something perhaps?
>
> My handkerchief. He threw it. I remember. Did I not take it up?

His hand groped vainly in his pockets. No, I didn't. Better buy one.

He laid the dry snot picked from his nostril on a ledge of rock, carefully. For the rest let look who will.

Behind. Perhaps there is someone.

He turned his face over a shoulder, rere regardant. Moving through the air high spars of a threemaster, her sails brailed up on the crosstrees, homing, upstream, silently moving, a silent ship. (U42)

[The schooner "homing upstream" is symbolic of the return of Odysseus, the father, to his home and his power, and in the *Odyssey,* the father needs the help of the son, Telemachus. That is the main theme in the passage above. The father comes home to the son in the schooner, and here the son also comes home.] In the prodigal-son motif, the son comes back to the father. But we're all prodigals. How are we going to return? The Stephen that we've been dealing with, the one in hell, is a person who doesn't have the courage to risk himself to save another.

So, the "Proteus" chapter ends with Stephen imagining himself going down into the water, and when we have followed him in that descent—he thinking, finally, in a mood of resignation: *Yes, evening will find itself in me, without me. All days make their end.*—we will turn the last page of the chapter and there, at the opening of the next, we will meet Mr. Leopold Bloom, who is Ulysses, the father, but also the drowned man in the sea of married life, with Molly, his wife, the sea-nymph hourly tolling his knell. Will Stephen, this day, have the courage and compassion to open his heart to this man, "poles apart," and to the life that through him calls? That is the prime question of *Ulysses.* And the answer is that he will. There will come a moment when Bloom is, as it were, drowning, and that is when the breakthrough will come for Stephen. His ego eliminated, he will move to save Bloom, and by the act, he will transform himself; and these two men—father and son, self-exiled from their traditions, moving through the hell of Dublin seeking each other—will finally come together. Indeed, Stephen has already prepared his heart to respond with the "Yes" of the line just cited, and from the side of the nymphs its world-echo will be heard in the deep of the night, at the end of the book, in Molly Bloom's symphony of "Yesses."

In the "Proteus" chapter are all the motifs of the experience of Dublin. Every single one of them carries over into a mythological motif, exactly the mythological motifs of the schizoid situation into which Stephen is moving. Stephen is going to disappear into the night at the end of *Ulysses*, but Joyce will survive.

## THE ODYSSEUS CHAPTERS

### *Introduction*

In *Ulysses*, these twelve chapters are not rendered in the order in which they come in the *Odyssey*. I'm going to start this [part of the analysis] with some remarks about Leopold Bloom, who like Odysseus is wandering, wandering, wandering; but unlike Odysseus, Bloom is an unaggressive gentle person, who solicits ads for a living.

Bloom has not had a very successful life; he is middle middle class and generally undistinguished. He is distinguished, however, by his generosity and compassion of spirit, qualities that are the exact opposite of Stephen's. In this respect, in fact, he and Stephen couldn't be more opposite. On the other hand, they are alike in their exclusion. Bloom is a Jew—well, he really isn't technically a Jew. His father is a Jew, but his mother is Irish.[41] In Dublin, however, he is regarded as a Jew, and so he is somewhat excluded by his society. As for Stephen, he has excluded himself from society. So, they are both excluded: one is self-excluded, the other is other-excluded.

As Bloom wanders, he is continually giving clues to people, somehow enlightening them, so to speak, without knowing that he is doing it. We'll see an example of this shortly, in the "Lotus-Eaters" chapter. Now, Bloom's dispensing boons without knowing he has the knowledge is the medieval idea of the wandering Jew, who has the book of illumination in his pocket, but is not himself illuminated. To the medieval mind, he has closed his eyes to the salvation which is the product of his own tradition.

Bloom is married to Molly, a buxom singer whom we see only in bed. Today, Bloom knows, Molly is going to have a consortium with her tour manager, whose name, significantly, is Blazes Boylan. He will visit 7 Eccles Street, and Molly will spend the day in bed entertaining him. Just as Odysseus had all the suitors in his house, so Bloom has suitors at home, and while he is off on his wanderings, he tries not to think about what he knows will be going on at home.

Now Bloom's problem isn't altogether Molly's fault. She is Penelope, the wife of Odysseus, from whom he has been away for twenty years. Bloom and Molly once had a little boy named Rudy, but the little boy is gone. When he died, their whole sensual life was, as it were, cut off; since then, they have had very little to do with each other in a primary way in their marriage. They also have a daughter, Milly, who has just turned fifteen—the proper age for marriage in traditional cultures, for in mythological thinking, the nymph is ready to be married on the day of the full moon. Milly, the little moon-girl, is what Molly was when Bloom was attracted to her. This Milly-Molly theme runs throughout the book.

Furthermore, in their bedroom Bloom has hung a picture:

> *The Bath of the Nymph* over the bed. Given away with the Easter number of *Photo Bits*...

...a cheap newspaper.

> ...splendid masterpiece in art colours.... Not unlike her...

...Molly...

> ...with her hair down: slimmer. Three and six I gave for the frame. She said it would look nice over the bed. Naked nymphs...(U53)

So, Bloom's accent in relationship to his wife Molly is (so to speak) a bit too high up. Molly is a little below that level, considerably more physical than that, and Bloom isn't really up to her. In fact, nobody is up to her, which is the point of the last chapter in the book. Meanwhile, Bloom, whose eye of address is turned on the little nymph above the bed, has used a pseudonym to advertise in the paper for anyone wishing to correspond with Henry Flower (*bloom* being a flower), and he has been carrying on a surreptitious pen-pal correspondence with a young girl. So, Bloom has set his mind on the pretty girl (the pin-up girl motif: the nymph over the bed), and while he's wandering, he's ogling every handsome female in Dublin. Yet Bloom, the wandering Jew, the one on the outskirts, so to say, is also saving souls. And he is going to save Stephen.

## Calypso

In this first Odysseus chapter, "Calypso," Bloom's mind is, you might say, more on the nymph than on Molly, so here Molly plays the role of Calypso, the middle-aged nymph with whom Odysseus spent years coming to understand the female principle. The chapter opens with Bloom in the kitchen of his house fixing breakfast for Molly:

> Mr Leopold Bloom ate with relish the inner organs of beasts and fowls. He liked thick giblet soup, nutty gizzards, a stuffed roast heart, liverslices fried with crustcrumbs, fried hencods' roes. Most of all he like grilled mutton kidneys which gave to his palate a fine tang of faintly scented urine.[42]
>
> Kidneys were in his mind as he moved about the kitchen softly, righting her breakfast things on the humpy tray. Gelid light and air were in the kitchen but out of doors gentle summer morning everywhere. Made him feel a bit peckish.
>
> The coals were reddening.
>
> Another slice of bread and butter: three, four; right. She didn't like her plate full. Right. He turned from the tray, lifted the kettle off the hob and set it sideways on the fire. It sat there, dull and squat, its spout stuck out. Cup of tea soon. Good. Mouth dry.
>
> The cat walked stiffly round a leg of the table with tail on high.
>
> —Mkgnao!
>
> —O, there you are, Mr Bloom said, turning from the fire. (U45)

He pours some milk for the cat, and while she drinks it, he thinks about what he is going to have for breakfast.

> He listened to her licking lap. Ham and eggs, no. No good eggs with this drouth. Want pure fresh water. Thursday: not a good day either for a mutton kidney at Buckley's. Fried with butter, a shake of pepper. Better a pork kidney at Dlugacz's. While the kettle is boiling. (U46)

Now, remember: the boys in the Martello tower—the Father, Son, and Holy Ghost—were eating eggs. They are totally in the masculine world, not in touch with the rhythm of Mother Nature. Bloom, on the other hand, who's not eating eggs, is in touch with the rhythm of nature. He's going to eat something else. Although he is a Jew, he decides to have a pork kidney for breakfast. He is not any better a Jew than Stephen is a Catholic.

So he goes out to get a pork kidney. As he leaves the house, he realizes that the key to the door is in his other pair of trousers—he has changed into black clothes for the funeral of Paddy Dignam today—so he closes the door just enough to make it look as if were locked. So, Bloom is dressed in black for a funeral; Stephen is wearing black because his mother is dead; and these two figures in black will be moving through the colorful world of Dublin.

Bloom goes to a Jewish pork butcher named Dlugacz. Boy, the religious system is working in this town! Dlugacz has a whole pile of advertisements for a Zionist project, Agendath Netaim. Bloom picks up a sheet and reads it, and again we have the theme of the exile: Bloom thinks about Palestine, as Odysseus thought about Ithaca. Then, going home with his kidney, Bloom hurries to walk behind the maidservant from next door—a hippy girl, as it were—and he follows this parcel of meat, you might say, back to his house.

When he arrives there [the ensuing domestic scene shows Bloom comfortably at home.] Well, not quite comfortably:

> Two letters and a card lay on the hallfloor. He stooped and gathered them. Mrs Marion Bloom. His quickened heart slowed at once. Bold hand. Mrs Marion.
> —Poldy!

Molly calls him.

> Entering the bedroom he halfclosed his eyes and walked through warm yellow twilight towards her tousled head.
> —Who are the letters for?
> He looked at them. Mullingar. Milly.
> —A letter for me from Milly, he said carefully, and a card to you. And a letter for you.
> He laid her card and letter on the twill bedspread near the curve of her knees.
> —Do you want the blind up?
> Letting the blind up by gentle tugs halfway his backward eye saw her glance at the letter and tuck it under her pillow.
> —That do? he asked, turning.
> She was reading the card, propped on her elbow.
> —She got the things, she said.
> He waited till she had laid the card aside and curled herself back slowly with a snug sigh.
> —Hurry up with that tea, she said. I'm parched.
> —The kettle is boiling, he said.

But he delayed to clear the chair: her striped petticoat, tossed soiled linen: and lifted all in an armful on to the foot of the bed.

As he went down the kitchen stairs she called:

—Poldy!

—What?

—Scald the teapot.

Downstairs, he makes tea and starts to cook the pork kidney.

Then he slit open his letter, glancing down the page and over. Thanks: new tam: Mr Coghlan: lough Owel picnic: young student: Blazes Boylan's seaside girls.

The tea was drawn....

He prodded a fork into the kidney and slapped it over: then fitted the teapot on the tray. Its hump bumped as he took it up. Everything on it? Bread and butter, four, sugar, spoon, her cream. Yes. He carried it upstairs, his thumb hooked in the teapot handle.

Nudging the door open with his knee he carried the tray in and set it on the chair by the bedhead.

—What a time you were! she said.

She set the brasses jingling as she raised herself briskly, an elbow on the pillow. He looked calmly down on her bulk and between her large soft bubs, sloping within her nightdress like a shegoat's udder. The warmth of her couched body rose on the air, mingling with the fragrance of the tea she poured.

A strip of torn envelope peeped from under the dimpled pillow. In the act of going he stayed to straighten the bedspread.

—Who was the letter from? he asked.

Bold hand. Marion.

—O, Boylan, she said. He's bringing the programme.

—What are you singing?

—*Là ci darem* with J. C. Doyle, she said, and *Love's Old Sweet Song.* (U50–52)

[Now Bloom is certain he is going to be cuckolded that very day by Molly and Blazes Boylan.] Back in the kitchen, Bloom eats his pork-kidney breakfast and reads the letter from Milly:

Dearest Papli

Thanks ever so much for the lovely birthday present. It suits me splendid. Everyone says I am quite the belle in my new tam. I got mummy's lovely box of creams and am writing. They are lovely. I am getting on swimming in the photo business now. Mr Coghlan took one of me and Mrs. Will send when developed. We did great biz yesterday. Fair day and all the beef to the heels were in....

... substantial women with heavy ankles.

We are going to lough Owel on Monday with a few friends to make a scrap picnic. Give my love to mummy and to yourself a big kiss and thanks. I hear them at the piano downstairs. There is to be a concert in the Greville Arms on Saturday. There is a young student comes here some evenings named Bannon his cousins or something are big swells and he sings Boylan's (I was on the pop of writing Blazes Boylan's) song about those seaside girls. Tell him silly Milly sends my best respects. I must now close with fondest love

Your fond daughter

Milly (U54)

So, Bloom's again been reminded of Molly's affair with Blazes Boylan, this time by his own daughter. Boylan's song, by the way, is:

*All dimpled cheeks and curls,*
*Your head it simply swirls.*
*Those girls, those girls,*
*Those lovely seaside girls.* (U55)

It's not much of a song.[43]

Now in the last chapter, Stephen realized at some deep level this is June 16th; the sun in a week will reach its apogee and start down toward winter, and his radiant, youthful, solo career will soon end. [Later in the book,] when Stephen thinks about marriage, Bloom becomes his model for a married man—and Bloom is a cuckold. Shakespeare was married and a cuckold. Bloom is married and cuckolded. A shoddy kind of life situation all around.

Bloom finishes breakfast and leaves the house. He will spend the day wandering about Dublin. As he does, he will try to keep his mind off what is going on at home, to think of something else, and his whole day, consequently, will be a kind of attempt to remain distracted. And so he will have adventures as he goes along.

## Lotus-Eaters

It is in the second chapter, the "Lotus-Eaters," that Bloom has a fanciful affair with the girl whom he has never met—the nymph, you might say, over the bed. He goes to the post office, picks up a letter from this young girl for Henry Flower, puts it in his pocket [and sets off to find a discreet place to read it, where he won't be discovered.] As he leaves the post office, he meets a friend.

> M'Coy. Get rid of him quickly. Take me out of my way. Hate company when you. (U60)

They talk about Paddy Dignam's funeral and about their wives. [Bloom is thinking about other women.] Then Bloom moves on.

> He drew the letter from his pocket and folded it into the newspaper he carried. Might just walk into her here. The lane is safer....
>
> He turned into Cumberland street and, going on some paces, halted in the lee of a station wall.... No-one.... Open it.... He opened the letter within the newspaper.
>
> A flower. I think it's a. A yellow flower with flattened petals. Not annoyed then? What does she say?

It's really a very amusing, funny letter.

> Dear Henry
>
> I got your last letter to me and thank you very much for it. I am sorry you did not like my last letter. Why did you enclose the stamps? I am awfully angry with you. I do wish I could punish you for that. I called you naughty boy because I do not like that other world. Please tell me what is the real meaning of that word?...

I don't know what word he used.

> Are you not happy in your home you poor little naughty boy? I do wish I could do something for you. Please tell me what you think of poor me. I often think of the beautiful name you have. Dear Henry, when will we meet? I think of you so often you have no idea. I have never felt myself so much drawn to a man as you. I feel so bad about. Please write me a long letter and tell me more. Remember if you do not I will punish you. So now you know what I will do to you, you naughty boy, if you do not wrote. O how I long to meet you. Henry dear, do not deny my request before my patience are exhausted.

Then I will tell you all. Goodbye now, naughty darling. I have such
a bad headache. today. and write *by return* to your longing
Martha

P. S. Do tell me what kind of perfume does your wife use. I want to
know.

This is a significant statement.44 Then there are kisses.

X X X X

He tore the flower gravely from its pinhold smelt its almost no smell
and placed it in his heart pocket. Language of flowers. They like it
because no-one can hear. Or a poison bouquet to strike him down.
(U63–64)

Well, nothing is going to come of this, as I have found out very well.
Nothing ever comes of this sort of thing. So that's that. Bloom moves on.

Fingering still the letter in his pocket he drew the pin out of it.
Common pin, eh? He threw it on the road. Out of her clothes some-
where: pinned together. Queer the number of pins they always have.
No roses without thorns....

Going under the railway arch he took the envelope, tore it swiftly
in shreds and scattered them towards the road. The shreds fluttered
away, sank in the dark air: a white flutter, then all sank. (U64–65)

Then, the letter in his pocket, Bloom passes a Catholic church:

The cold smell of sacred stone called him. He trod the worn steps,
pushed the swingdoor and entered softly by the rere.

Something going on: some sodality. Pity so empty. Nice discreet
place to be next some girl. Who is my neighbor? Jammed by the hour
to slow music. That woman at midnight mass. Seventh heaven.
Women knelt in the benches with crimson halters round their necks,
heads bowed. A batch knelt at the altarrails. The priest went along
by them, murmuring, holding the thing in his hands. He stopped at
each, took out a communion, shook a drop or two (are they in
water?) off it and put it neatly into her mouth. Her hat and head
sank. Then the next one. Her hat sank at once. Then the next one:
a small old woman. The priest bent down to put it into her mouth,
murmuring all the time. Latin. The next one. Shut your eyes and

> open your mouth. What? *Corpus:* body. Corpse. Good idea the
> Latin. Stupefies them first. Hospice for the dying. They don't seem
> to chew it: only swallow it down. Rum idea: eating bits of a corpse.
> Why the cannibals cotton to it.
>
> He stood aside watching their blind masks pass down the aisle,
> one by one, and seek their places. He approached a bench and seated
> himself in its corner, nursing his hat and newspaper. (U66)

Joyce has here associated the eating of the host with the eating of the
lotus in the *Odyssey*. [Bloom remains in church through the end of the Mass,
then moves on. He goes to the chemist's, and when he leaves there, he is
stopped by an acquaintance named Bantam Lyons.] And now here's an example of Bloom dispensing boons without knowing that he is doing so:

> At his armpit Bantam Lyons' voice and hand said:
> —Hello, Bloom. What's the best news? Is that today's? Show us
> a minute. . . .

He takes Bloom's newspaper.

> —I want to see about that French horse that's running today,
> Bantam Lyons said. Where the bugger is it?
> He rustled the pleated pages, jerking his chin on his high collar.
> Barber's itch. Tight collar he'll lose his hair. Better leave him the
> paper and get shut of him.
> —You can keep it, Mr Bloom said.
> —Ascot. Gold cup. Wait, Bantam Lyons muttered. Half a mo.
> Maximum the second.
> —I was just going to throw it away, Mr Bloom said.
> Bantam Lyons raised his eyes suddenly and leered weakly.
> —What's that? his sharp voice said.
> —I say you can keep it, Mr Bloom answered. I was going to
> throw it away that moment.
> Bantam Lyons doubted an instant, leering: then thrust the out-
> spread sheets back on Mr Bloom's arms.
> —I'll risk it, he said. Here, thanks.
> He sped off towards Conway's corner. (U70)

Well, the fellow takes Bloom's remark as a tip and, of course, a horse
named *Throwaway* will win, this story will get around, and later, we'll see
(U274–275), the incident will get Bloom in trouble.

## Hades

This next chapter, "Hades," is about Paddy Dignam's funeral, and it begins with Bloom riding in the funeral procession in a carriage with several men, including Simon Dedalus, Stephen's father.

Martin Cunningham, first, poked his silkhatted head into the creaking carriage, and, entering deftly, seated himself. Mr Power stepped in after him, curving his height with care.

—Come on, Simon.

—After you, Mr Bloom said.

Mr Dedalus covered himself quickly and got in, saying:

—Yes, yes.

—Are we all here now? Martin Cunningham asked. Come along, Bloom.

Mr Bloom entered and sat in the vacant place. He pulled the door to after him and slammed it twice till it shut tight. He passed an arm through the armstrap and looked seriously from the open carriagewindow at the lowered blinds of the avenue. . . .

All waited. Nothing was said. . . . Then wheels were heard from in front, turning: then nearer: then horses' hoofs. A jolt. Their carriage began to move, creaking and swaying. Other hoofs and creaking wheels started behind. The blinds of the avenue passed. . . .

All watched awhile through their windows caps and hats lifted by passers. Respect. . . . Mr Bloom at gaze saw a lithe young man, clad in mourning, a wide hat. (U72)

He catches a glimpse of Stephen, who's just left the beach.

—There's a friend of yours gone by, Dedalus, he said.

—Who is that?

—Your son and heir.

—Where is he? Mr Dedalus said, stretching over across.

The carriage, passing the open drains and mounds of rippedup roadway before the tenement houses, lurched round the corner and, swerving back to the tramtrack, rolled on noisily with clattering wheels. Mr Dedalus fell back, saying:

—Was that Mulligan cad with him? His *fidus Achates!*

—No, Mr Bloom said. He was alone. . . .

—He's in with a lowdown crowd, Mr Dedalus snarled. That Mulligan is a contaminated bloody doubledyed ruffian by all accounts. His name stinks all over Dublin. But with the help of God and His blessed mother I'll make it my business to write a letter one of those days to his mother or his aunt or whatever she is that will open her eye as wide as a gate. I'll tickle his catastrophe, believe you me. . . .

He ceased. Mr Bloom glanced from his angry moustache to Mr Power's mild face and Martin Cunningham's eyes and beard, gravely shaking. Noisy selfwilled man. Full of his son. He is right. Something to hand on. If little Rudy had lived. See him grow up. Hear his voice in the house. Walking beside Molly in an Eton suit. My son. Me in his eyes. Strange feeling it would be. From me. (U73)

What's happening is, these first three Odysseus chapters are overlapping in time with the first three Telemachus chapters: while Stephen is doing one thing, Bloom is doing another—1, 2, 3.

A bit later, as the funeral procession passes through Dublin, the mourners pass a figure in a white straw hat:

—How do you do? Martin Cunningham said, raising his palm to his brow in salute.

—He doesn't see us, Mr Power said. Yes, he does. How do you do?

—Who? Mr Dedalus asked.

—Blazes Boylan, Mr Power said. There he is airing his quiff.

Just that moment I was thinking.

Mr Dedalus bent across to salute. From the door of the Red Bank the white disc of a straw hat flashed reply: spruce figure passed.

Mr Bloom reviewed the nails of his left hand, then those of his right hand. The nails, yes. Is there anything more in him that they sees? Fascination. Worst man in Dublin. That keeps him alive. They sometimes feel what a person is. Instinct. But a type like that. My nails. I am just looking at them: well pared. And after: thinking alone. Body getting a bit softy. I would notice that: from remembering. What causes that? I suppose the skin can't contract quickly enough when the flesh falls off. But the shape is there. The shape is there still. Shoulders. Hips. Plump. Night of the dance dressing. Shift stuck between the cheeks behind.

He clasped his hands between his knees and, satisfied, sent his vacant glance over their faces. (U76)

The first three Bloom chapters, then, have to do with his life in the three realms: first, the realm of his home on earth; next, the ethereal realm, in his fancy with the invisible girl; and here, the underworld realm, where he goes to a cemetery and attends the funeral of Paddy Dignam.

### Aeolus

The next chapter, "Aeolus," takes place in a newspaper office, and here Bloom and Stephen pass each other closely for the first time. Now in Homer, Aeolus was Lord of the Winds, and "realm of the winds" is not a bad way to describe a newspaper. What we learn of this newspaper is that all the articles communicate misinformation; they are simply all slightly off center. Bloom has come to place an ad for Alexander Keyes.

WE SEE THE CANVASSER AT WORK

Mr Bloom laid his cutting on Mr Nannetti's desk.

—Excuse me, councillor, he said. This ad, you see. Keyes, you remember?

Mr Nannetti considered the cutting awhile and nodded.

—He wants it in for July, Mr Bloom said.

The foreman moved his pencil towards it.

—But wait, Mr Bloom said. He wants it changed. Keyes, you see. He wants two keys at the top.

Hell of a racket they make....

...the printing presses...

...He doesn't hear it. Nannan. Iron nerves. Maybe he understands what I.

The foreman turned round to hear patiently and, lifting an elbow, began to scratch slowly in the armpit of his alpaca jacket.

—Like that, Mr Bloom said, crossing his forefingers at the top. Let him take that in first.

Mr Bloom, glancing sideways up from the cross he had made, saw the foreman's sallow face, think he has a touch of jaundice, and beyond the obedient reels feeding in huge webs of paper. Clank it. Clink it. Miles of it unreeled. What becomes of it after? O, wrap up meat, parcels: various uses, thousand and one things.

Slipping his words deftly into the pauses of the clanking he drew swiftly on the scarred woodwork. (U99)

Stephen has come to bring a letter about hoof and mouth disease that Mr. Deasy has given him.

> Mr O'Madden Burke, tall in copious gray of Donegal tweed, came in from the hallway. Stephen Dedalus, behind him, uncovered as he entered.
>
> —*Entrez, mes enfants!* Lenehen cried.
>
> —I escort a suppliant, Mr O'Madden Burke said melodiously. Youth led by Experience visits Notoriety.
>
> —How do you do? the editor said, holding out a hand. Come in....
> Lenehan said to all:
>
> —Silence! What opera resembles a railwayline? Reflect, ponder, excogitate, reply.
>
> Stephen handed over the typed sheets, pointing to the title and signature.
>
> —Who? the editor asked....
>
> —Mr Garrett Deasy, Stephen said.
>
> —That old pelters, the editor said....
>
> —Good day, Stephen, the professor said, coming to peer over their shoulders. Foot and mouth? Are you turned...?...
>
> SHINDY IN WELLKNOWN RESTAURANT
>
> —Good day, sir, Stephen answered blushing. The letter is not mine. Mr Garrett Deasy asked me to...
>
> —O, I know him, Myles Crawford said, and I knew his wife too. The bloodiest old tartar God ever made. By Jesus, she had the foot and mouth disease and no mistake! The night she threw the soup in the waiter's face in the Star and Garter. Oho!
>
> A woman brought sin into the world. For Helen, the runaway wife of Menelaus, ten years the Greeks. O'Rourke, prince of Breffni.
>
> —Is he a widower? Stephen asked.
>
> —Ay, a grass one, Myles Crawford said, his eye running down the typescript. Emperor's horses. Habsburg. An Irishman saved his life on the ramparts of Vienna. Don't you forget! Maximilian Karl O'Donnell, graf von Tirconnell in Ireland. Sent his heir over to make the king an Austrian fieldmarshal now. Going to be trouble there one day. Wild geese. O yes, every time. Don't you forget that!
>
> —The moot point is did he forget it, J. J. O'Molloy said quietly, turning a horseshoe paperweight. Saving princes is a thankyou job.

Professor MacHugh turned on him.

—And if not? he said.

—I'll tell you how it was, Myles Crawford began. A Hungarian it was one day... (U109)

So Stephen and Bloom, who are destined to meet at the end of the day, first cross paths in "the realm of the winds." They do not seek each other out, but they are in the same place at the same time.

### *Lestrygonians*

Then comes the chapter of the "Lestrygonians," who in the *Odyssey* were cannibals. In this chapter, Bloom is going from one restaurant to another, wondering where he is going to eat lunch. The way the chapter is written, you come out smeared with pie and grease and fish and everything—it is all over you. It starts out like this:

Pineapple rock, lemon platt, butter scotch. A sugarsticky girl shovelling scoopfuls of creams for a christian brother. Some school treat. Bad for their tummies. Lozenge and comfit manufacturer to His Majesty the King. God. Save. Our. Sitting on his throne sucking red jujubes white. (U124)

This was the chapter where I first understood what Joyce was doing with his manner of writing. I suddenly realized that Joyce's style is meant really to give you the experience he is writing about: It is an experiential writing. Early in this chapter, he even gives us a clue about what he is doing. Bloom is standing on a bridge.

Looking down he saw flapping strongly, wheeling between the gaunt quaywalls, gulls....

He threw down among them a crumpled paper ball. Elijah thirty-two feet per sec is com. Not a bit. The ball bobbed unheeded on the wake of swells, floated under by the bridgepiers. Not such damn fools.... Live by their wits. They wheeled, flapping.

*The hungry famished gull*
*Flaps o'er the waters dull.*

That is how poets write, the similar sounds. But then Shakespeare has no rhymes: blank verse. The flow of the language it is. The thoughts. (U125)

As Bloom moves on, thinking about lunch, images of food and eating are everywhere, on nearly every page.

If you cram a turkey say on chestnut meal it tastes like that. Eat pig like pig. But then why is it that saltwater fish are not salty? (U126)

. . . a nice nun there, really sweet face. . . . Our great day, she said. Feast of Our Lady of Mount Carmel. Sweet name too: caramel. (U127)

Remember when we got home raking up the fire and frying those pieces of lap of mutton for her supper with the Chutney sauce she liked. And the mulled rum. (U128)

Hot mockturtle vapour and steam of newbaked jampuffs rolypoly poured out from Harrison's. The heavy noonreek tickled the top of Mr Bloom's gullet. Want to make good pastry, butter, best flour, Demerara sugar, or they'd taste it with the hot tea. (U129)

He looked still at her. . . . Pungent mockturtle oxtail mulligatawny. I'm hungry too. Flakes of pastry on the gusset of her dress: daub of sugary flour stuck to her cheek. Rhubarb tart with liberal fillings, rich fruit interior. (U130)

Round to Menton's office. His oyster eyes staring at the postcard. Be a feast for the gods. (U131)

Poor Mrs Purefoy! Methodist husband. Method in his madness. Saffron bun and milk and soda lunch in the educational dairy. Y. M. C. A. Eating with a stopwatch, thirtytwo chews to the minute. And still his muttonchop whiskers grew. (U132)

A squad of constables debouched from College street, marching in Indian file. Goosestep. Foodheated faces, sweating helmets, patting their truncheons. After their feed with a good load of fat soup under their belts. (U133)

Have your daughters inveigling them to your house. Stuff them up with meat and drink. Michaelmas goose. Here's a good lump of thyme seasoning under the apron for you. Have another quart of goosegrease before it gets too cold. (U134)

Charley Kavanagh used to come out on his high horse, cocked hat, puffed, powdered and shaved. Look at the woebegone walk of him. Eaten a bad egg. Poached eyes on ghost. (U135)

His eyes followed the high figure in homespun. . . . Coming from the vegetarian. Only weggebobbles and fruit. Don't eat a beafsteak. If you do the eyes of that cow will pursue you through all eternity. They say it's healthier. Windandwatery though. Tried it. Keep you on the run all day. Bad as a bloater. Dreams all night. Why do they call that thing they gave me nutsteak? Nutarians. Fruitarians. To give you the idea you are eating rumpsteak. Absurd. Salty too. They cook in soda. Keep you sitting by the tap all night. (U136)

Thick feet that woman has in the white stockings. Hope the rain mucks them up on her. Countrybred chawbacon. All the beef to the heels were in. . . .

Duke street. Here we are. Must eat. The Burton. Feel better then. . . .

His heart astir he pushed in the door of the Burton restaurant. Stink gripped his trembling breath: pungent meatjuice, slush of greens. See the animals feed. . . .

—Roast beef and cabbage.

—One stew.

Smells of men. Spaton sawdust, sweetish warmish cigarette-smoke, reek of plug, spilt beer, men's beery piss, the stale of ferment.

His gorge rose.

Couldn't eat a morsel here. Fellow sharpening knife and fork to eat all before him, old chap picking his tootles. Slight spasm, full, chewing the cud. Before and after. Grace after meals. Look on this picture then on that. Scoffing up stewgravy with sopping sippets of bread. Lick it off the plate, man! Get out of this. (U138–139)

After all there's a lot in that vegetarian fine flavour of things from the earth garlic of course it stinks after Italian organgrinders crisp of onions mushrooms truffles. Pain to the animal too. Pluck and draw fowl. Wretched brutes there at the cattlemarket waiting for the poleaxe to split their skulls open. Moo. Poor trembling calves. Meh. Staggering bob. Bubble and squeak. Butchers' buckets wobbly lights.

Give us that brisket off the hook. Plup. Rawhead and bloody bones. Flayed glasseyed sheep hung from their haunches, sheepsnouts bloodypapered snivelling nosejam on sawdust. Top and lashers going out. Don't maul them pieces, young one.

Hot fresh blood they prescribe for decline. Blood always needed. Insidious. Lick it up smokinghot, thick sugary. Famished ghosts.

Ah, I'm hungry.

He entered Davy Byrne's. Moral pub. . . .

What will I take now? . . .

. . . Let me see. I'll take a glass of burgundy and . . . let me see.

Sardines on the shelves. Almost taste them by looking. Sandwich? Ham and his descendants mustered and bred there. Potted meats. What is home without Plumtree's potted meat? Incomplete. What a stupid ad! Under the obituary notices they stuck it. All up a plumtree. Dignam's potted meat. Cannibals would with lemon and rice. White missionary too salty. Like pickled pork. Expect the chief consumes the parts of honour. (U140)

Like a few olives too if they had them. Italian I prefer. Good glass of burgundy take away that. Lubricate. A nice salad, cool as a cucumber, Tom Kernan can dress. Puts gusto into it. Pure olive oil. Milly served me that cutlet with a sprig of parsley. Take one Spanish onion. God made food, the devil the cooks. Devilled crab. (U141)

Mr Bloom ate his strips of sandwich, fresh clean bread, with relish of disgust pungent mustard, the feety savour of green cheese. Sips of his wine soothed his palate. (U142)

Mild fire of wine kindled his veins. I wanted that badly. Felt so off colour. His eyes unhungrily saw shelves of tins: sardines, gaudy lobsters' claws. All the odd things people pick up for food. Out of shells, periwinkles with a pin, off trees, snails out of the ground the French eat, out of the sea with bait on a hook. Silly fish learn nothing in a thousand years. If you didn't know risky putting anything into your mouth. Poisonous berries. Johnny Magories. Roundness you think good. Gaudy color warns you off. One fellow told another and so on. Try it on the dog first. Led on by the smell or the look. Tempting fruit. Ice cones. Cream. Instinct. Orangegroves for instance. Need artificial irrigation. Bleibtreustrasse. Yes but what about oysters. Unsightly like a clot of phlegm. Filthy shells. Devil to open them too. Who found them out? Garbage, sewage they feed on. Fizz and Red bank oysters. Effect on the sexual. Aphrodis. He was in the Red Bank this morning. Was he oysters old fish at table perhaps he young flesh in bed no June has no ar no oysters. But there are people like things high. Tainted game. Jugged hare. First catch your hare. Chinese eating eggs fifty years old, blue and green again. Dinner of thirty courses. Each dish harmless might mix inside. Idea for a poison mystery. That archduke Leopold was it no yes or was it Otto one of those Habsburgs? Or who was it used to eat the scruff off his own head? Cheapest lunch in town. Of course aristocrats, then the others copy to be in the fashion. Milly too rock oil and flour. Raw pastry I like myself. Half the catch of oysters they throw back in the sea to keep up the price. Cheap no-one would buy. Caviare. Do the grand. Hock in green glasses. Swell blowout. Lady this. Powdered bosom pearls. The *élite*. *Crème de la crème.* They want special dishes to pretend they're. Hermit with a platter of pulse keep down the stings of the flesh. Know me come eat with me. Royal sturgeon high sheriff, Coffey, the butcher, right to venisons of the forest from his ex. Send him back the half of a cow. Spread I saw down in the Master of the Rolls' kitchen area. Whitehatted *chef* like a rabbi. Combustible duck. Curly cabbage *à la duchesse de Parme.* Just as well to write it on the bill of fare so you can know what you've eaten. Too many drugs spoil the broth. I know it myself. Dosing it with Edwards' dessicated soup. Geese stuffed silly for them. Lobsters boiled alive. Do ptake some ptarmigan. Wouldn't mind being a waiter in a swell hotel. Tips, evening dress, halfnaked ladies. May I tempt you to a little more filleted lemon sole, miss Dubedat? Yes, do bedad. And she did bedad. Huguenot name I expect that. A miss Dubedat lived in Killiney, I remember. *Du de la* French. Still it's the same fish perhaps old Micky Hanlon of Moore street ripped the guts out of...

Stuck on the pane two flies buzzed, stuck.

Glowing wine on his palate lingered swallowed. Crushing in the winepress grapes of Burgundy. Sun's heat it is. Seems to a secret touch telling me memory. Touched his sense moistened remembered. Hidden under wild ferns on Howth below us bay sleeping: sky. No sound. The sky. The bay purple by the Lion's head. Green by Drumleck. Yellowgreen towards Sutton. Fields of undersea, the lines faint brown in the grass, buried cities. Pillowed on my coat she had her hair, earwigs in the heather scrub my hand under her nape, you'll toss me all. O wonder! Coolsoft with ointments her hand touched me, caressed: her eyes upon me did not turn away. Ravished over her I lay, full lips full open, kissed her mouth. Yum. Softly she gave me in my mouth the seedcake warm and chewed. Mawkish pulp her mouth had mumbled sweetsour of her spittle. Joy: I ate it: joy. Young life, her lips that gave me pouting. Soft warm sticky gumjelly lips. Flowers her eyes were, take me, willing eyes. Pebbles fell. She lay still. A goat. No-one. High on Ben Howth rhododendrons a nannygoat walking surefooted, dropping currants. Screened under ferns she laughed warmfooted. Wildly I lay on her, kissed her: eyes, her lips, her stretched neck beating, woman's breasts full in her blouse of nun's veiling, fat nipples upright. Hot I tongued her. She kissed me. I was kissed . . .

Stuck, the flies buzzed.

His downcast eyes followed the silent veining curve of the oaken slab. Beauty: it curves: curves are beauty. Shapely goddesses, Venus, Juno: curves the world admires. Can see them library museum standing in the round hall, naked goddesses. Aids to digestion. They don't care what a man looks. All to see. Never speaking. I mean to say to fellows like Flynn. Suppose she did Pygmalion and Galatea what would she say first? Mortal! Put you in your proper place. Quaffing nectar at mess with gods golden dishes, all ambrosial. Not like a tanner lunch we have, boiled mutton, carrots and turnips, bottle of Allsop. Nectar imagine it drinking electricity: gods' food. Lovely forms of women sculped Junonian. Immortal lovely. And we stuffing food in one hole and out behind: food, chyle, blood, dung, earth, food: have to feed it like stoking an engine. (U143–144)

Joyce's virtuosity with words is absolutely incredible. He can do anything he wants; and in this chapter, which is a sort of extended meditation on food and eating, he gives you a case of indigestion.

### Scylla and Charybdis

"Scylla and Charybdis," the next chapter, is a very interesting one. It is equated in Joyce's mind with the episode in the *Odyssey* where Odysseus sails between Scylla, the rock of logic, and Charybdis, the abyss, the vortex of mysticism. It takes place in a library. You will recall that Bloom and Stephen first crossed in the newspaper office, a place where information (or misinformation) is printed. Now, when Bloom and Stephen come together again, this time it's in a library—printing again, this time printing of books.

Stephen and his cronies are in the library having this intellectual argument about literature, and Stephen proposes an elaborate theory, a sort of joke theory (which, we will see, he claims he himself does not believe), about Shakespeare's plays being simply representations of his own life. Stephen starts talking about *Hamlet*. Stephen's theory is that, when the ghost of King Hamlet (the role played by Shakespeare) is talking to Prince Hamlet (the role played by Burbage), it is Shakespeare talking to his son Hamnet, who died shortly before Shakespeare wrote the play.

> —The play begins. A player comes on under the shadow, made up in the castoff mail of a court buck, a wellset man with a bass voice. It is the ghost, the king, a king and no king, and the player is Shakespeare who has studied Hamlet all the years of his life which were not vanity in order to play the part of the spectre. He speaks the words to Burbage, the young player who stands before him beyond the rack of cerecloth, calling him by a name:
>
> *Hamlet, I am thy father's spirit.*
>
> bidding him list. To a son he speaks, the son of his soul, the prince, young Hamlet and to the son of his body, Hamnet Shakespeare, who has died in Stratford that his namesake may live for ever.
> Is it possible that that player Shakespeare, a ghost by absence, and in the vesture of buried Denmark, a ghost by death, speaking his own words to his own son's name (had Hamnet Shakespeare lived he would have been prince Hamlet's twin), is it possible, I want to know, or probable that he did not draw or foresee the logical conclusion of those premises: you are the dispossessed son: I am the murdered father: your mother is the guilty queen, Ann Shakespeare, born Hathaway? (U155)

Then Stephen argues that the crucial event of Shakespeare's life is when he was cuckolded by Ann Hathaway:

> Do you think the writer of *Antony and Cleopatra*, a passionate pilgrim, had his eyes in the back of his head that he chose the ugliest doxy in all Warwickshire to lie withal? Good: he left her and gained the world of men. But his boywomen are the women of a boy. Their life, thought, speech are lent them by males. He chose badly? He was chosen, it seems to me. If others have their will Ann hath a way. By cock, she was to blame. She put the comether on him, sweet and twentysix. The greyeyed goddess who bends over the boy Adonis, stooping to conquer, as prologue to the swelling act, is a boldfaced Stratford wench who tumbles in a cornfield a lover younger than herself....
>
> The quaker librarian...creaked to and fro, tiptoing up nearer heaven by the altitude of a chopine, and, covered by the noise of the outgoing, said low:
>
> —Is it your view, then, that she was not faithful to the poet?...
>
> —Where there is a reconciliation, Stephen said, there must have been first a sundering. (U157–159)

While Stephen elaborates on his wonderfully intricate argument, Joyce describes the librarian as walking around like a kind of ibis; the descriptions are references to Thoth, the Egyptian god who is the lord of writing:

> Coffined thoughts around me, in mummycases, embalmed in spice of words. Thoth, god of libraries, a birdgod, moonycrowned. And I heard the voice of that Egyptian highpriest. *In painted chambers loaded with tilebooks.* (U159)

Then Stephen points out that the proof of his improvised theory is the fact that Shakespeare, in resentment, left Ann in his will his second-best bed:

> —He was a rich country gentleman, Stephen said, with a coat of arms and landed estate at Stratford and a house in Ireland yard, a capitalist shareholder, a bill promoter, a tithefarmer. Why did he not leave her his best bed if he wished her to snore away the rest of her nights in peace? (U167)

While Stephen continues, Buck Mulligan arrives with his obscenities, and Bloom comes in to look something up. Now all three of them are together in the library. Then, Stephen launches into the theme of the father and son, about how Shakespeare and both his father and his son were divided by the curtain of death by the time of the writing of *Hamlet,* so that Shakespeare may be "his own grandfather."[45] [Stephen is, of course,

speaking of himself and his preoccupations as he speaks of Shakespeare.]
Finally, Stephen reaches the conclusion of his argument:

—... The note of banishment, banishment from the heart, banishment from home, sounds uninterruptedly from *The Two Gentlemen of Verona* onward till Prospero breaks his staff, buries it certain fathoms in the earth and drowns his book. ... But it was the original sin that darkened his understanding, weakened his will and left in him a strong inclination to evil. The words are those of my lords bishops of Maynooth. An original sin and, like original sin, committed by another in whose sin he too has sinned. It is between the lines of his last written words, it is petrified on his tombstone under which her four bones are not to be laid. Age has not withered it. Beauty and peace have not done it away. It is in infinite variety everywhere in the world he has created, in *Much Ado about Nothing,* twice in *As You Like It,* in *The Tempest,* in *Hamlet,* in *Measure for Measure*—and in all the other plays which I have not read.

He laughed to free his mind from his mind's bondage.

Judge Eglinton summed up.

—The truth is midway, he affirmed. He is the ghost and the prince. He is all in all.

—He is, Stephen said. The boy of act one is the mature man of act five. All in all. In *Cymbeline,* in *Othello* he is bawd and cuckold. He acts and is acted on. Lover of an ideal or a perversion, like José he kills the real Carmen. His unremitting intellect is the hornmad Iago ceaselessly willing that the moor in him shall suffer.

—Cuckoo! Cuckoo! Cuck Mulligan clucked lewdly. O word of fear! ...

—Man delights him not nor woman neither, Stephen said. He returns after a life of absence to that spot of earth where he was born, where he has always been, man and boy, a silent witness and there, his journey of life ended. Gravediggers bury Hamlet *père* and Hamlet *fils.* A king and a prince at last in death, with incidental music. And, what though murdered and betrayed, bewept by all frail tender hearts for, Dane or Dubliner, sorrow for the dead is the only husband from whom they refuse to be divorced. ... Strong curtain. He found in the world without as actual what was in his world within as possible. Maeterlinck says: *If Socrates leave his house today he will find the sage seated on his doorstep. If Judas go forth tonight it is to Judas his steps will tend.* Every life is many days, day after day. We walk through ourselves, meeting robbers, ghosts, giants, old men, young men, wives, widows, brothers-in-love, but always meeting ourselves. The playwright who wrote the folio of this world and wrote it badly (He gave us light first and the sun two days later) . . . is doubtless all in all in all of us, ostler and butcher, and would be bawd and cuckold too but that in the economy of heaven, foretold by Hamlet, there are no more marriages, glorified man, an androgynous angel, being a wife unto himself.

—*Eureka!* Buck Mulligan cried. *Eureka!* . . .

—You are a delusion, said roundly John Eglinton to Stephen. You have brought us all this way to show us a French triangle. Do you believe your own theory?

—No, Stephen said promptly. (U174–175)

Then, moments later, as Mulligan and Stephen leave the library:

About to pass through the doorway, feeling one behind, he stood aside.

Part. The moment is now. Where then? If Socrates leave his house today, if Judas go forth tonight. Why? That lies in space which I in time must come to, ineluctably.

My will: his will that fronts me. Seas between.

A man passed out between them, bowing, greeting.

—Good day again, Buck Mulligan said.

The portico.

Here I watched the birds for augury. Aengus of the birds. They go, they come. Last night I flew. Easily flew. Men wondered. Street of harlots after. A creamfruit melon he held to me. In. You will see.

—The wandering jew, Buck Mulligan whispered with clown's awe. Did you see his eye? He looked upon you to lust after you. I fear thee, ancient mariner. O, Kinch, thou art in peril. Get thee a breechpad. . . .

A dark back went before them, step of a pard, down, out by the gateway, under portcullis barbs.

They followed. (U178–179)

Therefore, Stephen is following Bloom without Bloom's knowledge. Guided by Bloom, Stephen leaves Mulligan behind. From now on, Stephen will follow this dark father.

### The Wandering Rocks

The next chapter, "The Wandering Rocks," is written as a series of short cameo scenes that all add up to Dublin. Each scene is a brief re-rendering of a motif that is present in other chapters. This chapter has inspired a number of novels, including Dos Passos's *Manhattan Transfer,* where the city is the hero. In this chapter, there are nineteen different scenes that all add up to a giant portrait of the modern metropolis.[46] Here is one scene.

———

As they trod across the thick carpet Buck Mulligan whispered behind his Panama to Haines:

—Parnell's brother. There in the corner.

They chose a small table near the window, opposite a longfaced man whose beard and gaze hung intently down on a chessboard.

—Is that he? Haines asked, twisting round in his seat.

—Yes, Mulligan said. That's John Howard, his brother, our city marshall.

John Howard Parnell translated a white bishop quietly and his grey claw went up again to his forehead whereat it rested. An instant after, under its screen, his eyes looked quickly, ghostbright, at his foe and fell once more upon a working corner.

—I'll take a *mélange,* Haines said to the waitress.

—Two *mélanges,* Buck Mulligan said. And bring us some scones and butter and some cakes as well.

When she had gone he said, laughing:

—We call it D. B. C. because they have damn bad cakes. O, but you missed Dedalus on *Hamlet.*

Haines opened his newbought book.

—I'm sorry, he said. Shakespeare is the happy huntingground of all minds that have lost their balance.

The onelegged sailor growled at the area of 14 Nelson street:

—*England expects....*

Buck Mulligan's primrose waistcoat shook gaily in his laughter.

—You should see him, he said, when his body loses its balance. Wandering Aengus I call him.

—I am sure he has an *idée fixe,* Haines said, pinching his chin thoughtfully with thumb and forefinger. Now I am speculating what it would be likely to be. Such persons always have.

Buck Mulligan bent across the table gravely.

—They drove his wits astray, he said, by visions of hell. He will never capture the Attic note. The note of Swinburne, of all poets, the white death and the ruddy birth. That is his tragedy. He can never be a poet. The joy of creation. . . .

—Eternal punishment, Haines said, nodding curtly. I see. I tackled him this morning on belief. There was something on his mind, I saw. It's rather interesting because professor Pokorny of Vienna makes an interesting point out of that.

Buck Mulligan's watchful eyes saw the waitress come. He helped her to unload her tray.

—He can find no trace of hell in ancient Irish myth, Haines said, amid the cheerful cups. The moral idea seems lacking, the sense of destiny, of retribution. Rather strange he should have just that fixed idea. Does he write anything for your movement?

He sank two lumps of sugar deftly longwise through the whipped cream. Buck Mulligan slit a steaming scone in two and plastered butter over its smoking pith. He bit off a soft piece hungrily.

—Ten years, he said, chewing and laughing. He is going to write something in ten years.

—Seems a long way off, Haines said, thoughtfully lifting his spoon. Still, I shouldn't wonder if he did after all.

He tasted a spoonful from the creamy cone of his cup.

—That is real Irish cream I take it, he said with forbearance. I don't want to be imposed on.

Elijah, skiff, light crumpled throwaway, sailed eastward by flanks of ships and trawlers, amid an archipelago of corks, beyond new Wapping street past Benson's ferry, and by the threemasted schooner *Rosevean* from Bridgwater with bricks. (U204–205)

—◦◦◦—

"The Wandering Rocks" chapter, a virtuoso performance straight through, is a kind of microcosm of the *Finnegans Wake* macrocosm.

*Sirens*

Now we come to what I think are the three most delicious chapters of the book. The first of these chapters, "Sirens," shows Bloom at the time when he knows Blazes is with Molly. Remember, he has been wandering from place to place all day to evade this knowledge, and now he is taking some early afternoon refreshment in the bar of the Ormond Hotel, and the sirens are tending bar. There is singing going on in the next room, and Simon Dedalus, Stephen's father, a great tenor, is one of the singers:

> The harping chords of prelude closed. A chord, longdrawn, expectant, drew a voice away.
> —*When first I saw that form endearing...*
> Richie turned.
> —Si Dedalus' voice, he said.
> Braintipped, cheek touched with flame, they listened feeling that flow endearing flow over skin limbs human heart soul spine. Bloom signed to Pat, bald Pat is a waiter hard of hearing, to set ajar the door of the bar. The door of the bar. So. That will do. Pat, waiter, waited, waiting to hear, for he was hard of hear by the door.
> —*... Sorrow from me seemed to depart.*
> Through the hush of air a voice sang to them, low, not rain, not leaves in murmur, like no voice of strings or reeds or whatdoyoucallthem dulcimers touching their still ears with words, still hearts of their each his remembered lives. Good, good to hear: sorrow from them each seemed to from both depart when first they heard. When first they saw, lost Richie Poldy, mercy of beauty, heard from a person wouldn't expect it in the least, her first merciful lovesoft oftloved word.
> Love that is singing: love's old sweet song. Bloom unwound slowly the elastic band of his packet. Love's old sweet *sonnez la* gold. Bloom wound a skein round four forkfingers, stretched it, relaxed, and wound it round his troubled double, fourfold, in octave, gyved them fast.
> —*Full of hope and all delighted...*
> Tenors get women by the score. Increase their flow. Throw flower at his feet. When will we meet? My head it simply. Jingle all delighted. He can't sing for tall hats. Your head it simply swurls.

Perfumed for him. What perfume does your wife? I want to know. Jing. Stop. Knock. Last look at mirror always before she answers the door. The hall. There? How do you? I do well. There? What? Or? Phial of cachous, kissing comfits, in her satchel. Yes? Hands felt for the opulent.

Alas the voice rose, sighing, changed: loud, full, shining, proud.

—*But alas, 'twas idle dreaming...*

Glorious tone he has still. Cork air softer also their brogue. Silly man! Could have made oceans of money. Singing wrong words. Wore out his wife: now sings. But hard to tell. Only the two themselves. If he doesn't break down. Keep a trot for the avenue. His hands and feet sing too. Drink. Nerves overstrung. Must be abstemious to sing. Jenny Lind soup: stock, sage, raw eggs, half pint of cream. For creamy dreamy.

Tenderness it welled: slow, swelling, full it throbbed. That's the chat. Ha, give! Take! Throb, a throb, a pulsing proud erect.

Words? Music? No: it's what's behind.

Bloom looped, unlooped, noded, disnoded.

Bloom. Flood of warm jamjam lickitup secretness flowed to flow in music out, in desire, dark to lick flow invading. Tipping her tepping her topping her. Tup To pour o'er sluices pouring gushes. Flood, gush, flow, joygush, tupthrob. Now! Language of love.

—*... ray of hope is ...*

Beaming. Lydia for Lidwell squeak scarcely hear so ladylike the muse unsqueaked a ray of hope.

*Martha* it is. Coincidence. Just going to write. Lionel's song. Lovely name you have. Can't write. Accept my little pres. Play on her heartstrings pursestrings too. She's a. I called you naughty boy. Still the name: Martha. How strange! Today.

The voice of Lionel returned, weaker but unwearied. It sang again to Richie Poldy Lydia Lidwell also sang to Pat open mouth ear waiting to wait. How first he saw that form endearing, how sorrow seemed to part, how look, form, word charmed him Gould Lidwell, won Pat Bloom's heart.

Wish I could see his face, though. Explain better. Why the barber in Drago's always looked my face when I spoke his face in the glass. Still hear it better here than in the bar though farther.

—*Each graceful look....*

First night when I saw her at Mat Dillon's in Terenure. Yellow, black lace she wore. Musical chairs. We two the last. Fate. After her. Fate. Round and round slow. Quick round. We two. All looked. Halt. Down she sat. All ousted looked. Lips laughing. Yellow knees.

—*Charmed my eye...*

Singing. Waiting she sang. I turned her music. Full voice of perfume of what perfume does your lilactrees.... (U225–226)

The whole chapter is in this kind of a musical vein; it is a very interesting, musically composed chapter.

### Cyclops

Then comes a great work: the "Cyclops" chapter, which takes place in Barney Kiernan's pub. The narrator of this chapter is nameless; he's just a regular Irish tough guy. Here's how it begins:

I was just passing the time of day with old Troy of the D. M. P. at the corner of Arbour hill there and be damned but a bloody sweep came along and he near drove his gear into my eye. I turned around to let him have the weight of my tongue when who should I see dodging along Stony Batter only Joe Hynes.

—Lo, Joe, says I. How are you blowing? Did you see that bloody chimneysweep near shove my eye out with his brush?

—Soot's luck, says Joe. Who's the old ballocks you were to?

—Old Troy, says I, was in the force. I'm on two minds not to give that fellow in charge for obstructing the thoroughfare with his brooms and ladders.

—What are you doing round those parts? says Joe.

—Devil a much, says I. (U240)

That is the way the story is told, using the actual narrative that takes place in the bar; however, there are huge interjections, in different styles, inserted throughout the chapter. One example is the gigantic description of the Cyclops, a nationalist politician called "the citizen," a big Irish bully in the pub. For Joyce, a politician is a person with one eye, because he sees only one side of a problem. It takes another person to see the whole problem, and here Bloom supplies that other eye to this balance. Joyce describes the citizen as though he were an old hero in the Irish epics, where they build everybody up by piling on all kinds of adjectives:

The figure seated on a large boulder...

Only this giant is seated, not on a huge boulder, but in a pub.

> ...at the foot of a round tower was that of a broadshouldered deepchested stronglimbed frankeyed redhaired freelyfreckled shaggybearded widemouthed largenosed longheaded deepvoiced barekneed brawy-handed hairylegged ruddyfaced sinewyarmed hero. From shoulder to shoulder he measured several ells and his rocklike mountainous knees were covered, as was likewise the rest of his body wherever visible, with a strong growth of tawny prickly hair in hue and toughness similar to the mountain gorse (*Ulex Europeus*). The widewinged nostrils, from which bristles of the same tawny hue projected, were of such capaciousness that within their cavernous obscurity the fieldlark might easily have lodged her nest. The eyes in which a tear and a smile strove ever for the mastery were of the dimensions of a goodsized cauliflower. A powerful current of warm breath issued at regular intervals from the profound cavity of his mouth while in rhythmic resonance the loud strong hale reverberations of his formidable heart thundered rumblingly causing the ground, the summit of the lofty tower and the still loftier walls of the cave to vibrate and tremble. (U243)

In the bar, there is a dog named Garryowen. A poem is recited by this great big hairy dog, lying on the floor, while everybody is having drinks.[47]

> All those who are interested in the spread of human culture among the lower animals (and their name is legion) should make a point of not missing the really marvellous exhibition of cynanthropy given by the famous old Irish red setter wolfdog formerly known by the *sobriquet* of Garryowen and recently rechristened by his large circle of friends and acquaintances Owen Garry.... We subjoin a specimen [of canine poetry].... The metrical system of the canine original, which recalls the intricate alliterative and isosyllabic rules of the Welsh englyn, is infinitely more complicated but we believe our readers will agree that the spirit has been well caught. Perhaps it should be added that the effect is greatly increased if Owen's verse be spoken somewhat slowly and indistinctly in a tone suggestive of suppressed rancour.
>
> > *The curse of my curses*
> > *Seven days every day*

*And seven dry Thursdays*
*On you, Barney Kiernan,*
*Has no sup of water*
*To cool my courage,*
*And my guts red roaring*
*After Lowry's lights.*
(U256)

I'll bet that's what many a dog is thinking while you are enjoying yourself and he's lying on the ground. So, Bloom is in this pub, and the Cyclops, this giant Sinn Fein patriot, is big-mouthing, and making a lot of noise. Meanwhile:

Bloom was talking and talking with John Wyse, and he quite excited with his dunducketymudcoloured mug on him and his old plumeyes rolling about.

—Persecution, says he, all the history of the world is full of it. Perpetuating national hatred among nations.

—But do you know what a nation means? says John Wyse.

—Yes, says Bloom.

—What is it? says John Wyse.

—A nation? says Bloom. A nation is the same people living in the same place.

—By God, then, says Ned, laughing, if that's so I'm a nation for I'm living in the same place for the past five years.

So of course everyone had the laugh at Bloom and says he, trying to muck out of it:

—Or also living in different places.

—That covers my case, says Joe.

—What is your nation if I may ask? says the citizen.

—Ireland, says Bloom. I was born here. Ireland.

The citzen said nothing only cleared the spit out of his gullet and, gob, he spat a Red bank oyster out of him right in the corner. . . .

—And I belong to a race too, says Bloom, that is hated and persecuted. Also now. This very moment. This very instant.

Gob, he near burnt his fingers with the butt of his old cigar.

—Robbed, says he. Plundered. Insulted. Persecuted. Taking what belongs to us by right. At this very moment, says he, putting up his fist, sold by auction in Morocco like slaves or cattle.

—Are you talking about the new Jerusalem? says the citizen.

—I'm talking about injustice, says Bloom.

—Right, says John Wyse. Stand up to it then with force like men....

—But it's no use, says he. Force, hatred, history, all that. That's not life for men and women, insult and hatred. And everybody knows that it's the very opposite of that that is really life.

—What? says Alf.

—Love, says Bloom. I mean the opposite of hatred. I must go now, says he to John Wyse. Just round to the court a moment to see if Martin is there. If he comes just say I'll be back in a second. Just a moment. (U271–273)

And Bloom leaves. Earlier in the day, Bloom gave Bantam Lyons his newspaper, saying, "I was just going to throw it away." Well, here's what happens:

—I know where he's gone, says Lenehan, cracking his fingers.

—Who? says I.

—Bloom, says he. The courthouse is a blind. He had a few bobs on *Throwaway* and he's gone to gather in the shekels.... I met Bantam Lyons going to back that horse only I put him off it and he told me Bloom gave him the tip. Bet you what you like he has a hundred shilling to five on. He's the only man in Dublin has it. A dark horse.

—He's a bloody dark horse himself, says Joe.

—Mind, Joe, says I. Show us the entrance out.

—There you are, says Terry.

Goodbye Ireland I'm going to Gort. So I just went round the back of the yard to pumpship and begob (hundred shillings to five) while I was letting off my (*Throwaway* twenty to) letting off my load gob says I to myself I knew he was uneasy in his (two pints off of Joe and one in Slattery's off) in his mind to get off the mark in (hundred shillings is five quid) and when they were in the (dark horse) Pisser Burke was telling me card party and letting on the child was sick (gob, must have done about a gallon) flabbyarse of a wife speaking down the tube *she's better* or *she's* (ow!) all a plan so he could vamoose with the pool if he won or (Jesus, full up I was) trading without a licence (ow!) Ireland my nation says he (hoik! phthook!) never be up to those bloody (there's the last of it) Jerusalem (ah!) cuckoos.

So anyhow when I got back they were at it dingdong. John Wyse saying it was Bloom gave the ideas for Sinn Fein to Griffith to put in his paper all kinds of jerrymandering, packed juries and swindling the taxes off the government and appointing consuls all over the world to walk about selling Irish industries. Robbing Peter to pay Paul. Gob, that puts the bloody kybosh on it if old sloppy eyes is mucking up the show. Give us a bloody chance. God save Ireland from the likes of that bloody mouseabout. Mr Bloom with his argol bargol. And his old fellow before him perpetrating frauds, old Methusalem Bloom, the robbying bagman, that poisoned himself with the prussic acid after he swamping the country with his baubles and his penny diamonds. Loans by post on easy terms. Any amount of money advanced on note of hand. Distance no object. No security. Gob, he's like Lanty MacHale's goat that'd go a piece of the road with every one.

—Well, it's a fact, says John Wyse. And there's the man now that'll tell you all about it, Martin Cunningham....

So in comes Martin asking where was Bloom.

—Where is he? says Lenehan. Defrauding widows and orphans.

—Isn't that a fact, says John Wyse, what I was telling the citizen about Bloom and the Sinn Fein?

—That's so, says Martin. Or so they allege.

—Who made those allegations? says Alf.

—I, says Joe. I'm the alligator.

—And after all, says John Wyse, why can't a jew love his country like the next fellow?

—Why not? says J. J., when he's quite sure which country it is.

—Is he a jew or a gentile or a holy Roman or a swaddler or what the hell is he? says Ned. Or who is he?...

—He's a perverted jew, says Martin, from a place in Hungary...

—Isn't he a cousin of Bloom the dentist? says Jack Power.

—Not at all, says Martin. Only namesakes. His name was Virag, the father's name that poisoned himself. He changed it by deed-poll, the father did.

—That's the new Messiah for Ireland! says the citizen. Island of saints and sages!

—Well, they're still waiting for their redeemer, says Martin. For that matter so are we.

—Yes, says J. J., and every male that's born they think may be their Messiah. And every jew is in a tall state of excitement, I believe, till he knows if he's a father or a mother.

—Expecting every moment will be his next, says Lenehan.

—O, by God, says Ned, you should have seen Bloom before that son of his that died was born. I met him one day in the south city markets buying a tin of Neave's food six weeks before the wife was delivered.

—*En ventre sa mère,* says J. J.

—Do you call that a man? says the citizen.

—I wonder did he ever put it out of sight, says Joe.

—Well, there were two children born anyhow, says Jack Powers.

—And who does he suspect? says the citizen.

Gob, there's many a true word spoken in jest. One of those mixed middlings he is. Lying up in the hotel Pisser was telling me once a month with headache like a totty with her courses. Do you know what I'm telling you? It'd be an act of God to take a hold of a fellow the like of that and throw him in the bloody sea. Justifiable homicide, so it would. Then sloping off with his five quid without putting up a pint of stuff like a man. Give us your blessing. Not as much as would blind your eye.

—Charity to the neighbor, says Martin. But where is he? We can't wait.

—A wolf in sheep's clothing, says the citizen. That's what he is. Virag from Hungary! Ahasuerus I call him. Cursed by God. (U274–277)

Now the big buster is really boiling hot. And Bloom returns.

—I was just round at the courthouse, says he, looking for you. I hope I'm not....

—No, says Martin, we're ready.

Courthouse my eye and your pockets hanging down with gold and silver. Mean bloody scut. Stand us a drink itself. Devil a sweet fear! There's a jew for you! All for number one. Cute as a shithouse rat. Hundred to five....

[A scream is heard outside the lecture hall. Campbell quips, "Well, it's appropriate. Who has the courage to save a drowning man?]

—Don't tell anyone, says the citizen.

—Beg your pardon, says he.

—Come on boys, says Martin, seeing it was looking blue. Come along now.

—Don't tell anyone, says the citizen, letting a bawl out of him. It's a secret.

And the bloody dog woke up and let a growl.

—Bye-bye all, says Martin.

And he got them out as quick as he could, Jack Power and Crofton or whatever you call him and him in the middle of them letting on to be all at sea and up with them on the bloody jaunting car....

A jaunting car is a two-wheeled car, with the seat going in such a way that you are sitting sideways.

—Off with you, says Martin to the jarvey....

But begob I was just lowering the heel of the pint when I saw the citizen getting up to waddle to the door, puffing and blowing with the dropsy, and he cursing the curse of Cromwell on him, bell, book and candle in Irish, spitting and spatting out of him and Joe and little Alf round him like a leprechaun trying to pacify him.

—Let me alone, says he.

And begob he got as far as the door and they holding him and he bawls out of him:

—Three cheers for Israel!...

Now, as I pointed out earlier, Bloom isn't a Jew technically, but he identifies with the Jews. And he says:

—Mendelssohn was a jew and Karl Marx and Mercadante and Spinoza. And the Saviour was a jew and his father was a jew. Your God.

—He had no father, says Martin. That'll do now. Drive ahead.

—Whose God? says the citizen.

—Well, his uncle was a jew, says he. Your God was a jew. Christ was a jew like me....

Well, the Giant isn't having any of that.

Gob, the citizen made a plunge back into the shop.

—By Jesus, says he, I'll brain that bloody jewman for using the holy name. By Jesus, I'll crucify him so I will. Give us that biscuit-box here.

—Stop! Stop! says Joe....

Gob, the devil wouldn't stop him till he got hold of the bloody tin anyhow and out with him and little Alf hanging on to his elbow and he shouting like a stuck pig, as good as any bloody play in the Queen's royal theatre:

—Where is he till I murder him?

And Ned and J. J. paralysed with the laughing.

—Bloody wars, says I, I'll be in for the last gospel.

But as luck would have it the jarvey got the nag's head round the other way and off with im.

—Hold on, citizen, says Joe. Stop! (U279–281)

The tin is described as though it were the rock that the Cyclops threw at Odysseus, and its impact on the streets is described as an earthquake.

Begob he drew his hand and made a swipe and let fly. Mercy of God the sun was in his eyes or he'd have left him for dead, Gob, he nearly sent it into the county Longford. The bloody nag took fright and the old mongrel after the car like bloody Hell and all the populace shouting and laughing and the old tinbox clattering along the street.

Then the style changes, and there is a gigantic insertion in the style of a newspaper.

The catastrophe was terrific and instantaneous in its effect. The observatory of Dunsink registered in all eleven shocks, all of the fifth grade of Mercalli's scale, and there is no record extant of a similar seismic disturbance in our island since the earthquake of 1534, the year of the rebellion of Silken Thomas. The epicentre appears to have been that part of the metropolis which constitues the Inn's Quay ward and parish of Saint Michan covering a surface of fortyone acres, two roods and one square pole or perch. All the lordly residences in the vicinity of the palace of justice were demolished and that noble edifice itself, in which at the time of the catastrophe important legal debates were in progress, is literally a mass of ruins beneath which it is to be feared all the occupants have been buried alive. From the reports of eyewitnesses it transpires that the seismic waves were accompanied by a violent atmospheric perturbation of cyclonic character. An article of headgear since ascertained to belong to the much respected clerk of the crown and peace Mr George Fottrell and a silk umbrella with gold handle with the engraved initials, crest, coat of arms and house number of the erudite and worshipful chairman of quarter sessions sir Frederick Falkiner, recorder of Dublin, have been discovered by search parties in remote parts of the island respectively, the former on the third basaltic ridge of the giant's causeway, the latter embedded to the extent of one foot three inches in the sandy beach of Holeopen bay near the old head of Kinsale. Other eyewitnesses depose that they observed an incandescent object of enormous proportions hurtling through the atmosphere at a terrifying velocity in a trajectory directed southwest by west. Messages of condolence and sympathy are being hourly received from all parts of the different continents and the sovereign pontiff has been graciously pleased to decree that a special *missa pro defunctis* shall be celebrated simultaneously by the ordinaries of each and every cathedral church of all the episcopal dioceses subject to the spiritual authority of the Holy See in suffrage of the souls of those faithful departed who have been so unexpectedly called away from our midst.

Now the work goes into the clearing up of everything by certain various salvage firms:

The work of salvage, removal of *débris,* human remains etc has been entrusted to Messrs Michael Meade and Son, 159 Great Brunswick street, and Messrs T. and C. Martin, 77, 78, 79, and 80 North Wall, assisted by the men and officers of the Duke of Cornwall's light infantry under the general supervision of H. R. H., rear admiral, the right honourable sir Hercules Hannibal Habeas Corpus Anderson, K. G., K. P., K. T., P. C., K. C. B., M. P., J. P., M. B., D. S. O., S. O. D., M. F. H., M. R. I. A., B. L., Mus. Doc., P. L. G., F. T. C. D., F. R. U. I., F. R. C. P. I. and F. R. C. S. I.

Then the voice is again that of the toughy narrator.

You never saw the like of it in all your born puff. Gob, if he got that lottery ticket on the side of his poll he'd remember the gold cup, he would so, but begob the citizen would have been lagged for assault and battery and Joe for aiding and abetting. The jarvey saved his life by furious driving as sure as God made Moses. What? O, Jesus, he did. And he lets a volley of oaths after him.

—Did I kill him, says he, or what?

And he shouting to the bloody dog:

—After him, Garry! After him, boy!

The giant sics the great big dog (a poet as we saw) on Bloom.

> And the last we saw was the bloody car rounding the corner and old sheepsface on it gesticulating and the bloody mongrel after it with his lugs back for all he was bloody well worth to tear him limb from limb. Hundred to five! Jesus, he took the value of it out of him, I promise you.

Then, here at the end of the chapter, the style unexpectedly changes again, this time into that of the King James Bible:

> When, lo, there came about them all a great brightness and they beheld the chariot wherein He stood ascend to heaven. And they beheld Him in the chariot, clothed upon in the glory of the brightness, having raiment as of the sun, fair as the moon and terrible that for awe they durst not look upon Him. And there came a voice out of heaven, calling: *Elijah! Elijah!* And He answered with a main cry: *Abba! Adonai!* And they beheld Him even Him, ben Bloom Elijah, amid clouds of angels ascend to the glory of the brightness at an angle of fortyfive degrees over Donohoe's in Little Green street like a shot off a shovel. (U281–283)

I don't think you can beat that for literary bravado. Isn't that a show? Gargantuan: in the chapter you go rocking back and forth from one to another.

### Nausicaa

Bloom, after this shock, goes down to the beach to cool off. Now I just want to give you a shock. From the style that we've just heard, we now move into the style of a young girls' magazine:

> The summer evening had begun to fold the world in its mysterious embrace. Far away in the west the sun was setting and the last glow of all too fleeting day lingered lovingly on sea and strand, on the proud promontory of dear old Howth guarding as ever the waters of the bay, on the weedgrown rocks along Sandymount shore and, last but not least, on the quiet church whence there streamed forth at times upon the stillness the voice of prayer to her who is in her pure radiance a beacon ever to the stormtossed heart of man, Mary, star of the sea.

Bloom sees three girls playing on the beach with a baby and a couple of little kids.

The three girl friends were seated on the rocks, enjoying the evening scene and the air which was fresh but not too chilly. Many a time and oft were they wont to come there to that favourite nook to have a cosy chat beside the sparkling waves and discuss matters feminine, Cissy Caffrey and Edy Boardman with the baby in the pushcar and Tommy and Jacky Caffrey, two little curlyheaded boys, dresssed in sailor suits with caps to match and the name *H.M.S. Belleisle* printed on both. For Tommy and Jacky Caffrey were twins, scarce four years old and very noisy and spoiled twins sometimes but for all that darling little fellows with bright merry faces and endearing ways about them. They were dabbling in the sand with their spades and buckets, building castles as children do, or playing with their big coloured ball, happy as the day was long. And Edy Boardman was rocking the chubby baby to and fro in the pushcar while that young gentleman fairly chuckled with delight. He was but eleven months and nine days old and, though still a tiny toddler, was just beginning to lisp his first babyish words. Cissy Caffrey bent over to him to tease his fat little plucks and the dainty dimple in his chin.

—Now, baby, Cissy Caffrey said. Say out big, big. I want a drink of water.

And baby prattled after her:

—A jink a jink a jawbo. (U284)

Bloom starts ogling one of the young girls.

Gerty MacDowell who was seated near her companions, lost in thought, gazing far away into the distance was, in very truth, as fair a specimen of winsome Irish girlhood as one could wish to see. She was pronounced beautiful by all who knew her.... Her figure was slight and graceful, inclining even to fragility.... The waxen pallor of her face was almost spiritual in its ivorylike purity though her rosebud mouth was a genuine Cupid's bow, Greekly perfect. Her hands were of finely veined alabaster with tapering fingers and as white as lemonjuice and queen of ointments could make them.... There was an innate refinement, a languid queenly *hauteur* about Gerty which was unmistakably evidenced in her delicate hands and higharched instep. Had kind fate but willed her to be born a gentlewoman of high degree in her own right and had she only received the benefit of a good education Gerty MacDowell might easily have held her own beside any lady in the land and have seen herself exquisitely gowned with jewels on her brow and patrician suitors at her feet vying with one another to pay their devoirs to her. Mayhap it was this, the love that might have been, that lent to her softlyfeatured face at whiles a look, tense with suppressed meaning, that imparted a strange yearning tendency to the beautiful eyes, a charm few could resist. Why have women such eyes of witchery? Gerty's were of the bluest Irish blue, set off by lustrous lashes and dark expressive brows.... But Gerty's crowning glory was her wealth of wonderful hair. It was dark brown with a natural wave in it. She had cut it that very morning on account of the new moon and it nestled about her pretty head in a profusion of luxuriant clusters and pared her nails too, Thursday for wealth. And just now...a telltale flush, delicate as the faintest rosebloom, crept into her cheeks she looked so lovely in her sweet girlish shyness that of a surety God's fair land of Ireland did not hold her equal. (U285–286)

Meanwhile, in a church on the hill just behind the beach, there is a men's retreat in progress.

And then there came out upon the air the sound of voices and the pealing anthem of the organ. It was the men's temperance retreat conducted by the missioner, the reverend John Hughes S. J., rosary, sermon and bedediction of the Most Blessed Sacrament. They were there gathered together without distinction of social class (and a most edifying spectacle it was to see) in that simple fane beside the waves, after the storms of this weary world, kneeling before the feet of the immaculate, reciting the litany of Our Lady of Loreto, beseeching her to intercede for them, the old familiar words, holy Mary, holy virgin of virgins. (U290)

So while Bloom is fixated on these young girls on the beach, hymns to the virgin Mother are being sung by a male chorus. Then:

...Jacky Caffrey called out:
     And they looked was it sheet lightning but Tommy saw it too over the trees beside the church, blue and then green and purple.
     —It's fireworks, Cissy Caffrey said.
     And they all ran down the strand to see over the houses and the

church, helterskelter, Edy with the pushcar with baby Boardman in it and Cissy holding Tommy and Jacky by the hand so they wouldn't fall running.

—Come on, Gerty, Cissy called. It's the bazaar fireworks.

But Gerty was adamant. She had no intention of being at their beck and call. If they could run like rossies she could sit so she said she could see from where she was. Whitehot passion was in that face, passion silent as the grave, and it had made her his. At last they were alone without the others to pry and pass remarks and she knew he could be trusted to the death, steadfast, a sterling man, a man of inflexible honour to his fingertips. His hands and face were working and a tremor went over her. She leaned back far to look up where the fireworks were and she caught her knee in her hands so as not to fall back looking up and there was no-one to see only him and her. . . . (U299)

And while the fireworks explode, Bloom has this absurd little reverie: He is ogling Gerty, and his thoughts go in such a direction that finally he has an orgasm. Then Gerty begins to walk away to join the others.

Slowly, without looking back she went down the uneven strand to Cissy, to Edy, to Jacky and Tommy Caffrey, to little baby Boardman. It was darker now and there were stones and bits of wood on the strand and slippy seaweed. She walked with a certain quiet dignity characteristic of her but with care and very slowly because – because Getty MacDowell was . . .

Tight boots? No, She's lame! O!

Mr Bloom watched her as she limped away. Poor girl! That's why she's left on the shelf and the others did a sprint. Thought something was wrong by the cut of her jib. Jilted beauty. (U301)

Well, we can see, Bloom is a man of great sympathy. And so, we are now ready for the next two chapters, which are the great finale to the Odysseus section.

### Oxen of the Sun

This long, fantastic chapter, one of the most difficult ones in the book, is written in a series of styles that echo the development of English literature. Let me give you a few clues before we come to the big crisis.

Bloom has heard that a good soul named Mrs. Purefoy has been having a difficult time giving birth (note the wasteland theme), so he goes to the maternity hospital to sympathize and find out how she is doing. There, in the hospital visiting room, he encounters Stephen, sitting with a group of his medical-student cronies, talking irreverently about the mysteries of conception, gestation, birth, motherhood, marriage, God, the Church, and the universe.

Now, while these boys talk disrespectfully about women and birth and related subjects, Joyce's experiments in style are going on and on. As they discuss the different stages in the development of the foetus, the literary style itself is developing. Just as the baby is growing in the mother's womb, so the English language is growing in the womb of England. The chapter begins in the style of the ancient Celtic chronicles, becomes the style of the Anglo-Saxon epics, and then moves down through the ages of English literature. Further, just as there is the egg and the sperm, so is there the Celtic and Anglo-Saxon polarity.

[The chapter starts with a primitive invocation to the sun as the source of fertility.]

> Deshil Holles Eamus. Deshil Holles Eamus. Deshil Holles Eamus.
> Send us bright one, light one, Horhorn, quickening and wombfruit.
> Send us bright one, light one, Horhorn, quickening and wombfruit.
> Send us bright one, light one, Horhorn, quickening and wombfruit.
> Hoopsa boyaboy hoopsa! Hoopsa boyaboy hoopsa! Hoopsa boyaboy hoopsa! (U314)

*Deshil* is Irish, and it means to circumambulate in a clockwise direction;[48] *Holles* is the name of the street on which the hospital is located; *Eamus* is Latin and means "Let us go." So, the whole phrase, which is a kind of chant, means "Let us go to Holles street in the clockwise direction." *Send us bright one, light one, Horhorn, quickening and wombfruit* is a charm to ask for fertility. *Hoopsa boyaboy hoopsa!* is the interruption [: "Whoops! A boy! A boy!"].

Next there is an English translation of a Latin text, what you would get if you were translating literally an old Latin chronicle. The first sentence of this section boils down to: "There is no better sign of a decent society than the care that is taken of birthing mothers." Here is the [unfertilized egg of the English language], you might say, waiting for the sperm.

Universally that person's acumen is esteemed very little perceptive concerning whatsoever matters are being held as most profitably by mortals with sapience endowed to be studied who is ignorant of that which the most in doctrine erudite and certainly by reason of that in them high mind's ornament deserving of veneration constantly maintain when by general consent they affirm that other circumstances being equal by no exterior splendour is the prosperity of a nation more efficaciously asserted than by the measure of how far forward may have progressed the tribute of its solicitude for that proliferent continuance which of evils the original if it be absent when fortunately present constitutes the certain sign of omnipollent nature's incorrupted benefaction. (U314)

Now comes the sperm, in the style of the alliterative poetry of the Anglo-Saxons.[49]

Before born babe bliss had. Within womb won he worship. Whatever in that one case done commodiously done was. A couch by midwives attended with wholesome food reposeful, cleanest swaddles as though forthbringing were now done and by wise foresight set.... 

And so we are begot. Next, Bloom comes to the door of Horne's maternity hospital.

Some man that wayfaring was stood by housedoor at night's oncoming. Of Israel's folk was that man that on earth wandering far had fared. Stark ruth of man his errand that him lone led till that house.... (U315)
   In ward wary the watcher hearing come that man mildhearted eft rising with swire ywimpled to him her gate wide undid.

A nurse lets him in.

Lo, levin leaping lightens in eyeblink Ireland's westward welkin.

Some lightning flashes in the sky.

Full she drad that God the Wreaker all mankind would fordo with water for his evil sins.

It's as though a deluge were coming.

Christ's rood made she on breastbone and him drew that he would rathe infare under her thatch.

She blesses herself and says, "Come in."

> That man her will wotting worthful went in Horne's house.
>     Loth to irk in Horne's hall hat holding the seeker stood. On her
> stow he ere was living with dear wife and lovesome daughter that
> then over land and seafloor, nine years had long outwandered.

Bloom knows the nurse. He and his wife once lived with her, but he
hasn't seen her for nine years.

> Once her in townhithe meeting he to her bow had not doffed.

Once he hadn't tipped his hat to her bow.

> Her to forgive now he craved with good ground of her allowed that
> that of him swiftseen face, hers, so young then had looked.

Well, he knows how to get out.

> Light swift her eyes kindled, bloom of blushes his word winning.
>     As her eyes then ongot his weeds swart therefor sorrow she feared.

Remember: he's dressed in black because of the funeral.

> Glad after she was that there ere adread was.

She's glad when he tells her, "Everything's OK."

> Her he asked if O'Hare Doctor tidings sent from far coast and she
> with grameful sigh him answered that O'Hare Doctor in heaven was.

Doctor O'Hare, whom he thought to meet here, has died.

> Sad was the man that word to hear that him so heavied in bowels
> ruthful. All she there told him, ruing death for friend so young, al-
> gate sore unwilling God's rightwiseness to withsay. (U316)

God's ways are not our ways, and it's too bad.

Now, as I mentioned, Stephen and the medical students are in the
waiting room when Bloom arrives, so he goes in and joins them. He has
come simply out of sympathy for Mrs. Purefoy, and he is soon repelled by
their impious, barbarous, learned conversation about birth and conception
and monstrous foetuses. Bloom is thinking of Molly and the loss of their
child. While these young men are talking, the great crisis comes. This is,
you see, the middle of the book, and it's here that the wasteland motif is
going to yield, and the sterile, infernal self-containment of these main
characters will begin to crack.

So, Stephen has been making rather rude remarks about God when abruptly—BANG!—a prodigious thunderclap sounds.

> A black crack of noise in the street in the street here, alack, bawled back. Loud on left Thor thundered: in anger awful the hammer-hurler. Came now the storm that hist his heart. And Master Lynch bade him have a care to flout and witwanton as the god self was angered for his hellprate and paganry. And he that had erst challenged to be so doughty...
>
> ... Stephen, who has always been terribly afraid of thunder...
>
> ... waxed wan as they might all mark and shrank together and his pitch that was before so haught uplift was now of a sudden quite plucked down and his heart shook within the cage of his breast as he tasted the rumour of that storm. (U323)

Why is Stephen so terribly frightened? Because he hears in that sound, that noise in the street, the warning roar of an approaching god revealed through phenomenality; that is, a break-through of the transcendent-immanent *con-transmagnificandjew-BANG-tantiality* of his morning meditation.

This moment of Thor's awful anger thus corresponds, in Joyce's intention, to Vico's idea of man's first notion of God, of a higher power to which he had to submit, coming through the voice of thunder. Vico, in a work called *The New Science,* saw historical conditions as moving in a cycle that he called the four ages of man: the age of the giants, the age of the fathers, the age of the sons, and the age of the people; then the cycle comes around again to the age of the giants, the chaos.

Vico's cycle begins with the age of the giants, when people are godless barbarians: wild, brutal, savage animals fighting each other for various goods. Then the voice of thunder sounds, and some hear it as the voice of God, threatening and disciplining mankind; others don't. But those who recognize God's voice in the thunder realize that they have been living in a beastly and inhuman manner, and they turn to decent living. They become God-fearing, monogamous souls, who develop agriculture, raise families, piously toil and till the soil. Thus the next stage begins, the age of the fathers, the patriarchs who have heard the word of God and carry civilization to the stage beyond savagery. Vico sees this age as the beginning of the neolithic.

So, the founding fathers toil, they put energy into agriculture, and they build up property and gain wealth. Then comes the age of the sons, the aristocrats who have not heard the voice of God but inherit the knowledge that God spoke to their fathers, just as they have inherited their father's property. Meanwhile, the children of those savages who did not hear the voice of God are outside of the great estates and, seeing how prosperous everything is inside, they too want in. So they are allowed in with the understanding that they must work for the privilege of being there, and they become the slaves, the serfs, the servants.

Then the sons begin to hear from the people working for them: "Well, who are you to have all this property anyhow? Why shouldn't we have something too?" The people bring up all kinds of rational and moral arguments to support their claims. I think we recognize this motif. So now we have the fourth age, the age of the people, when all the property is distributed democratically, and nobody has heard the voice of God or even inherited the moral order, so to speak. And what are the people interested in? Just goods—property. So they start fighting again, and back we go to the age of the giants, when the voice of God in the thunder was first heard.

So, Joyce introduces Vico's theme here in the middle of *Ulysses* with the thunderclap that frightens Stephen. And when we come to *Finnegans Wake,* we will hear the thunderclap resound at the opening of the book, and we will see Joyce using Vico's story of the cyclical ages of man as a central organizing theme.

Now, returning to our story, when that "black crack of noise in the streets" bawls back at him, Stephen is terribly frightened.

> But the braggart boaster cried that an old Nobodaddy was in his cups...

*Nobodaddy* is Blake's name for the God of the Old Testament.

> ... it was muchwhat indifferent and he would not lag behind his lead.

"Aw, I'll get drunk, too," Stephen brags.

> But this was only to dye his desperation as cowed he crouched in Horne's hall. He drank indeed at one draught to pluck up a heart of any grace for it thundered long rumblingly over all the heavens so that Master Madden, being godly certain whiles, knocked him on his ribs upon that crack of doom...

Now Bloom turns to comfort Stephen.

> ... and Master Bloom, at the braggart's side, spoke to him calming words to slumber his great fear, advertising how it was no other thing but a hubbub noise that he heard, the discharge of fluid from the thunderhead, look you, having taken place, and all of the order of a natural phenomenon.

With that evocation of sympathy, the first inkling of compassion in the book, Bloom and Stephen begin to come together.

> But was young Boasthard's fear vanquished by Calmer's words? No, for he had in his bosom a spike named Bitterness which could not by words be done away. And was he then neither calm like the one nor godly like the other? He was neither as much as he would have liked to be either.

Stephen, who is assailed by pangs of conscience for his sort of "paganry," is not calmed by Bloom's words.

> But could he not have endeavoured to have found again as in his youth the bottle Holiness that then he lived withal? Indeed no for Grace was not there to find that bottle. Heard he then in that clap the voice of the god Bringforth or, what Calmer said, a hubbub of Phenomenon? Heard? Why, he could not but hear unless he had plugged him up the tube Understanding (which he had not done).

Stephen, you see, is aware of the implied mythical dimension of this event.[50]

> For through that tube he saw that he was in the land of Phenomenon where he must for a certain one day die as he was like the rest too a passing show. And would he not accept to die like the rest and pass away? By no means would he though he must nor would he make more shows according as men do with wives which Phenomenon has commanded them to do by the book Law. (U323–324)

So, with Bloom's gesture of fatherly compassion for Stephen, the youth who is clearly in spiritual trouble and could have been (given his age) Bloom's own son, the transformation of both men has begun. From this moment of expressed compassion onward, a progressive disintegration of Stephen's attitude of pride will open the way, finally, for a leap of reciprocal sympathy that carries him outward beyond his broken defenses, to an actual experience (for a couple of hours, at least) of that mystery of consubstantiality with another about which he has been brooding all day long—albeit in the purely cerebral terms of an abstract, theological, medieval jargon. This is the transformation that takes place in the characters in this book. There are critics who have written that *Ulysses* isn't a novel because there is no transformation of character. The transformation of character is right here: sympathy breaks the self-containment of Stephen and Bloom. In fact, this theme, this problem, is the main theme and concern of the work.

Now we come to another very interesting moment. Bloom is looking intently at a bottle of Bass Ale. A bass, of course, is a fish, one of the early symbols of Christ. Bass Ale has a red triangle on the label, and ale is, of course, an intoxicant, a spirit. As Bloom is staring at this red triangle, Lenehan is about to disturb him; but Buck Mulligan stops him from interrupting and says:

> ...preserve a druid silence. His soul is far away. It is as painful perhaps to be awakened from a vision as to be born. Any object, intensely regarded, may be a gate of access to the incorruptible eon of the gods. (U340)

I mentioned this basic theme before with respect to the esthetic experience: Any object can open back to the mystery of the universe. You can take any object whatsoever—a stick or stone, a dog or a child—draw a ring around it so that it is seen as separate from everything else, and thus contemplate it in its mystery aspect—the aspect of the mystery of its being, which is the mystery of all being—and it will have there and then become a proper object of worshipful regard. So, any object can become an adequate base for meditation, since the whole mystery of man and of nature and of everything else is in any object that you want to regard. This idea, which is the anagogical inspiration of Joyce's book and of his art, is what we are getting in that little moment in the maternity hospital.

Now then, shortly after the great thunderclap which breaks the impasse, word comes that the child has been born—analogously, a new man is now to be born of Stephen as well—and there is an amusing little piece describing the relief of the mother. The style by now has come all the way up to Dickens, so we read about this birth in Dickens's language:

Meanwhile the skill and patience of the physician had brought about a happy *accouchement*. It had been a weary weary while both for patient and doctor. All that surgical skill could do was done and the brave woman had manfully helped. She had. She had fought the good fight and now she was very very happy. Those who have passed on, who have gone before, are happy too as they gaze down and smile upon the touching scene. Reverently look at her as she reclines there with the motherlight in her eyes, that longing hunger for baby fingers (a pretty sight it is to see), in the first bloom of her new motherhood, breathing a silent prayer of thanskgiving to One above, the Universal Husband. And as her loving eyes behold her babe she wishes only one blessing more, to have her dear Doady there with her to share her joy, to lay in his arms that mite of God's clay, the fruit of their lawful embraces. He is older now (you and I may whisper it) and a trifle stooped in the shoulders yet in the whirligig of years a grave dignity has come to the conscientious second accountant of the Ulster bank, College Green branch. O Doady, loved one of old, faithful lifemate now, it may never be again, that faroff time of the roses! With the old shake of her pretty head she recalls those days. God! How beautiful now across the mist of years! But their children are grouped in her imagination about the bedside, hers and his, Charley, Mary Alice, Frederick Albert (if he had lived), Mamy, Budgy (Victoria Frances), Tom, Violet Constance Louisa, darling little Bobsy (called after our famous hero of the South African war, lord Bobs of Waterford and Candahar) and now this last pledge of their union, a Purefoy if ever there was one, with the true Purefoy nose. Young hopeful will be christened Mortimer Edward after the influential third cousin of Mr Purefoy in the Treasury Remembrancer's office, Dublin Castle. And so time wags on: but father Cronion has dealt lightly here. No, let no sigh break from that bosom, dear gentle Mina. And Doady, knock the ashes from your pipe, the seasoned briar you still fancy when the curfew rings for you (may it be the distant day!) and dout the light whereby you read in the Sacred Book for the oil too has run low, and so with a tranquil heart to bed, to rest. He knows and will call in His own good time. You too have fought the good fight and played loyally your man's part. Sir, to you my hand. Well done, thou good and faithful servant! thou good and faithful servant. (U343–344)

So, the child is born; and just as the child has left the mother's body, so the crowd in the waiting-room, with the announcement of the birth, goes tearing out of the maternity hospital—just as English breaks out of England into the various patois and dialects of the empire, including the United States.

Now, the young men are shouting and running down the street, some of them intending to go to the brothels. And there's a fire somewhere: we hear a fire contraption roaring past, and also, a sermon about Elijah by an American Methodist rabblerouser.[51]

Golly, whatten tunket's yon guy in the mackintosh? Dusty Rhodes. Peep at his wearables. By mighty! What's he got? Jubilee mutton. Bovril, by James. Wants it real bad. D'ye ken bare socks? Seedy cuss in the Richmond? Rawthere! Thought he had a deposit of lead in his penis. Trumpery insanity. Bartle the Bread we calls him. That, sir, was once a prosperous cit. Man all tattered and torn that married a maiden all forlorn. Slung her hook, she did. Here see lost love. Walking Mackintosh of lonely canyon. Tuck and turn in. Schedule time. Nix for the hornies. Pardon? Seen him today at a runefal? Chum o' yourn passed in his checks? Ludamassy! Pore piccaninnies! Thou'll no be telling me thot, Pold veg! Did ums blubble bigsplash crytears cos fren Padney was took off in black bag? Of all de darkies Massa Pat was verra best. I never see the like since I was born. *Tiens, tiens,* but it is well sad, that, my faith, yes. O, get, rev on a gradient one in nine. Live axle drives are souped. Lay you two to one Jenatzy licks him ruddy well hollow. Jappies? High angle fire, inyah! Sunk by war specials. Be worse for him, says he, nor any Rooshian. Time all. There's eleven of them. Get ye gone. Forward, woozy wobblers! Night. Night. May Allah the Excellent One your soul this night ever tremendously conserve.

Your attention! We're nae tha fou. The Leith police dismisseth us. The least tholice. Ware hawks for the chap puking. Unwell in his abominable regions. Yooka. Night. Mona, my thrue love. Yook. Mona, my own love. Ook.

Hark! Shut your obstropolos. Pflaap! Pflaap! Blaze on. There she goes. Brigade! Bout ship. Mount street way. Cut up! Pflaap! Tally ho. You not come? Run, skelter, run. Pflaaaap!

Lynch! Hey? Sign on long o' me. Denzille lane this way. Change here for Bawdyhouse. We two, she said, will seek the kips where

shady Mary is. Righto, any old time. *Laetabuntur in cubilibus suis.*
You coming long? Whisper, who the sooty hell's the johnny in the
black duds? Hush! Sinned against the light and even now that day is
at hand when he shall come to judge the world by fire. Pflaap! *Ut im-
plerentur scripturae.* Strike up a ballad. Then outspake medical Dick
to his comrade medical Davy. Christicle, who's this excrement
yellow gospeller on the Merrion hall? Elijah is coming! Washed
in the blood of the Lamb. Come on, you winefizzling, ginsizzling,
booseguzzling existences! Come on, you dog-gone, bullnecked,
beetlebrowed, hogjowled, peanutbrained, weaseleyed fourflushers,
false alarms and excess baggage! Come on, you triple extract of in-
famy! Alexander J. Christ Dowie, that's my name, thar's yanked to
glory most half this planet from Frisco beach to Vladivostok. The
Deity aint no nickel dime bumshow. I put it to you that He's on
the square and a corking fine business proposition. He's the grand-
est thing yet and don't you forget it. Shout salvation in King Jesus.
You'll need to rise precious early, you sinner there, if you want to
diddle the Almighty God. Pflaaaap! Not half. He's got a coughmix-
ture with a punch in it for you, my friend, in his back pocket. Just
you try it on. (U348–349)

As the chapter ends, then, Stephen is terribly drunk with this bunch of
roughnecks; and Bloom, with his fatherly interest in the lad, doesn't like to
see him going off in such a state with those fellows to that place. So he thinks,
"Well, I'll follow him and watch over him," and he follows Stephen and
his crony Lynch down to the whorehouses. There, in the next chapter, the
initations will take place that break both Stephen and Bloom past their fixes.

## Circe

### Introduction

We come now to the woman's view, to the "Circe" chapter, which takes
place in Nighttown, the brothel section of Dublin—in the realm of Circe,
the seductress. It runs 147 pages, about a fourth of the book.

Up to this point in *Ulysses,* each chapter has been a kind of little song
of its own, with its own style and rhythm. Joyce's general style, however, has
been basically a kind of old-style writing, pretty much in the realm of natural experience: complex, with many inflections and echoes of the *Odyssey*

throughout to give the sense that what is happening is something people have been experiencing one way or another all through the centuries. The "Circe" chapter, by contrast, is written in play form. Furthermore, when Bloom and Stephen go into the brothel world, their ego complexes are being dissolved, which releases energy that descends into the unconscious and activates what Jung calls "the autonomous complexes." Moreover, as they descend further into the ocean of the unconscious, they begin to hallucinate, and a kind of hallucinatory world amalgamates with the gross-object world. So what Joyce does, both in the text and in the imagery, is alternate imaginary experiences with actual ones, for we are in a realm where hallucination and objective fact intermingle. We are on the way to what we will get in *Finnegans Wake*.

Now [as a kind of guide to this immensely complex] chapter, I want to bring up several points that I think will bring out the main themes of Bloom's experience and Stephen's relationship to him.

The first point: Bloom is looking for a son. He had a son, Rudy, who died. Had the little boy lived, he would have been eleven years old in 1904. So Bloom is a father who has been deprived of a son. In his youth, however, Bloom had an affair with a girl, Bridie Kelly, and he might have begotten a son.[52] In Bloom's thoughts, then, Stephen plays the role of his possible son.

Another point: Bloom has a lot of pseudo-scientific thoughts in his mind, a lot of information and misinformation, and one theme, the law of falling bodies (thirty-two feet per second per second), continually returns to him. Bloom's son would now be eleven years old. The motif of these two numbers, 11 and 32, which is being built up here in *Ulysses,* is a theme that will repeatedly recur in amusing ways in *Finnegans Wake:* 1132, 1132, 1132. It comes up as a day, as a legal code, as an address—32 West 11th Street (I tip my hat whenever I walk past that house)—and in many other ways. And what does 1132 mean? Well, 32 (feet per second per second) lets us know there has been a fall, and 11 lets us know that there is a kind of resurrection. There is another aspect to this 1132 reference. One time when I was reading St. Paul's Epistle to the Romans (I don't recall why), I came across a passage that seemed to me to say just what *Finnegans Wake* was all about: "For God has consigned all men to disobedience that he may show his mercy to all." Give God a chance and be disobedient. Sin! As

Luther said, "Sin boldly!" For sin is what evokes God's mercy. This is associated with the text we read in the Catholic Mass for Holy Saturday: "*O felix culpa!*" ("Oh happy fault!"), that is, the fall of Adam and Eve, the Original Sin which evoked the Savior. There would have been no Savior had there been no fall: "Oh happy fall!" So when I read the passage in Paul's Epistle that I thought was the key to *Finnegans Wake,* I wrote down the reference. And guess what it was: Romans 11:32. So, that's another aspect to this 1132 motif.

A further point: Another theme in Bloom's mind as he wanders is that of parallax, a concept which governs the construction of the "Circe" chapter. Anybody who focuses a camera knows what parallax is: the camera lens is down below, but the viewer is up above, so you have to correct for that, and the angle of correction is the parallax. The parallax is also used in astronomy. Suppose you want to measure the distance from a star to, not where your telescope is, but to the center of the earth. How do you find what the angle should be? The way you get the parallax to the center of the earth is by viewing the star from the top of the earth and from the bottom. So, you sight the angle from where you are, then wait twelve hours until the earth has turned 180 degrees, and then sight from the new direction. The relation between the old angle and the new one is your parallax. Similarly, in *Ulysses,* Stephen and Bloom provide, as it were, the two parallactic angles, the top and the bottom points of view. When you put the view of Stephen and the view of Bloom together, you get the center of man. And that's how the "Circe" chapter is rendered—from those two parallactic angles: one, that of Stephen with his friend Lynch going into the brothel; and the other, that of Bloom following them.

Moreover, if you draw the parallax angle on a piece of paper, you have a figure that looks like a little bow, the bow of Ulysses, which sends the arrow to the mark. In the *Odyssey,* you recall, Penelope proposes a test to pick a husband from among the suitors. She will marry the one who can drive the arrow from the bow of Odyseus through twelve axes—twelve being the number of signs of the zodiac, as well as the number of chapters that Bloom is here surviving. It is Odysseus, who has returned in disguise, who draws the bow, sends the arrow through the axes, and then slays the suitors.

This bow image also suggests another of Joyce's motifs: the mystery of OM (or AUM), that great Sanskrit term of mystery that is spoken of in the

Māndūkya Upaniṣad:

> Affix to the Upaniṣad, the bow incomparable, the sharp arrow of devotional worship; then with mind absorbed and heart melted in love, draw the arrow and hit the mark—the imperishable *brahman.*
>
> OM is the bow, the arrow is the individual being, and *brahman* is the target. With a tranquil heart, take aim. Lose thyself in him, even as the arrow is lost in the target.[53]

AUM is also a word that, when analyzed, refers to three areas of the soul: consciousness, dream consciousness, and the dark realm of dreamless sleep. These three realms of the human psyche together must all be brought together, and when that happens, the arrow can be sent to the center. This idea is the ultimate significance of the parallax theme on which Bloom is meditating throughout *Ulysses.*

## Nighttown

So, Stephen has embarked with his companion, Lynch, on a veritable night-sea journey into the belly of the whale, into the night-street of brothels, the isle of magic of the nymph Circe and her sty of men-become-swine. And Joyce describes Dublin's brothel area as a really tawdry place, where people might very well be transformed into pigs. But as we know from the *Odyssey,* there is a certain advantage to being transformed into a pig: when Odysseus manages to compel Circe to turn his men back into men again, they are younger and more handsome and stronger than they ever were.

We are entering the brothel area now, and it is as though we were going into the underworld, a pretty grimy, unpleasant place:

> *(The Mabbot street entrance of nighttown, before which stretches an uncobbled tramsiding set with skeleton tracks, red and green will-o'-the-wisps and danger signals. Rows of grimy houses with gaping doors. Rare lamps with faint rainbow fans. Round Rabaiotti's halted ice gondola stunted men and women squabble. They grab wafers between which are wedged lumps of coral and copper snow. Sucking, they scatter slowly. Children. The swancomb of the gondola, highreared, forges on through the murk, white and blue under a lighthouse. Whistles call and answer.)*

### THE CALL

Wait, my love, and I'll be with you.

### THE ANSWER

Round behind the stable.

*(A deafmute idiot with goggle eyes, his shapeless mouth dribbling, jerks past, shaken in Saint Vitus' dance. A chain of children's hands imprisons him.)*

### THE CHILDREN

Kithogue! Salute!

### THE IDIOT

*(lifts a palsied left arm and gurgles.)* Grhahute!

### THE CHILDREN

Where's the great light?

### THE IDIOT

*(gobbling)* Ghaghahest. (U350)

*(Stephen, flourishing the ashplant in his left hand, chants with joy the introit for paschal time. Lynch, his jockeycap low on his brow, attends him, a sneer of discontent wrinkling his face.)*

### STEPHEN

*Vidi aquam egredientem de templo a latere dextro. Alleluia.* (U352)

Stephen is entering this underworld realm chanting the Latin for the mass at Pascal time, at Eastertime, the time of the death and resurrection of Christ, his leaving of the body behind and going to the Father in the spirit. Stephen is on his own track, indifferent to the area around him.

Meanwhile, Bloom patiently follows Stephen and Lynch into Nighttown to protect (and perhaps to rescue) Stephen, who has now evoked his concerned interest; but he loses the young men and has to go seeking them through the streets. Completely bewildered, he goes into a butcher shop to buy something to eat. Moments later, he is almost run over by a trolley car: that's the Symplegades—you know, the rocks that clash together—he's going through the pairs-of-opposites into the world beyond the light.

So now vulnerable Bloom is in the mystic realm, in the lewd suggestive nightland, where he comes under enchantment. His own activated imagination begins to spew from beneath the floors of his mind the whole sewer of what Jung has termed the "personal unconscious": the repressed, half-forgotten urgencies and memories of desire, shame, and libidinous fantasy that, throughout his life from infancy onward, have been running off below decks, so to speak, and accumulating there in a timeless, sloshing, fetid bilge. As he tries to find his way through the brothel district, he begins to imagine people he knows seeing him there—"What if so-and-so were to see me? What if so-and-so were to see me?"

Then curious little juxtapositions of fact and hallucination begin to occur. His dead father comes and spooks him for a while, then his dead mother. And while Bloom wanders amid all these different experiences [the dead, the living, and the imaginary, all join to act as an externalized commentary on his feelings of guilt in entering the illicit realms of Nighttown. Then he imagines that the police appear, and suddenly he fantasizes that he is on trial]. A group of imaginary character witnesses come to support him and to explain that he is on a charitable mission in the red-light district: "And he's doing good, and he has done good," and so forth, and so on. Then, in Bloom's fantasy, in come three fashionable ladies to "testify" against him.

MRS YELVERTON BARRY

*(in lowcorsaged opal balldress and elbowlength ivory gloves, wearing a sabletrimmed brickquilted dolman, a comb of brilliants and panache of osprey in her hair)* Arrest him, constable. He wrote me an anonymous letter in prentice backhand when my husband was in the North Riding of Tipperary on the Munster circuit, signed James Lovebirch. He said that he had seen from the gods my peerless globes as I sat in a box of the *Theatre Royal* at a command performance of *La Cigale.* I deeply inflamed him, he said. He made improper overtures to me to misconduct myself at half past four P.M. on the following Thursday, Dunsink time. He offered to send me through the post a work of fiction by Monsieur Paul de Kock, entitled *The Girl with the Three Pairs of Stays. . . .*

### THE HONOURABLE MRS MERVYN TALBOYS

*(in amazon costume, hard hat, jackboots cockspurred, vermilion waist-coat, fawn musketeer gauntlets with braided drums, long train held up and hunting crop with which she strikes her welt constantly)* Also me. Because he saw me on the polo ground of the Phoenix park at the match All Ireland versus the Rest of Ireland. My eyes, I know, shone divinely as I watched Captain Slogger Dennehy of the Inniskillings win the final chukkar on his darling cob *Centaur.* This plebeian Don Juan observed me from behind a hackney car and sent me in double envelopes an obscene photograph, such as are sold after dark on Paris boulevards, insulting to any lady. I have it still. It represents a partially nude señorita, frail and lovely (his wife, as he solemnly assured me, taken by him from nature), practicing illicit intercourse with a muscular torero, evidently a blackguard. He urged me to do likewise, to misbehave, to sin with officers of the garrison. He implored me to soil his letter in an unspeakable manner, to chastise him as he richly deserves, to bestride and ride him, to give him a most vicious horsewhipping.

### MRS BELLINGHAM

Me too.

### MRS YELVERTON BARRY

Me too.

*(Several highly respectable Dublin ladies hold up improper letters received from Bloom.)*

### THE HONOURABLE MRS MERVYN TALBOYS

*(stamps her jingling spurs in a sudden paroxysm of fury)* I will, by the God above me. I'll scourge the pigeonlivered cur as long as I can stand over him. I'll flay him alive.

### BLOOM

*(his eyes closing, quails expectantly)* Here? *(he squirms)* Again! *(he pants cringing)* I love the danger.

### THE HONOURABLE MRS MERVYN TALBOYS

Very much so! I'll make it hot for you. I'll make you dance Jack Latten for that.

### MRS BELLINGHAM

Tan his breech well, the upstart! Write the stars and stripes on it!

### MRS YELVERTON BARRY

Disgraceful! There's no excuse for him! A married man!

### BLOOM

All these people. I meant only the spanking idea. A warm tingling glow without effusion. Refined birching to stimulate the circulation.

### THE HONOURABLE MRS MERVYN TALBOYS

*(laughs derisively)* O, did you, my fine fellow? Well, by the living God, you'll get the surprise of your life now, believe me, the most unmerciful hiding a man ever bargained for. You have lashed the dormant tigress in my nature into fury.

### MRS BELLINGHAM

*(shakes her muff and quizzing-glasses vindictively)* Make him smart, Hanna dear. Give him ginger. Thrash the mongrel within an inch of his life. The cat-o'-nine-tails. Geld him. Vivisect him.

### BLOOM

*(shuddering, shrinking, joins his hands: with hangdog mien)* O cold! O shivery! It was your ambrosial beauty. Forget, forgive. Kismet. Let me off this once. *(he offers the other cheek)*

### MRS YELVERTON BARRY

*(severely)* Don't do so on any account, Mrs Talboys! He should be soundly trounced!

THE HONOURABLE MRS MERVYN TALBOYS

*(unbuttoning her gauntlet violently)* I'll do no such thing. Pigdog and always was ever since he was pupped! To dare address me! I'll flog him black and blue in the public streets. I'll dig my spurs in him up to the rowel. He is a wellknown cuckold. *(she swishes her huntingcrop savagely in the air)* Take down his trousers without loss of time. Come here, sir! Quick! Ready?

BLOOM

*(trembling, beginning to obey)* The weather has been so warm. (U379–382)

[In his generalized guilty fantasies, Bloom thinks the police will suspect that the package of pig's feet he has dropped is a bomb, and that he is wearing black clothes as camouflage for placing bombs under cover of night.]

SECOND WATCH

*(points to the corner)* The bomb is here.

FIRST WATCH

Infernal machine with a time fuse.

BLOOM

No, no. Pig's feet. I was at a funeral.

FIRST WATCH

*(draws his truncheon)* Liar!

*(The beagle lifts his snout, showing the grey scorbutic face of Paddy Dignam. He has gnawed all. He exhales a putrid carcasefed breath. He grows to human size and shape. His dachshund coat becomes a brown mortuary habit. His green eye flashes bloodshot. Half of one ear, all the nose and both thumbs are ghouleaten.)*

PADDY DIGNAM

*(in a hollow voice)* It is true. It was my funeral. Doctor Finucane pronounced life extinct when I succumbed to the disease from natural causes. (U385)

After the buried Paddy Dignam supports Bloom's assertions, his fantasies fade out, and he marches onward. Finally, outside one of the brothels, Bloom hears through an open window someone playing a piano in open fifths.

> (*... Bloom plodges forward again through the sump. Kisses chirp amid the rifts of fog. A piano sounds. He stands before a lighted house, listening. The kisses, winging from their bowers[,] fly about him, twittering, warbling, cooing.*)

### THE KISSES

(*warbling*) Leo! (*twittering*) Icky licky micky sticky for Leo! (*cooing*) Coo coocoo! Yummyyum, Womwom! (*warbling*) Big comebig! Pirouette! Leopopold! (*twittering*) Leeolee! (*warbling*) O Leo!

> (*They rustle, flutter upon his garments, alight, bright giddy flecks, silvery sequins.*)

### BLOOM

A man's touch. Sad music. Church music. Perhaps here....

He realizes he has found the place where Stephen and his friend have gone. As Bloom stands irresolutely in front of the brothel,

> (*Zoe Higgins, a young whore in a sapphire slip closed with three bronze buckles, a slim black velvet fillet round her throat, nods, trips down the steps and accosts him.*)

### ZOE

Are you looking for someone? He's inside with his friend.

### BLOOM

Is this Mrs Mack's?

Ho, ho. Well, he knows something about this place, doesn't he?

### ZOE

No, eightyone. Mrs Cohen's. You might go farther and fare worse. Mother Slipperslapper. (*familiarly*) She's on the job herself tonight with the vet her tipster that gives her all the winners and pays for her son in Oxford....

This bit of information is going to stand Bloom in good stead a little later in the evening.

Working overtime but her luck's turned today. (*suspiciously*) You're not his father, are you?

BLOOM

Not I!

ZOE

You both in black. Has little mousey any tickles tonight?

(*His skin, alert, feels her fingertips approach. A hand glides over his left thigh....Her hand slides into his left trouser pocket and brings out a hard black shrivelled potato. She regards it and Bloom with dumb moist lips.*)

BLOOM

A talisman. Heirloom.

ZOE

For Zoe? For keeps? For being so nice, eh?

(*She puts the potato greedily into a pocket then links his arm, cuddling him with supple warmth. He smiles uneasily. Slowly, note by note, oriental music is played. He gazes in the tawny crystal of her eyes, ringed with kohol. His smile softens.*)

In his imagination, he now sees her as some warm Oriental fantasy. And she says:

ZOE

You'll know me the next time.[54]

BLOOM

(*forlornly*) I never loved a dear gazelle but it was sure to....

(*Gazelles are leaping, feeding on the nountains. Near are lakes. Round their shores file shadows black of cedargroves. Aroma rises, a strong hairgrowth of resin. It burns, the orient, a sky of sapphire, cleft by the bronze flight of eagles. Under it lies the womancity, nude, white, still, cool, in luxury. A fountain murmurs among damask roses. Mammoth roses murmur of scarlet winegrapes. A wine of shame, lust, blood exudes, strangely murmuring.)*

Gazelles are leaping. Bloom in his imagination believes that he is going into some seraglio.[55] She conducts him upstairs.

ZOE

*(murmuring singsong with the music, her odalisk lips lusciously smeared with salve of swinefat and rosewater)* Schorach ani wenowach, benoith Hierushaloim.

"I am black but comely, O ye daughters of Jerusalem."[56]

BLOOM

*(fascinated)* I thought you were of good stock by your accent.

ZOE

And you know what thought did?

*(She bites his ear gently with little goldstopped teeth, sending on him a cloying breath of stale garlic. . . . )* (U387–389)

She begins to feel him up, and his imagination becomes inflamed. He feels himself to be in a strange situation certainly. As the two enter the building, church chimes sound midnight, and it's as though they were chiming for his entry into what is later called "the new Bloomusalem." (U395) The chimes help him feel that this adventure is a grand, grand thing. As he and the whore Zoe go up the brothel stairs he imagines that he is greeted by torch bearers.

AN ELECTOR

Three times three for our future chief magistrate!

*(The aurora borealis of the torchlight procession leaps.)* (U390)

[In Bloom's hallucination, his sexual excitement modulates into political megalomania.] He imagines that Lord Mayor Harrington, the Counselor

Lorcan Sherlock, and many other important people hail him going up the steps; and there's a grand illusory celebration:

> (*Prolonged applause. Venetian masts, maypoles and festal arches spring up. A streamer bearing the legends* Cead Mile Failte *and* Mah Ttob Melek Israel *spans the street. All the windows are thronged with sightseers, chiefly ladies. Along the route the regiments of the Royal Dublin Fusiliers, the King's Own Scottish Borderers, The Cameron Highlanders and the Welch Fusiliers, standing to attention, keep back the crowd. Boys from High school are perched on the lampposts, telegraph poles, windowsills, cornices, gutters, chimneypots, railings, rainspouts, whistling and cheering. The pillar of the cloud appears....*) (U391)

The festivities continue, with flags and banners, a fife and drum band, and all manner of people cheering and shouting. Then:

> (*...A sunburst appears in the northwest.*)

#### THE BISHOP OF DOWN AND CONNOR

I here present your undoubted emperor-president and king-chairman, the most serene and potent and very puissant ruler of this realm. God save Leopold the First!

#### ALL

God save Leopold the First! (U393)

Bloom is having quite an experience. It's a long, long affair that goes on for pages, and much of it picks up themes from his earlier experiences during the day. Then, suddenly, the euphoric tide begins to turn. The change starts with Father Farley.

#### FATHER FARLEY

He is an episcopalian, an agnostic, an anythingarian seeking to overthrow our holy faith.

#### MRS RIORDAN

(*tears up her will*) I'm disappointed in you! You bad man! (U400)

Then, as happened in the case of the Church and Aunt Dante turning against Parnell, the people begin to come down on him.

### THE MOB

Lynch him! Roast him! He's as bad as Parnell was. Mr Fox!

(*Mother Grogan throws her boot at Bloom. Several shopkeepers from upper and lower Dorset street throw objects of little or no commercial value, hambones, condensed milk tins, unsaleable cabbage, stale bread, sheep's tails, odd pieces of fat.*)

### BLOOM

(*excitedly*) This is midsummer madness, some ghastly joke again. By heaven, I am guiltless as the unsunned snow! It was my brother Henry. He is my double. He lives in number 2 Dolphin's Barn. Slander, the viper, has wrongfully accused me. Fellowcountrymen, *sgeul i mbarr bata coisde gan capall....*

You will recall that in the *Odyssey,* when Odysseus is being initiated to the female power—so that he is no longer the bully with respect to women, but is in an attitude of dialogue with an "equal but other"—he is sent into the underworld, where he meets Tiresias, who had been both man and woman. Now, as Bloom is about to cross the threshold into the brothel, it's Tiresias who appears. Listen to what happens in Bloom's imagination as he continues his defense.

...I call upon my old friend, Dr Malachi Mulligan, sex specialist, to give medical testimony on my behalf.

### DR MULLIGAN

(*in motor jerkin, green motorgoggles on his brow*) Dr Bloom is bisexually abnormal. He has recently escaped from Dr Eustace's private asylum for demented gentlemen. Born out of bedlock hereditary epilepsy is present, the consequence of unbridled lust. Traces of elephantiasis have been discovered among his ascendants. There are marked symptoms of chronic exhibitionism. Ambidexterity is also latent. He is prematurely bald from selfabuse, perversely idealistic in consequence, a reformed rake, and has metal teeth. In consequence of a family complex he has temporarily lost his memory and I believe him to be more sinned against than sinning. I have made a pervaginal examination and, after application of the acid test to

5427 anal, axillary, pectoral and pubic hairs, I declare him to be *virgo intacta.*

(*Bloom holds his high grade hat over his genital organs.*) ...

Some other doctors then offer their opinions.

### DR DIXON

(*reads a bill of health*) Professor Bloom is a finished example of the new womanly man. His moral nature is simple and lovable. Many have found him a dear man, a dear person. He is a rather quaint fellow on the whole, coy though not feebleminded in the medical sense.... I appeal for clemency in the name of the most sacred word our vocal organs have ever been called upon to speak. He is about to have a baby.

### BLOOM

O, I so want to be a mother.

### MRS THORNTON

(*in nursetender's gown*) Embrace me tight, dear. You'll be soon over it. Tight, dear.

> (*Bloom embraces her tightly and bears eight male yellow and white children. They appear on a redcarpeted staircase adorned with expensive plants. All the octuplets are handsome, with valuable metallic faces, well-made, respectably dressed and wellconducted, speaking five modern languages fluently and interested in various arts and sciences. Each has his name printed in legible letters on his shirtfront: Nasodoro, Goldfinger, Chrysostomos, Maindorée, Silversmile, Silberselber, Vifargent, Panargyros. They are immediately appointed to positions of high public trust in several different countries as managing directors of banks, traffic managers of railways, chairmen of limited liability companies, vicechairmen of hotel syndicates.*) (U402–403)

Bloom, in that moment when he asks to be a mother, is the dual male-female, the world center.[57] Nicolas Cusanus states that "God is an intelligible circle whose circumference is nowhere and whose center is everywhere." Every man is the center. In the *Rosarum Philosophorum,* an alchemical text dating from about the sixteenth century, there is a passage about the philosopher's stone:

> Out of man and woman make a round circle and extract the quadrangle from this and from the quadrangle the triangle. Make a round circle and you shall have the philosopher's stone.[58]

This figure will actually be drawn in *Finnegans Wake,* as we will see later. Jung also discusses the philosopher's stone. He says that the image of the deity dormant and concealed in matter was what the alchemists called the original chaos or the earth of paradise or the round fish in the sea or merely the rotundum or the egg. That round thing was in possession of the key which unlocked the closed doors of matter.[59]

So, returning now to Bloom's mad hallucinations, after his birth experience, his sexual megalomania again takes over [and he imagines himself "Bloom the Messiah."][60]

A VOICE

Bloom, are you the Messiah ben Joseph or ben David?

BLOOM

(*darkly*) You have said it.

BROTHER BUZZ

Then perform a miracle like Father Charles.

BANTAM LYONS

Prophesy who will win the Saint Leger.

(*Bloom walks on a net, covers his left eye with his left ear, passes through several walls, climbs Nelson's Pillar, hangs from the top ledge by his eyelids, eats twelve dozen oysters (shells included), heals several sufferers from the king's evil, contracts his face so as to resemble many historical personages, . . . turns each foot simultaneously in different directions, turns the tide back, eclipses the sun by extending his little finger.*)

The Papal Nuncio now appears and goes through a ceremony.

### BRINI, PAPAL NUNCIO

(*in papal zouave's uniform, steel cuirasses as breastplate, armplates, thigh-plates, legplates, large profane moustaches and brown paper mitre*) *Leopoldi autem generatio.* Moses begat Noah and Noah begat Eunuch and Eunuch begat O'Halloran and O'Halloran begat Guggenheim . . .

These are the generations of Leopold [in comic imitation of the genealogies of Jesus in Matthew and Luke,] and they continue right on down, until finally:

. . . and Virag begat Bloom *et vocabitur nomen eius Emmanuel.*

"And his name shall be called Emmanuel."

### A DEADHAND

(*writes on the wall*) Bloom is a cod. (U403–404)

And then all these little onanistic sins of Bloom's youth come up to accuse him. Finally:

(*Lieutenant Myers of the Dublin Fire Brigade by general request sets fire to Bloom. Lamentations.*) (U406)

[And thus Bloom achieves a megalomaniac climax; he suffers execution as the Messiah.] Now the great moment of his crossing the threshold into the brothel room at last arrives, and Bloom stumbles.

### ZOE

(*her lucky hand saving him*) Hoopsa! Don't fall upstairs.

### BLOOM

The just man falls seven times. (*he stands aside at the threshold*) After you is good manners.

### ZOE

Ladies first, gentlemen after.

(*She crosses the threshold. He hesitates. She turns and, holding out her hands, draws him over. He hops. On the antlered rack of the hall hang a man's hat and waterproof. . . .*)

This sort of nineteenth-century coatrack, the kind with antlers on either side of a mirror, will be important later.

> *Bloom uncovers himself but, seeing them, frowns, then smiles, pre-occupied. . . .*) (U409)

[Bloom's reaction is guarded: perhaps he sees a reflection of his status as a cuckold.] Bloom comes into the tawdry parlor, where there are three whores: Zoe, of course, whose name suggest zoology; Florry, suggesting botany; and Kitty [a collection of things,] the mineral world. Lynch, in a jockey cap, is in there, and Stephen, who

> (*. . . stands at the pianola on which sprawl his hat and ashplant. With two fingers he repeats once more the series of empty fifths. . . .*) (U410)

Now for the whole question of "empty fifths," open fifths.[61] The fifth is the furthest one can get from the tonic without being on the way back: *Do re mi fa sol la ti do,* then *do* begins to close again. At this point in *Ulysses,* Stephen knows that he is at the extreme of his departure from the base, of his separation from the father. The tonic is the father or the ground or the base or the drone, and he has separated himself as far as he can. The sun will cross [the Tropic of Cancer on] the June 22 summer solstice, and will then [start on its journey south,] to set. Stephen realizes that this episode is the end of his old life, the moment of crucifixion, the moment when the sun reaches the apogee of its climb in the heavens and begins its descent: "I have gone as far as I can in this egoistic single way of mine, and I am about to embark on my way home." He tries to explain to Lynch.

### STEPHEN

. . . The reason is because the fundamental and the dominant are separated by the greatest possible interval which . . .

### THE CAP

Which? Finish. You can't.

### STEPHEN

(*with an effort*) Interval which. Is the greatest possible ellipse. Consistent with. The ultimate return. The octave. Which. . . .

So, Stephen realizes that his mounting spiritual solo night (*do, re, mi, fa, sol*) is about to begin its return to earth (*la, ti, do*), the tonic. And just at this instant:

> (*Outside the gramophone begins to blare* The Holy City.)

A nice coincidence of an event and of the readiness to experience the event: he is about to see Bloom. Stephen goes on, drunkenly yet precisely, striving to give words to his dawning apprehension of the way to experience consubstantiality.

STEPHEN

(*abruptly*) What went forth to the ends of the world to traverse not itself, God, the sun, Shakespeare, a commercial traveller, having itself traversed in reality itself becomes that self. . . .

Bloom has traversed himself. The world that you experience is a projection of your own potentiality, and what you seek is yourself.

Wait a moment. Wait a second. Damn that fellow's noise in the street. Self which it itself was ineluctably preconditioned to become. *Ecco!*

LYNCH

(*with a mocking whinny of laughter grins at Bloom and Zoe Higgins*) What a learned speech, eh?

ZOE

(*briskly*) God help your head, he knows more than you have forgotten.

(*With obese stupidity Florry Talbot regards Stephen.*)

FLORRY

They say the last day is coming this summer. (U411–412)

So we're at the moment of the end of the world. And what is the end of the world? It is the end of your particular attitude toward the world. In the so-called fifth gospel, *The Gospel According to Thomas,* the disciples ask, "When will the kingdom come?"—when will this moment come that we're waiting for now? And Jesus says:

> The kingdom will not come by expectation. They will not say, "See here," or "See there." But the kingdom of the father is spread upon the earth and men do not see it.[62]

This text was dug up in 1945 in the Egyptian desert, but it suggests how Joyce is interpreting the symbology of the church: by translating it into the Gnostic mode, where the crisis is understood to be not literal and historical, but psychological: in your life.[63] When that happens, the normal differentiated world dissolves, and the unity of the world is experienced. Further, the experience of this unity is a function of art. Moreover, it is the function of [this chapter] to have Stephen experience this unity in relation to Bloom. Immediately after Florry's observation, he turns and sees Bloom. And just then the gramophone blares:

> Jerusalem!
> Open your gates and sing
> Hosanna...

> (*A rocket rushes up through the sky and bursts. A white star falls from it, proclaiming the consummation of all things and second coming of Elijah....*) (U413)

Here is the psychological crisis: Stephen has recognized himself in Bloom, and that's the end of his separateness in fact. He has already had a moment of compassion with Bloom in the maternity hospital where, you might say, this possibility was conceived. Now it actually takes place. Whereupon, among the various hallucinatory phenomena bewildering Stephen's drunken brain, The End of the World "with a Scotch accent" enters, dancing.[64] And Elijah comes, with an American accent, shouting a Billy-Sunday-like Hell-and-damnation tirade, of which the following is the climax:

ELIJAH

...Are you a god or a doggone clod? If the second advent came to Coney Island are we ready? Florry Christ, Stephen Christ, Zoe Christ, Bloom Christ, Kitty Christ, Lynch Christ, it's up to you to sense that cosmic force. Have we cold feet about the cosmos? No. Be on the side of the angels. Be a prism. You have that something within, the higher self. You can rub shoulders with a Jesus, a Gautama, an Ingersoll. Are you all in this vibration? I say you are.... (U414)

Joyce (I believe) says we all are in this vibration. The miracle of the Incarnation is the Magnificat of each one of us: Florry Christ, Stephen Christ, Zoe Christ, and so on—we are all particles of the Christ. Very frequently, you know, Joyce brings out key thoughts in a totally contrary kind of language and situation. So his essential message here—and this is the Gnostic message—is that the face of God is the face before you: your friend, a stranger, or whomever.

Now back to our story. Shortly after Elijah appears, the drunken Stephen sees arising from behind a coal scuttle the apparition of the Irish sea-god Mananaan MacLir, whose curling waves were the foam-maned steeds of his morning meditation on Sandymount shore. [Here we have a vision of great thematic importance.] The Greek counterpart of Mananaan MacLir is Poseidon, whose Latin counterpart is Neptune, Lord of the Abyssal Waters—not the salt waters, but the sweet life-informing waters. In India, the counterpart is Śiva, Lord of the Liṅgam, the fertilizing energy, the semen of the universe that comes pouring in. The consort of Śiva and of Neptune is the World Goddess, so here in the Abyssal Depths, they both link up and fuse with the image of the drowned man in the sea. This bearded spirit, looming in a cone of light, is seen sitting like a brooding bard, chin on knees:

> (*In the cone of the searchlight behind the coalscuttle, ollave, holyeyed, the bearded figure of Mananaun MacLir broods, chin on knees. He rises slowly. A cold seawind blows from his druid mouth. About his head writhe eels and elvers. He is encrusted with weeds and shells. His right hand holds a bicycle pump. His left hand grasps a huge crayfish by its two talons.*)

My friend Padraic Colum tells me that the Dublin poet AE—who was a contemporary and no favorite of Joyce—once appeared in just this way, as Mananaan, in a special production of his own play *Deirdre,* and that Joyce here is poking fun at him. But Joyce is also bringing to a climax a theme that he has been developing since early in the book: that of the consubstantial father, fathoms deep, and of seachange and transubstantiation. The bicycle pump in the god's right hand and the crayfish in his left are the tokens of his powers, conceived in caricature, yet mimicking correctly those Oriental gods who are depicted holding in their right hands tokens of their life-giving powers, and in their left, the life-taking.

As for the bicycle pump: The first principle of life is the breath: Greek *pneuma,* Sanskrit *prāṇa,* Latin *spiritus*—what God breathed into Adam to give him life—here, the bicycle pump. And the prime symbol of death in *Ulysses* is cancer, of which Stephen's mother died: here, the crab (cancer) in Mananaan's left hand. Cancer in the zodiac is the sign of the summer solstice, less than a week away, when the mounting sun—"which went forth to traverse not itself" will begin its return (*la, ti, do*) toward winter, humbling its course to death. Cancer, furthermore, is the astrological symbol assigned to the breast, that is, of Motherhood. Indeed, Joyce here is poking fun; but his mode throughout *Ulysses* is of irony; as Northrop Frye states of irony in his *Anatomy of Criticism,* its technique is that "of appearing to be less than one is."

So we have life in this sea-god's right hand, and in his left hand, death. We have seen Hindu images of Kālī, a goddess kilted with arms and legs, whose one hand bestows boons or holds a bowl of milk rice, signifying "Do not be afraid," while another hand holds a sword with which she cuts off heads; this goddess is wearing a necklace of seventy-two skulls and has her tongue out to lap up the blood of those to whom she has given birth. This is what life is. Life gives birth to us and eats us back. Joyce has already spoken of Ireland as a little old crone and as a sow that eats her farrow. And what does this weed- and shell-encrusted apparition of Mananaan say when he arises?

MANANAUN MACLIR

(*with a voice of waves*) Aum! Hek! Wal! Ak! Lub! Mor! Ma! White yoghin of the gods. Occult pimander of Hermes Trismegistos....

The intoned monosyllables suggest the mystic utterances of Indian Tantric mantras. *White yoghin of the gods* is, of course, a reference to Śiva, the Indian model of the ascetic life, who, however, was broken from his solitary meditations by the magic of the goddess Śakti, who became his spouse.[65] He thus affords a perfect mythological prototype of the prospect now before Stephen.

Now, *pimander:* This is the name of one of the most influential texts of the late Hellenistic *Corpus hermeticum,* all of which are credited traditionally to a legendary Hermes Trismegistus. The *Pimander,* translated for

Cosimo de' Medici in 1463 by Marsilio Ficino, became a veritable Bible for the poets and painters of the Renaissance. Indeed, as remarked by Frances Yates in her volume *Giordano Bruno and the Hermetic Tradition,* some even supposed that Hermes Trismegistus had been the occult teacher of Moses; in the Vatican itself, in the Borgia Apartments, there is a mural by the master Pinturicchio that shows Isis, seated on a Renaissance throne, instructing Hermes Trismegistus at her right hand and Moses at her left—which surely suggests (apparently with papal approval) that the wisdom shared by the pagan and the Hebrew sages was originally revealed neither by Yahweh nor by Jove, but by the consort of the dead-and-resurrected Egyptian Savior Osiris. And along with this there must also have gone the interesting implication (likewise with papal approval) that the shared symbols might be safely interpreted either in their mystical hermetic or in the authorized Christian senses—the ultimate wisdom being, I suppose, that, since the final secret of divinity transcends and resolves all contradictions, *either* reading will serve as a guide so long as it is not taken as final.

The burlesque sea-god's speech continues:

> (*with a voice of whistling seawind*) Punarjanam patsypunjaub! I won't have my leg pulled. It has been said by one: beware the left, the cult of Shakti. (*with a cry of stormbirds*) Shakti Shiva, darkhidden Father!...

*Punarjanam patsypunjaub!* is a caricature of the Sanskrit terms *punar* ("again") and *janam* ("birth"), refering to reincarnation; *pat* ("to fall") plus *pancha* ("five") becomes "to fall into five," which is a way of describing death: one returns to the five elements of which one is composed—earth, air, fire, water, and ether. So, out of death comes rebirth.

*Beware the left, the cult of Shakti:* Śakti is the female power incarnate in goddesses and in all females; and in the legend of Śiva's marriage, this energy was strong enough to break the god's meditation. *Beware the left:* that is, the "left hand path," the way of initiation through sexual rites, where the woman becomes the guru, the initiator of the male.

*Shakti Shiva, darkhidden Father!:* Śiva, joined to his Śakti, is the lord of that left-hand path. Śiva is the lord of eternal life, and as he lies prostrate, the goddess with her hands representing the life and the death principle is standing on him. She is, as it were, an emanation of his dream: the woman is the emanation of the man's image of his universe. His fulfillment consists in comprehending her and enlivening her. The female is the other half, you might say, of the deity. This is the mysticism of the dyad, male-female as one. In Stephen's case, the part of Śiva is to be played by Bloom, whose consort, Molly, is the Śakti of the book. Moreover, Bloom in his Tiresian fantasy was Śakti-Śiva, male and female combined.[66]

Further: Śiva is the god worshiped throughout India in the form of a stylized male organ (the *lingam*), which is generally represented as though emerging from beneath the earth to penetrate a stylized female organ (the *yoni*) symbolic of the cosmic mother-goddess within whose womb (space-time: the Kantian "*a priori* forms of sensibility") all creatures dwell. Also, like the classical Neptune-Poseidon, Śiva carries as symbol a trident, for he is actually, historically, an Oriental transformation of the same widely known divinity. I count it greatly to Joyce's credit that he not only recognized these relationships and equated as one power the Celtic Mananaan, Indian Śiva, and Mediterranean Neptune-Poseidon, but also employed the Indian vocabulary to suggest their relevance to his contransmagnificandjewbangtantiality theme.

I note, by the way, that this key word, which we have discussed already at some length, has exactly thirty-six letters; but 3 + 6 = 9; and 9, according to the Kabbala, is the number assigned to the mystic phallus of God (*Yesod,* the Foundation) by which the masculine aspect of the Lord who created Adam and Eve "in his own image... male and female" (Genesis 1:27) is joined to his feminine aspect, his creation (*Malkuth,* the Kingdom).[67]

Returning to Stephen's sea-god, we next read:

> (*He smites with his bicycle pump the crayfish in his left hand. On its cooperative dial glow the twelve signs of the zodiac. He wails with the vehemence of the ocean.*) Aum! Baum! Pyjaum! I am the light of the homestead. I am the dreamery creamery butter. (U416)

*He smites with his bicycle pump the crayfish in his left hand:* that is to say, he brings together these pairs of opposites. The bicycle pump, the vessel of wind, smites the crayfish, creature of the waters, and the lights appear of the world-bounding zodiac; for, as we learn from the Book of Genesis: "the spirit of God moved upon the face of the waters; and God said, 'Let there be Light': and there was light." Whereupon the waters, roused to turbulence by this Wind of God, rolling, breaking ineluctably, must have resounded with some such

sound as *Aum!,* the Indian sacred syllable said to be that of the immanent creative energy of the universe; and *Baum!,* which in German means "tree"—for
example, Yggdrasil, the World Ash—is then symbolic of the universe itself.

*Pyjaum,* obviously, is pyjama (from the Persian *pa,* "leg," plus *jamah,*
"garment"), and is here a burlesque reference to the phallic theme of the
lingam in the yoni, jewel in the lotus, spirit in the flesh, or (in Hebrew)
God's presence in Israel, the *Shekinah.*

*I am the light of the homestead:* He is the fire of life that burns on every
hearth, released equally from the coal of the coal scuttle and from the flesh
of the body's temperature. *I am the dreamery creamery butter:* In India, what
is consecrated (transubstantiated) and sacrificed on the altar is not bread or
wine, as in the Catholic Mass, but butter: they dip a bit of cotton in butter, put it on a little lamp to light it, and that is the sacrifice, the crucifixion,
the offering. And the miracle there is interpreted, not as a miraculous
*change* of substance—divinity *entering into* the sacrament—but as a "showing forth," *epiphany,* or special "manifestation" from within, of that universally present *brahman, ātman, brahman-ātman,* which is the ground and
hidden nature of all things. Remember: "Any object, intensely regarded,
may be a gate of access to the incorruptible eon of the gods." (U340)

Now there is a great scene. Zoe has taken Bloom's potato [his *moly*], so
he is not protected and is now going to be turned into a pig. The door
opens, and in comes Bella Cohen, the "mother superior" of this institution.

> (*The door opens. Bella Cohen, a massive whoremistress, enters. She is
> dressed in a threequarter ivory gown, fringed round the hem with tas-
> selled selvedge, and cools herself flirting a black horn fan like Minnie
> Hauck in* Carmen. *On her left hand are wedding and keeper rings.
> Her eyes are deeply carboned. She has a sprouting moustache. Her olive
> face is heavy, slightly sweated and fullnosed with orangetainted nos-
> trils. She has large pendant beryl eardrops.*)

BELLA

My word! I'm all of a mucksweat.

> (*She glances round her at the couples. Then her eyes rest on Bloom with
> hard insistence. Her large fan winnows wind towards her heated face-
> neck and embonpoint. Her falcon eyes glitter.*)

THE FAN

(*flirting quickly, then slowly*) Married, I see.


BLOOM

Yes. Partly, I have mislaid....


THE FAN

(*half opening, then closing*) And the missus is master. Petticoat government.


BLOOM

(*looks down with a sheepish grin*) That is so.


THE FAN

(*folding together, rests against her left eardrop*) Have you forgotten me?


BLOOM

Nes. Yo.


THE FAN

(*folded akimbo against her waist*) Is me her was you dreamed before? Was then she him you us since knew? Am all them and the same now me?

  (*Bella approaches, gently tapping with the fan.*)


BLOOM

(*wincing*) Powerful being. In my eyes read that slumber which women love.


THE FAN

(*tapping*) We have met. You are mine. It is fate.


BLOOM

(*cowed*) Exuberant female. Enormously I desiderate your domination. I am exhausted, abandoned, no more young. I stand, so to speak, with an unposted letter bearing the extra regulation fee before the too late box of the general postoffice of human life. The door and window open at a right angle cause a draught of thirtytwo feet per second according to the law of falling bodies. I have felt this instant a twinge of sciatica in my left gluteal muscle. It runs in our family. Poor dear papa, a widower, was a regular barometer from it. He believed in animal heat. A skin of tabby lined his winter waistcoat. Near the end, remembering king David and the Sunamite, he shared his bed with Athos, faithful after death. A dog's spittle as you probably.... (*he winces*) Ah!

In his imagination, another apparition passes. Now Bella moves closer to him.

#### THE FAN

(*tapping*) All things end. Be mine. Now.

#### BLOOM

(*undecided*) All now? I should not have parted with my talisman. Rain, exposure at dewfall on the searocks, a peccadillo at my time of life. Every phenomenon has a natural cause.

#### THE FAN

(*points downwards slowly*) You may.

#### BLOOM

(*looks downwards and perceives her unfastened bootlace*) We are observed.

#### THE FAN

(*points downwards quickly*) You must.

#### BLOOM

(*with desire, with reluctance*) I can make a true black knot. Learned when I served my time and worked the mail order line for Kellett's. Experienced hand. Every knot says a lot. Let me. In courtesy. I knelt once before today. Ah!

(*Bella raises her gown slightly and, steadying her pose, lifts to the edge of a chair a plump buskined hoof and a full pastern, silksocked. Bloom, stifflegged, aging, bends over her hoof and with gentle fingers draws out and in her laces*)

### BLOOM

(*murmurs lovingly*) To be a shoefitter in Manfield's was my love's young dream, the darling joys of sweet buttonhooking, to lace up crisscrossed to kneelength the dressy kid footwear satinlined, so incredibly impossibly small, of Clyde Road ladies. Even their wax model Raymonde I visited daily to admire her cobweb hose and stick of rhubarb toe, as worn in Paris.

### THE HOOF

Smell my hot goathide. Feel my royal weight.

### BLOOM

(*crosslacing*) Too tight?

### THE HOOF

If you bungle, Handy Andy, I'll kick your football for you.

### BLOOM

Not to lace the wrong eyelet as I did the night of the bazaar dance. Bad luck. Hook in wrong tache of her.... person you mentioned. That night she met.... Now!

(*He knots the lace. Bella places her foot on the floor. Bloom raises his head. Her heavy face, her eyes strike him in midbrow. His eyes grow dull, darker and pouched, his nose thickens.*)

### BLOOM

(*mumbles*) Awaiting your further orders we remain, gentlemen,....

### BELLO

(*with a hard basilisk stare, in a baritone voice*) Hound of dishonour!

BLOOM

(*infatuated*) Empress!

BELLO

(*his heavy cheekchops sagging*) Adorer of the adulterous rump!

BLOOM

(*plaintively*) Hugeness!

BELLO

Dungdevourer!

BLOOM

(*with sinews semiflexed*) Magmagnificence!

BELLO

Down! (*he taps her on the shoulder with his fan*) Incline feet forward! Slide left foot one pace back! You will fall. You are falling. On the hands down!

BLOOM

(*her eyes upturned in the sign of admiration, closing, yaps*) Truffles!

(*With a piercing epileptic cry she sinks on all fours, grunting, snuffling, rooting at his feet:...*) (U429–433)

So, Bloom imagines himself turning into a little female pig that scurries under the sofa, and peeks out through the fringe. During his utter degradation, which follows, the nymph [in the picture] over his bed appears and teases Bloom for having lusted after her. Then:

THE NYMPH

(*her features hardening, gropes in the folds of her habit*) Sacrilege! To attempt my virtue! (*a large moist stain appears on her robe*) Sully my innocence! You are not fit to touch the garment of a pure woman. (*she clutches again in her robe*) Wait. Satan, you'll sing no more lovesongs. Amen. Amen. Amen. (*she draws a poniard and, clad in the sheathmail of an elected knight of nine, strikes at his loins*) Nekum!

### BLOOM

(*starts up, seizes her hand*) Hoy! Nebrakada! Cat o' nine lives! Fair play, madam. No pruningknife. The fox and the grapes, is it? What do you lack with your barbed wire? Crucifix not thick enough? (*he clutches her veil*) A holy abbot you want or Brophy, the lame gardener, or the spoutless statue of the watercarrier, or good mother Alphonsus, eh Reynard?

### THE NYMPH

(*with a cry flees from him unveiled, her plaster cast crackling, a cloud of stench escaping from the cracks*) Poli...! (U451)

When the nymph cracks, her hold on Bloom's imagination vanishes. He is released, cleared [of Circe's spell], his submissive masochism is gone, and Bello becomes Bella again. What has happened here is that Bloom has undergone a psychological crisis. This whole crisis has taken place in Bloom's mind during the few seconds of time that he has been looking at Bella. These things can happen very, very secretly, and Joyce has rendered all of the imagery that underlies the crisis in Bloom's imagination. To do so, Joyce has used two time systems: one for the outer world, and the other for this inner world. Now it is a question, of course, as to whether or not this is a legitimate thing for a writer to do. But how else can you do it? Inner psychological time—where a minute, actually, can hold eons of sense—is very different from clock time outside.

Now Bella asks the men to pay, to put their money down.[68] [Bloom intervenes to prevent her from cheating the drunken Stephen, and she is not pleased. Bloom also offers to keep Stephen's money until he is less drunk; but Stephen says that money "doesn't matter a rambling damn."] Then Zoe takes Stephen's hand.

### ZOE

(*examining Stephen's palm*) Woman's hand.

STEPHEN

(*murmurs*) Continue. Lie. Hold me. Caress. I never could read His handwriting except His criminal thumbprint on the haddock....

Originally, on the beach, Stephen believed that he was intended to interpret "signatures of all things I am here to read...." (U31) But here in the brothel he seems to have despaired of ever being able to read those signatures. Zoe now examines his hand, which is to say, she "reads his signature."

ZOE

What day were you born?

STEPHEN

Thursday. Today.

ZOE

Thursday's child has far to go. (*she traces lines on his hand*) Line of fate. Influential friends.

FLORRY

(*pointing*) Imagination.

ZOE

Mount of the moon. You'll meet with a.... (*she peers at his hands abruptly*) I won't tell you what's not good for you. Or do you want to know?

BLOOM

(*detaches her fingers and offers his palm*) More harm than good. Here. Read mine.

The whores begin to read Bloom's palm.

BELLA

Show. (*she turns up Bloom's hand*) I thought so. Knobby knuckles for the women.

ZOE

(*peering at Bloom's palm*) Gridiron. Travels beyond the sea and marry money.

BLOOM

Wrong.

ZOE

(*quickly*) O, I see. Short little finger. Henpecked husband. That wrong?

(*Black Liz, a huge rooster hatching in a chalked circle, rises, stretches her wings and clucks.*)

BLACK LIZ

Gara. Klook. Klook. Klook. (*she sidles from her newlaid egg and waddles off*)

BLOOM

(*points to his hand*) That weal there is an accident. Fell and cut it twentytwo years ago. I was sixteen.

ZOE

I see, says the blind man. Tell us news.

As the whores start in on Bloom, suggesting that he is a cuckold whose wife runs the show, the poor man, suspecting an exposure, can only squirm and smile; the signatures of his life are not ineluctable to these night-world nymphs. But Stephen, now moved by a reciprocal sentiment of compassion toward Bloom, interrupts.

STEPHEN

See? Moves to one great goal. I am twentytwo. Sixteen years ago he was twentytwo too. Sixteen years ago I twentytwo tumbled. Twentytwo years ago he sixteen fell off his hobbyhorse. (*he winces*) Hurt my hand somewhere. Must see a dentist. Money? (U458–459)

Stephen, recognizing some kind of energy with Bloom, notes superstitiously a mystic correspondence between the numbers 22 and 16 that is bringing the two of them together; namely, that he himself, now twenty-two, had an accident sixteen years ago. Also, Stephen [on his way to the mystical estate of fatherhood,] is moving into Bloom's shoes and is going to get married, as Bloom is married: "I and the Father are One."

Bloom at this point sees in his mind a very bad image of Boylan with Molly in the apartment in their house. It is pretty ugly what he imagines going on there, and while he's having these thoughts, Lynch cruelly joins in the fun, laughing coarsely at an illusion he has spied in the coatrack mirror: the image of Bloom's head with antlers behind it—Bloom wearing the cuckold's horns.

LYNCH

(*points*) The mirror up to nature. (*he laughs*) Hu hu hu hu hu!

(*Stephen and Bloom gaze in the mirror. The face of William Shakespeare, beardless, appears there, rigid in facial paralysis, crowned by the reflection of the reindeer antlered hatrack in the hall.*)

SHAKESPEARE

(*in dignified ventriloquy*) 'Tis the loud laugh that bespeaks the vacant mind. (*to Bloom*) Thou thoughtest as how thou wastest invisible. Gaze. (*he crows with a black capon's laugh*) Iagogo! How my Oldfellow chokit his Thursdaymomum.[69] Iagogogo! . . . .

Stephen is making an analogy in his mind: himself and Bloom, Burbage and Shakespeare, the son and the father. While all this is going on, Bloom is terribly uncomfortable.

BLOOM

(*smiles yellowly at the three whores*) When will I hear the joke?

ZOE

Before you're twice married and once a widower.

BLOOM

Lapses are condoned. Even the great Napoleon when measurements were taken next the skin after his death. . . . (U463)

It is at this point that we are beginning to pick up important themes. The sore point and the joke is simply this: that [Molly has been with Blazes Boylan today,] and Bloom, all day, has been trying to keep this central fact of his life out of mind—like a Ulysses wandering the world-sea, while at home Penelope gives roof to her suitors, the usurpers in his house. In addition, you will recall that Stephen has earlier this day developed in the library his theory about Shakespeare having been cuckolded by Ann Hathaway, and corollary to that, his argument that Prince Hamlet was Shakespeare's own dead son Hamnet. Moreover, since Stephen sees himself as Hamlet, son of King Hamlet (the ghost part played by Shakespeare himself), he sees Bloom as Shakespeare, as the father. So the appearance of Shakespeare's antlered face in the whorehouse mirror as vulnerable, simple-hearted Leopold Bloom's counterpart, marks for Stephen, the cold hard aesthete who has been himself posing as a counterpart of Hamlet, a considerable spiritual crisis of human identification and compassion—at last! He feels sympathy for Bloom.

STEPHEN

*Et exaltabuntur cornua iusti.*[70] Queens lay with prize bulls. Remember Pasiphae for whose lust my grandoldgrossfather made the first confessionbox. Forget not Madam Grissel Steevens nor the suine scions of the house of Lambert. And Noah was drunk with wine. And his ark was open.

BELLA

None of that here. Come to the wrong shop.

The whore thinks that Stephen is going too far.

LYNCH

Let him alone. He's back from Paris.

ZOE

(*runs to Stephen and links him*) O go on! Give us some parleyvoo. (U464)

A very wild scene now develops. Stephen, recognizing Bloom's torture, leaps impulsively to his feet and breaks into an ecstatic kind of speech-making and a drunken dance in celebration of the intimate indecencies of all life, but especially of the married life into which he, too—consubstantial with Bloom, as the Father—is about to fall. In the midst, however, of his "dance of death" (U472), his crazy jig into the hilarity of which the others have gaily entered, he is brought up short by an appalling, horrible vision of his dead mother.

THE MOTHER

(*with the subtle smile of death's madness*) I was once the beautiful May Goulding. I am dead.

STEPHEN

(*horrorstruck*) Lemur, who are you? No. What bogeyman's trick is this?

BUCK MULLIGAN

(*shakes his curling capbell*) The mockery of it! Kinch dogsbody killed her bitchbody. She kicked the bucket. (*tears of molten butter fall from his eyes on to the scone*) Our great sweet mother! *Epi oinopa ponton.*

THE MOTHER

(*comes nearer, breathing upon him softly her breath of wetted ashes*) All must go through it, Stephen. More women than men in the world. You too. Time will come.

STEPHEN

(*choking with fright, remorse and horror*) They say I killed you, mother. He offended your memory. Cancer did it, not I. Destiny....

Why does Stephen feel remorse and fear and guilt? Because when his mother was dying, she asked him to kneel down and pray,[71] and he wouldn't do it. Stephen with his fierce rigor of mind would not break to that extent, so she died believing that her son was a lost soul. And now she comes to tell him of mother's love and to entreat him to repent.

THE MOTHER

(*a green rill of bile trickling from a side of her mouth*) You sang that song to me. Love's bitter mystery.

STEPHEN

(*eagerly*) Tell me the word, mother, if you know now. The word known to all men.

THE MOTHER

Who saved you the night you jumped into the train at Dalkey with Paddy Lee? Who had pity for you when you were sad among the strangers? Prayer is allpowerful. Prayer for the suffering souls in the Ursuline manual and forty days' indulgence. Repent, Stephen.

STEPHEN

The ghoul! Hyena!

THE MOTHER

I pray for you in my other world. Get Dilly to make you that boiled rice every night after your brainwork. Years and years I loved you, O, my son, my firstborn, when you lay in my womb.

ZOE

(*fanning herself with the gratefan*) I'm melting.

FLORRY

(*points to Stephen*) Look! He's white.

BLOOM

(*goes to the window to open it more*) Giddy.

THE MOTHER

(*with smouldering eyes*) Repent! O, the fire of hell.

STEPHEN

(*panting*) His noncorrosive sublimate! The corpsechewer! Raw head and bloody bones.

THE MOTHER

(*her face drawing near and nearer, sending out an ashen breath*) Beware! (*she raises her blackened withered right arm slowly towards Stephen's breast with outstretched finger*) Beware God's hand!

(*A green crab with malignant red eyes sticks deep its grinning claws in Stephen's heart.*)

STEPHEN

(*strangled with rage, his features drawn grey and old*) Shite!

BLOOM

(*at the window*) What?

STEPHEN

*Ah non, par exemple!* The intellectual imagination! With me all or not at all. *Non serviam!*

FLORRY

Give him some cold water. Wait. (*she rushes out*)

THE MOTHER

(*wrings her hands slowly, moaning desperately*) O Sacred Heart of Jesus, have mercy on him! Save him from hell, O Divine Sacred Heart!

STEPHEN

No! No! No! Break my spirit, all of you, if you can! I'll bring you all to heel!

THE MOTHER

(*in the agony of her deathrattle*) Have mercy on Stephen, Lord, for my sake! Inexpressible was my anguish when expiring with love, grief and agony on Mount Calvary.

STEPHEN

*Nothung!*

That's the name of Siegfried's sword.

(*He lifts his ashplant high with both hands and smashes the chandelier. Time's livid final flame leaps and, in the following darkness, ruin of all space, shattered glass and toppling masonry.*)

THE GASJET

Pwfungg!

BLOOM

Stop!

LYNCH

(*rushes forward and seizes Stephen's hand*) Here! Hold on! Don't run amok!

BELLA

Police!

(*Stephen, abandoning his ashplant, his head and arms thrown back stark, beats the ground and flies from the room, past the whores at the door.*)

BELLA

(*screams*) After him!

(*The two whores rush to the halldoor. Lynch and Kitty and Zoe stampede from the room. They talk excitedly. Bloom follows, returns.*)

THE WHORES

(*jammed in the doorway, pointing*) Down there.

ZOE

(*pointing*) There. There's something up.

### BELLA

Who pays for the lamp? (*she seizes Bloom's coattail*) Here, you were with him. The lamp's broken.

### BLOOM

(*rushes to the hall, rushes back*) What lamp, woman?

### A WHORE

He tore his coat.

### BELLA

(*her eyes hard with anger and cupidity, points*) Who's to pay for that? Ten shillings. You're a witness.

### BLOOM

(*snatches up Stephen's ashplant*) Me? Ten shillings? Haven't you lifted enough off him? Didn't he....?

### BELLA

(*loudly*) Here, none of your tall talk. This isn't a brothel. A ten-shilling house.

### BLOOM

(*His head under the lamp, pulls the chain. Puling, the gasjet lights up a crushed mauve purple shade. He raises the ashplant.*) Only the chimney's broken. Here is all he....

### BELLA

(*shrinks back and screams*) Jesus! Don't!

### BLOOM

(*warding off a blow*) To show you how he hit the paper. There's not sixpenceworth of damage done. Ten shillings!

FLORRY

(*with a glass of water, enters*) Where is he?

BELLA

Do you want me to call the police?

BLOOM

O, I know. Bulldog on the premises. But he's a Trinity student. Patrons of your establishment. Gentlemen who pay the rent. (*he makes a masonic sign*) Know what I mean? Nephew of the vicechancellor. You don't want a scandal.

BELLA

(*angrily*) Trinity. Coming down here ragging after the boatraces and paying nothing. Are you my commander here or? Where is he? I'll charge him! Disgrace him, I will! (*she shouts*) Zoe! Zoe!

BLOOM

(*urgently*) And if it were your own son in Oxford? (*warningly*) I know.

BELLA

(*almost speechless*) Who are. Incog!

ZOE

(*in the doorway*) There's a row on.

BLOOM

What? Where? (*he throws a shilling on the table and starts*) That's for the chimney. Where? I need mountain air. (U473–478)

And out he goes. Meanwhile, in the street, Stephen has come into collision with the two soldiers. They have one whore between them, and she tells them that Stephen has insulted her. It's not clear what he did—he may have bumped into her, or something like that—but in any case, by the time Bloom arrives, a crowd has gathered, and there's a confrontation in process.

### BLOOM

(*elbowing through the crowd, plucks Stephen's sleeve vigorously*) Come now, professor, that carman is waiting.

### STEPHEN

(*turns*) Eh? (*he disengages himself*) Why should I not speak to him or to any human being who walks upright upon this oblate orange? (*he points his finger*) I'm not afraid of what I can talk to if I see his eye. Retaining the perpendicular. (*he staggers a pace back*)

### BLOOM

(*propping him*) Retain your own.

### STEPHEN

(*laughs emptily*) My centre of gravity is displaced. I have forgotten the trick. Let us sit down somewhere and discuss. Struggle for life is the law of existence but human philirenists, notably the tsar and the king of England, have invented arbitration. (*he taps his brow*) But in here it is I must kill the priest and the king. . . .

### PRIVATE CARR

(*to Stephen*) Say it again.

### STEPHEN

(*nervous, friendly, pulls himself up*) I understand your point of view though I have no king myself for the moment. This is the age of patent medicines. A discussion is difficult down here. But this is the point. You die for your country. Suppose. (*he places his arm on Private Carr's sleeve*) Not that I wish it for you. But I say: Let my country die for me. Up to the present it has done so. I didn't want it to die. Damn death. Long live life! (U481–482)

While Stephen continues his drunken confrontation, we have the vision of the climax of a Black Mass being celebrated. We started this book with the words "*Introibo ad altare Dei*" ("I go unto the altar of God"), the opening words of the Mass. And now here at the climax, where the consecrated host is broken and eaten, they are echoed diabolically.

FATHER MALACHI O'FLYNN

*Introibo ad altare diaboli.*

THE REVEREND MR HAINES LOVE

To the devil which hath made glad my young days.

FATHER MALACHI O'FLYNN

(*takes from the chalice and elevates a blooddripping host*) *Corpus meum.*

THE REVEREND MR HAINES LOVE

(*raises high behind the celebrant's petticoat, revealing his grey bare hairy buttocks between which a carrot is stuck*) My body.

THE VOICE OF ALL THE DAMNED

Htengier tnetopinmo Dog Drol eht rof, Aiulella!

(*From on high the voice of Adonai calls.*)

ADONAI

Dooooooooooog!

THE VOICE OF ALL THE BLESSED

Alleluia, for the Lord God Omnipotent reigneth!

ADONAI

Goooooooooooood! (U489–490)

The Mass is supposed to be literally the enactment of the crucifixion on Mount Calvary. There, Christ on the cross, almost dead, was pierced by the lance of Longinus. Here, the soldier, the lance of Longinus, pierces Stephen. As Stephen is putting all these things together, what he is doing is dying to himself. He's being wiped out. Private Carr...

> (*... rushes towards Stephen, fist outstretched, and strikes him in the face. Stephen totters, collapses, falls, stunned. He lies prone, his face to the sky, his hat rolling to the wall. Bloom follows and picks it up.*) (U491)

Stephen is so weak and drunk, down he goes. Then there's a row on the street, the police arrive, and Bloom rescues Stephen [who is about to get into real trouble: the police, fearing that a riot might be starting, are about to arrest Stephen; but Bloom intervenes, telling them that he knows Stephen and that it's just some students making a fuss. Corny Kelleher, a police spy, appears, and Bloom gets him to jolly the police away from Stephen.] And now there is a lovely tender moment. Stephen is lying in the street, murmuring some lines from Yeats's poem about Fergus. Bloom, alone at last with his fallen charge, is standing over him. This is the end.

### STEPHEN

(*murmurs*)

> .... shadows ... the woods
> ... white breast ... dim sea,

(*He stretches out his arms, sighs again and curls his body. Bloom, holding the hat and ashplant, stands erect. A dog barks in the distance. Bloom tightens and loosens his grip on the ashplant. He looks down on Stephen's face and form.*)

### BLOOM

(*communes with the night*) Face reminds me of his poor mother. In the shady wood. The deep white breast. Ferguson, I think I caught. A girl. Some girl. Best thing could happen him. (*he murmurs*).... swear that I will always hail, ever conceal, never reveal, any part or parts, art or arts.... (*he murmurs*).... in the rough sands of the sea ... a cabletow's length from the shore.... where the tide ebbs.... and flows....

(*Silent, thoughtful, alert he stands on guard, his fingers at his lips in the attitude of secret master. Against the dark wall a figure appears slowly, a fairy boy of eleven, a changeling, kidnapped, dressed in an Eton suit with glass shoes and a little bronze helmet, holding a book in his hand. He reads from right to left inaudibly, smiling, kissing the page.*)

### BLOOM

(*wonderstruck, calls inaudibly*) Rudy!

### RUDY

*(gazes, unseeing, into Bloom's eyes and goes on reading, kissing, smiling. He has a delicate mauve face. On his suit he has diamond and ruby buttons. In his free left hand he holds a slim ivory cane with a violet bowknot. A white lambkin peeps out of his waistcoat pocket.)* (U497)

Bloom, protecting Stephen, sees before him his own little dead son Rudy, who, had he lived, would have been eleven now, exactly half Stephen's age. And that ends the great odyssey of the twelve middle chapters of *Ulysses*. There is a relevant thought expressed by Schopenhauer in one of the most wonderful of his many wonderful writings, "On an Apparent Intention in the Fate of the Individual."[72] He observes that, whereas while living of our lives we may regard the occurrences of many events as largely accidental, when we approach the end of our days and look back, our whole lifetime shows an order, as though composed like a novel by an author with a hidden plan. All that formerly seemed to be the product of mere chance is recognized in the panorama of years as having been required for the orderly unfolding of a structured plot. All those miscellaneous parcels come together surprisingly. Schopenhauer compares this not unusual experience to the effect of the once popular toy known as an anamorphoscope; whereby a picture, broken up and scattered on a page in such a way as not to be identifiable, is brought together by a conical mirror to compose a recognizable image.

That is the way this novel is composed. Throughout its pages appear the scattered figures of apparently tawdry, fragmentary lives, to which the magical composing mirror is the title of the novel itself: *Ulysses*. This applied, the apparently trivial, accidental incidents of this undistinguished day of Bloom, Stephen, Molly, and the rest are seen as reflexes of the archetypes of classic myth: epic destinies of heroic quest, metamorphosis, and fulfillment.

## THE TELEMACHUS, ODYSSEUS, AND PENELOPE CHAPTERS

### *Eumaeus*

[The next two chapters show Bloom and Stephen discussing many matters, and finally parting. Then, in the final chapter, we hear from Molly, the Eternal Feminine, who ends the book as the sun is rising.]

Joyce's style in the "Eumaeus" chapter reflects the condition of Stephen and Bloom at this time of night. How Joyce can do this, I don't know: it's the kind of sloppy, imprecise language you get from prep school boys writing essays. Here's the opening passages to give you an idea of the style:

> Preparatory to anything else Mr Bloom brushed off the greater bulk of the shavings and handed Stephen the hat and ashplant and bucked him up generally in orthodox Samaritan fashion which he very badly needed. His (Stephen's) mind was not exactly what you would call wandering but a bit unsteady and on his expressed desire for some beverage to drink Mr Bloom in view of the hour it was and there being no pump of Vartry water available for their ablutions let alone drinking purposes hit upon an expedient by suggesting, off the reel, the propriety of the cabman's shelter, as it was called, hardly a stones-throw away near Butt bridge where they might hit upon some drinkables in the shape of a milk and soda or a mineral. (U501)

Bloom suggests they go to the cabman's shelter, an all-night stand where the cabmen refresh themselves, and what follows is a strange and wonderful scene.

There are all these fall-out fellows, a lot of old men, driftwood people, the jetsam thrown up by the sea at the dead hours of the night—it's just the shag ends of the night, the shag ends of the world. An old sailor tells a long tale, and Stephen and Bloom talk. It's a simple, mutually considerate, undistinguished conversation.

> Over his untastable apology for a cup of coffee, listening to this synopsis of things in general, Stephen stared at nothing in particular. He could hear, of course, all kinds of words changing colour like those crabs about Ringsend in the morning burrowing quickly into all colours of different sorts of the same sand where they had a home somewhere beneath or seemed to. Then he looked up and saw the eyes that said or didn't say the words the voice he heard said, if you work.
> —Count me out, he managed to remark, meaning work.
> The eyes were surprised at this observation because as he, the person who owned them pro tem. [,] observed or rather his voice speaking did, all must work, have to, together.
> —I mean, of course, the other hastened to affirm, work in the widest possible sense. Also literary labour not merely for the kudos of

the thing. Writing for the newspapers which is the readiest channel nowadays. That's work too. Important work. After all, from the little I know of you, after all the money expended on your education you are entitled to recoup yourself and command your price. You have every bit as much right to live by your pen in pursuit of your philosophy as the peasant has. What? You both belong to Ireland, the brain and the brawn. Each is equally important.

—You suspect, Stephen retorted with a half laugh, that I may be important because I belong to the *faubourg Saint Patrice* called Ireland for short.

—I would go a step further, Mr Bloom insinuated.

—But I suspect, Stephen interrupted, that Ireland must be important because it belongs to me.

—What belongs, queried Mr Bloom bending, fancying he was perhaps under some misapprehension. Excuse me. Unfortunately, I didn't catch the latter portion. What was it you....?

Stephen, patently crosstempered, repeated and shoved aside his mug of coffee or whatever you like to call it none too politely, adding:

—We can't change the country. Let us change the subject. (526–527)

Here in this all-night shelter, for the first time in the book, Stephen is candid and open, not trying to be impressive, not trying to defend himself against somebody. He has felt sympathy for Bloom, Bloom has felt sympathy for him—there has been this consubstantiality, so to speak. Bloom shows Stephen a photograph.

—Do you consider, by the by, he said, thoughtfully selecting a faded photo which he laid on the table, that a Spanish type?

Stephen, obviously addressed, looked down on the photo showing a large sized lady with her fleshy charms on evidence in an open fashion as she was in the full bloom of womanhood in evening dress cut ostentatiously low for the occasion to give a liberal display of bosom, with more than a vision of breasts, her full lips parted and some perfect teeth, standing near, ostensibly with gravity, a piano on the rest of which was *In Old Madrid,* a ballad, pretty in its way, which was then all the vogue. Her (the lady's) eyes, dark, huge, looked at Stephen, about to smile about something to be admired, Lafayette of Westmoreland street, Dublin's premier photographic artist, being responsible for the esthetic execution.

—Mrs Bloom, my wife, the *prima donna* Madam Marion Tweedy, Bloom indicated. Taken a few years since. In or about ninety six. Very like her then. (U533)

As they sit there, Bloom is thinking about Stephen:

The vicinity of the young man he certainly relished, educated, *distingué* and impulsive into the bargain, far and away the pick of the bunch though you wouldn't think he had it in him yet you would....

It was a thousand pities a young fellow, blessed with an allowance of brains as his neighbor obviously was, should waste his valuable time with profligate women who might present him with a nice dose to last him his lifetime. In the nature of single blessedness he would one day take unto himself a wife when Miss Right came on the scene but in the interim ladies' society was a *conditio sine qua non* though he had the gravest possible doubts, not that he wanted in the smallest to pump Stephen . . . as to whether he would find much satisfaction basking in the boy and girl courtship idea and the company of smirking misses without a penny to their names bi or triweekly with the orthodox preliminary canter of complimentplaying and walking out leading up to fond lovers' ways and flowers and chocs. To think of him house and homeless, rooked by some landlady worse than any stepmother, was really too bad at his age. The queer suddenly things he popped out with attracted the elder man who was several years the other's senior or like his father but something substantial he certainly ought to eat even were it only an eggflip made on unadulterated maternal nutriment or, failing that, the homely Humpty Dumpty boiled.

—At what o'clock did you dine? he questioned of the slim form and tired though unwrinkled face.

—Some time yesterday, Stephen said.

—Yesterday! exclaimed Bloom till he remembered it was already tomorrow Friday. Ah, you mean it's after twelve!

—The day before yesterday, Stephen said, improving on himself.

Literally astounded at this piece of intelligence Bloom reflected. Though they didn't see eye to eye in everything a certain analogy there somehow was as if both their minds were travelling, so to speak, in the one train of thought....

Anyhow upon weighing the pros and cons, getting on for one, as it was, it was high time to be retiring for the night. The crux was it was a bit risky to bring him home as eventualities might possibly ensue (somebody having a temper of her own sometimes) and spoil the hash altogether as on the night he misguidedly brought home a dog (breed unknown) with a lame paw (not that the cases were either identical or the reverse though he had hurt his hand too) to Ontario Terrace as he very distinctly remembered, having been there, so to speak. On the other hand it was altogether far and away too late for the Sandymount or Sandycove suggestion so that he was in some perplexity as to which of the two alternatives....At all events he wound up by concluding, eschewing for the nonce hidebound precedent, a cup of Epp's cocoa and a shakedown for the night plus the use of a rug or two and overcoat doubled into a pillow at least he would be in safe hands and as warm as a toast on a trivet he failed to perceive any very vast amount of harm in that always with the proviso no rumpus of any sort was kicked up....

Finally, Bloom decides to invite Stephen to his house for a cup of cocoa.

—I propose, our hero eventually suggested after mature reflection while prudently pocketing her photo, as it's rather stuffy here you just come home with me and talk things over. My diggings are quite close in the vicinity. You can't drink that stuff. Do you like cocoa? Wait. I'll just pay this lot....

All kinds of Utopian plans were flashing through his (B's) busy brain, education (the genuine article), literature, journalism, prize titbits, up to date billing, concert tours in English watering resorts packed with hydros and seaside theatres, turning money away, duets in Italian with the accent perfectly true to nature and a quantity of other things, no necessity, of course, to tell the world and his wife from the housetops about it, and a slice of luck. An opening was all [that] was wanted. Because he more than suspected he had his father's voice to bank his hopes on which it was quite on the cards he had so it would be just as well, by the way no harm, to trail the conversation in the direction of that particular red herring just to. (U534–538)

So Bloom is making all these grand plans, thinking, "Stephen knows Italian, and Molly sings in Italian, and Stephen likes to sing, so perhaps Stephen could room with us and teach Molly Italian, and she could cultivate his singing." Then, with unsteady Stephen leaning on Bloom, they leave the cabman's shelter; and as they make their way to Bloom's house, Stephen begins to sing.

As for the promised cup of cocoa: When they arrive at Bloom's, the cocoa he will prepare for Stephen will be made from milk that had been for Molly; so in a sense, Bloom has now conquered Molly, and he and his son are now on their own.

### Ithaca

This wonderful chapter, written in the form of questions and answers in scientific language, shows the end of Bloom and Stephen. They are being (as it were) disintegrated, analyzed into the ground. It starts this way, with Bloom and Stephen walking to Bloom's house:

> What parallel courses did Bloom and Stephen follow returning?
>
> Starting united both at normal walking pace from Beresford place they followed in the order named Lower and Middle Gardiner streets and Mountjoy square, west: then, at reduced pace, each bearing left, Gardiner's place by an inadvertence as far as the farther corner of Temple street: then, at reduced pace with interruptions of halt, bearing right, Temple street, north, as far as Hardwicke place. Approaching disparate, at relaxed walking pace, they crossed both the circus before George's church diametrically, the chord in any circle being less than the arc which it subtends. (U544)

At last they arrive at Bloom's house.

> What act did Bloom make on their arrival at their destination?
>
> At the housesteps of the 4th of the equidifferent uneven numbers, number 7 Eccles street, he inserted his hand mechanically into the back pocket of his trousers to obtain his latchkey.
>
> Was it there?
>
> It was in the corresponding pocket of the trousers which he had worn on the day but one preceding.
>
> Why was he doubly irritated?
>
> Because he had forgotten and because he remembered that he had reminded himself twice not to forget.
>
> What were then the alternatives before the, premeditatedly (respectively) and inadvertently, keyless couple?
>
> To enter or not to enter. To knock or not to knock.
>
> Bloom's decision? (U546)

He has to go in by the cellar door. Bloom is the secret master: he knows this door is open. The door is open to the goddess of the world—namely, Molly—but only the one who knows how to enter can enter. So Bloom enters.

> A stratagem. Resting his feet on the dwarf wall, he climbed over the area railings, compressed his hat on his head, grasped two points at the lower union of rails and stiles, lowered his body gradually by its length of five feet nine inches and a half to within two feet two inches of the area pavement and allowed his body to move freely in space by separating himself from the railings and crouching in preparation for the impact of the fall. (U546)

This meticulous description of what they are doing and saying goes on and on, and as you can imagine, their conversation is not very interesting. Stephen has let his hair down. He's not defending himself; he's not being the bright smart-guy he was in the first part of the book; he's just a beaten-up young man. He and Bloom talk on about this, that, and the other thing—nothing adds up to very much. Then, after they've had a drink of cocoa, Bloom makes a suggestion.

> What proposal did Bloom, diambulist, father of Milly, somnambulist, make to Stephen, noctambulist?
> To pass in repose the hours intervening between Thursday (proper) and Friday (normal) on an extemporised cubicle in the apartment immediately above the kitchen and immediately adjacent to the sleeping apartment of the host and hostess.

It's late, so why doesn't Stephen stay with him for the night?

> What various advantages would or might have resulted from a prolongation of such an extemporisation?
> For the guest: security of domicile and seclusion of study. For the host: rejuvenation of intelligence, vicarious satisfaction. For the hostess: disintegration of obsession, acquisition of correct Italian pronunciation. (U570)

However, Stephen "inexplicably" refuses to stay, and both men go out into the yard to urinate—another echo of the dog theme that runs throughout the book.[73] Dog spelled backwards is God. Then Stephen departs into the night.

What sound accompanied the union of their tangent, the disunion of their (respectively) centrifugal and centripetal hands?

The sound of the peal of the hour of the night by the chime of the bells in the church of Saint George.

They hear churchbells.

What echoes of that sound were by both and each heard?

BY STEPHEN:

> *Liliata rutilantium. Turma circumdet.*
> *Iubilantium te virginum. Chorus excipiat.*

BY BLOOM:

> *Heigho, heigho,*
> *Heigho, heigho.*

Stephen vanishes into the night, and that is the end of Stephen Dedalus. As for Bloom:

Where were the several members of the company which with Bloom that day at the bidding of that peal had travelled from Sandymount in the south to Glasnevin in the north?

Martin Cunningham (in bed), Jack Power (in bed), Simon Dedalus (in bed), Ned Lambert (in bed), Tom Kernan (in bed), Joe Hynes (in bed), John Henry Menton (in bed), Bernard Corrigan (in bed), Paddy Dignam (in the grave).

Alone, what did Bloom hear?

The double reverberation of retreating feet on the heavenborn earth, the double vibration of a jew's harp in the resonant lane.

Alone, what did Bloom feel?

The cold of interstellar space, thousands of degrees below freezing point or the absolute zero of Fahrenheit, Centigrade, or Réaumur: the incipient intimations of proximate dawn.

The dead come into his mind.

Of what did bellchime and handtouch and footstep and lonechill remind him?

Of companions now in various manners in different places defunct: Percy Apjohn (killed in action, Modder River), Philip Gilligan (phthisis, Jervis Street hospital), Matthew F. Kane (accidental drowning, Dublin Bay), Philip Moisel (pyemia, Heytesbury street), Michael Hart (phthisis, Mater Misericordiae hospital), Patrick Dignam (apoplexy, Sandymount). (U578–579)

He then goes upstairs to Molly. As he enters the room...:

> What suddenly arrested his ingress?
>
> The right temporal lobe of the hollow sphere of his cranium came into contact with a solid timber angle where, an infinitesimal but sensible fraction of a second later, a painful sensation was located in consequence of antecedent sensations transmitted and registered. (U579)

He has bumped his head, because Molly has changed the whole room around. The female is energy, she is mover, she is change. We have noted that Ramakrishna says that Brahmā is *brahman* when he is quiet, and Māyā is *brahman* in movement. So Molly has changed all the scenery in the room, and when Bloom comes in, the chair that used to be here is there and the bureau is somewhere else, so he bumps into the furniture.[74]

Then Bloom undresses, and in detail he undresses: almost twenty pages have to do with his getting undressed and analyzing the contents of the bureau drawer and of the house and of everything else, so that by the end we know pretty much everything there is to know about Bloom. And then Bloom enters the bed:

> How?
>
> With circumspection, as invariably when entering an abode (his own or not his own): with solicitude, the snakespiral springs of the mattress being old, the brass quoits and pendent viper radii loose and tremulous under stress and strain: prudently, as entering a lair or ambush of lust or adders: lightly, the less to disturb: reverently, the bed of conception and of birth, of consummation of marriage and of breach of marriage, of sleep and of death.
>
> What did his limbs, when gradually extended, encounter?
>
> New clean bedlinen, additional odours, the presence of a human form, female, hers, the imprint of a human form, male, not his, some crumbs, some flakes of potted meat, recooked, which he removed.
>
> If he had smiled why would he have smiled?
>
> To reflect that each one who enters imagines himself to be the first to enter whereas he is always the last term of a preceding series even if the first term of a succeeding one, each imagining himself to be first, last, only and alone whereas he is neither first nor last nor only nor alone in a series originating in and repeated to infinity.

What preceding series?

Assuming Mulvey to be the first term of his series, Penrose, Bartell D'Arcy, professor Goodwin, Julius Mastiansky, John Henry Menton, Father Bernard Corrigan, a farmer at the Royal Dublin Society's Horse Show, Maggot O'Reilly, Matthew Dillon, Valentine Blake Dillon (Lord Mayor of Dublin), Christopher Callinan, Lenehan, an Italian organgrinder, an unknown gentleman in the Gaiety Theatre, Benjamin Dollard, Simon Dedalus, Andrew (Pisser) Burke, Joseph Cuffe, Wisdom Hely, Alderman John Hooper, Dr Francis Brady, Father Sebastian of Mount Argus, a bootblack at the General Post Office, Hugh E. (Blazes) Boylan and so each and so on to no last term.

What were his reflections concerning the last member of this series and late occupant of the bed?

Reflections on his vigour (a bounder), corporal proportion (a billsticker), commercial ability (a bester), impressionability (a boaster).

Why for the observer impressionability in addition to vigour, corporal proportion and commercial ability?

Because he had observed with augmenting frequency in the preceding members of the same series the same concupiscence, inflammably transmitted, first with alarm, then with understanding, then with desire, finally with fatigue, with alternating symptoms of epicene comprehension and apprehension.

With what antagonistic sentiments were his subsequent reflections affected?

Envy, jealousy, abnegation, equanimity.

Envy?

Of a bodily and mental male organism specially adapted for the superincumbent posture of energetic human copulation and energetic piston and cylinder movement necessary for the complete satisfaction of a constant but not acute concupiscence resident in a bodily and mental female organism, passive but not obtuse.

Jealousy?

Because a nature full and volatile in its free state, was alternately the agent and reagent of attraction. Because attraction between agent(s) and reagent(s) at all instants varied, with inverse proportion of increase and decrease, with incessant circular extension and radial reentrance. Because the controlled contemplation of the fluctuation of attraction produced, if desired, a fluctuation of pleasure.

Abnegation?

In virtue of a) acquaintance initiated in September 1903 in the establishment of George Mesias, merchant tailor and outfitter, 5 Eden Quay, b) hospitality extended and received in kind, reciprocated and reappropriated in person, c) comparative youth subject to impulses of ambition and magnanimity, colleagual altruism and amorous egoism, d) extraracial attraction, intraracial inhibition, supraracial prerogative, e) an imminent provincial musical tour, common current expenses, net proceeds divided.

Equanimity?

As as natural as any and every natural act of a nature expressed or understood executed in natured nature by natural creatures in accordance with his, her and their natured natures, of dissimilar similarity. As not so calamitous as a cataclysmic annihilation of the planet in consequence of a collision with a dark sun. As less reprehensible than theft, highway robbery, cruelty to children and animals, obtaining money under false pretences, forgery, embezzlement, misappropriation of public money, betrayal of public trust, malingering, mayhem, corruption of minors, criminal libel, blackmail, contempt of court, arson, treason, felony, mutiny on the high seas, trespass, burglary, jailbreaking, practice of unnatural vice, desertion from armed forces in the field, perjury, poaching, usury, intelligence with the king's enemies, impersonation, criminal assault, manslaughter, wilful and premeditated murder. As not more abnormal than all other parallel processes of adaptation to altered conditions of existence, resulting in a reciprocal equilibrium between the bodily organism and its attendant circumstances, foods, beverages, acquired habits, indulged inclinations, significant disease. As more than inevitable, irreparable.

Why more abnegation than jealousy, less envy than equanimity?

From outrage (matrimony) to outrage (adultery) there arose nought but outrage (copulation) yet the matrimonial violator of the matrimonially violated had not been outraged by the adulterous violator of the adulterously violated.

What retribution, if any?

Assassination, never, as two wrongs did not make one right.

Duel by combat, no. Divorce, not now. Exposure by mechanical artifice (automatic bed) or individual testimony (concealed ocular witnesses), not yet. Suit for damages by legal influence or simulation of assault with evidence of injuries sustained (selfinflicted), not impossibly. Hushmoney by moral influence, possibly. If any, positively, connivance, introduction of emulation (material, a prosperous rival agency of publicity: moral, a successful rival agent of intimacy), depreciation, alienation, humiliation, separation protecting the one separated from the other, protecting the separator from both. (U601–603)

He is going to let it go. He has killed the suitors in his mind. Let it be. Now when Bloom enters the bed, Molly is roused, and she asks him about his day. He says, "Well, I had a bad time, and this young man, Stephen Dedalus..." "Oh, yes," she says. So she knows about Stephen having been there. Now we have a very interesting moment. Bloom and Molly are to be turned into cosmic entities.

What moved visibly above the listener's and the narrator's invisible thoughts?
The upcast reflection of a lamp and shade, an inconstant series of concentric circles of varying gradations of light and shadow. (U606)

Above them on the ceiling are circular reflections of shadows and light from a nightlamp. Now in the *Commedia,* when Dante at last beholds the Beatific Vision of the Trinity (three male figures) in a blaze of reflected Living Light, "within the clear subsistence of that lofty Light," he states, "there appeared to me three circles of three colors and of one dimension...."

Here in *Ulysses,* Joyce gives us the earthly paradise equivalent of the Beatific Vision: the beatific mystery of the sacred androgyne—the male and female in bed; not a triad of male figures (as we had at the beginning with the three fried eggs), but male and female; and above them are the circles of light, imperfect, shadowed, inconstant. We are not in heaven, so the circles are not perfect. But in Joyce's final image of the man and the woman together in this way, we find the image of humanity, and these little circles of shadow and light tell us that this is Joyce's image of the Beatific Vision on earth.

In what directions did listener and narrator lie?

Listener, S.E. by E.: Narrator, N.W. by W.: on the 53rd parallel of latitude, N., and 6th meridian of longitude, W. at an angle of 45° to the terrestrial equator.

Molly is sleeping in one direction, and Bloom is sleeping the other way.

In what state of rest or motion?

At rest relatively to themselves and to each other. In motion being each and both carried westward, forward and rereward respectively, by the proper perpetual motion of the earth through everchanging tracks of neverchanging space.

In what posture?

Listener: reclined semilaterally, left, left hand under head, right leg extended in a straight line and resting on left leg, flexed, in the attitude of Gea-Tellus, fulfilled, recumbent, big with seed. Narrator: reclined laterally, left, with right and left legs flexed, the indexfinger and thumb of the right hand resting on the bridge of the nose, in the attitude depicted in a snapshot photograph made by Percy Apjohn, the childman weary, the manchild in the womb.

Womb? Weary?

He rests. He has travelled.

With?

Sinbad the Sailor and Tinbad the Tailor and Jinbad the Jailer and Ninbad the Nailer and Finbad the Failer and Binbad the Bailer and Pinbad the Pailer and Minbad the Mailer and Hinbad the Hailer and Rinbad the Railer and Dinbad the Kailer and Vinbad the Quailer and Linbad the Yailer and Xinbad the Phthailer.

When?

Going to dark bed there was a square round Sinbad the Sailor roc's auk's egg in the night of the bed of all the auks of the rocs of Darkinbad the Brightdayler.

Where?

(U606–607)

Leopold Bloom has gone into the night of Molly's womb.

### Penelope

And then it starts, that great chapter of Molly. Her two key words are *yes* and *because*.

Yes because he never did a thing like that before as ask to get his breakfast in bed with a couple of eggs since the City Arms hotel when he used to be pretending to be laid up with a sick voice doing his highness to make himself interesting for that old faggot Mrs Riordan that he thought he had a great leg of and she never left us a farthing all for masses for herself and her soul greatest miser that ever was.... (U608)

And on and on and on. Then she begins to think about her various lovers; she comes up to Boylan, and then she thinks about Stephen. Wouldn't it be nice [if Stephen came to stay with them,] and how Stephen is so much more refined than this bunch that she's been with. Then she thinks, "Oh, yes, and there's something of that in Leopold, too." [The thought of Leopold] leads her to think of her girlhood in Gibraltar among the flowery realm down there. When she then thinks of Bloom in that sense, she thinks of the time she first gave herself to him on Howth Head, which extends out into Dublin Bay, and there are great rhododendrons [growing up the face of the cliff] there. [The thought of making love on Howth leads Molly to think of the time when she was a girl in Gibraltar and of her first love, whom she confuses with Bloom on Howth.]

...I love flowers Id love to have the whole place swimming in roses God of heaven theres nothing like nature the wild mountains then the sea and the waves rushing then the beautiful country with the fields of oats and wheat and all kinds of things and all the fine cattle going about that would do your heart good to see rivers and lakes and flowers all sorts of shapes and smells and colours spring-ing up even out of the ditches primroses and violets nature it is as for them saying theres no God I wouldnt give a snap of my two fingers for all their learning why dont they go and create some-thing I often asked him atheists or whatever they call themselves go and wash the cobbles off themselves first then they go howling for the priest and they dying and why why because theyre afraid of hell on account of their bad conscience ah yes I know them well who was the first person in the universe before there was anybody that made it all who ah that they dont know neither do I so there you are they might as well try to stop the sun from rising tomor-row the sun shines for you he said the day we were lying among the rhododendrons on Howth head in the grey tweed suit and his straw hat the day I got him to propose to me yes first I gave him the bit of seedcake out of my mouth and it was leapyear like now yes 16 years ago my God after that long kiss I near lost my breath yes he said I was a flower of the mountain yes so we are flowers all a womans body yes that was one true thing he said in his life and the sun shines for you today yes that was why I liked him because I saw he understood or felt what a woman is and I knew I could always get round him and I gave him all the pleasure I could leading him on till he asked me to say yes and I wouldnt answer first only looked out over the sea and the sky I was thinking of so many things he didnt know of Mulvey and Mr Stanhope and Hester and father and old captain Groves and the sailors playing all birds fly and I say stoop and washing up dishes they called it on the pier and the sentry in front of the governors house with the thing round his white helmet poor devil half roasted and the Spanish girls laughing in their shawls and their tall combs and the auctions in the morning the Greeks and the jews and the Arabs and the devil knows who else from all the ends of Europe and Duke street and the fowl market all clucking outside Larby Sharons and the poor donkeys slipping half asleep and the vague fellows in the cloaks asleep in the shade on the steps and the big wheels of the carts of the bulls and the old castle thousands of years old yes and those handsome Moors all in white and turbans like kings asking you to sit down in their little bit of a shop and Ronda with the old windows of the posadas 2 glancing eyes a lattice hid for her lover to kiss the iron and the wineshops half open at night and the castanets and the night we missed the boat at Algeciras the watchman going about serene with his lamp and O that awful deepdown torrent O and the sea the sea crimson sometimes like fire and the glorious sunsets and the figtrees in the Alameda gardens yes and all the queer little streets and the pink and blue and yellow houses and the rosegardens and the jessamine and geraniums and cactuses and Gibraltar as a girl when I was a Flower of the mountain yes when I put the rose in my hair like the Andalusian girls used or shall I wear a red yes and how he kissed me under the Moorish wall and I thought well as well him as another and then I asked him with my eyes to ask again yes and

then he asked me would I yes to say yes my mountain flower and
first I put my arms around him yes and drew him down to me so
he could feel my breasts all perfume yes and his heart was going
like mad and yes I said yes I will Yes. (U642–644)

And that's how Ulysses ends: *Yes.*

I shall never understand how so many of our fashionable critics can for
so long have written of *Ulysses* as a pessimistic negative work. I think there
are twenty *Yesses* in that last passage. Further, loud and clear, throughout
the book, comes Joyce's message of the bliss-in-being that is one in fact,
though many in its apparitions, broken, multiplied, and reflected in this
spirit-tossed ocean of tears that is the element of our apparently separated
lives, *neben-* and *nacheinander,* as they are. And therein lies the justification
of the symphony of "yesses" of Leopold's *śakti* (and Joyce's *śakti* also)
Molly Bloom, at the conclusion of the book, remembering their own sweet
day of thunder, sixteen years ago... *Yes.*

The affirmation of life is what Joyce represents. Joyce did not have a
happy life, but he said *Yes* to the life he had. What I find in this book is
that we have all said *Yes* and given ourselves. Bloom has given himself in
his way, Stephen has given himself his way, Molly has given herself her
way, and we're melting now into that wonderful ocean and all these memories, and she's thinking of Gibraltar even while she's thinking of the
rhododendrons and this man and that one and it all melts into one big big
dominant experience... *Yes.*

This *Yes,* however, comes from an element of life that is not rational.
While going through *Ulysses,* we have been in the realm of separate individuals, and there has been nothing that anyone would rationally say was
to be greatly affirmed. Then Stephen and Bloom are opened to compassion, which brings them together, and with that opening, we find that all
of life is to be affirmed. Both then vanish into darkness. They are the two
poles: the adolescent youth and the mature man, introvert and extrovert in
Jungian terms. Neither occupies the middle station, and each is inadequate
to the full call of life, Molly there, who is (so to speak) the unawakened life
really, and yet she does support the world, she is good enough... *Yes.*

Molly has not yet been waked to full flower because there is no man in
all the series [of men who have desired her] that is up to her. In India, there

is a goddess with eighteen hands, and in each hand is a weapon that was taken from a different god. This image is, as it were, Molly. When we come to *Finnegans Wake,* however, there *will* be a man equal to her—not an actual man, but the archetypal man, for she is the archetypal woman. And it is on the edge of that realm out of which life stems that we hear... *Yes.*

The Hindus speak of two modes of consciousness. The first, "waking consciousness," reveals the world of gross bodies, which has to be illuminated from without, which changes forms slowly, where an Aristotelian logic prevails: *I am not you; this is not that; A is not not-A.* In *Ulysses,* we have journeyed from waking consciousness, the realm of gross objects, to the realization with Bloom and Stephen of *tat tvam asi* ("thou art that"): *you and the other are one.* We are approaching the realm of "dream consciousness," the Hindu's second mode of consciousness, wherein subject and object, though they seem to be separate, are one: *I as dreamer am surprised by my dream, yet the dream is I.* Objects in dream consciousness are self-luminous: they shine of themselves. They are what is called "subtle matter." And as we'll soon see, *Finnegans Wake* is subtle matter. In *Ulysses,* we are now in an intermediate realm, between waking consciousness and the dream, between the world of hard facts and the paradise where duality is transcended and all things are one. And we are being led into that next realm, into *Finnegans Wake,* by Molly's affirmation from the edge of the realm of dream... *Yes.*

When you read an ordinary novel, there is a usually a narrative purpose—the hero is trying to get somewhere or do something—and everything in the novel is written to carry you further toward either fulfillment or an obstruction that complicates the situation, so that something more has to be done. That is not what Joyce had in mind for *Ulysses.* There is no movement in this book. It is absolutely static. Unless you enjoy the miracle of the prose, everything lasts too long. In fact, that's one characteristic of *Ulysses,* part of the idea of the book: everything is a bit too long. It's a fagging, tiring thing, although every detail is precise. It takes a little while to realize that the fun of the thing is the thing itself, just here and now. Every single paragraph is worth your attention and pleasure. I tell you, when you read *Ulysses* again and then again, it just gets to be more and more alive. All the way through, you hear echoes of what is going to come later. And when you move into the world of *Finnegans Wake*—the very alive, subtle world of wonderful rippling Anna Livia and HCE—all of the motifs in *Ulysses* will come to life in a wonderful dancing way, and *Ulysses* will then seem composed of heaviness, made up of gross matter—really like the hell it is supposed to be . . . *Yes.*

## CHAPTER IV

# FINNEGANS WAKE

## INTRODUCTION

### *Approaching the Wake*

Before we enter the dream realm of *Finnegans Wake,* let me remind you of my understanding of John Weir Perry's description of the the schizophrenic process, since we began this journey into Joyce with the idea that these themes underlie his major works.

The first, Stephen's situation through much of *A Portrait,* is the individual's inability to link affects of sentiments with appropriate images. Affect images are split: one has affects without proper images with which to communicate and images from which one cannot receive the message. One has a sense of conflict between contending principles on many levels (black and white, democracy and communism, and so on) and behind that is fear of the opposite sex, as well as fear of being transformed into the opposite sex and a sense of collision with the opposite sex. These tensions lead to a split self-image. Feeling himself to be an outcast, a clown, a good-for-nothing, the person with a split self-image acts that role, and yet, at the same time, in his unconscious, he has the notion of himself as the world-saving hero. He is living on two levels, and there is a sense of everything in the world being a kind of drama or play.

Second is the theme of the outsider seeking to establish a new center. Stephen decides to fly on the wings of art. Being in a realm of fierce controls, he seeks a loosening experience: the erotic principle, the play of trust and love, which involves an experience of the imagery of death and sacrifice. Recall Stephen and Bloom in Nighttown: the individual, thinking of himself as a crucified redeemer, experiences the imagery either as a regression back into the past, where the beginning took place, or as a dropping down into the abyss, the source out of which all things spring.

Then come the resolving experiences, the third theme, which is rendered as apotheosis: the experience of oneself as the divine out of which all comes. The image may be of oneself as the savior of the world (the Christ or the Buddha) or as the universal king, lord of the four quarters. Along with this image comes the motif of the sacred marriage: the resolution of opposition through the conjunction of sexual opposites.

Finally, out of this fulfillment motif (which takes place in the abyss) comes the theme of new birth, the dawn of a new society, and the imagery of a quadrated world—like the Garden of Eden, with rivers flowing from the center into the four directions. As we will see, *Finnegans Wake* is a quadrated world: it is divided into four books, within which the cycle of the river, the cycle of the day, the cycle of the year, and the cycle of the eon are all divided into four.

Jung speaks of this quadrated image as the totally functioning psyche, with the four psychological functions—sensation, intuition, feeling, and thinking—all perfectly available to the individual, so that one is working on all four cylinders, so to speak. Now the tendency in most people, and in nearly all traditional mythologies, is to project these images outward; but the problem of the modern human being is to interiorize the symbology: to realize that heaven, purgatory, and hell are not places somewhere out there to which you will be going when you die, but aspects of the human experience. They are aspects of one's immediate experience now, so that all the gods and all the heavens and hells are within us.

Thus far, as I have said, Joyce has carried us through the hell ranges, where all these little egos are holding onto themselves and defending themselves. He starts us moving toward the coming of love against control in the middle of *Ulysses,* when the thunder sounds and Bloom opens and tries to console the frightened Stephen. Then Stephen opens to Bloom in the brothel, and by the time Bloom takes Stephen home, their self-contained characters have been, as it were, blown away. They have theoretically annihilated themselves in this process. So when we move into the *Wake,* we will be in the realm of the two who have become one.

Finally, we have seen how Joyce is amalgamating into a great archetypal system this range of mythologies: the Mesopotamian systems (the classical, Hebrew, and Egyptian) pulled together with primitive material and Celtic, Germanic, and Oriental traditions. Now recall the "Circe" chapter of *Ulysses,* when Stephen, in the throes of hallucination, sees the image of Mananaan MacLir arising from behind a coal scuttle [u416]. I noted that this Irish lord of the abyss is the precise equivalent of Neptune-Poseidon and, in India, of Śiva. Now an attribute of the lord of the abyss is the trident, the sense of which is the middle between the pairs of opposites. And remember, the trident is the pitchfork of Satan, also the lord of the abyss, who has been turned into a devil in the Christian tradition, which regards Nature as corrupt and rejects its power and glory. But with the appearance of Mananaan MacLir, Nature pushes up from the depths within Stephen and begins to show its divine power again. This apparition with his bicycle pump and crayfish trumpets the motif of the pairs of opposites, the main theme in *Finnegans Wake.*

### Archetypal Opposition

The great archetypal duad in the *Wake* is father/mother: Humphrey Chimpden Earwicker (HCE) and Anna Livia Plurabelle (ALP).

*Livia* suggests Liffey, the name of the river that flows through Dublin and out into the sea, where the water of the ocean is heated by the sun, evaporates into the blue sky, and becomes the clouds drifting over Glendalough, the hill area south of Dublin, where rain falls and rivulets unite into a stream that becomes the River Liffey. The river is ALP in the various stages of her life: first, this bubbling little stream is a dancing girl, flowing east for a certain way, then westward into lovely gentle countryside; next she turns north and is a matron, mother of a family, a suburban decency; then she turns eastward again and is an old crone, a scrubwoman flowing through Dublin and carrying away all the filth and dirt of the city, all the load of her life, back into the sea, Father Ocean, her father—her cold, mad, feary father. Then the sun, the solar power, lifts the vapor from the sea, and up in the heavens clouds form like children in the womb of the mother universe, and the clouds drift, and the rain comes down over Glendalough, and the cycle starts over again. ALP is the *mārga* (the "path"), the river.

Now, the name of our hero is Humphrey Chimpden Earwicker: the "Hump" in his name suggests a hill, the hill of Howth, a headland jutting out into the sea just to the north of where Anna flows. The word *howth* means "head." In the *Wake,* Howth Head poking out into the sea is thought of as the head of a great sleeping giant. If Howth is the giant's head, then Dublin is his belly, and his toes and feet turn up in Phoenix Park.

Humphrey Chimpden Earwicker: An earwig is a bug that gets in your ear and keeps buzzing. This can be compared to the Egyptian scarab, which is put on the heart of a person being buried in a sarcophagus and represents the reawakened. "Earwicker" can be read as *the awaker,* and the word *Buddha* means "the one who is awake," that is, the one who wakes the sleeper from sleep and the world dream goes with him. So we are in the dream world, waiting for the waker. We do not want only the waker, however, we also want the dream to go on. Miserable, horrible as it is, it is our bliss, our lives.

The giant sleeping in the Irish landscape is named Finn. He [is the great warrior from Irish legend, and] can be compared to the Hindu god Viṣṇu, who sleeps on the great serpent Ananta. The serpent, whose name means "unending," represents in animal form the source, the water out of which all comes. As Viṣṇu sleeps, he dreams the world: the world is Viṣṇu's dream, growing from his navel in the form of a lotus. If you see an image of Viṣṇu dreaming with the lotus, you often seen his consort Lakṣmī massaging his feet. She is also the lotus (*padmā*). She is in two roles. In one, she massages his feet, irritating him a little—just "Mmm, here I am dear...." Then, when he thinks about her, she is the dream, the lotus.

In Hinduism, the activating principle (Sanskrit: *śakti*) is female energy; the quiescent is male. What the man really wants is to be left alone: "I just want to be alone and quiet." The man is asleep. It is the passing of this phenomenon, the woman, that wakes him to action. So in the *Wake,* the river Liffey is the female power, the giant's consort, his wife, Anna Livia Plurabelle. This twinkling female ripples past and "With lipth she lithpeth to him all to time of thuch on thuch and thow on thow." [23.23] She says, "What a life that was in the last eon. Let's have another eon." And, "Wouldn't it be nice to start the world again?" And the man thinks, "Yes, it would." Then he is activated, and they start to work. We are going to see this irritating moment, this flowing river rippling along past the sleeping giant and activating his imagination, throughout the *Wake*. These themes go flickering by; something begins to happen, and we are summoned to life.

### The Dream

*Finnegans Wake* is written on the level of dream, and the perspective is that of dream consciousness. The Spanish dramatist Calderón wrote a play entitled *La Vida es Sueño, Life is a Dream,* and in the same period Shakespeare is saying: "We are such stuff as dreams are made on/ And our little life is rounded with a sleep."[75] We are all aspects of the world dreamer. When you go to sleep you return to the condition of the world dreamer, for everything in your dream is an aspect of yourself. In the *Wake*, we have all been dissolved into dream and move in a dream realm, where all the characters and the landscape are aspects of the dreamer, where forms in a mysterious way manifest their identity even through their separateness.

That is the meaning of Finnegan, the father, the central figure in the *Wake*, the world dreamer who is dreaming through us all. The principal objects of his dream are the members of his family: his wife and daughter, Anna Livia and Issy, who are essentially Molly and Milly in *Ulysses*, seen now in the way of dream radiance; and two sons—Shem the Penman, the loser; and Shaun the Post, the successful political guy, the winner. The sons are, you might say, concretizations or realizations of the dream that the father had when he begot them. Who are they? Stephen and Mulligan; though in the *Wake* they are just shadows, grotesque "charictures" playing over the surface of the "drame."[76]

Now a human dreamer has two orders of dream. Using Jung's terms, one is the personal, and the other, the collective. When you go into sleep, you carry with you a residual recollection of personal experiences. The personal aspect of your dream—"Am I going to pass the exam? Should I marry Susie or Betty?"—has to do with those experiences of your personal life. You can remember dreams of that sort: just personal things. But, says Jung, below the personal level, the energies of your dream are those of the human body, of biology. Your biology is related to the biology of plants and animals: they too share the life energies—what we might term "body wisdom," in contrast to mental wisdom. When you move deeper in dream, when you move into the sphere of the permanent energies of your body, your mental wisdom is gradually extinguished, body wisdom (as it were) rises, and you experience the collective order of dream, where the imagery is identical with the imagery of myth. And since some of these images have not been allowed to play a role in your life, you come into relation to them with surprise.

The personal and the collective, then, are the two levels of dream: the peculiar, ever-changing, historical moment associated with this, that or another person; and the eternal archetypal process common to all. When one listens to Indian music, it never has a beginning and it has no end. You know that the music is going on all the time, and the consciousness of the musician just dips down into the music, picks it up with the instrument, and reads it again. That's the way the *Wake* is: the same thing is going on, always the same way, yet ever changing. No matter. The whole book is based on this process: the more something changes, the more it remains the same—the round, the riverrun circle, the vortex of rebirth.

## The Hereweareagain Gaieties

The riverrun cycle, round and round and round and round, is the flow of the river of time: the coming into being of the world and its going out of being. Joyce calls the process "the Hereweareagain Gaieties" [455.25] and "the Royal Revolver" [455.26]. Everything keeps going round and round one way after another. Joyce compares this round with the Hesiod cycle of the four ages (the ages of gold, silver, bronze, and iron) and with Vico's cycle of the four ages of man. *Finnegans Wake* is, accordingly, divided into four books.

Book I is divided into eight chapters, all of which have to do with the hero's character as it appears to others. This is Vico's age of the patriarchs who heard the voice of God in thunder, the age of gold. Book II, with four chapters, is Vico's age of the aristocratic sons, the age of silver. Book III, with four chapters, is the age of the people, the bronze age, when all the property is distributed and everybody wants more. And this leads to Book IV, a single chapter, which is the *ricorso,* the return to beginnings—exactly the moment of transition we are in now (as Joyce sees it), for the dreamer in the *Wake* is living in our day. With the *ricorso*, the Hereweareagain Gaities starts anew, and we are back in the age of the battling giants slugging each other all over the place, back in the iron age, in chaos.

In Hindu India this vortex is represented on a cosmic level by the four *yugas* (the "world ages"), which run in a descending cycle: the *yuga* of four, of three, of two, and of one—of Kālī ("strife"), when everything ends in mush and must be restored. In this tradition that final mush will come when the caste system is broken, for the caste system represents the differentiated system of the society as an organism: the *brahman* caste, the priests, is the head; the *kṣatriya,* the governing caste of princes and warriors, is the shoulders; the *vaiśya* caste (what we would think of as the middle class), is the torso; and the *śudra,* the suffering serving class, is the legs. These castes constitute the unit body, which (viewed in this way) can be augmented to be a counterpart of the body of the universe. So when the caste system disintegrates, it is as though the body structure were breaking down and turning into a single thing—what happens with cancer, which is why Joyce uses that motif—everything disintegrating into the abyss, the beginning, the chaos out of which all comes and back into which it goes, the Alpha and the Omega, the divine union. Ovid speaks in the *Metamorphoses* of this system of disintegration into the abyss as a situation where the pairs of opposites are not distinguished from each other any more, for the world comes into being only when the distinctions come into being.

So eons come and go, come and go. That great cycle is marked every year by the solstices and equinoxes. The world comes and goes. Every day the great round is represented in small measure by dawn, noonday, sunset, night, the beginning of a new day. Nothing happens that has not happened a million times before. This vortex of death and rebirth, what in Buddhism is known as the *saṃsāra,* operates on the cosmic and on the individual level. Nietzsche brings up this theme in the *Zarathustra*—in fact, this concept of eternal return is the inspiration of the book: every moment that you live is a moment that is going to come back. Not only will it come back, but it will come back infinitely often. It will be here again in an eon, in an eon, and in an eon after. It is an eternal moment. Every moment that you are living is an eternal moment because it is going to be back again. Each moment is one that you will have to live again. It is not a moment that leads to something else.

With this perspective, your whole accent shifts. You no longer think of the moment you are living as leading to something else, but realize it as the final term. It is just a moment, an end in itself, that moment which it is and no other moment. When we say the end justifies the means, we are denying this principle. The thing that you are doing is not a means to some end. The means has to be justified in itself. That does not mean that it has to be justified morally, because it is impossible to be moral according to this principle.

## Finnegan's Fall

The number "1132" runs all through the *Wake*. It's the number of fall and renewal—the speed of falling bodies being 32 feet per second per second and 11 being the number of the renewal of the decade. And recall Paul's Epistle to the Romans, where he says at 11:32: "...for God has consigned all men to disobedience that he may show his mercy to all." Our disobedience, our sinning—the Fall—gives God the chance to show and bring forth his character, which is mercy.

About the Fall: the fall in the Garden of Eden starts everything going. Our whole world, the world of life, is based on that fall. Were it not for the fall in the Garden of Eden, there would be no time, there would be no death and birth. We are Adam's children, consuming the substance of his sinful life, living (as it were) on his fall. Now suppose sinning were to stop. Suppose the sleeping giant on whose sleep we depend were to wake up. That would be the end of the world. So the last thing we want is for sinning to cease, because the waking of the sleeping giant would bring about the end of life. Joyce depicts this sinful giant in the image of Finnegan.

There is an Irish-American vaudeville song called "Finnegan's Wake," and it is a story of an Irish hod carrier.[77] I don't know whether anyone knows any more what a hod carrier was. Before there were buildings made of metal with wonderful mechanical elevators going up and down, buildings were made of bricks. When a building was being built, the bricks had to be carried up, and so men went up scaffolds and ladders using a hod, this pole with a carrier on the top, to carry the bricks. Hod carriers were mostly Irishmen (it was just at the time of the Irish coming over here), so you had a lot of Irishmen going up with bricks on their shoulder and coming down with an empty hod. They were circulating matter and the spirit:

carrying matter up to heaven and bringing *spiritus* ("air") back to earth. Here we have the circle again, this wonderful cycle.

One of these hod carriers was named Tim Finnegan, and his favorite pastime, like that of many Irishmen, was drinking Irish whiskey. The word *whiskey* is a Celtic word that means "the water of life," and this activates the spirit in what we still call "spirits." Jameson's Whiskey is made in Dublin from the water of the River Liffey, so it is (you might say), the delicious extract, the radiance (as it were) of Anna Livia; and a radiance makes you drunk. So, full of radiance, the spirit which induces ecstacy and rapture, Tim Finnegan one day tumbles from the top of his ladder and falls down the ladder—boom! boom! boom!—and that sound of his fall is the thunderous sound of God's voice in Vico's cycle saying, "This is not the way for you old barbarians to live." His friends find him at the bottom of the ladder, and they take him home to have his wake. In the midst of his wake, someone begins flinging around a bottle of whiskey. It pours over Finnegan's body, and he jumps up and tries to join in the dance at his own wake. Now if that were to happen—if the dreamer were to wake, if the sinner were to stop sinning—it would, of course, end the party. Since Joyce uses Finnegan as the man representing the Fall, the whole world is based on his remaining asleep. So all the anxious mourners press down on him and say, "Stay down there! You just stay where you are." And they reassure him that all is being taken care of in his absence: "There's already a big rody ram lad at random on the premises" [28.36]—that is to say, HCE, the father of this family, is on the premises.

HCE is a tavern keeper. He is serving spirit all the time in a tavern in Chapelizod, which was once a town outside of Dublin, but now is a tiny suburb. Chapelizod: the chapel of Isolde—that is, the place where Isolde lived when Tristan came from Cornwall to fetch her to King Mark; and then, of course, they cuckolded King Mark. So here we have the motif of the father (Mark), his nephew/son (Tristan), and his young wife (Isolde), whom the son is taking away—this is the Oedipus complex, is it not!

In this family there is a daughter, who is the younger version of her mother, the girl her father actually married. So she is both the daughter and the wife—and there is a wonderful incest situation that Joyce defines, in recondite legal terms in Book III of the *Wake,* as a fantastic sea of iniquity in the unconscious of this family. Then there are the two sons, Shem, the writer, and Shaun, the fair-haired hero boy. They are, as I said, the counterparts of Mulligan and Stephen in *Ulysses,* but those two are only shadows here. Joyce treats Shem and Shaun, who are always quarreling, in a playful, disrespectful way.

In addition to the family—father and mother, two sons, and a daughter—there are a few minor characters: an old man who helps out at the bar and an old woman, Kate the Slop, the servant in the house who was "put in with the bricks" [245.34]—she has been there forever. Now all of these people live right on the edge of Phoenix Park: the park of the phoenix, the bird that burns itself to death and is resurrected—the Hereweareagain Gaieties theme again. Phoenix Park is, of course, the Garden of Eden.

There is one more thing that I should point out before we move into the *Wake.* The tavern keeper has run for election to an office and lost, because of a rumor about his having committed some kind of impropriety in Phoenix Park. But nobody can figure out what he did. Well, what was it that Adam and Eve did? That always has been a matter of debate. The dominant opinion about HCE's crime seems to be that he was a voyeur, that he had been watching two servant girls urinating in the bushes in the dark. How could he have been watching anything at all at midnight? Three soldiers witnessed his transgression in the dark, but they were drunk, so the whole thing is a mess. Nobody knows what happened in the park, what HCE's sin was. Nobody knows what went wrong in Eden, what brought about the great Fall that has evoked the mercy of God. Nobody knows.

Now with that little introduction, we can enter the rivverun round. As we tour the subtle dream realm of *Finnegans Wake,* we will have, if not a complete guide to the landscape, then at least a few landmarks to help us figure out where we are.

## THE WAKE

### Book I

> riverrun, past Eve and Adam's, from swerve of shore to bend of bay, brings us by a commodius vicus of recirculation back to Howth Castle and Environs. (3.1–3)

*riverrun. . .:* *Finnegans Wake* opens with a small letter, the last half of a sentence. If you want to find the beginning of that sentence, you turn to the end of the book, where you find this phrase: *a way alone a last a loved a long the* Then you return to the beginning of the book and finish the phrase with *riverrun past Eve and Adam's*... You can go round the circle and come to the end, or you can go out of the book. You don't have to come back into this book, but you will probably be tempted back in; and you will begin the round again, the whole thing will start all over again. So it is with being reincarnated.

Alternatively—you know the Buddha's posture pointing to the juncture?—you can leave the ring, *nirvāṇa,* pass out, not come back, dissociate yourself from it. The choice of leaving the cycle would lead us to Joyce's *Paradiso,* his last great book, which (had it been written) would have represented heaven and release. If we don't pass out of the cycle, however, then we are back in the *Wake,* back in this round of reincarnation that is equivalent to the Christian purgatory, where the soul is purged of its limitations and its ignorances, and finally *waked,* enlightened

*riverrun,*...: the river Liffey.... *past Eve and Adam's*...: the river of time comes down to us as Adam and Eve, father and mother of all life, and in Dublin the Liffey runs past a little church named Adam and Eve's.... *from swerve of shore to bend of bay,*...: the swerve of the shore is where the Liffey runs around Howth Head and into Dublin Bay; and it's there, at Island Bridge where tide and riverwater mingle, that the tavern of HCE is to be found.

Joyce, however, plays a game here: *swerve of shore* suggests a serpent (the temptation theme), and you can hear in "s-s-s" of the phrase the whisk of the dress of the woman, the temptress who wakes you and makes you follow. The girls in the park appear as this tempting aspect of the woman. The woman, however, is also the restorer of her husband. Here are two aspects of the woman: one knocks you down, the other puts you together again. The second of these aspects is, of course, a female symbol of God's mercy.

Another game: *bend of bay* suggests a "bey," a Turkish noble, who is here bending, just as the waves of Dublin Bay come in and bend onto the beach. The bey, then, is the invading male going broke on the shore of Mother Ireland—going smash, smash, smash on the *swerve of shore.* So, the bay is the hero, and the shore is the heroine. And this interplay between the sea and the land (the salt water of the sea and the sweet water of Ireland) is analogous in *Finnegans Wake* to the interplay between the male figures and the female throughout the work.

The ultimate image of Man is that of Adam before Eve was drawn from his rib: it is an androgynous image. But once she is withdrawn, the two are against each other in a kind of antagonistic cooperation. So also here at the beginning of the *Wake:* these two are against each other, yet it is that opposition which supplies the energy to generate the activities of the book. The waters of the bay, breaking on the shore, represent a counterpart on the elemental level of HCE, Here Comes Everybody, our hero, falling. He may fall as Adam in the Garden, he may fall as Humpty Dumpty from the wall, when Alice bedazzles him, or he may fall as Finnegan, the hod carrier who got drunk and fell from the wall that he was helping to build.

... *brings us by a commodius vicus of recirculation* ...: a *vicus* is a road, and there is actually a Vico Road in Dalkey; here the vicus is the road of return[78]... *back to Howth Castle and Environs.*

Howth Castle is a castle that sits on Howth Head, the head of the giant whose feet are the hills in Phoenix Park. Howth Castle was founded by Sir Almeric Tristram, who came to Ireland with Henry II at the time of the English conquest of Ireland. *Howth Castle and Environs* contain the initials of the hero (HCE), who is represented at Howth Castle and Environs, to which the riverrun has brought us back. It is as though (an important matter in the book) we were on a tour. Here we have the blue book of Ireland. Following the riverrun, we follow the tour and, in time, we come back to Howth Castle and Environs and start the round again.

Now, having returned to the beginning, with this account of the first sentence in mind, we can read the rest of the first page of the *Wake*. The next paragraphs will tell us, as did the first sentence, that those things that did take place are going to take place again, but they have not yet taken place, for we are at the beginning of the book—so every sentence is going to speak in doubletalk (as it were), saying both yes and no, meaning more than one thing. And as we go through this next passage, recall that the tavern is in Chapelizod, so the Tristan and Isolde motif will appear here, as will the theme of conquest, of the invader against the native Irish.

> Sir Tristram, violer d'amores, fr'over the short sea, had passencore rearrived from North Armorica on this side the scraggy isthmus of Europe Minor to wielderfight his penisolate war: nor had topsawyer's

rocks by the stream Oconee exaggerated themselse to Laurens County's gorgios while they went doublin their mumper all the time: nor avoice from afire bellowsed mishe mishe to tauftauf thuart-peatrick: not yet, though vennissoon after, had a kidscad buttended a bland old isaac: not yet, though all's fair in vanessy, were sosie ses-thers wroth with twone nathandjoe. Rot a peck of pa's malt had Jhem or Shen brewed by arclight and rory end to regginbrow was to be seen ringsome on the aquaface. (3.4–14)

*Sir Tristram,* . . . : he appears in two senses: one, the epic Tristan, and the other, the historical Sir Almeric Tristram. The word *Tristram*—there are many plays on this word throughout the *Wake.* Here it seems to be com-posed of *triste,* meaning "sad," plus *tram,* a kind of vehicle: the hero is a vehicle of divine revelation and manifestation, and he is very sad. . . . *violer d'amores,* . . . : the violater of love; *violer* is an old French word describing one who plays the violin in praise of love. . . . 79 *fr'over the short sea,* . . . : he has come from across the sea between England and Ireland—Saint George's Channel. . . . *had passencore rearrived* . . . : had passing again (*pass-encore*) and had not yet again (*pas-encore*) and had in the past yet again (*passe-encore*) arrived once more[80]. . . *from North Armorica* . . . : *Armorica* is a medieval name of Brittany, but the word also suggests America. . . . *on this side the scraggy isthmus of Europe Minor* . . . : Europe can be regarded as an isthmus projecting from Asia. Also implied here is a connection between Asia Minor and Europe. Snorri Sturluson in the *Prose Edda* proposes that Celtic and Nordic gods are simply historical characters who came from Troy. The medieval story of the origins of the British race declares that the British orig-inally came from Troy, which was in Asia Minor. . . . *to wielderfight his penisolate war:* . . . : *penisolate* war could be read as the Peninsular War, in which [British troops commanded by] Dublin-born Arthur Wellesley [later first] duke of Wellington, drove back and expelled Napoleon's armies; further, this war's designation as *penisolate* sounds the brother battle motif, for they are at war with each other in the same word—it can be read as *pen-isolate,* referring to Shem, and as penis-olate, referring to Shaun.

. . . *nor had topsawyer's rocks* . . . : America having appeared in *North Armorica, topsawyer* brings to mind the American hero Tom Sawyer, whom we associate, of course, with Mark Twain (Mark the Second, after Tristan's King Mark); also with Huckleberry Finn—which brings up Finnegan and the great Irish hero Finn McCool, who in Irish legend lived for a hundred years defending Dublin Bay with his great band of warriors, the *Fianna*, for whom the Irish Fenian movement is named. All of this is evoked by *topsawyer*.

What is a *topsawyer?* Well, in lumbering days, a big tree was cut up in a saw pit by two men with a huge saw. The one standing up on top was the top sawyer, and the one down in the pit was the bottom sawyer. In the *Wake*, the topsawyer is Shaun, of course, and the pit sawyer who is getting all the sawdust in his eyes is his brother, Shem—the two fighters in the brother battle motif. And who is the tree—the *tree-stem*—Tristan? Of course, it is daddy, so here also is the theme of the destruction of the father. Before moving on, there is in *rocks* a slang reference to testicles, and also to money; the Irish come to America dead broke, they make money, and they become wealthy people like the Kennedys.

...*by the stream Oconee exaggerated themselse to Laurens County's gorgios*...A curious fact: *Laurens* echoes *Lawrence,* and the Lawrence family owns Howth Castle right now. Further, in Georgia there is a county named Laurens, where there is a stream called *Oconee—Oconee* can be read as *ochone,* an Irish word meaning "alas"—and on the banks of the Oconee stream in Laurens county Georgia stands the town of Dublin. The American Dublin is on the stream Oconee in which are topsawyer's rocks.

...*while they went doublin their mumper all the time:*...: that is, always doubling their number (*mumber*); "mum" is a type of beer first brewed in [Germany in] 1492, a significant date for America.

...*nor avoice from afire*...: Here is the voice from the fire—recall Moses; and this voice from the burning bush...*bellowsed mishe mishe*...: a greeting in Irish from the female side of the system, and it suggests what you hear every time you pick up the telephone in Japan—"*mushimushi,*" which effectively means, "Hello, hello, who is there?...*to tauftauf thuartpeatrick:*...: the primary reference here is to St. Patrick's baptizing Ireland—*tauftauf* suggests the German *taufen,* "to baptize"; *peatrick* (peatreek) brings to mind the legend of St. Patrick's Purgatory. St. Patrick once drew a circle on the ground, and the earth opened, and the flames of purgatory appeared.

...*not yet, though venissoon after, had a kidscad buttended a bland old isaac:*...: Isaac was fooled (*buttended*) by Jacob, the younger (*cadet* in

French) brother who put on a kid-skin and offered himself as his older brother; in addition, Isaac Butt was an Irish revolutionary who got into a "brother battle" with Parnell.[81]

... *not yet, though all's fair in vanessy*...: a reference to Thackeray's *Vanity Fair*.[82] ... *were sosie sesthers wroth*...: refers to Susanna, Esther, and Ruth, three women in the Bible associated with older men.[83] ... *with twone nathandjoe*....: *nathanjoe* is an anagram for Jonathan, and Dublin-born Jonathan Swift was turned on his head by his two young beloveds, both named Esther.

... *Rot a peck of pa's malt*...: Noah's liquor; after the Flood, Noah got drunk and was exposed, and his three sons saw him naked which was forbidden.[84] ... *had Jhem or Shen*...: Noah's three sons were Shem, Ham, and Japheth: Shem (*Shen*), the one the Bible puts in command, was the son favored by Noah, and the other two, Ham and Japheth, are run together into *Jhem* (Shaun).... *brewed by arclight*...: that is, by the light of the rainbow.... *and rory end to the regginbrow was to be seen ringsome on the aquaface*....: after the Flood, the rainbow appeared in the east (the *rory end*—which also refers to Rory O'Connor, the last High King of Ireland, when the royal brow [*regginbrow*] of the conqueror, Henry II, was seen coming from across the sea to Ireland).

All of these references are in the first full paragraph, and they form the nuclear statement of all of the themes that are going to open up in this book. Here they are all running together. The second paragraph refers to Finnegan's fall.

> The fall (bababadalgharaghtakamminarronnkonnbronntonnerronntuonnthunntrovarrhounawnskawntoohoohoordenenthurnuk!) of a once wallstrait oldparr is retaled early in bed and later on life down through all christian minstrelsy. The great fall of the offwall entailed at such short notice the pftjschute of Finnegan, erse solid man, that the humptyhillhead of humself promptly sends an unquiring one well to the west in quest of his tumptytumtoes: and their upturnpikepointandplace is at the knock out in the park where oranges have been laid to rust upon the green since devlinsfirst loved livvy. (3.15–24)

*The fall (bababadalgharaghtakamminarronnkonnbronntonnerronntuonnthunntrovarrhounawnskawntoohoohoordenenthurnuk!)*...: This is the thunder sound of Finnegan's fall, which was the fall... *of a once wallstrait oldparr...*, a reference to the Wall Street crash, as well as to the fall of Finnegan down the ladder. However, there was an old, old man in the seventeenth and eighteenth centuries named Old Parr, who was all covered with hair and lived to be something like two hundred years old.[85]

This old hairy man went to court to see Charles I, and the story of this old, old man ... *is retaled early in bed and later on life down through all christian minstrelsy. The great fall of the offwall...*: fall of the offal, the fall of Adam, also the fall that ... *entailed at such short notice the pftjschute of Finnegan,...* put a tail on Finnegan, once a solid man ... *erse solid man, that the humptyhillhead of humself...* Howth Head, which when seen in the east ... *prumptly sends an unquiring one well to the west in quest of his tumptytumtoes:...* his toes ... *and their upturnpikepointandplace is at the knock out in the park...* so, he fell like Humpty Dumpty, and as I have already said, his toes turn up in Phoenix Park, where there is a place called Castle Knock,... *where oranges have been laid to rust upon the green...* that is, where Protestant invaders, Orangemen (*oranges*), have been laid to rest (*to rust*) upon the earth, where they will disintegrate and become Irish fertilizer, more or less; but there is a bit of anguish before they end calmly in the *green;* and this has been going on ... *since devlinsfirst... devlins* suggests devil, but in Gottfried von Strassburg's Tristan, *Dyflin* is the medieval name for Dublin[86] ... *loved livvy.*

What do you think of that? That's the first page of the book; there are 628 pages. Actually, there's nothing in the *Wake* that's as difficult as the first two full paragraphs until much later in the book.

On the next page, after a paragraph about early wars, there is a passage about Primordial Master Finnegan, a bricklayer living in prehistoric times, before there were any great estates. Now Ibsen's masterbuilder was named Bygmester Solness, and he was urged by a young girl to climb a tower that he had built; and when he was at the top, she waved her scarf, he got dizzy and fell—Humpty Dumpty's fall—and that was the end of the masterbuilder. Further, Joyce had a theory that language began from gestures, from pantomime, and since the hero HCE is a stutterer, the masterbuilder with stuttering hand gestures in this delightful paragraph is:

> Bygmester Finnegan, of the Stuttering Hand, freeman's maurer, lived in the broadest way immarginable in his rushlit toofarback for

messuages before joshuan judges had given us numbers or Helviticus
committed deuteronomy (one yeastyday he sternely struxk his tete in
a tub for to watsch the future of his fates but ere he swiftly stook it
out again, by the might of moses, the very water was eviparated and
all the guenneses had met their exodus so that ought to show you
what a pentschanjeuchy chap he was!) and during mighty odd years
this man of hod, cement and edifices in Toper's Thorp piled buildung supra buildung pon the banks for the livers by the Soangso. He
addle liddle phifie Annie ugged the little craythur. Wither hayre in
honds tuck up your part inher. Oftwhile balbulous, mithre ahead,
with goodly trowel in grasp and ivoroiled overalls which he habitacu-
larly fondseed, like Haroun Childeric Eggeberth he would caligulate
by multiplicables the alltitude and malltitude until he seesaw by
neatlight of the liquor wheretwin 'twas born, . . .

Here comes the building of a skyscraper:

his roundhead staple of other days to rise in undress maisonry up-
standed (joygrantit!), a waalworth of a skyerscrape of most eyeful
hoyth entowerly, erigenating from next to nothing and celescalating
the himals and all, hierarchitectitiptitoploftical, with a burning bush
abob off its baubletop and with larrons o'toolers clittering up and
tombles a'buckets clottering down. (4.18–5.4)

*. . . larrons o'toolers clittering up and tombles a'buckets clottering down. . . . :*
this is a reference is to the historical cycle, particularly to building the skyscraper of the British Empire—when Henry II came to Ireland, Lawrence
O'Toole (*larrons o'toolers*), the Bishop of Dublin, rose in the church, and
about the same time Thomas à Becket (*tombles a'buckets*) fell.

In the sixth paragraph, we read of the hero's heraldic insignia:

Of the first was he to bare arms and a name: Wassaily Booslaeugh of
Riesengeborg. His crest of huroldry, in vert with ancillars, troublant,
argent, a hegoak, poursuivant, horrid, horned. . . .

This is heraldic language.

His scutschum fessed, with archers strung, helio, of the second.
Hootch is for husbandman handling his hoe. Hohohoho, Mister
Finn, you're going to be Mister Finnagain! Comeday morm and, O,
you're vine! Sendday's eve and, ah, you're vinegar! Hahahaha, Mister
Funn, you're going to be fined again! (5.5–12)

The paragraph that follows opens with the great question:

> What then agentlike brought about that tragoady thundersday this municipal sin business? Our cubehouse still rocks as earwitness to the thunder of his arafatas but we hear also through successive ages that shebby choruysh of unkalified muzzlenimiissilehims that would blackguardise the whitestone ever hurtleturtled out of heaven. . . .

He is praying to the Virgin for information.[87]

> Stay us wherefore in our search for tighteousness, O Sustainer, what time we rise and when we take up to toothmick and before we lump down upown our leatherbed and in the night and at the fading of the stars! For a nod to the nabir is better than wink to the wabsanti. Otherways wesways like that provost scoffing bedoueen the jebel and the jypsian sea. Cropherb the crunchbracken shall decide. Then we'll know if the feast is a flyday. She has a gift of seek on site and she all-casually ansars helpers, the dreamydeary. Heed! Heed! It may half been a missfired brick, as some say, or it mought have been due to a collup-sus of his back promises, as others looked at it. (There extand by now one thousand and one stories, all told, of the same). But so sore did abe ite ivvy's holired abbles,(what with the wallhall's horrors of rollsrights, carhacks, stonengens, kisstvanes, tramtrees, fargobawlers, autokino-tons, hippohobbilies, streetfleets, tournintaxes, megaphoggs, circuses and wardsmoats and basilikerks and aeropagods and the hoyse and the jollybrool and the peeler in the coat and mecklenburk bitch bite at his ear and the merlinburrow burrocks and his fore old porecourts, the bore the more, and his blightblack workingstacks at twelvepins a dozen and the noobibusses sleighding along Safetyfirst Street and the derry-jellybies snooping around Tell-No-Tailors' Corner and the fumes and the hopes and the strupithump of his ville's indigenous romekeepers, homesweepers, domecreepers, thurum and thurum in fancymud mu-rumd and all the uproor from all the aufroofs, a roof for may and a reef for hugh butt under his bridge suits tony) wan warning Phill filt tip-pling full. His howd feeled heavy, his hoddit did shake. (There was a wall of course in erection)[.] Dimb! He stottered from the latter. Damb! he was dud. Dumb! Mastabatoom, mastabadtomm, when a mon merries his lute is all long. For whole the world to see. (5.13–6.12)

That is how he fell, amid all that noise in the city street. Now we are at his wake, an Irish wake, a grand party based on death:

Shize? I should shee! Macool, Macool, orra whyi deed ye diie? of a trying thirstay mournin? Sobs they sighdid at Fillagain's chrissormiss wake, all the hoolivans of the nation, prostrated in their consternation and their duodisimally profusive plethora of ululation. There was plumbs and grumes and cheriffs and citherers and raiders and cinemen too. And the all gianed in with the shoutmost shoviality. Agog and magog and the round of them agrog. To the continuation of that celebration until Hanandhunigan's extermination! Some in kinkin corass, more kankan keening. Belling him up and filling him down. He's stiff but he's steady is Priam Olim! 'Twas he was the dacent gaylabouring youth. Sharpen his pillowscone, tap us his bier! E'erawhere in the whorl would ye hear sich a din again? With their deepbrow fundigs and the dusty fidelios. They laid him brawdawn alanglast bed. With a bockalips of finisky fore his feet. And a barrowload of guenesis hoer his head. Tee the tootal of the fluid hang the twoddle of the fuddled, O!

The corpse is lying there, and all of his companions and old friends are drinking and eating his widow out of house and home.

Hurrah, there is but young gleve for the owl globe wheels in view which is tautaulogically the same thing. . . .

Then a strange thing happens: the wake starts to disintegrate and another theme begins to emerge:

Well, Him a being so on the flounder of his bulk like an overgrown babeling, let wee peep, see, at hom, well, see peegee ought he ought, platterplate. . . .

Finnegan's body becomes the landscape of the countryside.

Hum! From Shopalist to Bailywick or from ashtun to baronoath or from Buythebanks to Roundthehead or from the foot of the bill to ireglint's eye he calmly extensolies. And all the way (a horn!) from fjord to fjell his baywinds' oboboes shall wail him rockbound (hoahoahoah!) in swimswamswum and all the livvylong night, the delldale dalppling night, the night of bluerybells, her flittaflute in tricky trochees (O carina! O carina!) wake him. With her issavan essavans and her patterjackmartins about all them inns and ouses. Tilling a teel of a tum, telling a toll of a teary turty Taubling. Grace before Glutton. . . .

All the world is living on him. In his death, he becomes that which is consummed by his own children. It is as if he were an egg that has fallen and broken; his widow simply scrambles him up and serves him as the food at the wake.[88]

> For what we are, gifs à gross if we are, about to believe. So pool the begg and pass the kish for crawsake. Omen. So sigh us. Grampupus is fallen down but grinny sprids the boord....

The old man is depicted as spread out on the table

> Whase on the joint of a desh? Finfoefom the Fush. Whase be his baken head? A loaf of Singpantry's Kennedy bread. And whase hitched to the hop in his tayle? A glass of Danu U'Dunnell's foamous olde Dobbelin ayle. But, lo, as you would quaffoff his fraudstuff and sink teeth through that pyth of a flowerwhite bodey behold of him as behemoth for he is noewhemoe. Finiche!...

Then he fades out

> Only a fadograph of a yestern scene. Almost rubicund Salmosalar, ancient fromout the ages of the Agapemonides, he is smolten in our mist, woebecanned and packt away. So that meal's dead off for summan, schlook, schlice and goodridhirring....

Disappearing, melting into the archetypes, his form can still be seen in the landscape.

> Yet may we not see still the brontoichthyan form outlined aslumbered, even in our own nighttime by the sedge of the troutling stream that Bronto loved and Brunto has a lean on. *Hic cubat edilis. Apud libertinam parvulam.*... (6.13–7.23)

The whole scene fades into the past, and he becomes Dublin and is memorialized in the giant lying there with all of us living our lives in his belly and eating him.

Then for a number of pages: Not only the landscape is to be reviewed (pp. 7, 10, 12, 14, 23) but typical epochs of human history: modern history (pp. 8–11), medieval history (pp. 13–14), prehistory (pp. 15–20); also, a few fragments of folklore (pp. 20–23); a comical vaudeville song; and the dump heap in our own backyard (p. 19). As the eye regards each, it slightly disintegrates to reveal an unmistakable trait or two of the grotesque Finnegan within.[89]

Then we are back at the wake, and now the whiskey is spilled on Finnegan, and he stirs and hollers in his native tongue:

Anam muck an dhoul! Did ye drink me doornail?

"Soul of the devil, did ye think me dead?" He moves to get up, but nobody wants him to get up, of course, for he is the great dreamer of our lives. We are his dream, and if he wakes, all of us are gone. So the mourners try to persuade him to lie down again:

Now be aisy, good Mr Finnimore, sir. And take your laysure like a god on pension and don't be walking abroad.

They tell him, "Stay where you are. You wouldn't want to be up anyhow, the way the world has changed."

Sure you'd only lose yourself in Healiopolis now the way your roads in Kapelavaster are that winding there after the calvary, the North Umbrian and the Fivs Barrow and Waddlings Raid and the Bower Moore and wet your feet maybe with the foggy dew's abroad. Meeting some sick old bankrupt or the Cottericks' donkey with his shoe hanging, clankat-achankata, or a slut snoring with an impure infant on a bench. 'Twould turn you against life, so 'twould. And the weather's that mean too.

They continue to try to persuade him to stay where he is. They tell him they'll tend his grave, bring roses:

... And we'll be coming here, the ombre players, to take your gravel and bringing you presents, won't we, fenians? And it isn't our spittle we'll stint you of, is it, druids? Not shabbty little imagettes, penny-dirts and dodgemyeyes you buy in the soottee stores. But offerings of the fields. Mieliodories, that Doctor Faherty, the madison man, taught to gooden you. Poppypap's a passport out. And honey is the holiest thing ever was, hive, comb and earwax, the food for glory, (mind you keep the pot or your nectar cup may yield too light!) and some goat's milk, sir, like the maid used to bring you.

"Just stay where you are. We will bring you flowers and honey and goat's milk. You are great."

... Your fame is spreading like Basilico's ointment since the Fintan Lalors piped you overborder and there's whole households beyond the Bothnians and they calling names after you. ...

"You are great, and we'll say so."

The menhere's always talking of you sitting around on the pig's cheeks under the sacred rooftree, over the bowls of memory where every hollow holds a hallow, with a pledge till the drengs, in the Salmon House.... (24.15–25, 35–36, 25.11–15)

"We'll sing your praises throughout the ages. You just stay there for a while, and let us have our life. Besides, your old primordial pagan days are all over. They are past." Recall that were it not for the fall of Adam, there would be no time, no birth, no death, and we would be in the children's paradise, in Eden. But look how exciting the world is that resulted from Adam's fall! We don't want Finnegan to wake up. And so:

...Repose you now! Finn no more!

For, be that samesake sibsubstitute of a hooky salmon, there's already a big rody ram lad at random on the premises of his haunt of the hungred bordles, as it is told me.

There is a new, powerful character on the premises now.

Shop Illicit, flourishing like a lordmajor or a buaboabaybohm, litting flop a deadlop (aloose!) to lee but lifting a bennbranch a yardalong (ivoeh!) on the breezy side (for showm!), the height of Brewster's chimpney and as broad below as Phineas Barnum; humphing his share of the showthers is senken on him he's such a grandfallar, with a pocked wife in pickle that's a flyfire and three lice nittle clinkers, two twilling bugs and one midgit pucelle. (28.33–29.8)

This new man who has a wife and a daughter and two sons will now be in charge. Old Finn, the old Adam on whose sin we live, has been left behind, and we have a new historical character: HCE. However, every now and then throughout the book we will hear echoes of the prehistoric Finnegan. He and HCE are the two aspects of the dream: the traditional/biological and the personal/historical.

Joyce tells us that his text has many meanings: "We seem to us (the real Us!) to be reading our Amenti in the sixth sealed chapter of the going forth by black." [62.26–27] Reading this book we seem to be reading the story of our own death and resurrection, the mystery of our own lives. And Joyce constantly tries to help us read his text, to help us dig into the *Wake* as archeologists dig into the middens of history. So our archeological expedition has been digging back into the past, sinking a shaft into those aspects of the dream which stem from old Finn's time long ago.

In the first chapter, as we have seen, we had a description of Finnegan and his fall. Now, in the second chapter, we begin to learn more about HCE and his sin:

> They tell the story (an amalgam as absorbing as calzium chloereyedes and hydrophobe sponges could make it) how one hapygogusty Ides-of-April morning (the anniversary, as it fell out, of his first assumption of his mirthday suit and rights in appurtenance to the confusioning of human races) ages and ages after the alleged misdemeanour when the tried friend of all creation, tigerwood roadstaff to his stay, was billowing across the wide expanse of our greatest park in his caoutchouc kepi and great belt and hideinsacks and his blaufunx fustian and ironsides jackboots and Bhagafat gaiters and his rubberised inverness, he met a cad with a pipe. (35.1–11)

So, as the story goes, HCE was walking in Phoenix Park, when a cad (the youngest son—the *cadet*) came up to him, said his watch had stopped, and asked, "What time is it?" It seems that the old fellow, instead of answering, launched into an interminable, nervous defense of his conduct. He said, "I didn't do it. No, I swear I didn't," and so forth and so on. When the cad got that for an answer, he went off scratching his head:

> ...as a metter of corse (one could hound him out had one hart to for the monticules of scalp and dandruff droppings blaze his trail)... (37.10–12)

So, leaving a trail of dandruff behind him, the cad goes home and tells his wife. She then goes to confession and tells the priest that something has happened. The priest then goes to the races, where he was overheard:

> ...to pianissime a slightly varied version of Crookedribs confidentials, (what Mère Aloyse said but for Jesuphine's sake!) hands between hahands, in fealty sworn (my bravor best! my fraur!) and, to the strains of *The Secret of Her Birth*, hushly pierce the rubiend aurellum of one Philly Thurnston, a layteacher of rural science and orthophonethics of a nearstout figure and about the middle of his forties during a priestly flutter for safe and sane bets... (38.30–39.1)

The disreputable characters who overhear the priest spread the story around everywhere, of course, until it is all over town and finally appears as a scurrilous ballad written by Hosty, a street singer. The first verse goes:

> Have you heard of one Humpty Dumpty
> How he fell with a roll and a rumble
> And curled up like Lord Olofa Crumple
> By the butt of the Magazine Wall... (45.1–4)

The verses goes on and on, relating in detail the many crimes and misdemeanors of the hero. One refrain describes his children and his wife's problems with a husband like that:

> 'Tis sore pity for his innocent poor children
> But look out for his missus legitimate!
> When that frew gets a grip of old Earwicker
> Won't there be earwigs on the green? (47.13–18)

And it's with this long song that the second chapter ends.

The third chapter describes his trial and incarceration. Here the central question is: What *was* his sin? What happened to him in the park? It seems he made some kind of sexual mistake and was caught at it, or seems to have been caught at it. Anyway, rumors have been going around of a sexual scandal, in every form that such a scandal can take. Now, in the twenties, there was one such scandal that was very amusing: the Daddy Browning affair. It seems an old geezer named Daddy Browning was infatuated with a young skirt, a girl named Peaches, and a goose was somehow involved. So, to describe one aspect of the hero's sin, Joyce tells the story of Daddy and Peaches as an American movie of the period.

> ... *Cherchons la flamme!* Fammfamm! Fammfamm!
>
> Come on, ordinary man with that large big nonobli head, and that blanko berbecked fischial ekksprezzion Machinsky Scapolpolos, Duzinascu or other. Your machelar's mutton leg's getting musclebound from being too pulled. Noah Beery weighed stone thousand one when Hazel was a hen. Now her fat's falling fast. Therefore, chatbags, why not yours? There are 29 sweet reasons why blossomtime's the best. Elders fall for green almonds when they're raised on bruised stone root ginger though it winters on their heads as if auctumned round their waistbands. If you'd had pains in your hairs you wouldn't

look so orgibald. You'd have Colley Macaires on your lump of lead. Now listen, Mr Leer! And stow that sweatyfunnyadams Simper! Take an old geeser who calls on his skirt. Note his sleek hair, so elegant, *tableau vivant.* He vows her to be his own honeylamb, swears they will be papa pals, by Sam, and share good times way down west in a guaranteed happy lovenest when May moon she shines and they twit twinkle all the night, combing the comet's tail up right and shooting popguns at the stars. Creampuffs all to dime! Every nice, missymackenzies! For dear old grumpapar, he's gone on the razzledar, through gazing and crazing and blazing at the stars. Compree! She wants her wardrobe to hear from above by return with cash so as she can buy her Peter Robinson trousseau and cut a dash with Arty, Bert or possibly Charley Chance (who knows?) so tolloll Mr Hunker you're too dada for me to dance (so off she goes!) and that's how half the gels in town has got their bottom drars while grumpapar he's trying to hitch his braces on to his trars. But old grum he's not so clean dippy between sweet you and yum (not on your life, boy! not in those trousers! not by a large jugful!) for someplace on the sly, where Furphy he isn't by, old grum has his gel number two (bravevow, our Grum!) and he would like to canoodle her too some part of the time for he is downright fond of his number one but O he's fair mashed on peaches number two so that if he could only canoodle the two, chivee chivoo, all three would feel genuinely happy, it's as simple as A. B. C., the two mixers, we mean, with their cherrybum chappy (for he is simply shamming dippy) if they were all afloat in a dreamlifeboat, hugging two by two in his zoo-doo-you-doo, a tofftoff for thee, missymissy for me and howcameyou-e'enso for Farber, in his tippy, upindown dippy, tiptoptippy canoodle, can you? Finny. (64.28–65.33)

After the story of HCE has appeared in various forms, we move into the problem of the fighting brothers, the two contending sons. In the fourth chapter, Joyce makes this very important statement about the mysterious nature of their relationship:

The hilariohoot of Pegger's Windup cumjustled as neatly with the tristitone of the Wet Pinter's a were they *isce et ille* equals of opposites, evolved by a onesame power of nature or of spirit, *iste,* as the sole condition and means of its himundher manifestion and polarised for reunion by the symphysis of their antipathies. (92.6–11)

The one nature of their antipathies is what holds them together in battle. Much later, well into the book, there is a moment when the atom explodes and they are annihilated. This novel, however, was published and written long before the atom bomb did explode.

> [The abnihilisation of the etym by the grisning of the grosning of the grinder of the grunder of the first lord of Hurtreford expolodoto-nates through Parsuralia with an ivanmorinthorrorumble fragorom-boassity amidwhiches general uttermosts confussion are perceivable moletons skaping with muliculies while coventry plumpkins fairly-gosmotherthemselves in the Landaunelegants of Pinkadindy....]
> (353.22–28)

Immediately after annihilation, however, these two antipathetic entities appear again, still fighting, but the one who had brown eyes now has the blue eyes, and the one who had blue eyes now has the brown. They have changed in little details, but the same old thing goes on forever. These two fighting males are aspects of one being, in the same way that male and female are.

Various forms of such dual relationship appear throughout the book, but as we've noted, the archetypal duad is HCE and ALP, father and mother, Father Ocean and his river goddess, Viṣṇu and his all-embracing consort, the dreamer and his dream. [Here again, we remember that] Ramakrishna said at one time, "Brahmā (the Creator) is *brahman* (the infinite) in its quiescent state, and Māyā is *brahman* in movement." He is the still state, and she is *māyā,* the active movement that brings about all of our involvement in the delusions in the world, and both are aspects of the same being.

The first four chapters, then, have been concerned with HCE, the father-hero. The following four introduce the mother-heroine ALP, their contending sons and little daughter, as well as the other characters in this dream drama.

Chapter five opens with a prayer addressed to the one whose fascination holds us to the world, to *māyā,* the veil of illusion.

> In the name of Annah the Allmaziful, the Everliving, the Bringer of Plurabilities, haloed be her eve, her singtime sung, her rill be run, unhemmed as it is uneven!

Her untitled mamafesta memorialising the Mosthighest has gone by many names at disjointed times. (104.1–5)

Then there is a three-page-long list of various names that have been given to ALP's manifesto (*mamafesta*) (104–107), a letter she wrote memorializing the old man that was scratched up in a rubbish heap by a wonderful little hen named Belinda. The rest of chapter five is a lengthy exegesis by a pedantic scholar-professor who guides us through an elaborate interpretation of this mangled document dug up from a dung heap. This letter, it seems, will help us understand what's going on, but at every point in the text where we are about to find out some important answer, it turns out that there is a tea stain or a hole from the hen's beak or whatever. It's like the experience you have doing philological work. You get a manuscript and begin asking questions: Where did this come from? Who wrote it anyhow? And just when the text is about to tell you that it was written by...there is a gap. But as I once noted:

> Meticulous study of this manuscript will enable us to reconstruct a picture of what must have been the setting and cast of grand primeval drama. But this is by no means a simple three-dimensional task. The original letter proliferates into a banyan of footnotes, scholarly comments, explanations by a presumed original author, psychological analyses, Marxian commentary, and palimpsest research, until at last we have under our eye, not a scrap of letter, but a magnificent ferment of personages, places, and ideas, which Joyce calls the "Tiberiast duplex." (123.30–31) [90]

This letter we are trying to read is *Finnegans Wake,* of course. Here Joyce offers us some advice on how to read a difficult text:

> Now, patience; and remember patience is the great thing, and above all else we must avoid anything like being or becoming out of patience. A good plan used by worried business folk who may not have had many momentums to master Kung's doctrine of the meang or the propriety codestruces of Carprimustimus is just to think of all the sinking fund of patience possessed in their conjoint names by both brothers Bruce with whom are incorporated their Scotch spider and Elberfeld's Calculating Horses. If after years upon years of delving in ditches dark one tubthumper more than others, Kinihoun or Kahanan, giardener or mere measonmanonger, has got up for the

darnall same purpose of reassuring us with all the barbar of the Carrageehouse that our great ascendant was properly speaking three syllables less than his own surname (yes, yes, less), that the ear of Fionn Earwicker aforetime was the trademark of a broadcaster with wicker local jargon for an ace's patent (Hear! Calls! Everywhair!) then as to this radiooscillating epiepistle to which, cotton, silk or samite, kohol, gall or brickdust, we must ceaselessly return, whereabouts exactly at present in Siam, Hell or Tophet under that glorisol which plays touraloup with us in this Aludin's Cove of our cagacity is that bright soandsuch to slip us the dinkum oil?

Naysayers we know. . . .

We readers trying to get at this great dark secret know there are negative people saying, "Oh, it's nothing but this, it's nothing but that." We are now going to go past all these naysayers and really find the mystery in this text.

To conclude purely negatively from the positive absence of political odia and monetary requests that its page cannot ever have been a penproduct of a man or woman of that period or those parts is only one more unlookedfor conclusion leaped at, being tantamount to inferring from the nonpresence of inverted commas (sometimes called quotation marks) on any page that its author was always constitutionally incapable of misappropriating the spoken words of others. (108.8–36)

The letter this scholar is trying to elucidate is the one that you wrote to yourself in childhood, the one that the psychiatrist is now pulling out of you in therapy.

Luckily there is another cant to the questy. Has any fellow, of the dime a dozen type, it might with some profit some dull evening quietly be hinted—has any usual sort of ornery josser, flatchested fortyish, faintly flatulent and given to ratiocination by syncopation in the elucidation of complications, of his greatest Fung Yang dynasdescendanced, only another the son of, in fact, ever looked sufficiently longly at a quite everydaylooking stamped addressed envelope? Admittedly it is an outer husk: its face, in all its featureful perfection of imperfection, is its fortune: it exhibits only the civil or military clothing of whatever passionpallid nudity or plaguepurple nakedness may happen to tuck itself under its flap. Yet to concentrate solely on the literal sense or even the psychological contents of any document to the sore neglect of the enveloping facts themselves circumstantiating it is just as hurtful to sound sense (and let it be added to the truest taste) as were some fellow in the act of perhaps getting an intro from another fellow turning out to be a friend in need of his, say, to a lady of the latter's acquaintance, engaged in performing the elaborative antecistral ceremony of upstheres, straightaway to run off and vision her plump and plain in her natural altogether, preferring to close his blinkhard's eyes to the ethiquethical fact that she was, after all, wearing for the space of the time being some definite articles of evolutionary clothing, inharmonious creations, a captious critic might describe them as, or not strictly necessary or a trifle irritating here and there, but for all that suddenly full of local colour and personal perfume and suggestive, too, of so very much more and capable of being stretched, filled out, if need or wish were, of having their surprisingly like coincidental parts separated don't they now, for better survey by the deft hand of an expert, don't you know? Who in his heart doubts either that the facts of feminine clothiering are there all the time or that the feminine fiction, stranger than the facts, is there also at the same time, only a little to the rere? Or that one may be separated from the other? Or that both may then be contemplated simultaneously? Or that each may be taken up, and considered in turn apart from the other? (109.1–36)

The scholar describes circumstantiating facts surrounding the discovery of this letter. This hen that found it may be She who will lead us to the explication of this mystery dug up from the deep.

Lead, kindly fowl! They always did: ask the ages. What bird has done yesterday man may do next year, be it fly, be it moult, be it hatch, be it agreement in the nest. For her socioscientific sense is sound as a bell, sir, her volucrine automutativeness right on normalcy: she knows, she just feels she was kind of born to lay and love eggs (trust her to propagate the species and hoosh her fluffballs safe through din and danger!); lastly but mostly, in her genesic field it is all game and no gammon; she is ladylike in everything she does and plays the gentleman's part every time. Let us auspice it! Yes, before all this has time to end the golden age must return with its vengeance. Man will become dirigible, Ague will be rejuvenated, woman with her ridiculous white burden will reach by one step sublime incubation, the manewanting human lioness with her dishorned discipular manram will lie down together publicly flank upon fleece. No, assuredly, they are not justified, those gloompourers who grouse that letters have never been quite their old selves again since that weird weekday in bleak Janiveer (yet how palmy date in a waste's oasis!) when to the shock of both, Biddy Doran looked at literature. (112.9–27)

There are many ways this letter can be interpreted, just as there are many levels on which you can read the *Wake*. Here, in a passage about the event in the park, is the psychological aspect.

And, speaking anent Tiberias and other incestuish salacities among gerontophils, a word of warning about the tenderloined passion hinted at. Some softnosed peruser might mayhem take it up erogenously as the usual case of spoons, *prostituta in herba* plus dinky pinks deliberatively summersaulting off her bisexycle, at the main entrance of curate's perpetual soutane suit with her one to see and awoh! who picks her up as gingerly as any balmbearer would to feel whereupon the virgin was most hurt and nicely asking: whyre have you been so grace a mauling and where were you chaste me child? Be who, farther potential? and so wider but we grisly old Sykos who have done our unsmiling bit on 'alices, when they were yung and easily freudened, in the penumbra of the procuring room and what oracular comepression we have had apply to them! could (did we care to sell our feebought silence *in camera*) tell our very moistnostrilled one that *father* in such virgated contexts is not always that undemonstrative relative (often held up to our contumacy) who settles our hashbill for us and what an innocent allabroad's adverb such as Michaelly looks like can be suggestive of under the pudendascope and, finally, what a neurasthene nympholept, endocrine-pineal typus, of inverted parentage with a prepossessing drauma present in her past and a priapic urge for congress with agnates before cognates fundamentally is feeling for under her lubricitous meiosis when she refers with liking to some feeler she fancie's face. And Mm. We could. Yet what need to say? 'Tis as human a little story as paper could well carry... (115.11–36)

So that's the psychological interpretation—we ... *were yung and easily freudened*...—and then, of course, there's the political aspect:

...for we also know, what we have perused from the pages of *I Was a Gemral,* that Showting up of Bulsklivism by 'Schottenboum', that Father Michael about this red time of the white terror equals the old regime and Margaret is the social revolution while cakes mean the party funds and dear thank you signifies national gratitude. (116.5–10)

So on it goes, and in the course of the chapter we learn of many levels on which ALP's letter (and the *Wake*) can be read.

In the sixth chapter [the professor examines his class on the problem of this Tiberiast duplex. This chapter supplies a handy list of the chief characters and themes of *Finnegans Wake.*][91] At one point (148.33–149.10), pompous Professor Jones (a Shaun type) is asked this question: If a poor drunken exile with his aching eyes (Joyce himself, as Shem) were piteously to beg the professor for the wherewithal with which to save his soul, would the respectable gentleman care to today?

The answer is simply, "No!" The professor, however, feels it necessary to spin out an elaborate justification of his refusal. The result is a very scholarly discussion, but the argument is obscured by the professor's parenthetical remarks. A man who has taken all learning for his province, the professor seizes the occasion to baffle his classroom with demonstrations of his scope. As a result, his audience is everywhere going to sleep on him, and he is frequently compelled to scold and insult them back to at least the appearance of alert interest[92]

> As my explanations here are probably above your understandings, lattlebrattons, though as augmentatively umcomparisoned as Cadwan, Cadwallon and Cadwalloner, I shall revert to a more expletive method which I frequently use when I have to sermo with muddle-crass pupils. Imagine for my purpose that you are a squad of urchins, snifflynosed, goslingnecked, clothyheaded, tangled in your lacings, tingled in your pants, etsitaraw etcicero. And you, Bruno Nowlan, take your tongue out of your inkpot! As none of you knows javanese I will give all my easyfree translation of the old fabulist's parable. Allaboy Minor, take your head out of your satchel! *Audi,* Joe Peters! *Exaudi,* facts!

The fable he is going to translate freely from the Javanese is:

> The Mookse and The Gripes.
>
> Gentes and laitymen, fullstoppers and semicolonials, hybreds and lubberds!...

This piece, one of the sections from the *Wake* that was published early, is one of the gems in the book. Two boys, the Mookse and the Gripes (Shaun and Shem), are playing.

> Eins within a space and a wearywide space it wast ere wohned a Mookse. The onesomeness wast alltolonely, archunsitslike, broady oval, and a Mookse he would a walking go (My hood! cries Antony Romeo), so one grandsumer evening, after a great morning and his good supper of gammon and spittish, having flabelled his eyes, pilleoled his nostrils, vacticanated his ears and palliumed his throats, he put on his impermeable, seized his impugnable, harped on his crown and stepped out of his immobile *De Rure Albo* (socolled becauld it was chalkfull of masterplasters and had borgeously letout gardens strown with cascadas, pintacostecas, horthoducts and currycombs) and set off from Ludstown *a spasso* to see how badness was badness in the weirdest of all pensible ways.
>
> As he set off with his father's sword, his *lancia spezzata,* he was girded on, and with that between his legs and his tarkeels, our once in only Bragspear, he clanked, to my clinking, from veetoes to threetop, every inch of an immortal....

In this fable, the Mookse is the hero type; particularly, a cross between Pope Adrian IV, the only English-born Pope, and Henry II, who was advised by Adrian to go into Ireland and straighten things out there.

> He had not walked over a pentiadpair of parsecs from his azylium when at the turning of the Shinshone Lanteran near Saint Bowery's-without-his-Walls he came (secunding to the one one oneth of the propecies, *Amnis Limina Permanent*) upon the most unconsciously boggylooking stream he ever locked his eyes with. Out of the colliens it took a rise by daubing itself Ninon. It looked little and it smelt of brown and it thought in narrows and it talked showshallow. And as it rinn it dribbled like any lively purliteasy: *My, my, my! Me and me! Little down dream don't I love thee!*
>
> And, I declare, what was there on the yonder bank of the stream that would be a river, parched on a limb of the olum, bolt downright,

but the Gripes? And no doubt he was fit to be dried for why had he not been having the juice of his times?

His pips had been neatly all drowned on him; his polps were charging odours every older minute; he was quickly for getting the dresser's desdaign on the flyleaf of his frons; and he was quietly for giving the bailiff's distrain on to the bulkside of his *cul de Pompe.* In all his specious heavings, as be lived by Optimus Maximus, the Mookse had never seen his Dubville brooder-on-low so nigh to a pickle.

Adrian (that was the Mookse now's assumptinome) stuccstill phiz-à-phiz to the Gripes in an accessit of aurignacian. But Allmookse must to Moodend much as Allrouts, austereways or wastersways, in roaming run through Room. Hic sor a stone, singularly illud, and on hoc stone Seter satt huc sate which it filled quite poposterously and by acclammitation to its fullest justotoryum and whereopum with his unfallable encyclicling upom his alloilable, diupetriark of the wouest, and the athemystsprinkled pederect he always walked with, *Deusdedit,* cheek by jowel with his frisherman's blague, *Bellua Triumphanes,* his everyway addedto wallat's collectium, for yea longer he lieved yea broader he betaught of it, the fetter, the summe and the haul it cost, he looked the first and last micahlike laicness of Quartus the Fifth and Quintus the Sixth and Sixtus the Seventh giving allnight sitting to Lio the Faultyfindth.

—Good appetite us, sir Mookse! How do you do it? cheeped the Gripes in a wherry whiggy maudelenian woice and the jackasses all within bawl laughed and brayed for his intentions for they knew their sly toad lowry now. I am rarumominum blessed to see you, my dear mouster. Will you not perhopes tell me everything if you are pleased, sanity? All about aulne and lithial and allsall allinall about awn and liseias? Ney?

Think of it! O miserendissimest retempter! A Gripes!

—Rats! bullowed the Mookse most telesphorously, the concionator, and the sissymusses and the zozzymusses in their robenhauses quailed to hear his tardeynois at all for you cannot wake a silken nouse out of a hoarse oar. Blast yourself and your anathomy infairioriboos! No, hang you for an animal rurale! I am superbly in my supremest poncif! Abase you, baldyqueens! Gather behind me, satraps! Rots!

—I am till infinity obliged with you, bowed the Gripes, his
whine having gone to his palpruy head. I am still always having a
wish on all my extremeties. By the watch, what is the time, pace?

Figure it! The pining peever! To a Mookse! (152.4–154.17)

They are going to get into an extremely intricate and beclouded theological argument.[93] The Mookse is essentially the Roman Catholic Church,
full of authority and dogma, while the Gripes is something of a Gnostic and
rather unclear in his definitions. The argument escalates to this:

—Efter thousand yaws, O Gripes con my sheepskins, yow will be
belined to the world, enscayed Mookse the pius.

—Ofter thousand yores, amsered Gripes the gregary, be the goat
of MacHammud's, yours may be still, O Mookse, more botheared.

—Us shall be chosen as the first of the last by the electress
of Vale Hollow, obselved the Mookse nobily, for par the unicum of
Elelijiacks, Us am in Our stabulary and that is what Ruby and Roby
fall for, blissim.

The Pills, the Nasal Wash (Yardly's), the Army Man Cut, as
british as bondstrict and as straightcut as when that broken arched
traveller from Nuzuland...

—Wee, cumfused the Gripes limply, shall not even be the last
of the first, wee hope, when oust are visitated by the Veiled Horror.
And, he added: Mee are relying entirely, see the fortethurd of
Elissabed, on the weightiness of mear's breath. Puffut!

Unsightbared embouscher, relentless foe to social and business
success! (Hourihaleine) It might have been a happy evening but...

And they viterberated each other, *canis et coluber* with the
wildest ever wielded since Tarriestinus lashed Pissasphaltium.

—Unuchorn!

—Ungulant!

—Uvuloid!

—Uskybeak!

And bullfolly answered volleyball....

Their little sister, Nuvoletta, the Little Cloud Girl, has been watching
their battle.

Nuvoletta in her lightdress, spunn of sisteen shimmers, was looking
down on them, leaning over the bannistars and listening all she

childishly could. How she was brightened when Shouldrups in his glaubering hochskied his welkinstuck and how she was overclused when Kneesknobs on his zwivvel was makeacting such a paulse of himshelp! She was alone. All her nubied companions were asleeping with the squirrels. Their mivver, Mrs. Moonan, was off in the Fuerst quarter scrubbing the backsteps of Number 28. Fuvver, that Skand, he was up in Norwood's sokaparlour, eating oceans of Voking's Blemish. Nuvoletta listened as she reflected herself, though the heavenly one with his constellatria and his emanations stood between, . . .

Like all little sisters, she wants to get in on her brothers' game. You possibly know about this kind of thing.

and she tried all she tried to make the Mookse look up at her (but he was fore too adiaptotously farseeing) and to make the Gripes hear how coy she could be (though he was much too schystimatically auricular about *his ens* to heed her) but it was all mild's vapour moist. Not even her feignt reflection, Nuvoluccia, could they toke their gnoses off for their minds with intrepifide fate and bungless curiasity, were conclaved with Heliogobbleus and Commodus and Enobarbarus and whatever the coordinal dickens they did as their damprauch of papyrs and buchstubs said. As if that was their spiration! As if theirs could duiparate her queendim! As if she would be third perty to search on search proceedings! She tried all the winsome wonsome ways her four winds had taught her. . . .

Now she tries to attract their attention, to make them see what a pretty little thing she is.

She tossed her sfumastelliacinous hair like *la princesse de la Petite Bretagne* and she rounded her mignons arms like Mrs. Cornwallis-West and she smiled over herself like the beauty of the image of the pose of the daughter of the queen of the Emperour of Irelande and she sighed after herself as were she born to bride with Tristis Tristior Tristissimus. But, sweet madonine, she might fair as well have carried her daisy's worth to Florida. For the Mookse, a dogmad Accanite, were not amoosed and the Gripes, a dubliboused Catalick, wis pinefully obliviscent. . . .

The brothers are so involved in their argument that they have no eyes for her.

—I see, she sighed. There are menner. (156.19–158.5)

"They are stupid," she sighs. They represent all the conflicts of history, and she is a cloud in the sky that is overlooking it all. But it is her own sorrow that brings all this about: she rains down and starts the whole riverrun process.

> Oh, how it was duusk! From Vallee Maraia to Grasyaplaina, dormimust echo! Ah dew! Ah dew! It was so duusk that the tears of night began to fall, first by ones and twos, then by threes and fours, at last by fives and sixes of sevens, for the tired ones were wecking, as we weep now with them. *O! O! O! Par la pluie!* . . .
>
> . . . And there were left now an only elmtree and but a stone. Polled with pietrous, Sierre but saule. O! Yes! and Nuvoletta, a lass.
>
> Then Nuvoletta reflected for the last time in her little long life and she made up all her myriads of drifting minds in one. She cancelled all her engauzements. She climbed over the bannistars; she gave a childy cloudy cry: *Nuée! Nuée!* A lightdress fluttered. She was gone. And into the river that had been a stream (for a thousand of tears had gone eon her and come on her and she was stout and struck on dancing and her muddied name was Missisliffi) there fell a tear, a singult tear, the loveliest of all tears (I mean for those crylove fables fans who are 'keen' on the prettypretty commonface sort of thing you meet by hopeharrods) for it was a leaptear. But the river tripped on her by and by, lapping as though her heart was brook: *Why, why, why! Weh, O weh! I'se so silly to be flowing but I no canna stay!*
>
> No applause, please! Bast! The romescot nattleshaker will go round your circulation in *diu dursus.*
>
> Allaboy, Major, I'll take your reactions in another place after themes. Nolan Browne, you may now leave the classroom. Joe Peters, Fox. (158.19–24, 159.3–23)

In chapter seven, Shaun continues his violent attack on his brother Shem. Here Joyce satirizes himself as the writer-son, just as he did not spare Stephen Dedalus from light satire. In this section, Joyce, while describing Shem, is also describing himself.

> Shem's bodily getup, it seems, included an adze of a skull, an eight of a larkseye, the whoel of a nose, one numb arm up a sleeve, fortytwo hairs off his uncrown, eighteen to his mock lip, a trio of barbels from his megageg chin (sowman's son), the wrong shoulder higher than the right, all ears, an artificial tongue with a natural curl, not a foot

to stand on, a handful of thumbs, a blind stomach, a deaf heart, a loose liver, two fifths of two buttocks, one gleetsteen avoirdupoider for him, a manroot of all evil, a salmonkelt's thinskin, eelsblood in his cold toes, a bladder tristended, so much so that young Master Shemmy on his very first debouch at the very dawn of proto-history seeing himself such and such, when playing with thistlewords in their garden nursery, Griefotrofio, at Phig Streat III, Shuvlin, Old Hoeland, (would we go back there now for sounds, pillings and sense? would we now for annas and annas? would we for fullscore eight and a liretta? for twelve blocks one bob? for four testers one groat? not for a dinar! not for jo!) dictited to of all his little brothron and sweestureens the first riddle of the universe: asking, when is a man not a man? Telling them take their time, yungfries, and wait till the tide stops (for from the first his day was a fortnight) and offering the prize of a bittersweet crab, a little present from the past, for their copper age was yet unminted, to the winner. (169.11–170.9)

That is a description of Joyce himself: whenever there is a battle cry, he retreats into his study (called the Haunted Inkbottle), locks the door, and peers through the keyhole. Once, when looking out through the keyhole to see what is going on, he has the shocking experience of looking right into the barrel of a revolver, with, as Joyce says, "his cheeks and trousers chang-ing colour every time a gat croaked" (177.6–7). Meanwhile, his brother, the young hero, is out winning all the great prizes. And what is the writer doing inside the inkbottle house? Looking for the words of wisdom and finding them, he is writing "on the only foolscap available, his own body" (185.35–36). He uses his body as paper and his excrement as ink in a sort of effervescent fermentation of writing—that's the way modern art works— which is the book that Joyce is writing here.

The lectures of Shaun lead us to chapter eight, the Anna Livia Plurabelle chapter, which ends Book I. Joyce made a recording of the end of this chapter. Two old washerwomen, one on either side of a stream, are gossiping while doing the laundry. Here is how this "river chapter" begins.

O
tell me all about
Anna Livia! I want to hear all
about Anna Livia. Well, you know Anna Livia? Yes, of course, we all

know Anna Livia. Tell me all. Tell me now. You'll die when you hear. Well, you know, when the old cheb went futt and did what you know. Yes, I know, go on. Wash quit and don't be dabbling. Tuck up your sleeves and loosen your talktapes. And don't butt me—hike!—when you bend. Or whatever it was they threed to make out he thried to two in the Fiendish park. He's an awful old reppe. Look at the shirt of him! Look at the dirt of it! He has all my water black on me. And it steeping and stuping since this time last wik. How many goes is it I wonder I washed it? I know by heart the places he likes to saale, duddurty devil! Scorching my hand and starving my famine to make his private linen public. Wallop it well with your battle and clean it. My wrists are wrusty rubbing the mouldaw stains. And the dneepers of wet and the gangres of sin in it! What was it he did a tail at all on Animal Sendai? And how long was he under loch and neagh? It was put in the newses what he did, nicies and priers, the King fierceas Humphrey, with illysus distilling, exploits and all. But toms will till, I know he well. Temp untamed will hist for no man. As you spring so shall you neap. (196.1–23)

And as they talk on, the stream gets wider and wider. And on and on and on it goes, and these two Washers at the Ford become the banshees, washing linen and predicting a death, a calamity. On and on and on, and as we come now toward the end, it is getting dark, and they are losing touch with each other.

Well, you know or don't you kennet or haven't I told you that every telling has a taling and that's the he and the she of it. Look, look, the dusk is growing! My branches lofty are taking root. And my cold cher's gone ashley. Fieluhr! Filou! What age is at? It saon is late. 'Tis endless now senne eye or erewone last saw Waterhouse's clogh. They took it asunder, I hurd thum sigh. When will they reassemble it? O, my back, my back, my bach! I'd want to go to Aches-les-Pains. Pingpong! There's the Belle for Sexaloitez! And Concepta de Send-us-pray! Pang! Wring out the clothes! Wring in the dew! Godavari, vert the showers! And grant thaya grace! Aman. Will we spread them here now? Ay, we will. Flip! Spread on your bank and I'll spread mine on mine. Flep! It's what I'm doing. Spread! It's churning chill. Der went is rising. I'll lay a few stones on the hostel sheets. A man and his bride embraced between them. Else I'd have sprinkled and

folded them only. And I'll tie my butcher's apron here. It's suety yet.
The strollers will pass it by. Six shifts, ten kerchiefs, nine to hold to
the fire and this for the code, the convent napkins, twelve, one baby's
shawl. Good mother Jossiph knows, she said. Whose head? Mutter
snores? Deataceas! Wharnow are alle her childer, say? In kingdome
gone or power to come or gloria be to them farther? Allalivial, al-
laluvial! Some here, more no more, more again lost alla stranger. I've
heard tell that same brooch of the Shannons were married into a
family in Spain. And all the Dunders de Dunnes in Markland's
Vineland beyond Brendan's herring pool takes number nine in
yangsee's hats. And one of Biddy's beads went bobbing till she
rounded up last histereve with a marigold and a cobbler's candle in
a side strain of a main drain of a manzinahurries off Bachelor's Walk.
But all that's left to the last of the Meaghers in the loup of the years
prefixed and between is one kneebuckle and two hooks in the front.
Do you tell me that now? I do in troth. Orara por Orbe and poor
Las Animas! Ussa, Ulla, we're umbas all. Mezha, didn't you hear it a
deluge of times, ufer and ufer, respund to spond? You deed, you
deed! I need, I need! It's that irrawaddyng I've stoke in my aars. It all
but husheth the lethest zswound. Oronoko! What's yorr trouble? Is
that the great Finnleader himself in his joakimono on his statue riding the high horse there forehengist? Father of Otters, it is himself!
Yonne there! Isset that? On Fallareen Common? You're thinking of
Astley's Amphitheayter where the bobby restrained you making sug-
arstuck pouts to the ghostwhite horse of the Peppers. Throw the cob-
webs from your eyes, woman, and spread your washing proper! It's
well I know your sort of slop. Flap! Ireland sober is Ireland stiff. Lord
help you, Maria, full of grease, the load is with me! Your prayers. I
sonht so! Madammangut! Were you lifting your elbow, tell us, glazy
cheeks, in Conway's Carrigacurra canteen? Was I what, hobbledy-
hips? Flop! Your rere gait's creakorheuman bitts your butts disagrees.
Amn't I up since the damp dawn, marthared mary allacook, with
Corrigan's pulse and varicoarse veins, my pramaxle smashed, Alice
Jane in decline and my oneeyed mongrel twice run over, soaking and
bleaching boiler rags, and sweating cold, a widow like me, for to deck
my tennis champion son, the laundryman with the lavandier flan-
nels? You won your limpopo limp from the husky hussars when
Collars and Cuffs was heir to the town and your slur gave the stink

to Carlow. Holy Scamander, I sar it again! Near the golden falls. Icis on us! Seints of light! Zezere! Subdue your noise, you hamble creature! What is it but a blackburry growth or the dwyergray ass them four old codgers owns. Are you meanam Tarpey and Lyons and Gregory? I meyne now, thank all, the four of them, and the roar of them, that draves that stray in the mist and old Johnny MacDougal along with them. Is that the Poolbeg flasher beyant, pharphar, or a fireboat coasting nyar the Kishtna or a glow I behold within a hedge or my Garry come back from the Indes? Wait till the honeying of the lune, love! Die eve, little eve, die! We see that wonder in your eye. We'll meet again, we'll part once more. The spot I'll seek if the hour you'll find. My chart shines high where the blue milk's upset. Forgivemequick, I'm going! Bubye! And you, pluck your watch, forgetmenot. Your evenlode. So save to jurna's end! My sights are swimming thicker on me by the shadows to this place. I sow home slowly now by own way, moyvalley way. Towy I too, rathmine.

Ah, but she was the queer old skeowsha anyhow, Anna Livia, trinkettoes! And sure he was the quare old buntz too, Dear Dirty Dumpling, foostherfather of fingalls and dottergills. Gammer and gaffer we're all their gangsters. Hadn't he seven dams to wive him? And every dam had her seven crutches. And every crutch had its seven hues. And each hue had a differing cry. Sudds for me and supper for you and the doctor's bill for Joe John. Befor! Bifur! He married his markets, cheap by foul, I know, like any Etrurian Catholic Heathen, in their pinky limony creamy birnies and their turkiss indienne mauves. But at milkidmass who was the spouse? Then all that was was fair. Tys Elvenland! Teems of times and happy returns. The seim anew. Ordovico or viricordo. Anna was, Livia is, Plurabelle's to be. Northmen's thing made southfolk's place but howmulty plurators made eachone in person? Latin me that, my trinity scholard, out of eure sanscreed into oure eryan! *Hircus Civis Eblanensis!* He had buckgoat paps on him, soft ones for orphans. Ho, Lord! Twins of his bosom. Lord save us! And ho! Hey? What all men. Hot? His tittering daughters of. Whawk?

Can't hear with the waters of. The chittering waters of. Flittering bats, fieldmice bawk talk. Ho! Are you not gone ahome? What Thom Malone? Can't hear with bawk of bats, all thim liffeying waters of. Ho, talk save us! My foos won't moos. I feel as old as yonder elm. A tale told of Shaun or Shem? All Livia's daughter-sons. Dark hawks hear us. Night! Night! My ho head halls. I feel as heavy as yonder stone. Tell me of John or Shaun? Who were Shem and Shaun the living sons or daughters of? Night now! Tell me, tell me, tell me, elm! Night, night! Telmetale of stem or stone. Beside the rivering waters of, hitherandthithering waters of. Night! (213.11–216.5)

Book I, which has taken us into the past, ends here. We were archaeologists digging in the ground, finding signs of old times. Moving on to Book II, we will be in the here and now, actually in the tavern of HCE.

## Book II

In the beginning of Book II, the three children are playing in the garden, and there's a whole chapter here having to do with games of children. [There is a good little boy, Chuff, a really angelic child, and another one, a bad little boy, Glugg, and the devil himself was in him:]

Chuffy was a nangel then and his soard fleshed light like likening. Fools top! Singty, sangty, meekly loose, defendy nous from prowlabouts. Make a sign on the curst. Emen.

But the duvlin sulph was in Glugger, that lost-to-lurning. Punct. He was sbuffing and sputing, tussing like anisine, whipping his eyc-soult and gnatsching his teats over the brividies from exiters and the outher liubbocks of life. (222.22–28)

The lucky boy wins all the kisses from the girls:

The youngly delightsome frilles-in-pleyurs are now showen drawen, if bud one, or, if in florileague, drawens up consociately at the hinder sight of their commoner guardian. (224.22–24)

The other one is [laughed at and rejected by the girls,] thrown out and has a bad time:

Her boy fiend or theirs, if they are so pluriented, cometh up as a tra-padour, sinking how he must fand for himself by gazework what their colors wear as they are all showen drawens up....Apun which his poohoor pricoxity theirs is a little tittertit of hilarity (lad-o'-me-soul! Lad-o'-me-soul, see!) and the wordchary is atvoiced ringsoundinly by their toots ensembled, though not meaning to be clever, but just with a shrug of their hips to go to troy and harff a freak at himself by all that story to the ulstramarines. Otherwised, holding their noises, they insinuate quiet private, Ni, he make peace in his preaches and play with esteem.

Warewolff! Olff! Toboo! (224.23–26, 36; 225.1–8)

Then the mother calls and comes to fetch them. She is described now as Eve, who was born, as you know, from Adam's rib, and so she is called "the cutlet-sized consort." [Joyce gives you all her physical proportions, as he likes to do with his characters, and she turns out to be a sweet, plump little creature.]

> For the producer (Mr John Baptister Vickar) caused a deep abuliousness to descend upon the Father of Truants and, at a side issue, pluterpromptly brought on the scene the cutletsized consort, foundling filly of fortyshilling fostertailor and shipman's shopahoyden, weighing ten pebble ten, scaling five footsy five and spanning thirtyseven inchettes round the good companions, twentynine ditties round the wishful waistress, thirtyseven alsos round the answer to everything, twentythree of the same round each of the quis separabits, fourteen round the beginning of happiness and nicely nine round her shoes for slender. (255.27–36)

[The children, who have been playing in the street, are gathered by their mother and brought into the house, where they do their homework and go to sleep. However, they have been growing up and acquiring dangerous knowledge, mainly knowledge about adults and adult sexuality. The ringleader in the conspiracy of the children is Shem.]

Shem the introvert, rejected of man, is the explorer and discoverer of the forbidden. He is an embodiment of dangerously brooding, in-turned energy. He is the uncoverer of secret springs and, as such, the possessor of terrific, lightning powers. The books he writes are so mortifying that they are spontaneously rejected by the decent; they threaten, they dissolve the protecting boundary lines of good and evil. Provoked to action (and he must be provoked before he will act) he is not restrained by normal human laws, for they have been dissolved within him by the too powerful elixirs of the elemental depths; he may let loose a hot spray of acid; but, on the other hand, he may let loose such a magical balm of forgiveness that the battle-lines themselves become melted in a bacchanal of general love. Such absolute love is as dangerous to the efficient working of society as absolute hate. The possessor of the secrets, therefore, is constrained to hold his fire. Nobody really wants to hear what he has to say: the shepherds of the people denounce him from their pulpits, or else so dilute and misrepresent his teachings as to render them innocuous. Thus Shem is typically in retreat from society; he is the scorned and disinherited one, the Bohemian, or criminal outcast, rejected by Philistine prosperity. Under the title of Shem the Penman he is the seer, the poet, Joyce himself in his character of misunderstood, rejected artist. His characteristic behavior is to take refuge in his own room, where, on the foolscap of his own body, he writes a phosphorescent book in a corrosive language which Shaun cannot understand.

[In the third chapter of the second book, the children come to HCE's pub as a vengeful mob and destroy their father, the Winter King. The mob of grown children shout at HCE, "You thought we would never grow up!" (375.18–19). HCE, crouching in terror, looks with his hump like the guilty Richard the Third:]

> —He shook be ashaped of hempshelves, hiding that shepe in his goat. And for rassembling so bearfellsed the magreedy prince of Roger. Thuthud. Heigh hohse, heigh hohse, our kindom from an orse. Bruni Lanno's woollies on Brani Lonni's hairyparts. And the hunk in his trunk it would be an insalt foul the matter of that cellaring to a pigstrough. Stop his laysense. Ink him! . . . Just press this cold brand against your brow for a mow. Cainfully! The sinus the curse. . . . Glue on to him, Greevy! Bottom anker, Noordeece! And kick kick killykick for the house that juke built! . . . One bully son growing the goff and his twinger read out by the Nazi Priers. You fought as how they'd never woxen up, did you, crucket? (373.13–19,374.32–33,375.3–4,17–19)

[Then the young men and women merge as the lovers Tristan and Isolde, and they celebrate their physical maturing with ecstatic and athletic lovemaking, over the body of their deposed father.]

## Book III

In Book III, as the daylight begins to come through, the dream thins out, and we see the father's hopes for his sons, what he foresees as their future.

In this book, we find [the story of Shaun's maturing.] The matured Shaun, [containing a concealed Shem] takes on the burden of guilt and the powers of creation of the new Daedalus [the new father. Eventually he shows that he has become his father, as the generations succeed each other.]

The character of Shaun (Kevin), the folk-shepherd brother, the political orator, prudent, unctuous, economically successful favorite of the people, careful to preserve them from the causes and effects of immorality, policeman of the planet, conqueror of rebels, bearer of the white man's burden, is developed by Joyce elaborately and broadly. He is the contrapuntal opposite of Shem: the two brothers are the balanced ends of the human dumb-bell. And if it is the typical lot of Shem to be whipped and despoiled, Shaun is typically the whipper and despoiler. When he turns from making empires and preserving the peace of the world to the writing of best-sellers, the favored son does not himself descend to those dangerous, obscene, and forbidden depths from which the other brings forth his mad productions; his works are never in danger of censorship and rejection; they are the censors and rejectors.

Indeed, Shaun is not concerned with spiritual or esthetic matters except in so far as he can exploit them; the life of the flesh and senses is good enough for him. In a diverting passage beginning on page 429, Shaun addresses the little day-girls of St. Brigid's Academy, smiting their tender ears with admonitions of good counsel and very practical advice. "Collide with man, collude with money" (433.32–33) is a typical Shaunian saw. In sum: Shaun is man naively and shrewdly outgoing, where as Shem, his brother, has been touched by the "agenbite" which probes back again to the source. Shaun execrates Shem, maligns him, with the frank but not altogether unfearful disdain of the man of action for the man of thought. Under the title of Shaun the Postman, he delivers to mankind the great message which has been actually discovered and penned by Shem; but Shaun, who judges all things by their envelope, misdelivers the message. Yet he enjoys all the rewards of those who deliver good tidings.

Shem's business is not to create a higher life, but merely to find and utter the Word. Shaun, on the other hand, whose function is to make the Word become flesh, misreads it, fundamentally rejects it, limits himself to a kind of stupid concretism, and, while winning all the skirmishes, loses the eternal city.

Toward the close of the work (specifically, during the third section of Book III), the forms of the son-world dissolve and the everlasting primal form of HCE resurges. The all-father is reunited with his wife in a diamond-wedding anniversary, as if to demonstrate that behind the complexity of their children's lives they still continue to be the motive-givers. Together, they constitute the primordial, androgynous (man-woman) angel, which is Man, the incarnate God.

## *Book IV*

In Book IV, the night is over, and the risen sun, Humpty Dumpty put together again at last, shines on the old landscape, newly arisen from night. This book contains some of the funniest and most beautiful writing in the *Wake*. What seems to me to be one of the most successful short scenes in the book is written like a medieval saint's life from the seventh, eighth, and ninth centuries—the time when Ireland was saintly Ireland, the Isle of Saints, and St. Kevin and St. Patrick and all of the others were in their great day—the period when the little honey beehive huts and the round towers were built.

This is the last chapter now. Dawn has come, and in a little church the stained-glass windows, lit by the rising sun, are showing those pretty scenes of the lives of the saints. One window [a south window, shows the story of Saint Kevin and] Glendalough south of Dublin, where Saint Kevin lived. Kevin was a very saintly person, so saintly that when a girl came to tempt him, he pushed her off the rock and into the water, where she drowned. Then he was troubled with conscience. Here he has a bathtub which can be used also as a boat, or as a holy water or baptismal font. He is going out now on his saintly duty to an island in the middle of the lake, where there is a lake in the middle of the island. [He ends up, in fact, inside seven circles of water.]

> Yad. Procreated on the ultimate ysland of Yreland in the enclyclical Yrish archipelago, come their feast of precreated holy whiteclad angels, whomamong the christener of his, voluntarily poor Kevin, having been graunted the pravilege of a priest's postcreated portable *altare cum balneo,* when espousing the one true cross, invented and exalted, in celibate matrimony at matin chime arose and westfrom went and

came in alb of cloth of gold to our own midmost Glendalough-le-vert by archangelical guidance where amiddle of meeting waters of river Yssia and Essia river on this one of eithers lone navigable lake piously Kevin, lawding the triune trishagion amidships of his conducible altar super bath, rafted centripetally, diaconal servent of orders hibernian, midway across the subject lake surface to its supreem epicentric lake Ysle, whereof its lake is the ventrifugal principality, whereon by prime, powerful in knowledge, Kevin came to where its center is among the circumfluent watercourses of Yshgafiena and Yshgafiuna, an enysled lakelet yslanding a lacustrine yslet, whereupon with beach raft subdiaconal bath *propter* altar, with oil extremely anointed, acoompanied by prayer, holy Kevin bided till the third morn hour but to build a rubric penitential honeybeehivehut in whose enclosure to live in fortitude, acolyte of cardinal virtues, whereof the arenary floor, most holy Kevin excavated as deep as to the depth of a seventh part of one full fathom, which excavated, venerable Kevin, anchorite, taking counsel, proceded towards the lakeside of the ysletshore whereat seven several times he, eastward genuflecting, in entire ubidience at sextnoon collected gregorian water sevenfold and with ambrosian eucharistic joy of heart as many times receded, carrying that privileged altar *unacumque* bath, which severally seven times into the cavity excavated, a lector of water levels, most venerable Kevin, then effused thereby letting there be water where was theretofore dry land, by him so concreated, who now, confirmed a strong and perfect christian, blessed Kevin, exorcised his holy sister water, perpetually chaste, so that, well understanding, she should fill to midheight his tubbathaltar, which han[d]bathtub, most blessed Kevin, ninthly enthroned, in the concentric centre of the translated water, whereamid, when violet vesper vailed, Saint Kevin, Hydrophilos, having girded his sable *cappa magna* as high as to his cherubical loins, at solemn compline sat in his sate of wisdom, that handbathtub, whereverafter, recreated *doctor insularis* of the universal church, keeper of the door of meditation, memory *extempore* proposing and intellect formally considering, recluse, he meditated continuously with seraphic ardour the primal sacrament of baptism or the regeneration of all man by affusion of water. Yee. (605.4–606.12)

The last pages of the book are created by ALP. What has happened is that the scandal has ripped to pieces the reputation of HCE, and his good wife has stood up for him by preaching his virtues to the world and writing letters that excoriate those scallywags who would spread the scandal. She realizes, however, that there is something to the charges:

> All men has done something. Be the time they've come to the weight of old fletch. (621.32–33)

And now she is old. The night is ending, the dream is finishing, and she is about to wake, about to pass out of the dream. She is the old water of the old river going out to sea, returning to her father. In the literal story, she is in bed with her husband. The bed is the cosmic bed; its four posts are the four points of the compass, the four Evangelists (Matthew, Mark, Luke, and John), the four sages, the four winds, and everything else that occurs in fours. And here is her meditation as she is waking:

> But you're changing, acoolsha, you're changing from me, I can feel. Or is it me is? I'm getting mixed. Brightening up and tightening down. Yes, you're changing, sonhusband, and you're turning, I can feel you, for a daughterwife from the hills again. Imlamaya. And she is coming. Swimming in my hindmoist. Diveltaking on me tail. Just a whisk brisk sly spry spink spank sprint of a thing theresomere, saultering. Salterella come to her own. I pity your oldself I was used to. Now a younger's there. Try not to part! Be happy, dear ones! May I be wrong! For she'll be sweet for you as I was sweet when I came down out of me mother. My great blue bedroom, the air so quiet, scarce a cloud. In peace and silence. I could have stayed up there for always only. It's something fails us. First we feel. Then we fall. And let her rain now if she likes. Gently or strongly as she likes. Anyway let her rain for my time is come. I done me best when I was let. Thinking always if I go all goes. A hundred cares, a tithe of troubles and is there one who understands me? One in a thousand of years of the nights? All me life I have been lived among them but now they are becoming lothed to me. And I am lothing their little warm tricks. And lothing their mean cosy turns. And all the greedy gushes out their small souls. And all the lazy leaks down over their brash bodies. How small it's all! And me letting on to meself always. And lilting on all the time. I thought you were all glittering with the noblest of carriage. You're only a bumpkin. I thought you the great in all things, in guilt and in glory. You're but a puny. Home! My people were not their sort out beyond there so far as I can. For all the bold and bad and bleary they are blamed, the seahags. No! Nor for all our wild

dances in all their wild din. I can seen meself among them, allaniuvia pulchrabelled. How she was handsome, the wild Amazia, when she would seize to my other breast! And what is she weird, haughty Niluna, that she will snatch from my ownest hair! For 'tis they are the stormies. Ho hang! Hang ho! And the clash of our cries till we spring to be free. Auravoles, they says, never heed of your name! But I'm loothing them that's here and all I lothe. Loonely in me loneness. For all their faults. I am passing out. O bitter ending! I'll slip away before they're up. They'll never see. Nor know. Nor miss me. And it's old and old it's sad and old it's sad and weary I go back to you, my cold father, my cold mad father, my cold mad feary father, till the near sight of the mere size of him, the moyles and moyles of it, moananoaning, makes me seasilt saltsick and I rush, my only, into your arms. I see them rising! Save me from those therrble prongs! Two more. Onetwo moremens more. So. Avelaval. My leaves have drifted from me. All. But one clings still. I'll bear it on me. To remind me of. Lff! So soft this morning, ours. Yes. Carry me along, taddy, like you done through the toy fair. If I seen him bearing down on me now under whitespread wings like he'd come from Arkangels, I sink I'd die down over his feet, humbly dumbly, only to washup. Yes, tid. There's where. First. We pass through grass behush the bush to. Whish. A gull. Gulls. Far calls. Coming far! End here. Us then. Finn, again! Take. Bussoftlhee, mememormee! Till thousendsthee. Lps. The keys to. Given! A way a lone a last a loved a long the (626.35–628.16)

The river has gone out to sea, come back to the Father. Daylight has come, the dream has dissolved, and we are ready for the next night.

## EMERGING FROM THE WAKE

*Finnegans Wake* is written in a circle. You will recall that the book began with a small letter, in the middle of a sentence: *riverrun past Eve and Adam's...* The beginning of that sentence is at the end of the book: *A way a last a loved a lone a long the* We can come back, as we do in the *Wake*, and go round the round of reincarnations and rebirth. If certain things you read interest you, you will come back, go around again with the *Wake*. You can, however, read the book to the end [stay with "the,"] remain in the sea with Father Ocean, and not come round to the beginning. Then you are in heaven; you are out, released into the black silence, which is what was to have been the topic of Joyce's unwritten Fourth Work, his heaven book. Some images of the Buddha show him in the teaching posture, teaching about the round of rebirth. In these images, the hand points to a break. You can go out through the break, but most people will not; they will be back to go round and round again. This is an inexhaustible theme: you go round and round. The *Wake* is the Purāṇa of modern man. For their world, the old Indians had the Purāṇas and the Mahābhārata—they say in India, "If it isn't in the Mahābhārata, it isn't in the world." A great deal has happened since the days of the Purāṇas and the Mahābhārata, and for our world we have the *Wake*.

The miracle to me is that any man could have written *Finnegans Wake*. The languages! About two years after I finished the *Skeleton Key*, I received a letter from Africa from a German, who wrote and asked me if I would like to have a list of the Swahili words in *Finnegans Wake*. I wrote back and said I certainly would, and he sent me about ten pages. In his letter he said that the Swahili words that Joyce used were not what you would pick up from a dictionary; they are the words used in the street. In the *Wake*, the Swahili words appear in specific places; wherever the dark mother motif was [the mother as the mud of the fertile river,] Africa references and Swahili began to appear in hidden puns. There is also Sanskrit in the *Wake*. Now I happen to know a bit of Sanskrit, and the Sanskrit comes in with the motif of the avatar. The last section is full of Sanskrit material. And Irish Gaelic runs all through the *Wake*. There is also a great deal of Scandinavian material, because it is from Scandinavia that the raiders of Dublin came. The great Viking kingdom in Dublin is one of the themes in the book; Brian Boru, another little hero of the book, drove them out from Dublin, in the year 1014, so the *Wake* is [an epic] that takes everything in.

What, finally, is *Finnegans Wake* all about? Stripping away its accidental features, the book may be said to be all compact of *mutually supplementary antagonisms:* male-and-female, age-and-youth, life-and-death, love-and-hate; these, by their attraction, conflicts, and repulsions, supply polar energies that spin the universe. Wherever Joyce looks in history or human life, he discovers the operation of these basic polarities. Under the seeming aspect of diversity—in the individual, the family, the state, the atom, or the cosmos—these constants remain unchanged. Amid trivia and tumult, by prodigious symbol and mystic sign, obliquely and obscurely (because these manifestations are both oblique and obscure), James Joyce presents, develops, amplifies, and recondenses nothing more nor less than the eternal dynamic implicit in birth, conflict, death, and resurrection.

In *Finnegans Wake,* everything is brought together in what Joyce calls a sound compound to form one great miracle master through which shines always the radiance of HCE and ALP, the divine couple who generate the world, the dark hidden father and his *śakti,* come alive again by virtue of the magic of the left-hand path. It is they who are the substance, the consubstantiality that Stephen was seeking when he was walking by the sea. We have plunged into the sea. We have found the old man of the sea, lone and lonely there, "loonely in me loneness" (627.34), the father-mother, and that is what Joyce had to give us.

So there we have the great Daedalus flight of James Joyce. In the three major novels of Joyce, the hero, while wandering in Dublin, his labyrinthine environment, breaks loose from his own ego, yields with compassion to the world in all of its manifestations, and identifies himself finally with the great common ground that shines with radiance through all the forms of our lives. In his works, Joyce speaks for our lives.

To give you a personal example: I worked every minute of something like four years writing the *Skeleton Key to Finnegans Wake,* and when I finished, I found that everything I read, no matter what—newspapers, ads, the great works of literature—everything, no matter when it had been written, was just a quotation from the *Wake.* It was the funniest thing: I was bumping into Joyce all over the place. I'd read a newspaper account of something, and it read like one of the comic passages in the *Wake.* So I made a vow that I wouldn't read Joyce any more. I wanted to have my own life, after all. And then some years later, my wife, who during my years of working on the *Wake* had had imprinted on her tender mind my own zeal for the book, was traveling around the country performing her dances, and she took *Finnegans Wake* with her. She fell in love with the book and decided to do a kind of dance-play based on Anna Livia Plurabelle, the heroine. So I found myself back in *Finnegans Wake* again. But there had been enough of a span between these two periods for me to feel reconciled to a return to Joyce, particularly since it was my pretty wife who was representing Anna Livia, and the whole thing came back to me again, this time in terms of our own life together. It is a magical thing James Joyce has done, and I hope I have given you some sense of that in these talks.

## FINNEGAN THE WAKE[94]

### *I*

> riverrun, past Eve and Adam's, from swerve of shore to bend of bay, brings us by a commodius vicus of recirculation back to Howth Castle and Environs. (3.1–3)

*Finnegans Wake* breaks open like a Baedeker: a bulky guidebook to a portentous, queerly somnolent, unstable landscape: the interior of a dreaming being. James Joyce begins the book, parodying the manner of a learned and fervid professor-guide—a cicerone solicitous to unfold every legend inhering in the details of the scene to which he is introducing us. And though the sleeping being in whose interior we perambulate would never himself have guessed how cosmic the connotations of the figments of his dream, nevertheless we, the tourist party, thanks to the inexhaustible erudition of our garrulous courier, behold, in a spun-out version, the whole history and form of the macrocosm, their correspondence to the biography and anatomy of the microcosm, and the permanence within all of the immanent Father, Son, and Holy Ghost. "It was allso agreeable," we are moved to exclaim, as our luminous night-charabanc—gearless, clutchless—draws to the close of its instructive round:

> It was allso agreeable in our sinegear clutchless, touring the no placelike no timelike absolent..., like so many unprobables in their poor suit of the improssable. (609.1–2,5–6)

And so indeed it was. And so it will be again, next time we peer into this "most dantellising...lingerous longerous book of the dark." (251.23–24)

The guide, like everything else in the volume, undergoes a series of metamorphoses; the tourist-party correspondingly becomes now a class of attentive urchins, "snifflynosed, goslingnecked, clothyheaded, tangled in your lacings, tingled in your pants, etsitaraw, etcicero" (152.9–10), now the invisible radio public, or again, a rural sleuth's dull-witted assistant, a cringing native porter bearing the white man's burden of some ranging Mungo

Park, or a beady-eyed Huck Finn observing shadows on somebody's bedroom blind. Paleontology, archeology, paleography, and landscape-gardening are among the professor's favorite themes of discourse. He manipulated the "pudendascope" of psychoanalysis "on 'alices when they were yung and easily freudened," so that he knows that "father...is not always that undemonstrative relative who settles our hashbill for us." (115.30, 22–23, 26–28) And his ever-ready learning so abounds in folklore, myth, fable, theology, and metaphysics, that he finds himself competent to refer every scintilla of phenomenal experience, whether objective or subjective, back to its noumenon in the mind of God.

Behind the multifarious, sometimes annoying masquerade, sits the author, Joyce; now and then he sets the marionette aside to talk in person, still jokingly, with the reader. One is puzzled to guess where he is teasing, where serious, until at last it begins to dawn that the mode of disorderly burlesque is precisely James Joyce's deepest seriousness. This shocking realization opens the secret of his fundamentally dreamlike, anti-tragical, *mythological* craft[95]—an ambiguous, paradoxical art, of which François Rabelais was perhaps the last considerable Occidental practitioner.

"If there is any difficulty in reading what I write," James Joyce once observed to his friend Frank Budgen, "it is because of the material I use. In my case the thought is always simple."[96] The thought is that of the symbolic archetypes of mythology and metaphysics, familiar for millennia to mankind throughout the world. Mythology being the traditional picture-language of metaphysics (a disillusioning, entirely unsentimental, ideographic presentation of the formal principles of the cosmos), it is informed throughout by repose, even though its modes are variously whimsical, ludicrous, grandiose, and horrific. This is the case, likewise, in Joyce's *Finnegans Wake*. A prodigous anonymity of feeling, indifferent alike to vice and virtue, a readiness to permit not only civilizations, but universes, galaxies of universes, to be generated and annihilated in the wheeling rounds of time, is the sign of the apocalypse of this trans-humanistic, biologico-astronomical revelation. "The oaks of ald now they lie in peat yet elms leap where askes lay" (4.14–15). "Teems of times and happy returns. The seim anew" (215.22–23). "All's set for restart after the silence." (382.14) "The Hearweareagain Gaieties" (455.25). The atom "explodotonates" at 353.23–24; no minutes, no seconds later, the two annihilated parties are shaking hands again. "Mere man's mime: God has jest. The old order changeth and lasts like the first" (486.9–10). "Weeping shouldst not thou be when man falls but that divine scheming ever adoring be" (563.31–33). "We may catch ourselves looking forward...in that multimirror megaron of returningties, whirled without end to end" (582.18, 20–21).

The peoples of India know the myth of Viṣṇu, whose dream is the history of the world. He reposes on the waters of eternity, couched on Ananta ("Endless"), the Cosmic Serpent. From his navel grows a great lotus: the golden corolla is the flower of the world. In its center is the mountain of the gods, Mount Sumeru; the petals are the radiating continents. Mankind, the gods, and the demons that inhabit the underside of the petals come into existence, love and battle, undergo the vicissitudes of history, and—the lotus having completed the cycle of its natural season—presently dissolve again. Everything in the universe then disintegrates into the organism of the sleeping, blissful, macrocosmic giant. And during the subsequent night only the god exists, reposing on the boundless, everlasting waters. The lotus reappears; the golden bud expands. The goddess Padmā ("Lotus") opens to the dawn, and the history of the universe begins anew: "his goldwhite swaystick aloft ylifted, umbrilla-parasoul" (569.19–20). "Umbrella history," it is termed at 573.36.

> Now day, slow day, from delicate to divine, divases. Padma, brighter and sweetster, this flower that bells, it is our hour or risings. Tickle, tickle. Lotus spray. Till herenext. Adya. (598.11–14).[97]

The universe as dream is a dominant theme of metaphysics and myth: forms of the phenomenal world are regarded as unsubstantial metamorphoses of a primal conscious substance that never dies, was never born, is omnipresent, and is the seed-life of all things.[98] "*La vida es sueño*" (Calderón): "we are such stuff as dreams are made on" (Shakespeare's Prospero).[99] The phantasms (ourselves included) become manifest and disappear again, but are nothing in themselves. "*Alles vergängliche ist nur ein Gleichnis*" (Goethe). The wise, the completely disillusioned, are attached to nothing at all.

## II

The state of the Cosmic Dreamer is approximated in sleep—where the phantasmagoria that passes before the sleeper's eye is a little counterpart of the Creator's vision of the world. The concept of deep dream as oracle we know from many literary and religious documents. It is basic to the works of Dante, Joyce's pre-eminent model. "I found myself in a dark wood . . . I cannot well report how I entered it, so full was I of slumber at that moment" (*Inferno* I.2, 10–11). The prophetic vision was a favorite subject with Irish writers of the Middle Ages.[100] And Chaucer, following the tradition of his medieval craft, respected one sort of dream (the "Sweven") as a kind of minor revelation.

> God turne us every drem to goode!
> For hyt is wonder, by the roode.
> To my wyt, what causeth swevenes
> Eyther on morwes, or on evenes,
> And why th'effect folweth of somme,
> And of somme hit shal never come;
> Why that is an avision,
> And why this a revelacion,
> Why this a drem, why that a sweven,
> And noght to every man lyche even;
> Why this a fantome, why these oracles,
> I not; but who-so of these miracles
> The causes knoweth bet than I,
> Devyne he. . . . (*The House of Fame* I.1–14.)

Apparently it is a universal belief that when our powers of attention become detached, in sleep, from the commitment of the bodily organs and senses to the incoherent impressions and necessities of daily living, they subside into a supernatural stillness that unites the individual with the primal life that is his essential being. "At that time the Seer rests in his own state" (Patanjali). "The mind of the Sage at rest becomes the mirror of the universe" (Chuang Tzu).

> There, in clairvoyant-sleep, that divinity intuits Greatness. Whatever has been seen he proximately sees, whatever has been heard he proximately hears. Whatever has been and has been heard intuitively-known or unknown, good or evil, whatever has been directly-experienced in any land of airt, again and again he directly-experiences; he sees it all, he sees it all. (*Praśna Upaniṣad* 4.5).[101]

This is the sense of the sleep of the tavern keeper, Humphrey Chimpden Earwicker (HCE, Mr. Here Comes Everybody), the hero of

*Finnegans Wake.* Though in daytime he is muffled in the "sleep of igno-
rance in which most people pass their conscious lives,"[102] nevertheless,
within the depth of dream his spirit partakes of the wisdom of the All in
all of us. When he awakes he will have forgotten again, but for a time—
the time of dreaming—visions are presented to his inner eye that match,
in both quality and detail, the symbolical apparitions vouchsafed to
the seers.[103] And just as the psychoanalyst following the thread of the
dreams of his patient penetrates into the subconscious that supports, yet
remains unknown to, the citizen before him, so likewise do we, following
the "riverrun" of the nightmare of HCE—"this nonday diary, this allnights
newseryreel" (489.35)—enter awake the instructive zone of the hero's sleep.
We are like that miraculous old yogi Mārkandeya, who survived the dissolution of the world and went intact into the corpus of the Cosmic Giant
when the flower of the universe completed its day and was reabsorbed.[104]
Alert, we wander in the somnolent, queer landscape of memories disintegrating, ideals becoming reconstituted, portentous premonitions, desires
remarkably fulfilled. Houris of delight, jinns of dread, are there; as well as
figures laboring at purgatorial tasks "most dantellising." And our guide, it
now appears, is Virgil, opening our minds to the meaning of these incredible, yet intimately recollected, circles of torture, toil, and joy.[105]

### *III*

Dante's progress had its ancient counterpart in the ordeal of the Egyptian
mummy-soul in Amenti, on its lonely and dangerous journey to the throne
room of Osiris. And as the poet-visionary was guided through the spheres
of trial by the instructions of the initiator Virgil, so the departed "Osiris
N."[106] by the instructions of the Egyptian *Book of the Dead,* a copy of
which was placed in the mummy-case before the lid was closed. James
Joyce once suggested to his friend Frank Budgen that he should compose
an article on *Finnegans Wake* and title it "James Joyce's Book of the
Dead."[107] The interminable lecturing of Joyce's hermetic guide frequently
resounds with dim re-echoings from the musty Chapters of the Praises of
Re, the Chapter of Giving a Mouth to Osiris N., the Chapter of Coming
Forth by Day in the Underworld, and the Chapter of the Negative
Confession. Our cicerone actually transforms himself momentarily into the

brittle-dry papyrus, and "we seem to us (the real Us!) to be reading our Amenti in the sixth sealed chapter of the going forth by black" (62.26–27):

> Thou hast closed the portals of the habitations of thy children and thou hast set thy guards thereby, even Garda Didymus and Garda Domas, that thy children may read in the book of the opening of the mind to light and err not in the darkness which is the afterthought of thy nomatter by the guardiance of those guards which are thy bodemen. (258.28–34)

> The keykeeper of the keys of the seven doors of the dreamadoory in the house of the household of Hecech saysaith. (377.1–3)

> O, lord of the barrels, comer forth from Anow (I have not mislaid the key of Efas-Taem), O, Ana, bright lady, comer forth from Thenanow (I have not left temptation in the path of the sweeper of the threshold), O! (311.11–14)

> I have performed the law in truth for the lord of the law, Taif Alif. I have held out my hand for the holder of my heart in Annapolis, my youthrib city. Be ye then my protectors unto Mussabotomia before the guards of the city. (318.22–26)

> For (peace peace perfectpeace!) I have abwaited me in Elin and I have placed my reeds intectis before the Registower of the perception of tribute in the hall of the city of Analbe. (364.20–22)

> You are pure. You are pure. You are in your puerity. You have not brought stinking members into the house of Amanti. Elleb Inam, Titep Notep, we name them to the Hall of Honour. Your head has been touched by the god Enel-Rah and your face has been brightened by the goddess Arue-Ituc. (237.24–29)

> ... upon the night of the things of the night of the making to stand up the double tet of the oversear of the seize who cometh from the mighty deep and on the night of making Horuse to crihumph over his enemy... (328.31–35)

> ... forgetting to say their grace before chambadory, before going to boat with the verges of the chaptel of the opering of the month of Nema Knatut... (395.21–23)

> Amen, ptah! (411.11)

> Irise, Osirises! Be thy mouth given unto thee!... The overseer of the house of the oversire of the seas, Nu-Men, triumphant, sayeth: Fly

as the hawk, cry as the corncrake, Ani Latch of the postern is thy name; shout! (493.28, 30–33).

The eversower of the seeds of light to the cowld owld sowls that are in the domnatory of Defmut after the night of the carrying of the word of Nuahs and the night of making Mehs to cuddle up in a coddlepot, Pu Nuseht, lord of risings in the yonderworld of Ntamplin, tohp triumphant, speaketh. (593.20–24)

Bosse of Upper and Lower Byggotstrade, Ciwareke, may he live for river! (602.20)[108]

## IV

Hell, purgatory, and heaven are within: Dante's progress through the (macrocosmic) spheres outwardly evidences the profounding of his (microcosmic) being. His coming to the Father on high corresponds to his knowledge of the Son within: the two are consubstantial.

In Egypt, the conception of the problem was apparently identical. The papyrus guided the voyager past the chambers of peril (the chapter of Beating Back the Crocodile; the chapter of Repulsing Serpents; the chapter of Driving Back the Two Merti Goddesses; the chapter of Driving Away the Slaughterings which are Performed in the Underworld; the chapter of not letting the Soul of a Man be taken from him in the Underworld), and brought him safely to the throne room of the God. Then he who had been named "Osiris" on his deathbed beheld Osiris, and comprehended that he and the divinity, the knower and the known, creature and creator, the Son and the Father, were consubstantial. "He is I, and I am he."

This problem beset James Joyce from the beginning[109] and is a dominant theme in the *Wake:* developed, opened out, collapsed, inverted, parodied, and profoundly sounded in illustrations from an astonishing number of the world's mythologies, sacred writings, and secular literary productions; and as though to show that it inhabits, not only the sublime formulae of the saints and sages, but the playful imageries of popular life as well, the author has strung all the gathered pearls of his eclectic "monomyth" (581.24) on the simple coarse thread of a comical Irish-American song.

Hod carrier Tim Finnegan, a very hard drinker, one morning at the top of his ladder "filt tippling full. His howd feeled heavy, his hoddit did shake. (There was a wall of course in erection.) Dimb! He stottered from

the latter. Damb! he was dud. Dumb! Mastabatoom, mastabadtomm..."
(6.8–11) At Finnegan's wake were "all the hoolivans of the nation...And
the all gianed in with the shoutmost shoviality. Agog and magog and the
round of them agrog...Tee the tootal of the fluid hang the twoddle of the
fuddled, O!" (6.15, 18–19, 28) A gush of whisky ("Usqueadbaugham!" 24.14)
was accidentally dashed over the corpse:

> "Och, he revives! See how he raises!"
>   And Timothy, jumping from the bed,
> Cried out, while he lathered round like blazes,
>   "Soul of the divil! Did ye think me dead?"
>
> Whack, hurroo. Now take up your partners;
>   Welt the flure; your trotters shake.
> Isn't all the truth I've told ye;
> Lots of fun at Finnegan's wake.[110]

The relationship of this vivacious scene to the mystery and Saturnalia
of the killed and resurrected God (as described, for example, by Frazer in
*The Golden Bough*) is obvious. The *Wake* resounds with echoes of the
world's dying divinities: Bacchus, John Barleycorn, Osiris, the little wren
of St. Stephen's Day ("Wreneagle Almighty"—383.4; "The wren, the wren,
the king of all birds" 44; 340; 348; 363; 376; 430; 504; etc.). And just as the
death of the god is the life of his communion, so likewise that of Tim.
"Life...is a wake, livit or krikit, and on the bunk of our breadwinning lies
the cropse of our seedfather" (55.5, 7–8). Prostrate, "dead," Finnegan is our
world-sustaining landscape. "From Shopalist to Bailywick or from ashtun
to baronoath or from Buythebanks to Roundthehead or from the foot of
the bill to ireglint's eye he calmly extensolies" (6.33–35); particularly, the
landscape stretching westward under Dublin, from the Hill of Howth to
the grassy hillocks of Phoenix Park. "The cranic head on him, caster of his
reasons, peer yuthner in yondmist. Whooth? His clay feet, swarded in
verdigrass, stick up starck where he last fellonem, by the mund of the
magazine wall..." (7.29–32). Finnegan is the past; what was; the dimly
remembered; the forgotten; upon which the present is constructed and
continuously feeding. Megaliths (menhirs, cromlechs, dolmens, "giant
beds" and "giant graves") from the Neolithic are his handiwork. And he is
of the sacred number of those titanic legendary heroes who sleep within the

living mountains (Ireland's Finn McCool, for example) awaiting the day when they shall rise to set their people free.

> Liverpoor? Sot a bit of it! His braynes coolt parritch, his pelt nassy, his heart's adrone, his bluidstreams acrawl, his puff but a piff, his extremities extremely so....Words weigh no more to him than raindrips to Rethfernhim. Which we all like. Rain. When we sleep. Drops. But wait until our sleeping. Drain. Sdops. (74.13–15, 16–19)

In Joyce's version of the wake, when the whisky was splashed and the corpse stirred to rise, the company pressed the old man down again. "Now be aisy, good Mr. Finnimore, sir. And take your laysure like a god on pension and don't be walking abroad." (24.17). The present—the quick moment of the NOW—had passed him and already presented itself in another incarnation: "A big rody ram lad...with a pocked wife in pickle...two twilling bugs and one midgit pucelle" (28.36–29.7, 8).[111] Finnegan is of the generation of the grandfathers: "Move up Mumpty! Mike room for Rumpty! By order, Nickekellous Plugg" (99.19–21); the whole order of the present has been founded on the supposition of his demise.

## V

"I am Yesterday, Today, and Tomorrow," the mummy-soul perceives when awakened in the throne hall of Osiris.[112] The veil of time, as well as that of space, dissolves. But the mortal in life is implicated in the spectacle of the Manifold. (This is the meaning of the mythological image of the Fall: the One has become dispersed in and occluded by the contraries ("here and there," "then and now," "cause and effect," "means and ends," "good and evil," etc.) of Its cosmic manifestation: the Fall coincides with the blossoming of the lotus of the world.) What in eternity IS, now can be known only successively, as a process: past, present, and future.

Finnegan is past, Earwicker present; Earwicker's children are the future: the differing bodies are born and die. Yet when we peer with the eye of clairvoyant-sleep (Chaucer's "sweven") into the ephemeral individual, then the living moment, NOW, is perceived to be all that ever was ("O my shining stars and body!" 4.12–13); and it is as though a hole had been opened through the wall of the flux that separates our minds from the forgotten Paradise in which God is dwelling.[113]

Under conduct of our omniscient guide we rediscover "that One Man who sings in all of us";[114] that undisjointed Self, which is disjointed in the procession of the world. Through the quick of the sleeping Earwicker (that thread of life on which the millenniums have been strung like beads) we can peer back (and forward) through the ages: all are instant in one luminous moment. And we behold in a single "stable somebody" those past heroes who once were the present which our modern man now is; who are identical with him in the eon, though in history they have long since passed away.

This is how and why HCE both is and is not the same as Finnegan. As tavern keeper of Chapelizod (Humphrey Chimpden Earwicker) he is not the titanic builder of the past, but as the Monad (Here Comes Everybody; Haveth Childers Everywhere) he *is* what Finnegan *was.* Fathoming the images of *Finnegans Wake* we are sounding not merely the fantasies of Earwicker's dreaming, but the powers, the presences, within the genes of his cells.[115]

We can plumb through them the abyss of the history of man, back to the moment when Adam left the finger of God. HCE is that first mortal. He is also the survivor of the Deluge, the culture hero, the city founder, the patriarch, the king, and the marauder. He is the conquered. He is the vagabond, the voluptuary, and the saint. HCE, through the prism of time and space, has appeared, appears, and will go on reappearing, as though he were of many forms.[116]

## VI

But beneath and supporting this fluent self-multiplication in dream reposes the dreamlessness of Finnegan, whose resurrection was foretold in the comic song. He is death, the past, dreamless sleep: the dark and mysterious substratum of the dream of life. His mummy is all that we can see. But in the throne room of Osiris he is consubstantial with the God; and when that is discovered (that deep point within him touched where the contraries of death and life, past and future, come together), then Tomorrow, Today, and Yesterday will be one again, Finnegan will rouse, and the wake will end.

> The whole thugogmagog, including the portions understood to be oddmitted as the results of the respective titulars neglecting to

produce themselves, to be wound up for an afterenactment by a
Magnificent Transformation Scene showing the Radium Wedding
of Neid and Moorning and the Dawn of Peace, Pure, Perfect and
Perpetual, Waking the Weary of the World. (222.14–20)

"Life...is a wake" (55.5, 7); but when the Waked wakes what then of
Earwig the Awaker?

# · THE WILDER AFFAIR ·

## CHAPTER V

# The Skin of Whose Teeth?[117]

[On November 18, 1942, a play by Thornton Wilder, *The Skin of Our Teeth,* opened at the Plymouth Theatre in New York. It quickly became a hit. Almost exactly a month later, on December 19, 1942, the following article by Joseph Campbell and Henry Morton Robinson appeared in *The Saturday Review of Literature* claiming that the play was "an Americanized re-creation of *Finnegans Wake.*" Another article followed on February 13, 1943.]

## The Skin of Whose Teeth? Part I: The Strange Case of Mr. Wilder's New Play and Finnegans Wake

While thousands cheer, no one has yet pointed out that Mr. Thornton Wilder's exciting play *The Skin of Our Teeth* is not an entirely original creation, but an Americanized re-creation, thinly disguised, of James Joyce's *Finnegans Wake.* Mr. Wilder himself goes out of his way to wink at the knowing one or two in the audience, by quoting from and actually naming some of his characters after the main figures of Joyce's masterpiece. Important plot elements, characters, devices of presentation, as well as major themes and many of the speeches, are directly and frankly imitated, with but the flimsiest veneer to lend an American touch to the original features.

*The Skin of Our Teeth* takes its circular form from *Finnegans Wake,* closing and opening with the cycle-renewing, river-running thought-stream of the chief female character. The main divisions of the play are closed by periodic catastrophes (ice age, deluge, war), devices which are borrowed from the cosmic dissolutions of *Finnegans Wake.* Furthermore, Mr. Antrobus, Thornton Wilder's hero, is strangely reminiscent of Joyce's protagonist, H. C. Earwicker, "that homogenius man" (34.14) who has endured throughout all the ages of the world, though periodically overwhelmed by floods, wars, and other catastrophes. The activities, talents, and troubles of the two characters have significant resemblances. In both works they are Adam, All-Father of the world. They are tireless inventors and land-conquerors; both are constantly sending communiqués back home; both run for election, broadcast to the world, and are seen on television. Moreover, their characters have been impugned. In each case the hero repudiates the charges against him, but the secret guilt which each seeks to hide is constantly betrayed by slips of the tongue. To add to the long list of similarities, both are seduced under extenuating circumstances by a couple of temptresses, and are forever "raping home" the women of the Sabines.

Sabine leads both authors to Sabina, the name of Mr. Wilder's housekeeper, who had been "raped home" by Mr. Antrobus from one of his war expeditions. Her prototype is the garrulous housekeeper of *Finnegans Wake.* "He raped her home," says Joyce, "Sabrine asthore, in a parakeet's cage, by dredgerous lands and devious delts." (197.21–22)[118] To this delicious Joycean line Mr. Wilder is apparently indebted for his rape theme and the name of the Antrobus housekeeper.

The conversation between Mrs. Antrobus and Sabina in Act I carries the lilt of the Anna Livia Plurabelle chapter, and rehearses some of its themes, notably the patience of the wife while younger love beguiles her husband; and again, the little feminine attentions lavished on the man while he broods in melancholy (198.9–200.32).

The wonderful letter which the wife of Mr. Antrobus throws into the ocean at the close of Act II—that letter which would have told him all the secrets of her woman's heart and would have revealed to him the mystery of why the universe was set in motion—is precisely the puzzling missive of *Finnegans Wake,* tossed into the sea, buried in the soil, ever awaited, ever half-found, ever reinterpreted, misinterpreted, multifariously over-and-under interpreted, which continually twinkles, with its life-riddle, through every page of Joyce's work.

In Mr. Wilder's play, the wife's name is Maggy—which is one of her names in *Finnegans Wake* (III.II, 15, 16). She has borne innumerable children—again see *Finnegans Wake* 201.27–202.3. Her daughter aspires to powder and rouge and fancies herself in silks (143.31–148.32). The two sons, Cain and Abel, the abominated and the cherished, supply a fratricidal battle-theme that throbs through the entire play, precisely as it does in *Finnegans Wake.* Cain in both works is a peeping-tom and publisher of forbidden secrets. In Mr. Wilder's work he spies on and speaks out about the love-makings in the beach cabana. In Joyce's, he tattles the whole story of the love life of his parents (241.1–243.36).

The ingenious and very amusing scene at the close of Act I in which Tallulah Bankhead turns to the audience and begs for wood—chairs, bric-à-brac, anything at all—with which to feed the fire that will preserve humanity during the approaching ice-age, is a clever re-rendering of a passage in *Finnegans Wake.* In Joyce's work, when elemental catastrophe has almost annihilated mankind, the heroine goes about gathering into her knapsack various odds and ends, to be reanimated by the fire of life. As Joyce puts it:

> ...she'll loan a vesta [i.e., borrow a light] and hire some peat and sarch the shores her cockles to heat and she'll do all a turfwoman can...To puff the blaziness on. (12.9–12)

Mr. Wilder here follows Joyce's lead even to the point of having his actress borrow a light with which to ignite the preserving hearth.

There are, in fact, no end of meticulous unacknowledged copyings. At the entrance of Mr. Antrobus, for instance; his terrific banging at the door duplicates the fantastic thumpings of Joyce's hero at the gate of his own home (63.30–64.15), where he is arrested for thus disturbing the peace of the whole community. The great swathing of scarfs and wrappings which Mr. Antrobus removes when he comes in follows the mode of Joyce's hero, who is characteristically enveloped in no end of costumery. In the famous passage on 35.8–10, HCE is seen in heaped-up attire:

caoutchouc kepi and great belt and hideinsacks and his blaufunx fustian and ironsides jackboots and Bhagafat gaiters and his rubberised inverness.

Perhaps the chief difference between the protean HCE and the rigid Mr. Antrobus is revealed when the latter's wrappings are removed, leaving only a thin reminder of Joyce's grotesque folk-hero.

Throughout the work there are innumerable minor parallelisms. The razzing which Mr. Antrobus endures at the Shriners' Convention repeats the predicament of H. C. Earwicker throughout Book II, Chapter III (309–382). The "Royal Divorce" theme for *Finnegans Wake* reappears in the wish of Mr. Antrobus to be divorced from his wife. Neither of the heroes achieves his end, the wish itself being liquidated by catastrophe. The fortune-teller in Act II plays the role of Joyce's heroine, ALP, who assigns to all at the Masquerade the tokens of their fate (207.29–215.30). Later Mr. Wilder's gypsy coaches the seductress of Mr. Antrobus, just as in *Finnegans Wake* Isabelle learns from "gramma's grammar" how to "decline and conjugate" young men (268.9–270.28). Trivia-wise, the key-word "commodius" occurs in the second line of *Finnegans Wake* and within the first two minutes of Mr. Wilder's play. Finally, at the end of Mr. Wilder's play, the Hours pass across the stage intoning sublime instructions. This is a device conspicuous both in *Ulysses* and *Finnegans Wake*. Many further similarities could be cited.

It is a strange performance that Mr. Wilder has turned in. Is he hoaxing us? On the one hand, he gives no credit to his source, masking it with an Olsen and Johnson technique. On the other hand, he makes no attempt to conceal his borrowings, emphasizing them rather, sometimes even stressing details which with a minimum of ingenuity he could have suppressed or altered. But if puzzlement strikes us here, it grows when we consider the critics—those literary advisors who four years ago dismissed *Finnegans Wake* as a literary abortion not worth the modern reader's time, yet today hail with rave notices its Broadway reaction. The banquet was rejected but the Hellzapoppin's scrap that fell from the table they clutch to their bosom. Writes Alexander Woollcott, "Thornton Wilder's dauntless and heartening comedy stands head and shoulders above anything ever written for our stage." And why not, since in inception and detail the work springs from that "dauntless and heartening" genius, James Joyce!

## THE SKIN OF WHOSE TEETH? PART II: THE INTENTION BEHIND THE DEED

> There are certain charges that ought not to be made, and I think I may add, ought not to be allowed to be made. (*The Skin of Our Teeth*, 5)

> There are certain statements which ought not to be, and one should like to hope to be able to add, ought not to be allowed to be made. (*Finnegans Wake*, 33.19–21).

Several weeks ago we made charges. We indicated a relationship between Thornton Wilder's current Broadway play *The Skin of Our Teeth* and that big black book *Finnegans Wake*. Our first article, based on a single evening at the play, no more than broached the problem of Mr. Wilder's indebtedness to James Joyce. But now the appearance of the play in book form[119] offers abundant evidence that Mr. Wilder not only vigorously adapted *Finnegans Wake* to the Broadway temper, but also intended that someone, somewhere, someday, should recognize his deed for what it is.

The author had good reason to expect that this would not happen immediately. He realized fully that *Finnegans Wake* has not yet been assimilated by the larger public, and that the chances of explicit protest during the run of the play were slight. For in Joyce's work the themes are multidimensional and queerly interwoven, developing bit by bit throughout the obscure text. Even the studious eye is baffled by their intricacy. Mr. Wilder, having mastered the elaborate web, has selected a few structural strands, reduced them in size and weight, and presented them, neatly crocheted to box-office taste. Many of the Joyce-Wilder correspondences are so subtle and extended that it would require a vast wall for their exhibition. Nevertheless, within the compass of a brief article it is possible to present a series of eye-openers even to the most languid observer.

These correspondences amount to much more than a mere sharing of great and constant human themes. Character by character, Act by Act, unmistakable re-renderings are evident. Both works have for a setting modern suburban homes not yet detached from the archaic past. The fathers of both families are about forty-five years old; they have both just survived election campaigns, during which certain charges have been made against their character—charges indignantly denied, yet not ill-founded. Mr.

Antrobus pinches servant girls when he meets them in a dark corridor; HCE, too, is guilty of ungentlemanly conduct with maidservants. And they both indulge in extramarital sex adventures.

Such philanderings, it may be objected, are the common stuff of literature. But in *Finnegans Wake* and *The Skin of Our Teeth* the circumstances which surround them are Horrendous, Characteristic, and Especial. Mark what happens directly upon the husbands' stumbling into sin:—a thunder clap is heard (ST 86; FW 80 and elsewhere). Barely has Antrobus entered the cabana with the seductress, barely has HCE entered the bushes, when the thunder clap resounds and the hurricane signals go up. In both works this omen is a pronouncement of God's judgment on erring man, soon to be followed by deluge. The heroes' self-apologetic radio broadcasts to the world, describing their statesmanlike contributions to humanity, along with the worlds which they celebrate, dissolve in the engulfing catastrophe.

It is not enough to fob off this complex of themes, this curious telescoping of Adam and Noah, as "something out of Genesis." Quaintly enough, this merging of patriarchs does not occur in the Bible. It does occur, however, in *Finnegans Wake*—and now in *The Skin of Our Teeth*. Furthermore, Genesis 4 relates that the first son of Adam was Cain, the second Abel. But Joyce reverses this order in the *Wake;* so, oddly enough, does Wilder (ST 5). Is our Broadway playwright deriving his themes from the Hebrew or the Irish?

Mr. Wilder's maid-seductress Sabina assumes the traits, at one time or another, of all the temptress masks of *Finnegans Wake.* She is the servant girl, fond of movies (166.13–14), the Napoleonic *fille du regiment* (8–9), the worn out soubrette (531.13–26), the popular beauty (58–59), the captive "raped" home from her Sabine hills (197.21). With Joyce she is "the rainbow girl": Sabina's costume in Act I suggests the colors of the rainbow. In *Finnegans Wake,* too, all these seductress traits play over the basic personality of a gossipacious maid.

The role of maid-temptress is counterbalanced by the wife-mother, whose function it is to rebuild and preserve the life fires which, through Sabina, have gone out. In the play, as in the book, the wife borrows the light with which she kindles the hearth; even further, she borrows the light from a character who is called the Postman in the Joyce work, and in the Wilder work, Telegraph Boy. In her speeches she recalls the times when there were no weddings (FW 78–79; ST 59). One of her manifestations in *Finnegans Wake* is as a mother hen: as Joyce puts it, "she just feels she was kind of born to lay and love eggs" (112.13–14). Mr. Antrobus calls *his* wife a "broken down old weather hen." The umbrella that the wife carries through Wilder's Act II is the famous umbrella of *Finnegans Wake* (7, and elsewhere). Mrs. Antrobus re-echoes Mrs. Earwicker's railings against the candidate and scandalmongers who opposed her husband in the election.

The great letter that she throws into the sea is precisely the letter of *Finnegans Wake,* thrown away under identical circumstances (80, 92–93, 111, 113, 615–619). (Mr. Wilder's description of this letter is the most sensitive, most complete, most convincing interpretation yet to appear of this great Joycean theme.)[120] The divorce which threatens the Antrobus household is the Royal Divorce of *Finnegans Wake.* The circumstances which postpone the divorce, and forever will postpone it, are those of *Finnegans Wake.* And again, as in *Finnegans Wake,* the mother's love for the evil, rejected Cain, reconciles the male antagonisms within the family. (194–195, etc.). With these parallels and the many more, it is not surprising that Mrs. Antrobus's name is Maggie—written "Maggy" in the *Wake.*

So much for character comparisons; now for chronology. Skillfully and without essential dislocation, Mr. Wilder has adapted the four books of *Finnegans Wake* to the exigencies of a three-act play. Both works are composed in the form of a circle. Book I of *Finnegans Wake* and Act I of the play summon up the deepest past—the glacial age, dinosaurs, and mammoths (Joyce mentions both), as well as the dawn inventions of man— the alphabet, mechanics, and brewing. Book II and Act II take place in the present. Wilder's Act II is based specifically upon Book II, Section 3, of *Finnegans Wake;* Wilder simply transplants Joyce's Irish-tavern bacchanal to an Atlantic City convention. The last book of *Finnegans Wake* and the last Act of the play treat of the world's brave re-beginnings, following almost total catastrophe; they do not conclude, but circle back again to the start of all.

It is Book III of *Finnegans Wake* which would at first appear to have been omitted. But no. We find that this material has been telescoped retrospectively into the recitals of Mr. Antrobus in Act III, when he rehearses the fine ideals which he broodingly cherished during the years of struggle and war. These broodings and their return to the realities of peace correspond to HCE's dream for a future ideal and its dissolution into workaday fact. We cannot praise too highly what Mr. Wilder has here achieved in the way of re-creative interpretation. From these passages in his play a light goes back over great and very obscure sections of *Finnegans Wake.*

If the major correspondences are inescapable, minor similarities are numberless. Open the work to any page, and echoes vibrate from all directions. Some are highly esoteric and it is not improbable that Mr. Wilder is giving the wink of the fraternity to any Finnegan fan who may chance to be in the theatre. For instance, the play opens with an announcement that the sun arose at 6:32 A.M. Why precisely 32? This number, of all possible digits, is one of the ubiquitous puzzlers throughout the *Wake:* it appears during the course of the book some forty times in various combinations. Directly following the sunrise, we are shown three scrubwomen who have found Adam and Eve's wedding ring in the X Theatre. This literally reeks of Finnegan. No less than a dozen connotations spring immediately to mind: the scrubwoman theme, the entr'acte-scavenger theme, the "found article" theme, the ring theme, the wedding theme, the Phoenix Theatre theme, the "X" theme-complex (Xmas, CrissCross, Crucifixion-Resurrection, Crossbones, Cross-keys, XXX kisses, exwife, etc.), the Adam and Eve theme, etc.

An early stage direction bids Sabina to dust Mr. Antrobus's chair, "including the under side." In Mr. Earwicker's tavern the man-of-all-work "dusts the bothsides of the seats of the bigslaps" (370.26–29). In Act I, in his conversation with the fish, Mr. Antrobus leans over the bowl and says, "How've things been, eh? Keck-keck-keck." When we try to remember where we have heard "keck" before, we recall the "Brekkek Kekkek" of the Aristophanes frog chorus in the diluvian passage of *Finnegans Wake* (4.2). In *The Skin of Our Teeth* "Keck" undergoes further Joycean development by appearing five times in the speeches of Esmeralda, fortune teller, who is called "Mrs. Croaker" by the convention delegates.

But why should Mr. Antrobus give special attention to a fish? Well, the fish is HCE's totem animal, as well as the giant Finn's Salmon of Knowledge.

Wilder's little girl, like Joyce's, is papa's darling, his "little star" (ST 23). Mr. Antrobus is revived from a mood of most desperate melancholy on hearing that she has recited Wordsworth's "The Star" in school. In *Finnegans Wake,* one of the daughter's principal manifestations is Stella (Stella—star) who revives life interest in the melancholy old man. When questioned by

Mr. Antrobus, the daughter gives the exact dimensions of the ocean—a precocious knowledge suggestive of her "ocean origin" in *Finnegans Wake.*

To heap up resemblances: The message delivered by Mr. Wilder's Telegraph Boy has come by a wildly circuitous route, suggesting the peregrinations of the famous Finnegan missive (93–94, 420–421). The children are called "little smellers" by Mr. Antrobus: the phrase "the nice little smellar" is remembered from *Finnegans Wake* (444.13). Among the refugees of the end of Act I, four old men, Doctor, Professor, Moses, and Homer, predominate; these are certainly the Four Old Men among the frequenters of Mr. Earwicker's hostel (94, etc.). The Antrobus inventions of beer brewing, alphabet, and mechanics are precisely those of the hero in *Finnegans Wake.*

Mr. Wilder is a man who has entered an uninventoried treasure cave and who emerges with a pouch full of sample sparklers. Only the lapidary who has himself paid a secret visit to the wonder-hoard is in a position to gasp at the authentic Joycean glitter of Mr. Wilder's re-settings.

As yet, Captain Wilder has not deigned to make public comment. But in the play itself he very cryptically pronounces as harsh an evaluation of his work as will ever be made. This prouncement comes in Act I of *The Skin of Our Teeth,* when Mr. Antrobus comes home with his epochal invention, the wheel, which his son seizes with delight. Playing with the wheel, the son says: "Papa, you could put a chair on this." To which the father replies, broodingly: "Ye-e-s, any booby can fool with it now,—but I thought of it first." (ST, 29–30).

The wheel is James Joyce's circular book of cyclewheeling history, "the Book of Doublends Jined" (20.16); Mr. Wilder has cleverly fixed a chair to it, wherein the public can ride.

## Two Accounts: Editor's Afterword

[Wilder always denied the charges of undue influence. After the Campbell and Robinson articles, *Saturday Review* asked Wilder for a reply. He began a response, but eventually filed it away. Gilbert Harrison, in his biography of Wilder, describes the statement:

> In that unpublished statement he explained that in deciphering Joyce's novel the idea had come to him that one aspect of it might be expressed in drama: the method of representing mankind's long

journey by superimposing different epochs of time simultaneously. He even made sketches employing Joyce's characters and locale but soon abandoned the project. The slight element of plot in Joyce's novel was so thinly glimpsed amid the distortions of nightmare and the polyglot distortions of language that any possibility of dramatization was "out of the question." The notion about mankind in *The Skin of Our Teeth* and the viewing of the Antrobus family through several simultaneous layers of time did persist, however, and began to surround itself with many inventions of his own. From Joyce, he had "received the idea of presenting ancient man as an ever-present double to modern man. The four fundamental aspects of *Finnegans Wake* were not to my purpose and are not present in my play. Joyce's novel is primarily a study of Original Sin, and the role it plays in the life of the conscience. Its recurrent motto is St. Augustine's *O felix culpa.* Nor could I use its secondary subject, the illustration of Vico's theory of the cyclic seasonal repetitions of human culture. Nor could I find any place for its primary literary intention, the extraordinary means Joyce found for representing the thoughts of the mind while asleep, the famous 'night-language.' Nor could I employ his secondary literary intention, the technical tour-de-force whereby through puns and slips of the tongue he was able to represent several layers of mental activity going on at the same time and often contradictory to one another. If I had been able to transfer to the stage several or any one of these four basic aspects of the book, wherein its greatness lies, I would have done it and would have gladly published the obligation at every step of the way."[121]

In 1948, Wilder described the genesis of the play in a note prepared for the English production of the play, which starred Laurence Olivier.[122] In this note, he emphasized the prevalence of the theme of *Skin of Our Teeth* in the minds of everyday people:

It is hard to imagine a man who occasionally does not see himself as both All Men and the First Man. The two points of view are expressed for us by myths: at his marriage he may be reminded of Adam; when he goes about his house shutting the windows against a rainstorm he is Noah; when he goes hunting he calls himself Nimrod. The play tries to put this idea in dramatic form; and since it deals with both the Individual Man and the Type Man, and deals with them in great trouble, isn't it right that it should be indifferent to the smaller credibilities, be full of anachronisms, and should telescope all times and periods, and that it should be full of interruptions and accidents; and since Man is brave and long-enduring, isn't it right that every now and then it should be gay?[123]

Wilder made a further statement in 1948, to an interviewer who asked about the charges of influence:

I embedded one phrase of *Finnegans Wake* into the text as a salute and a bow of homage....

Sabina mockingly defending her employer, Mr. Antrobus[,] who is also Adam and Everyman, says, "There are certain charges that ought not to be made and, I think I may say, ought not to be allowed to be made." This speech, with its feeble cadence and insecure indignation, is a wonderful example of Joyce's miraculous ear.

"There are no other lines from Joyce?"

"None," said Mr. Wilder.[124]

Wilder enlarged on his description of the genesis of *Skin of Our Teeth* in 1955, during a revival of the play. When asked about "the circumstances under which you conceived the double time situation in *The Skin of Our Teeth*," Wilder replied:

[T]he treatment of several simultaneous levels of time was borrowed from Joyce's *Finnegans Wake* and Henry James' *A Sense of the Past*[,] and is even in Mark Twain's *Connecticut Yankee at King Arthur's Court.*[125]

Finally, in 1957 Wilder republished the text of *Skin of Our Teeth,* in which he inserted a notice:

This play is deeply indebted to James Joyce's *Finnegans Wake.* I should be very happy if, in the future, some author should feel similarly indebted to any work of mine. Literature has always more resembled a torch race than a furious dispute among heirs.[126]]

# · DIALOGUES ·

CHAPTER VI

# DIALOGUES[127]

QUESTION: *Is Joyce in his work trying to illustrate a dialectic pattern?*

JOSEPH CAMPBELL: Yes. There is a double dialectic here. There is the one dialectic on the biological level of the male and female, and the other dialectic on the historical level of the two inevitable antagonists in any historical circumstance. Equals of opposites: each one implies the other, and taking sides really commits you to a half view. The political man, Joyce [implies in the "Cyclops" episode of *Ulysses*], is a man with only one eye. He sees only one side, and is for only one side. The poet, having two eyes, sees both. But there would be no game if somebody didn't take sides. In fact, in terms of the opposition between poet and deedsman, one-eyed vision and two-eyed vision constitute a polarity, and it is already a choice to favor the way of two-eyed vision.

Life is a game. And so the attitude that Joyce has in his work is not that of withdrawing but affirming; yet in the affirmation, having lined up on one side, you are not to identify yourself with God and the other side with the Devil; the two represent a polarity. Or if you do identify yourself with God and the other with the Devil, then you must realize that there is a higher principle, higher than the duality of God and Devil of which they themselves are the polarized aspects. This is Joyce's theology: that God and

Devil are polarized for action. That the world is, as it were, spun between these two poles.

QUESTION: *If there is a dialectic, why is there a cycle?*

CAMPBELL: You may have in mind the model of the Hegelian-Marxian dialectic of historical thesis-antithesis-synthesis, with the synthesis manifest as a historical form. Joyce's dialectic, rather, is of a continuous historical conflict and alternation of thesis and antithesis, with the synthesis always present as the very foundation, or metaphysical ground, of the dual manifestation. Finnegan underlies the whole play of the city: should he sit up— that is, should he appear above ground historically—the play would dissolve. Analogy: the play of Yang and Yin, as a manifestation of the ever-present Tao.

---

QUESTION: *I was puzzled by your reference to compassion having some relationship to Purgatory.*

CAMPBELL: Well, Purgatory is a purging of ego, and compassion is the purging of ego. Passion is ego, it's ego-bound. Compassion is the opening. It's love, and ego is just the opposite to love.

QUESTION: *I thought Purgatory had something to do with hell.*

CAMPBELL: No. Hell is hell. Purgatory is purgatory. Hell is a place of ego-bondage. The souls in hell are those who have closed themselves to grace, to God's love, to the transpersonal, and are bound by the seven capital sins. Purgatory is a place of gradual clearance of this bondage. As the seven capital sins—pride, covetousness, lust, anger, envy, gluttony, and sloth—are opened one after another, one opens to beyond oneself. Pride is what must first be overcome. When pride is broken, then progressively one goes higher and higher. St. Augustine says, "Oh, Lord, thou hast made us *ad te,*" "tending to thee"; that is what is known as the transpersonal mystery which informs all things. The ego is exactly what holds you away from the experience of that mystery, and so the ego represents a bondage from the very nature of our nature, which is to move toward the transcendent.

In Dante, Purgatory is represented as a mountain. In his time, no one had ever journeyed south of the great western bulge of Africa that juts out into the Atlantic. All known continents were in the Northern Hemisphere, and it was thought that the lower half of the globe was water. Moreover, the belief was that Satan, when he was thrown out of heaven, hit the earth with such force that he plunged down to the center of the sphere—his genitals are exactly at the center—and that his fall first made the world turn. When Satan was thrown down like that, all the stages of his descent were marked as circles, the circle of hell, and the land he displaced was forced out the other end of the earth and became the mountain of Purgatory, rising from the waters of the Southern Hemisphere. At the summit of that mountain is the Earthly Paradise, the place of the union of the spiritual and material worlds, where Dante beheld Beatrice again. And she, then, led him through the highest sphere to Heaven.

In Joyce, we don't get to heaven, because he intended to write another work, but died before he wrote it. When he realized he was dying and would not complete this work to which he had put all of his life, it must have been a very dismal moment. I read somewhere that all he said was, "It's God's will." A saintly man, really. I'll tell you later what I think his last work would have to have been.

QUESTION: *Does that inward light contain the ego? What is the relationship between the inward light and the ego?*

CAMPBELL: The ego is the center of your consciousness. The energies that are the source of your life, the inward light you speak of, is below the level of your mental consciousness. For example, we will soon eat lunch, and then we will be digesting the lunch; but I don't think there is anyone here who knows consciously just *how* to digest a lunch, although we are all going to do it. There's more to you than your mental consciousness knows about. The vocabulary that relates and links our mental consciousness to the energies that inform our body and move our lives and give us our sentiments of love and hate and despair is the vocabulary of myth.

Now ego is protective of the physical body, but it's possible not to stay with that. The key is Schopenhauer's idea of compassion. You will recall that he asks, "How can it be that self-protection, the first law of ego-nature, is sometimes suddenly liquidated and a person spontaneously moves to another's rescue?" He says this is a breakthrough of a metaphysical realization: that you and the other are one. The notion of separateness is simply a function of the way our senses experience us here in time and space. We are separate in this room because of space. We are separate from the group that was here last night because of time. Time and space are the separating factors, what Nietzsche calls the *principium individuationis,* the individuating factors. Schopenhauer says that these factors are secondary, that the notion of you and the other is a secondary one, and that every now and then this other realization comes up. That is how compassion releases you from ego orientation. The actual realization of identity happens only in precious moments that come very seldom. When this identity is not actually realized, then one acts on the basis of altruism or some other such sentiment. But that's only an idea. True compassion is an experience.

QUESTION: *Is it Western man, Western ego, still talking in Joyce when the recognition of his own powers comes: when he makes Stephen dedicate himself to the forging of the uncreated conscience of his race? I can't imagine an Eastern artist conceiving to go forth into the world like that.*

CAMPBELL: I don't think an Eastern artist would make as big a jump as that. Artists in the East work within given and fixed lines—or, at least they do now. Perhaps back in the great creative periods of China there were artists with aspirations like Joyce's, but I don't get that impression from Oriental art now; it has all been in the past. But Joyce is doing it, and he's jumping far.

When Stephen determines "to forge . . . the uncreated conscience of my race," the question that arises is: What does he think his race is? I think there are two answers. His race is the Irish race, but his race is also the human race. Joyce knows, of course, that the Irish were knocked down by the British as early as the twelfth century. In this ordeal, they were actually deprived of their own life system, and the English language was imposed on them. But beyond that, I think Joyce felt that what Ireland had to give in the way of a revelation of the transpersonal and transcendent had not been given, and he was going to do it. That's why his esthetic is focused on the grave and constant, on identification with the human sufferer, the human race. So, "the uncreated conscience of my race" is both the Irish experience and the Irish inflection of the human revelation, which Joyce saw hadn't come through. Yet he saw potentials, and he determined that he was going to realize those potentials.

———◦/◦/◦———

QUESTION: *I don't understand Stephen Dedalus's definition of tragic terror:*

> *Terror is the feeling which arrests the mind in the presence of whatsoever is grave and constant in human sufferings and unites it with the secret cause.* [P204]

*What I don't understand is: if one has a sense of union with something secret and mysterious, why doesn't that give a sense of reassurance, or wonder, as opposed to terror?*

CAMPBELL: The tragic emotion is not fright. You know the *mysterium tremendum et fascinans.* This is an experience of the *tremendum* of life, of the fact that death inheres in life. And the terror is the sense of the breakthrough. It's the terror of the knowledge when God breaks through. That terror is something that explodes the whole ego system.

QUESTION: *From tragedy I understand that there is no God.*

CAMPBELL: Well, I use the word *God* in just a familiar way. God isn't a fact. God is a symbol. As soon as you interpret God as a fact, you are off the beam. That's one of our problems. As I have said, deities in mythological systems are personifications of energies; but in our system, God is personified as the source of energies: God says. "Here I am," you know. Of course, when you have a personification of God, you have a limitation. But where I have used the word *God,* let us simply say *brahman,* a neuter noun that refers past itself to the mystery of the total energy of life. And who are you? And where are you as a little historical person when that energy breaks through? That's the terror, and to realize that that energy is in you and all around you is the terror Joyce is talking about.

Aristotle says that the experience of pity and terror yields a "*catharsis,*" which in the Greek context is a ritual word meaning the purging of one's ego, the purging of one's rational orientation.[128] And with this catharsis, this breakthrough either of terror or of pity, where you unite with the human—not just with the historically conditioned—creature, you have depersonalized yourself. That's when you are in touch with the dynamics of the world. That's as I understand it.

QUESTION: *I don't think I've ever had that experience.*

CAMPBELL: Well, if you haven't had the experience, you can hope for it. That's the best I can say on that. It's supposed to be the effect of the experience of tragedy. I'll never forget seeing a Greek presentation of *Oedipus,* where he enters with his hands like this and his eyes out and blood streaming—you know, the Greeks like a lot of blood—and the Chorus, with its back to the audience, was facing him; and after everything was over, you felt a breakthrough rapture.

The experience of beauty and the experience of the sublime are two totally different experiences. The experience of the sublime is an ego-annihilating experience: the ego is just totally diminished and wiped out. The sublime is rendered through the experience of either enormous space or prodigious power. The greatest experience of the sublime that I have heard is from an astronaut who was given an E.V.A., an extra-vehicular activity. He was outside of the module with just the umbilical connecting his space suit to the module, when something went wrong inside the module and he had to wait to do the work he was supposed to do. So he was out there in space for five minutes with nothing to do. (Those chaps were given a lot to do, not only because there was a lot to be done, but so that they shouldn't get spaced out.) And here he was out there all alone, floating along at 18,000 miles an hour; and there was no wind and no sound; and up here was the earth, and over there was the moon; and he later said, "I just had to ask myself what I had ever done to deserve this experience." That's the sublime.

There are degrees of this release from ego-commitment that one can experience. Tragedy is one way to experience it, and there are others, although perhaps none as potent as what that astronaut was facing when he was floating out there in space and everything that he had identified with was wiped out. That's the best I can do on that.

QUESTION: *Can that also happen in the negative sense? Some Vietnam veterans . . .*

CAMPBELL: There's no doubt about it. At the root of life is bliss, you know; and in our temporal experiences, we have pain and pleasure, but the bliss underlies both. You can have degrees of pain that break right through to the bliss.

———⌇⌇⌇———

QUESTION: *Was Sylvia Beach a kind of mother figure?*

CAMPBELL: Well, I went to her bookshop two or three times during the fifteen months I was in Paris, but I never knew her intimately enough to say what her relationships were to other people. I didn't cultivate any relationship with anybody in Paris. It was a very solitary time for me; I was working something out. Sylvia Beach was very generous, a simple person to talk with, quite helpful and open, but she didn't make a big thing of it at all. I bought this copy of *Ulysses* from her.

You know, I had to smuggle this book into the United States. When I went to Paris as a student in 1928, nobody here had ever heard of Joyce. But in Paris: "*Ulysses?*" "*Mais oui!*" And here's the copy I bought. The first printing was on February 20, 1922, by Shakespeare & Co., Paris, 1,000 numbered copies, very, very elegant. Second printing, Egoist Press, London, October 1922, 2,000 numbered copies, of which 500 copies were burned by the New York Post Office Authorities. Third printing, Egoist Press, London, January 1923, 500 numbered copies of which 499 were seized by the Custom Authorities of the Post Office. What the hell is this? You're supposed to work for society, and this is what society does. Then a fourth printing, a fifth, a sixth, seventh, eighth, and this is the ninth printing, 1947.

———⌇⌇⌇———

QUESTION: *Would you comment on Jung's doubletake on* Ulysses?

CAMPBELL: This is one of the worst jobs Jung did. I mean, he never got what was going on in *Ulysses*. He got angry and wrote this tantrum because he wasn't getting it. As a matter of fact, psychiatrists don't have very good relationships to art of any kind. They always see it as symptomatic. That's what happened with Jung and *Ulysses.*

Both Joyce and Jung were in Zurich, and they knew each other. But I don't know how seriously Jung took his critique of *Ulysses,* or how much time he spent on it. Joyce's young daughter was brought to Jung at one time, and then one of Joyce's patronesses wanted him to be psychoanalyzed by Jung. What a ridiculous thing! Can you imagine an artist going to a psychiatrist for improvement! What Jung said about Joyce's daughter was that she was drowning in the very water in which Joyce was swimming. You have to be prepared for that domain of the powers of the psyche and the spirit. You have to be able to take it, and she couldn't. And as the constant presence in the house, he was, as it were, pulling her into the water.[129]

QUESTION: *That is the myth of Daedalus; his son Icarus didn't escape.*

CAMPBELL: That's right. Icarus fell into the water.

---

QUESTION: *I have a question about didactic art, which Joyce felt was improper art. It seems to me that great art does teach you something. Did he mean there should be no intent to teach?*

CAMPBELL: Didacticism isn't necessarily teaching. Didacticism is putting forth a program. The novels written mostly around the twenties that had to do with social improvement, for instance, all this leftist writing that is criticizing capitalism and furthering the new society and so forth, this is didactic writing.

I don't know if great art is supposed to instruct. Does a Picasso painting instruct? *I'm* instructing. I'm telling you what the hell they are put together with, and what's in there, and all that kind of thing. But when you are reading Joyce, what you get is radiance. You become harmonized, and that is what it's about. It is not teaching you a lesson. It is feeding you, giving you spiritual balance and spiritual harmony.

We are in our schooling so oriented to sociology and rational philosophy and so on that we think that's what art is about. It isn't. That word "esthetic" means having to do with the senses. What the artwork does is present you with a balanced organization, and while you are looking at it in esthetic arrest, for a moment you are in balance and breakthrough to transcendence. Is that instruction? That is a revelation. When Joyce was a young man, he wrote "epiphanies," his stories in *Dubliners.* Artwork should produce an epiphany, a revelation. That's not didacticism. Do you see the difference? I think it's an important distinction for a young artist to understand, because, as I said, we're so heavily instructed in sociology that we're intent on improving the world instead of affirming it. This is the problem with our mythology. All of the early mythologies, as well as the high mythologies, are concerned, not with improving the world, but with putting you in harmony with it.

The first example of a didactic mythology is Zoroastrianism. There you have a good world, and then an evil power breaks it, and it falls. So the world in which we live is a combination of good and evil—that's an old Manichean idea: the light has been swallowed by darkness, and we must release the light from the darkness. Our whole tradition says, "No. No. No. No, you don't yield to nature. Nature is fallen. Nature is corrupt. You correct nature." Joyce and the artist have a totally different mythology. They are saying, "Yes. Yes. Yes. Yes." And then the critic says, "Oh that's negative. You shouldn't say 'Yes' to anything like this."

QUESTION: *About "proper and improper art" in* A Portrait: *is Joyce suggesting that the opening up to transcendence is not possible in a kinetic narrative? If this is so, aren't most myths, including* Ulysses, *very kinetic? Don't the characters, with symbols or objects in them, draw you and repel you?*

CAMPBELL: Kinesis in the way of desire means desire for the object. Desire to do something about something moves you into action. If you have a flowing action in the piece, that's not the kinesis that we're talking about. If in reading a novel you are just following that action and getting the rhythm of the cycles, the rise and the fall of the cycles of tension and *détente,* that is not the kinesis that Joyce is talking about. When Joyce talks about kinetic art, he is talking either about the novel that tells you, "Society is rotten and needs fixing, so go out and fix it," or about the other sort of kinetic art, the kind which presents an apple that you want to eat. Who would want to eat Cézanne's apples? If you are filled with desire for the object represented, then you have the kinetic, pornographic relationship.

I understand the problem, because it took me a while to realize what Joyce was talking about. The word "kinesis" just means movement. We like to be moved, and the action of the novel moves, gets going. However, that's not what Joyce is talking about when he describes kinesis. He's talking about being filled with desire for possession and use of the object. That's pornography. The artwork is understood to refer to something else. And even a portrait is in danger of this. The standard definition of a portrait is "a picture with something wrong about the mouth." It doesn't look like Suzy, so we don't want it. Now nobody wanted to look like any of Picasso's portraits. Especially later on. But they are art; the object is there in and for itself. As Joyce says: "It is that thing which it is and no other thing." (P213)

Joyce gives us very precise and clear definitions of the difference between proper and improper art. Art in service of advertising or of sociology is improper art. Proper art has *integritas, consonantia,* and *claritas.* Then, further, with narrative art, you have the comic and the tragic. Now the Hindus recognize moods other than the comic and the tragic. They have the various *rasas,* or tastes, and the whole function of an artwork is to render a particular *rasa*—that taste, that flavor. But that's not the same as kinesis.

QUESTION: *The confusion really comes from realizing that you are drawn. It's a different kind of drawing. The symbols within the stories obviously refer to something else, but that doesn't mean that you might become involved with movement. It's not static.*

CAMPBELL: Oh yes, it's nothing like esthetic arrest. Time and space disappear, but you are held in the rapture. Dying can be a rapture too, I'm told.

---

QUESTION: *You spoke of the gift of prophecy as being a familiarity with the great morphological processes that shape and terminate life forces. If that is what we mean by prophecy, do you regard Joyce as a prophet? If so, could you say something about the nature of his prophecy as you understand it?*

CAMPBELL: I don't see Joyce as a prophet. The word "prophet" usually refers to prophecies into the future. I don't see any specific prophecies in

Joyce. I think of him as what he said he was: one revealing—revealing the essence of life. Of course, in that, there is an inevitable prophetic moment; that is to say, if death is in life, then death is coming. That's about as far as it goes.

QUESTION: *What about his use of Vico's ideas?*

CAMPBELL: Well, he uses Vico, but that's not his prophecy, it's Vico's. What Joyce sees in Vico is this cycle. And you can see the cycle. It's very interesting to read Yeats's wonderful book *A Vision,* where he gives a cycle for the history of a culture. Ezra Pound pointed out to Yeats that Yeats's definition of the culture cycle and the dating of the different stages correspond almost precisely to Spengler's, although Yeats and Spengler came from two totally different positions on this matter.

The recognition of cultural cycles is a recognition that there is in the history of a culture a beginning, a middle, and an end. A culture begins with a youthful impulse, comes to a moment of maturation, and then problems start, and it begins to decline, to disintegrate. That is the pattern for all organic forms. Recognizing cultural cycles means one sees culture as an organism and cultural history as an organic history.

We are going through the cycle and have to say "Yes" to it. It is hard to resist. You know I'm trying to get a club going—the Club for Stopping the Continental Drift. You see what I mean?

———

QUESTION: *The artist is always finding something by totally losing what so-ciety calls reality, the thing that is accepted. The artist is never accepting. And isn't that where his self-teaching becomes the art that Joyce was speaking of?*

CAMPBELL: That's the going off into the forbidden, the unknown, and coming out with your own discoveries. Students in art, of course, have to learn a technique from another artist. Then there comes that crisis when, having practiced and practiced, they begin to feel their own demon coming through. Some artist-teachers—I know a couple—don't like to see that happen and are too hard on the student. What that creates is a bad attitude: the student becomes negative to his own teacher. The worst thing that can happen, I think, is fighting the one who has given you the gift, because you should use the gift in the way of your discovery. You must go out beyond the teacher.

QUESTION: *I worked with a teacher, Hans Hoffman, who never did that. He started to free you. You made your inner discoveries first; you weren't influenced; you weren't told how to paint.*

CAMPBELL: Well, good for Hans Hoffman! But there are other painters who don't. I know at least two. They just hang on.

———

QUESTION: *I'm a bit confused. I was waiting to hear what would happen with Stephen and Bloom, and [then Molly provides the end of the book.] Stephen goes to Bloom's house. But what happens?*

CAMPBELL: When Joyce has Stephen go out into the night, that's the end of the Stephen that we have known throughout the book. [Yet Stephen has changed within the "Circe" chapter.] Because of his compassion for Bloom, Stephen clowns in Nighttown to distract people from laughing at Bloom, you see, and then his mother comes to him. [By that event, Joyce symbolizes that something crucial has occurred to the writer of *Ulysses*.] Something else[, the changed compassionate creator,] is coming.

Joyce ends up after writing *Ulysses* a totally different man from the writer who began *Ulysses*. He is another man when he is doing *Finnegans Wake*. *Ulysses* is heavy with earth. All of the precise details hold you down all the way. Molly is heavy, and *Ulysses* is heavy. I love the book, but by God, I get tired with it. You know, Joyce loads it in on you. He really does. And this is what was intended. *Finnegans Wake* flows. It just ripples along. Molly becomes Anna Livia Plurabelle, this wonderful, tripping, lively female power in the book.

QUESTION: *You say that Joyce himself was changed in this book as Stephen was. In the "Circe" chapter, there were things other than Tiresias blinded and having the insight, and the children with the metal faces who knew five languages. Bella became Bello—that was interesting.*

CAMPBELL: Female becomes male, just in his mind at that time. The male is the aggressor, and the female is the submissive one. Bloom turns into a little submissive pig—he has a kind of masochistic attitude, you know: "Enormously I desiderate your domination." (U430) It's hard to know how much of this is Joyce's experience. How could he write the experience of Molly Bloom as she lies there? I understand he did—that it's a valid picture of what a woman's mind would be. Of course, he had a wife, Nora Barnacle, and that poor soul was a courageous, heroic woman. What they went through, just because he wouldn't write books that anybody would buy.

⚬⚬⚬

QUESTION: *You talked about the Jew in exile. Is that related to the idea that you must go into exile to discover yourself?*

CAMPBELL: No I wouldn't say that. The story of the Wandering Jew is a medieval legend: as Christ was carrying the cross, one of the people standing along the line watching him said, "Go faster." Jesus looked at him and said, "I will; tarry until I return. You will be here when I return." Here is the one condemned to be in the world and of the earth forever. The Wandering Jew, therefore, represents the earthly virtues, of which compassion is the noblest.

Bloom is not trying for spiritual exaltation. He is living on earth; he has very nice attitudes towards people and the capacity for sympathy and compassion that Stephen never had. Stephen is off on a trajectory into outer space, you might say. Bloom is tied to the earth; he is, as it were, the moon-man, the one who is bound to the world of death and resurrection and has an understanding of it and pays attention to it. Bloom's interest in the physical details of life is all part of this theme of the Wandering Jew.

QUESTION: *What is the difference between involvement with the world and engagement?*

CAMPBELL: Engagement means, in its strongest sense, "You are this, which is all you've got." I had a funny thought a few weeks ago—I started talking about it earlier today, and then I didn't finish it. It was about the fall. Man has fallen. We are in a world of exile and fall. But the image of the savior which comes to us through Buddhism, through Zoroastrianism, through the Greek mystery religions, and through the idea of Christ is an image of voluntary entrance into the world. The savior comes in a voluntary way. He doesn't fall even to the death upon the cross. This is voluntary affirmation. It is not a fall, it is a voluntary act. If you get inside this idea and feel it in that way, then a very important transformation of consciousness takes place, and you are saved. You are no longer in exile, no longer in the fallen world; rather, you are saying, "Yes." This is Nietzsche's *amor fati,* the love of your fate—you say "Yes" to it. This what Joyce does in *Finnegans Wake.*

QUESTION: *Is this what you suppose Joyce the artist does in approaching his demon: a voluntary descent to examine the demon, but holding onto something, and then coming back up through the tip of the mountain, rather than climbing up the other side?*

CAMPBELL: Fine. That's what you get when Stephen goes into the brothels chanting the *Introit* for paschal time. He knows he is going to, and he intends to, lose himself in a consciousness-expanding experience. It is quite intentional. And then, when Bloom comes in, Stephen is playing open fifths on the piano—that's it.

QUESTION: *Does he intend to lose himself, or is he consciously hanging on?*

CAMPBELL: He is losing himself, the self he has been. When the transformation of consciousness occurs, the one that was there before isn't there any more. It is as extreme as that. And as we have seen when going from *Ulysses* to *Finnegans Wake,* it is another man writing, it's not the same man at all.

---

QUESTION: *I'd like to ask, talking about the legacy of Joyce: Is there any kind of contribution you feel he's made to the work of Samuel Beckett and, specifically, is there a relationship between* Waiting for Godot *and any of the work of Joyce?*

CAMPBELL: Well, I remember seeing a wonderful production of *Waiting for Godot*—I think it was the first one that was done—with Bert Lahr. And when I saw Pozzo and Lucky, I thought, "This is James Joyce." There is certainly an influence of Joyce. But Beckett has assimilated it to himself. I don't think you spot James Joyce throughout, but Joyce is there in the boldness of Beckett's imagery. I don't know if I have a right to say this, but Beckett seems to me rather dismal in a way that Joyce isn't. I find a dismal quality in Beckett's image of the terminal age that we're in now. Of course, Pozzo is the church, you know, and we are Lucky; we are so lucky to be Pozzo's slave. This is certainly Joyce's way of thinking about the church, which he called "a conspiracy of morbid bachelors."

QUESTION: *In* Godot, *there is a leaf which is a radiant thing that goes unnoticed. They wait for Godot, who came and left. It perhaps could be said that Joyce himself created bodies of work that were radiant and yet might not have been noticed at all were it not for a few scholars.*

CAMPBELL: Well, that might be, yes. As for the leaf, I think of the last words of Anna Livia: The stream is running through Dublin back to the ocean; day is dawning; the dream is fading; and as Anna Livia passes out, she says, "My leaves have drifted from me. All. But one clings still. I'll bear it on me. To remind me of. Lff!" (628.6–7) That's the leaf on the tree in *Godot* that was mentioned.

———※———

QUESTION: *I may be saying the obvious here, but it seems that Joyce is doing with words what Picasso is doing with his forms, just fracturing them and putting them together in new ways.*

CAMPBELL: That's certainly true. That was what I was hoping would come through: the smashing, recomposing, and putting together—in Joyce, in associations with dream; and in Picasso, in associations with the visual. Moreover, I'm trying to point out, with almost the same dates coming all along the line, that this is something that was happening right across the board.

QUESTION: *There's a thread running through your remarks that suggests that there's some larger unifying theme—turmoil or war or whatever it is—in the work of Picasso and Joyce. You keep referring to the same year in each artist's development, as if they were going forth in parallel. Can you illuminate that?*

CAMPBELL: Perhaps it is the *zeitgeist,* the spirit of the time. The minds of these men—and this is true also for Spengler and Yeats—seize the implications of the conditions of the civilization. They really perceive what is happening; and in their art, there is a progression from the nineteenth-century mechanistic way of thinking into what might be called (by people who don't care for this kind of thing) a "mystical" point of view.

I would say that the sciences are moving that way right now. In the field of consciousness research—and also in physics and astronomy—we are breaking past the cause-and-effect, mechanistic way of interpreting things. In the biological sciences, there is a vitalism coming in that goes much further toward positing a common universal consciousness of which our brain is simply an organ. Consciousness does not come from the brain. The brain is an organ of consciousness. It focuses consciousness and pulls it in and directs it through a time and space field. But the antecedent of that is the universal consciousness of which we are all just a part.

Schopenhauer, I would say, is the key philosopher for understanding these artists. Thomas Mann is full of Schopenhauer. Nietzsche is full of Schopenhauer. And Joyce's "Proteus" chapter—"Ineluctable modality of the visible"—just translates Schopenhauer. Schopenhauer wrote a wonderful paper on "An Apparent Intention in the Fate of the Individual," "*Transzcendente Spekulation über die anscheinende Absichtlichkeit im Schicksale des Einzelnen,*" which I don't think has been translated. At least, I can't find it.[130] He says that when you go through life, this character appears, that character appears, and it all seems accidental at the time it is happening. Then when you get on in your sixties or seventies and look back, your life looks like a well-planned novel with a coherent theme. Things have happened, you realize, in an appropriate way. Incidents that seemed to be accidental, pure chance, turn out to be major elements in the structuring of this novel. Schopenhauer says, "Who wrote the novel? You did."

Here a new consideration comes in. Just as people influenced you and played an important role in your life, so you are influencing others and playing an important role in their lives. There is a reciprocal influence, a network of interlocked novels. Who wrote all of these? Schopenhauer says, "It's as though the world were a dream dreamed by a single dreamer in which all the dream characters dreamed you." There is the clue to *Finnegans Wake.* Here is the world dream. And the world dreamer, who is he? Let's call him Finnegan. We are all particles of his dream. The *Wake* is like a hologram. The hologram is now a kind of metaphor for some of the problems the scientists are running into.[131]

QUESTION: *Would you talk further about science and mental consciousness?*

CAMPBELL: I'm not really competent to talk about that. You see, I'm totally an amateur in those fields. But my friends working in those fields tell me that, for instance, the problem with sub-atomic particles is that no one knows what those things are. They can be looked at as waves, and they can be looked at as particles. Nobody has seen them. We can only see their traces on the screen. There is a laboratory at Stanford that's two and a half miles long where they shoot these things. And nobody knows what they are.

When you have a possibility of two ways of talking about sub-atomic entities—one as a wave, and another as particles—this gets you into the same kind of problems that we have in describing our mentality. There is a man named David Birtram who speaks of there being no locus for memory in the mind. A memory seems to be spread all over the place—in the way, almost, of waves—until a specific act of focusing brings it into manifestation. Another man, David Bohm in London, sees the whole universe that way. So scientists are talking about both the universe and the mind as being comparable to a hologram.

There is something fantastic about the mind that Kant recognized when he asked, "How is it that we can make calculations for space here and know with certainty that these calculations will work for space out there, where man has never been?" During the spaceshot, the one just before Armstrong came down on the moon, the space module was on the way back, and Houston Ground Control asked, "Who's navigating now?" And the answer was, "Newton." The laws of space that were in Newton's head work out where the moon is. Nobody had ever been there, but by following those laws, by turning the jet in a certain direction and emitting a certain amount of energy, that module, that little peapod, was brought back to within a mile of a boat in the Pacific Ocean. When Armstrong's shoe came down on the moon, however, nobody knew how deeply it was going to go into moondust, because that was *a posteriori* knowledge, knowledge learned "after the fact." By contrast, knowledge of what space is like is *a priori* knowledge, knowledge we have "before the fact."

So, space out there is the same as space in here—the same mystery. You can work it all out in your head. How much can you work out in your head? A lot. Who knows? We are particles of space. It was from the hydrogen in space from a big bang that the constellations came, and then the planets, and we are the fruit of one of the planets. We are beginning to develop a mythology of spirit: what we call "spirit" may be an aspect of matter. I think this is in Joyce's books. Wordsworth had a touch of it in those wonderful lines about Tintern Abbey:

> For I have learned
> To look on nature, not as in the hour
> Of thoughtless youth; but hearing oftentimes
> The still sad music of humanity,
> Nor harsh nor grating, though of ample power
> To chasten and subdue.[132]

That is what Joyce is doing when Finnegan fades into the countryside. When the countryside is Finnegan, we have a tour that's telling us about ourselves. You remember Stephen saying in *Ulysses,* "What went forth to the ends of the world to traverse not itself becomes that self which it itself was ineluctably preconditioned to become." (U412) We see this idea of a set of principles that informs all life and all being. [We are] ourselves, but we are in perfect harmony with the world.

Now I have the image, for example, of a little baby, just born, being placed on the mother's body and immediately nursing there. The baby has an impulse and a universe which, at that time, is the mother. The mother is ready and responds. The baby is ready for what nature has to offer and responds. Nature is ready for the baby. Similarly, in a larger way, the whole of Mother Nature is ready for us, and we are made for it—there is this echo.

That is what Schopenhauer is talking about when he speaks about the world as a dream dreamed by a single dreamer. This is a metaphor to say something about the mystery, a deep mystery. Schopenhauer then has a chapter on death and the indestructibility of our being. What dies is the phenomenal manifestation of our true being, which is one with that which is in turn.[133] It sounds mysterious because we are used to thinking of things in nineteenth-century mechanistic terms, but that is what is going on. And I think that is what Joyce means. I think of the *Wake* as a modern *purāṇa,* a modern translation of the fundamental mythic form into a contemporary context, where the contemporary world is around you instead of the old world of 2000 B.C. which you get with the Book of Genesis. Joyce was a modern man. He knew it all, and he's bringing this revelation on.

—*~~*—

QUESTION: *You talked about elemental ideas and their ethnic expression, but I don't recall you ever describing what the elemental ideas are.*

CAMPBELL: Elementary ideas. Well, *boy and girl* is one. The relationships are differently rendered in different cultures. Take the notion of marriage. Think of the different kinds of marriages there are in the different cultures. There are elemental ideas in *Finnegans Wake:* the conflict between two males, the one who continually loses and the one who continually wins. Then there is the whole aura of victory, the whole aura of loss––these are elementary things that go on throughout nature. Then there are the different modes of male relating to female, and female relating to male. There are three modes here: one is the seductress; another is the wife, who puts the husband together again; and the third is the young girl, the daughter who then becomes in a way identical with the seductress. This is an idea that came to Joyce already from the *Odyssey.* And I did mention Circe, Calypso, and Nausicaa.

Those are the elementary ideas that are coming through this book. In relation to human life, there are certain elementary ideas such as the idea of sacrifice and the idea of God. But the notion of God is one that is culturally conditioned, and so any particular God is a folk idea. In principle, a god refers to something beyond itself. If you get stuck with a folk idea, you have not opened fully to your own humanity. This is the whole problem in cults. You can't have a cult unless you have a folk idea, a limitation of the elementary; but if you get stuck with the image, then you have lost the message in the object, the symbol, and you are stuck with the symbol. Everything is a symbol. Goethe says, "*Alles vergängliche ist nur ein Gleichnis*": "Everything phenomenal is a metaphor."[134] Look at it that way, and you are a poet.

—*~~*—

QUESTION: *What did you feel Joyce's Fourth Book, his* Paradiso, *was going to be?*

CAMPBELL: All we have for the new form are a couple of little sentences that Joyce let drop. It was going to be a short book. It was going to be simple. It was going to have to do with the ocean.[135]

*Finnegans Wake* ends, as you will recall, with the main female figure, the river Liffey flowing back out into the sea, returning to Father Ocean, to stasis. History has come to an end, you might say. We've transcended history. And if you don't want to go round and round and round again, then you can stay out there in the ocean. So, that would have to have been the setting of the next book.

Joyce said the Fourth Book was going to be short and simple and about the ocean. All the clues are found in this statement. And when Joyce says that the Fourth Book was to have been about the ocean, we know what it was to have been about. It comes out where Joyce speaks about "lotus spray" ("let us pray") as being what this book is. (598.14) Joyce calls the *Wake* an "umbrella history" (573.36); the opening out of rebirth is like that. So, the unwritten book would have to have been related to Viṣṇu's dream.

I'm very sure that the image—because he uses this image in *Finnegans Wake*—is of Viṣṇu sleeping on the cosmic serpent resting on the cosmic water dreaming the dream of the universe which rises in the form of a lotus from his navel; and there sits Brahmā, the so-called Creator, flooding with consciousness this world dream that has come from the navel of Viṣṇu. This universe, the lotus, is the world dream of the world dreamer. It is his bride, the goddess Padmā. She is what is in movement. She is Anna Livia, you see.

Now Viṣṇu's dream has two aspects. First, in its historical aspect, the dream goes through the cycle of world history: the lotus comes forth from his navel, grows, and will depart. In its other aspect, it goes back into him again, and in the intervals between worlds, it is potential in its simple form within the god himself. And then it comes forth again and is in process in time. I think that in his *Paradiso* Joyce was going to give us the second aspect, what the potential was, not the complexities of history. He would write about what might be called archetypal forms.

There is an Indian *purāṇa* called the Mārkandeya Purāṇa. It is about Mārkandeya, a sage who, when the world ended, didn't die; instead, he went into Viṣṇu's belly with the dream and wandered around inside Viṣṇu looking at the dream. Mārkandeya at one point slips out of Viṣṇu's mouth and falls out into the cosmic black ocean. There was nothing there. Viṣṇu just reaches out and puts him back into his mouth. I think that was what Joyce's next book was going to be. He was going to be inside the god, not showing history taking place, but with all the potentials of history now in potential form. I think Joyce was going to get put into Viṣṇu's mouth and, in some way or other, was going to take us with him.

# CHAPTER NOTES

## EDITOR'S FOREWORD

1  [From an early-afternoon question-and-answer session on December 18, 1982, part of the seminar "James Joyce and Pablo Picasso: Mythology in 20th Century Literature and Art," presented at the Theater of the Open Eye in New York City, December 18–19, 1982. This lecture appears as L820 in the Joseph Campbell Foundation's database of Campbell's lectures.]

2  [From a discussion on the morning of December 18, 1982, part of "James Joyce and Pablo Picasso." (L820)]

3  [From "The Mythology and Art of James Joyce," a lecture series by Campbell for the C. G. Jung Society of San Francisco at the California Historical Society on December 13–14, 1982 (L986–989); subsequently edited and released as the videotape series *Wings of Art* (Oakland, CA: Brightline, 1990).]

## JAMES JOYCE 1882–1941: AN OBITUARY NOTICE

4  [From the Sarah Lawrence College newspaper *The Campus,* Wednesday, January 22, 1941, p. 2.]

5  [This sentence is a version of FW 129.7–8.]

259

## CHAPTER I

6  ["The Novels of James Joyce" section is a conflation of various lectures by Campbell, including: "James Joyce and Pablo Picasso" (L820); "The Mythology

and Art of James Joyce," presented at Indiana University on April 25, 1968 (195 ff.); and "Imagery of Vision in the Novels of James Joyce," presented at Esalen Institute in November 1968 (L210–213). Also interwoven herein are Campbell's paper "Contransmagnificandjewbangtantiality," from *Studies in the Literary Imagination,* Volume III, No. 2 (October, 1970); parts of "Unlocking the Door to Joyce: Two Experts Present a Skeleton Key to *Finnegans Wake,*" by Campbell and Henry Morton Robinson, in *The Saturday Review of Literature,* Vol. 26 (June 19, 1943); and several selections from Campbell's unpublished papers, including article notes and fragments that appear in the Joseph Campbell Foundation archives as "Coincidence of Opposites" (MC17), "Joyce Fragments" (MC18), "Joyce/Dog-God" (MC25), and "Dante/Gafurius/Stephen/Leopold" (MC26).]

7    [For a detailed examination of these ten motifs in the hero's journey, see Campbell, *The Hero with a Thousand Faces,* Bollingen Series XVII (Princeton, NJ: Princeton Univeristy Press, 1949).]

8    [This is the cry of Wendy in J. M. Barrie's *Peter Pan,* which premiered in the autumn of 1904, so the reference here is a bit anachronistic. Of course, Wendy does not have obstetrical details in mind when she utters this cry.]

9    [The German *Alp* means "demon " or "goblin," and "nightmare" is *Alpdruck* or *Alptraum.*]

10   [Release from the cycle of rebirth is also found in Vico. The Vichian cycle is exclusively a *pagan* cycle. See Fáj Attila, "Vico's Basic Law of History in *Finnegans Wake,*" in Donald Phillip Verene, *Vico and Joyce* (Albany: State University of New York, 1987), p. 22:

> … Vico maintains that there were in the past, and will be in the future, exoduses, breakouts from the eternal *corsi* and *ricorsi,* even if in all these cases temporary relapses into the general law valid for the pagan peoples occurred or may occur. The ancient chosen people evaded the recurring historical cycles, and the same will come about to the new chosen people if it follows its Master's commandments. In front of the leaders of the Jews "the river Jordan was driven back" (Psalm 114.3); and the same flowing back of that river happened in front of the Messiah—as is to be seen on the old icons representing Christ's baptism. A similar phenomenon will occur in the future: the hopelessly and tragically recurrent *corsi* and *ricorsi* will be stopped by Christ's true followers, who will never again let their community or state relapse into barbarism.

The main passages from Vico referred to in the above passage are sections 1109ff from Vico, *La Scienza Nuova,* in the edition translated as *The New Science* by M. H. Fisch and T. G. Bergin (Ithaca: Cornell University Press, 1970).]

11   There is a very interesting paper by Thomas Mann, written just about the time Joyce was working these things out, called "*Versuch über das Theater,*" "About the Theatre" [in Mann, *Gesammelte Werke in zwölf Banden, Band X: Reden und Aufsätze* (S. Fischer Verlag), pp. 23–62, esp. pp. 27–35.]

## CHAPTER II

12  Guiraut de Borneilh, *Tam cum los oills el cor...*, in John Rutherford, *The Troubadors* (London: Smith, Elder and Company, 1861), p. 34.

13  [Ellsworth Mason and Richard Ellmann, editors, *The Critical Writings of James Joyce* (New York: Viking Press, 1959), p. 143: from the Paris notebooks (1903).]

14  ["Those things are beautiful the apprehension of which pleases."—*Critical Writings,* op. cit. p. 147; translating Aquinas, *Summa Theologica* I, q. 5, art. 4: "*Pulchra enim dicuntur ea quae visa placent.*"

—He uses the word *visa,* said Stephen, to cover esthetic apprehensions of all kinds, whether through sight or hearing or through any other avenue of apprehension. (P207)

Father William Noon, S.J., in his definitive *Joyce and Aquinas* (New Haven: Yale University Press, 1957), p. 26n, agrees with Joyce's application of the term: "The word 'sight,' for Aquinas, referred to all knowledge obtained through the intellect."]

15  [In the Paris notebooks of 1903 (see *The Critical Writings,* p. 144), Joyce writes:

And now of comedy. An improper art aims at exciting in the way of comedy the feeling of desire but the feeling which is proper to comic art is the feeling of joy. Desire, as I have said, is the feeling which urges us to go to something but joy is the feeling which the possession of some good excites in us.... For desire urges us from rest that we may possess something but joy holds us in rest so long as we possess something.... From this it may be seen that tragedy is the imperfect manner and comedy the perfect manner in art.]

16  [See Heinrich Zimmer, *Myths and Symbols in Indian Art and Civilization,* edited by Joseph Campbell, Bollingen Series VI (Princeton: Princeton University Press, 1972), pp. 147–149.]

17  [For an extended analysis of these same passages, see E. L. Epstein, *The Ordeal of Stephen Dedalus: The Conflict of the Generations in James Joyce's "A Portrait of the Artist as a Young Man"* (Carbondale, IL: Southern Illinois University Press, 1971), pp. 26–35.]

18  [It is sometimes described as having been a kind of "boneless" dance. Nora Joyce described it as "flinging your legs over your neck and kicking the furniture to pieces." See Ole Vinding, "James Joyce in Copenhagen," in *Portraits of the Artist in Exile: Recollections of James Joyce by Europeans,* edited by Willard Potts (Seattle: University of Washington Press, 1979), p. 150.]

19  [The phrase "He broke his glasses" is a linguistic subtlety, syntactically ambiguous: "He deliberately broke his glasses" and "His glasses became broken accidentally." Father Arnall does not correct the prefect of studies's interpretation of the phrase, and so Stephen is punished. See Edmund L. Epstein, "James Joyce and Language," in *Joyce Centenary Essays,* edited by Richard F. Peterson,

Alan M. Cohn, and Edmund L. Epstein (Carbondale and Edwardsville, Illinois: Southern Illinois University Press, 1983), pp. 62–63.]

20  [The Tsar was advocating, among other things, universal peace and an international court of arbitration to adjudicate conflicts between nations. Some historians now believe that he was merely attempting to give Russia more time to build up its armies.]

## CHAPTER III

21  [The Corrected Edition of *Ulysses* restores the reading of U35.199 as "Nother dying come home father." "Nother" was apparently overcorrected by the various printers of *Ulysses* until the Corrected Edition.]

22  From Joseph Campbell's unpublished papers, "Joyce Fragments" (MC18).

23  *Finnegans Wake* starts with the thunder: "bababadalgharaghtakamminarronn-konnbronntonnerronntuonnthunntrovarrhounawnskawntoohoohoordenen-thurnuk!" appears on the first page, and there are repetitions of these thunderwords throughout the book.

24  For a more detailed discussion of this motif, see Joseph Campbell, *The Masks of God: Creative Mythology* (New York: Viking Penguin, 1968), pp. 283–285.

25  In Homer there is no actual mention of rape: Odysseus reports that they slew the men of the Cicones and "took their wives...and divided them among us" (Book IX, ll. 40–42).]

26  [In Homer, there is no mention of a swamp, although Circe's isle is described as "lying low" (χθαμαλὴ κεῖται), and Circe's palace is in a "place of wide outlook" (περισκέπτῳ ἐνὶ χώρῳ); see Book X, ll. 196, 211.]

27  [Thomas Hardy, under the title of his long dramatic monologue "Panthera," published in 1909, comments:

> (For other forms of this legend—first met with in the second century—
> see Origen contra Celsum; the Talmud; Sepher Toldoth Jeschu;
> quoted fragments of lost Apocryphal gospels; Strauss, Haeckel; etc.)

In fact, the accusation originated, not among the Jews, but among the pagans. The earliest account of the matter is to be found in the second century A.D. In an anti-Christian tract, the pagan Celsus, pretending to be a Jew, argued that a Roman centurion named Panther or Panthera was the real father of Jesus. We do not have Celsus's original attack on Christianity, but being based heavily on Gnosticism, it was arguably very like Campbell's.

The entire material on "Panthera" is transmitted in Origen's third-century response to Celsus, in which Origen scornfully rejects Celsus's pretense to be a Jew. See *Origenis contra Celsum*, I, 28, 32, in J-P. Migne, *Patrologiae Cursus Completus*, Series Graeca, Vol. 11 (Turnhout, Belgium-Brepols), pp. 719–722; see also N. R. M. De Lange, *Origen and the Jews: Studies in Jewish-Christian Relations in Third-Century Palestine* (Cambridge/London: Cambridge University Press, 1976), pp. 66, 69.

Campbell's comment that the accusation occurs "in the Talmud or the Midrash, one or the other" is, therefore, inaccurate. Although there are a few references in the Talmud of the early Christian era to someone who could be identified with Jesus, they are all vague and unspecified. Jesus is called "Jeshu ben Pantiri," or "Jeshua ben Pandira" only in two or three places, apparently without explanation of the designation. "Of the name Ben Pandira ... no satisfactory explanation has been given." ("Jesus in Rabbinical Literature," in *The Universal Jewish Encyclopedia,* Vol. 6, p. 88). It is clear that the *origin* of the accusation is either completely pagan, or derives from "heretics inimical to Jesus, as the Ophites and Cainites..." ("Jesus," in *The Jewish Encyclopedia,* Vol. 7, p. 170). See also *Encyclopedia Judaica,* "Jesus," Vol. 10, pp. 13–17.

It is only later, after the period of "the Talmud or the Midrash," in the *Sefer Toledoth Jeshu,* the medieval Jewish document to which Hardy refers, that the story of Panthera is repeated and expanded to the form with which Hardy and Joyce were familiar.]

28 [Campbell pronounces "Deasy" as "daisy," the way some Irish do. "Deasy," however, is also frequently pronounced as "deezy."]

29 [The drowned-man theme appears prominently in *The Waste Land,* with the figure of the drowned Phoenician sailor, but this is not the first appearance of the undersea as a symbol of a type of smothered semi-existence. Eliot himself treats this symbol in "Prufrock." The theme of submerged human lives seems to have originated with the Symbolists. In *Bruges la Morte* (1892), the Belgian Symbolist Georges Rodenbach presents the "Ophelianization" of his home town when he drowns a town, Bruges, to represent the half-existence of automatized life, which he repeats in his *Vies Encloses;* see A. G. Lehmann, *The Symbolist Aesthetic in France* (Oxford: Blackwell's, 1968), p. 288. The theme plays a prominent part in Mallarmé's *Un Coup de Dés.* In our own time, Lawrence Durrell in his novel *Clea* has a woman dive into a wreck, and there she is pinned by her own harpoon gun: a symbol of the dangers of the half-life and of the past. The symbol is repeated by Adrienne Rich in *Diving into the Wreck.*]

30 [*Preisschrift über die Grundlage der Moral,* "On the Foundation of Morality," in Arthur Schopenhauer's *Sämtliche Werke,* Dritter Band (Munich: R. Piper Verlag, 1912), pp. 699–700.

A later passage in this work is relevant for Joyce's work. On pp. 701–702 Schopenhauer gives an example of compassion (*Mitleid*) preventing a crime. Two young men, Caius and Titus, are in love (with different girls), but they each have rivals for the love of the girls. Each is confronted with a dilemma: What shall I do about this situation? They both are tempted to take the short way out of the dilemma—murder. However, Caius works his way through the recommendations of a number of contemporary philosophical moralists— Fichte, Wollaston, Hutcheson, Adam Smith, Christian Wolff—and even evokes the Bible and Spinoza, to no avail. Titus, on the other hand, simply says, "When it came to making the arrangements, and so for the moment I had to concern myself not with my passion but with that rival, I clearly saw for the first time what would happen to him. But then I was seized with compassion and pity (*Aber nun ergriff mich Mitleid und Erbarmen*); I felt sorry for him; I had not the heart to do it, and could not.[*Ich konnte es nicht übers Herz bringen: ich habe es nicht thun können*]"; from E. F. J. Payne, trans., *On the Basis of Morality* (Indianapolis: Bobbs-Merrill, 1965), p. 169.

In *Finnegans Wake*, two young men have a moral dilemma: shall they or shall they not shoot their father, now in the guise of a Russian General? One son, Butt, the designated assassin, sees the General in a vulnerable position—in an act of defecation—and explains to the other son, Taff, that "I adn't the arts to"; he did not have the heart to shoot a man who was in such a humanly pathetic position:

> But,...when I looked upon the Saur of all the Haurousians with the weight of his arge fullin upon him from the travaillings of his tommuck and rueckenased the fates of a bosser, there was fear on me the sons of Nuad for him and it was heavy he was for me then the way I immingled my Irmenial hairmaierians ammongled his Gospolis fomiliours till, achaura moucreas, I adn't the arts to. (344.31, 33–36—345.1–3)]

31  [Stephen's musings on perception generally owe more to Berkeley and Aristotle than to Locke.]

32  [Aristotle was traditionally considered to be bald and rich.]

33  [There is room for debate on the source of these terms underlying Stephen's theorizing on space and time. The source for Joyce's *nacheinander* (time) and *nebeneinander* (space) may have been Lessing's *Laocoön*, which in 1766 defined the difference in the arts as matters of time, as in music and poetry, and space, as in painting and sculpture (Chapter XVI). See Don Gifford with Robert J. Seidman, editors, *Ulysses Annotated: Notes for James Joyce's Ulysses*, revised and expanded edition (Berkeley and Los Angeles: University of California Press, 1988), p. 45. Stephen himself identifies his source as Lessing at U456. However, Lessing used the word *aufeinander*, not *nacheinander*. (See also P214.)]

34  [The socks and brogues come from Mulligan, the trousers do not; Mulligan wonders whether some syphilitic drunkard wore them before Stephen (U5). "My two feet in his boots are at the end of his legs," therefore, does not seem to make sense as it stands; "his" has an ambiguous reference. Perhaps the line should read "My two feet in his boots are at the end of my legs."]

35  [It is not completely certain that these women *are* midwives. Stephen may be exercising his creative power here, attempting to write a *Dubliners* sketch; later on we see that the "midwife's bag" contains some shellfish (U199). Would a midwife, even in 1904 Dublin, take a misbirth out to the sands of the bay to bury it and then use the soiled bag to gather shellfish?]

36  There is also an ominous note of guilt here; the Greeks called the central altar at Delphi the *omphalos* ("navel") of the world, and it was at this altar that the guilty Orestes, driven mad by his guilt for having killed his mother, seeks refuge.]

37 [The phrase is from Thomas Traherne's *Centuries of Meditations*, first written in the seventeenth century and rediscovered in 1896 or 1897, but first published in 1908, so Joyce's use of the phrase may be an anachronism. See Gifford and Seidman, p. 47.]

38 [Gifford and Seidman, p. 47, locate the source of the phrase "made not begotten" in the Nicene Creed, in which Jesus was the only creature who was "begotten" by God the Father, not "made," as were all other human creatures. Stephen here accepts his merely human status.]

39 Shakespeare, *The Tempest,* I. ii., lines 394–401.

40 The sea, for Joyce, is the Father of Life, the Form of forms, who is to be sought and found beyond or within the wave of the sea of being. In sleep one enters into Nature—one's own nature—in the ultimate heart and depth of which, according to this philosophy, the immanent Godhood of one's being, the World Being, the Form of forms, is to be joined. But that Form is at once male and female. It is broken up, furthermore, and scattered over all the earth in what appears to be innumerable singularities, separate from, and even dangerous to, each other. It is opposed to itself, not only as male and female, but also, on the male side, as this male against that; on the female side, this female against that; and more generally, still further, as youth against age, heat against cold, light against dark, nature against spirit, fertilizing rain against desiccating drought, life against death, or what you will.

Giordano Bruno regarded the terms of all such polarities, not merely as counterpoised manifestations of the one transcendent yet immanent power, but also in their interaction, as the energy source of the world process. Bruno the Nolan wrote:

> The beginning, the middle, and the end, the birth, the growth, and the perfection of all that we see, come from contraries, through contraries, into contraries, to contraries. And where there is contrariety, there is action and reaction, there is motion, there is diversity, there is number, there is order, there are degrees, there is succession, there is vicissitude. (Giordano Bruno, as cited in Arthur D. Imerti, editor, *The Expulsion of the Triumphant Beast* [New Brunswick, N.J.: Rutgers University Press, 1964], pp. 90–91.)

Joyce not only has concurred in this view, but has even established and developed it as the paramount ground principle of both *Ulysses* and *Finnegans Wake.*

In *Finnegans Wake,* the Fall and scattering of the One into the Many is allegorized as the fall and scattering of the World Egg, Humpty Dumpty, from atop his wall—the wall of space-time, *māyā,* from beyond or above which the One descends.

Joyce, presenting a mythological rendering of these theories of reality in *Finnegans Wake,* produces a colorful compound of various phantasmagoric deities in a protean dream figure, the first appearance of which, in the first words of the book's first full paragraph, is under the name and guise of "Sir

Tristram, violer d'amores, fr'over the short sea." ["The short sea" is the Irish sea, in this context, from which ALP sees her own Mananaan sea-god rising, "moananoaning," at the end of the *Wake*.] The sea-god Mananaan, as well as Wotan, Hermes, Śiva, and much more, open out, beyond and within, this mercurial form that is not form, leading finally, in the last eleven syllables of the work to the void: "A way a lone a last a loved a long the

41  [For an approach to the problem of Bloom as a Jew, see Bernard Benstock, editor, *The Seventh of Joyce* (Bloomington, Indiana: Indiana University Press/Sussex, England: The Harvester Press, 1982), pp. 221–237.]

42  [Joyce here connects Bloom closely with Stephen, who just one page before had declared: "Dead breaths I living breathe, tread dead dust, devour a urinous offal from all dead." (U42) "Offal" is a term for "the inner organs of beasts and fowls." Stephen's "urinous offal" is exactly what Bloom loves to eat.]

43  [Gifford and Seidman, p. 76, note Zack Bowen's discovery of the text of the actual song, which was not of course written by Blazes Boylan, but by Harry Norris in 1899. On the other hand, Joyce never actually says that Boylan *wrote* the song; perhaps it is regarded by Milly as Boylan's song because Boylan often sings it.]

44  [The question shows a considerable strategic sense in "Martha": if anything develops with Bloom, she does not want Bloom going back to his wife smelling of alien scents!]

45  [Joyce's point is that Shakespeare, having lost his actual father to death before the writing of *Hamlet*, and having succeeded in an act of creation, which only a mature creator, a Daedalian "father," could accomplish, now occupies the "mystical estate" of fatherhood. (U170) Since fatherhood is an eternal state, like the fatherhood of God the Father, Shakespeare has moved into an eternity of fatherhood: His own father in the flesh is dead, so that he is no longer in the position of a son. In addition, a successful act of creation has made him a "father" of works of art.

> When Rutlandbaconsouthamptonshakespeare...wrote *Hamlet* he was not the father of his own son merely but, being no more a son, he was and felt himself the father of all his race, the father of his own grandfather, the father of his unborn grandson... (U171)]

46  [In addition, Virginia Woolf's *Mrs. Dalloway* is modeled closely on the "Wandering Rocks" chapter of *Ulysses*. See also Hugh Kenner, "Notes Toward an Anatomy of 'Modernism,'" in E. L. Epstein, editor, *A Starchamber Quiry* (New York and London: Methuen, 1982), pp. 4–42.]

47  [The dog, Garryowen, however, does not belong to "the citizen." Gerty MacDowell mentions "grandpapa Giltrap's lovely dog Garryowen that almost talked it was so human" (U289).]

48  ["*Deshil* is from the Irish *deasil, deisiol*: turning to the right, clockwise, sunwise: a ritual gesture to attract good fortune, and an act of consecration when

repeated three times." (See Gifford and Seidman, p. 408) It also means "south," however, and refers to ancient fire ceremonies performed by ancient peoples at the winter solstice, when they feared that the sun was going to continue its southward journey into extinction and would dance clockwise around ritual fires, from south to north, to entice the sun to follow them northward. Witches, of course, being perverse and evil, would also build fires, but they would dance around them *widdershins* (from the German *wieder der Sonne,* "against the sun") to drive the sun even further into southward extinction. The intimate association of this ceremony with the sun makes it appropriate for a chapter dealing with the Oxen of the Sun as symbols of fertility.]

49 [The high degree of alliteration in these selections is not really justified. Joyce is writing prose in this section of the *Oxen of the Sun,* and Old English prose is not noticeably alliterative. Joyce's parodies resemble Old English *poetry* more than they do prose, but actually Joyce's prose here is much more alliterative than even Old English poetry ever gets. In the actual Old English poetry there are never more than three alliterative particles in any line, and frequently there are no more than two. In addition, since all vowels alliterate with all other vowels, the alliteration is sometimes not really noticeable. Joyce's prose here is much closer in style to the poetry of the alliterative revival of the fourteenth century; see the works of the Pearl Poet, for example.]

50 [Stephen thinks that God is threatening him. "A black crack of noise in the street" is reminiscent of his definition of God in the "Nestor" chapter: "A shout in the street." (U28)]

51 [The sermon is not like the sermons of the evangelist John Alexander Dowie (1847–1907), but is in fact a close copy of a sermon by the internationally famous American evangelist and former baseball player Billy Sunday, even down to his characteristic cry of "Come on!" Billy Sunday's heyday was during the composition and publication of *Ulysses.*]

52 [The reference here is to U337–338:

> Now he [Bloom] is himself paternal and these about him might be his sons. Who can say? The wise father knows his own child. He thinks of a drizzling night in Hatch street, hard by the bonded stores there, the first. Together (she is a poor waif, a child of shame, yours and mine and of all for a bare shilling and her luckpenny), together they hear the heavy tread of the watch as two raincaped shadows pass the new royal university. Bridie! Bridie Kelly! He will never forget the name, ever remember the night, the bridenight. They are entwined in nethermost darkness, the willer with the willed, and in an instant (*fiat!*) light shall flood the world. Did heart leap to heart? Nay, fair reader. In a breath 'twas done but – hold! Back! It must not be! In terror the poor girl flees away through the murk. She is the bride of darkness, a daughter of night. She dare not bear the sunnygolden babe of day. No, Leopold. Name and memory solace thee not. That youthful

illusion of thy strength was taken from thee – and in vain. No son of thy loins is by thee. There is none now to be for Leopold what Leopold was for Rudolph.

From this passage, it is clear that Bridie Kelly is a prostitute, not a girlfriend of Leopold. It is not quite so clear whether or not the sexual act was accomplished; "In a breath 'twas done" suggests that it was, but "Hold! Back! It must not be" might suggest *coitus interruptus,* as does "In terror the poor girl flees away through the murk." However, it *is* clear that Bloom had no son (or indeed a "babe" of any sex) from the encounter with Bridie Kelly.]

53  [Māndūkya Upaniṣad 2.2.3–4; from Swami Prabhavananda and Frederick Manchester, *The Upanishads* (New York: Mentor Books/New American Library, 1957), p. 46.]

54  [The phrase is a truculent commonplace of British criminals; it corresponds to the American equivalent, "Who the hell do you think you're lookin' at?" The implication is that the viewer is going to report the activities of the viewed to the police.]

55  [Here Zoe's body, complete with the black velvet fillet, and the sapphire slip with the bronze clasps, has become Jerusalem, which is for Bloom the object of desire; whenever he thinks of women's bodies the East comes into his mind. The complex symbol developed during the day becomes a giant metaphor here, with Zoe's body as the tenor and Jerusalem as the vehicle.]

56  [Joyce makes a mistake in the Hebrew: *schorach* should be *shekhor,* "black, dark, (sun)burnt." The entire quotation should read *"shekhor ani ve novach."* The quotation is, of course, from The Song of Songs 1:5.]

57  [Regardless of the philosophical and religious overtones that Campbell finds in the phrase "O, I so want to be a mother" (U403), the main use of the phrase (as I say in note 8 above) is comic and parodic; Joyce here is importing the cry of Wendy in *Peter Pan,* who also yearns to be a mother.]

58  A quotation attributed to Pseudo-Aristotle, but not traceable, in "Tractatis Aristotelis alchymistae ad Alexandrum Magnum de lapide philosphico," *Theatrum Chemicum, praecipuos selectorum tractatus...continens,* Vol. V, pp. 88off. (Argentorati [Strasbourg], 1622). See C. G. Jung, *Psychology and Alchemy,* (second edition, completely revised), Vol. 12 in *The Collected Works of C. G. Jung,* Bollingen Series XX (Princeton, N.J.: Princeton University Press, 1953), p. 128.

59  [See *Psychology and Alchemy,* especially. pp. 317–344 (Part III, "Religious Ideas in Alchemy," Chapter 4, "The Prima Materia").]

60  [For a detailed discussion of the relationship between the philosopher's stone (the "lapis") and the Messiah, see *Psychology and Alchemy,* pp. 345–431 (Part III, Chapter 5, "The Lapis-Christ Parallel").]

61  ["Open fifths" cannot refer to *melodies* made up of notes a fifth apart. *All* melodic fifths are "open fifths." It is more likely that they are *harmonic* fifths, simply two-note chords, with the two notes a fifth apart——for example, C–G,

D–A, E–B, and so on. Stephen is trying to play a setting of the nineteenth psalm by the Venetian composer Benedetto Marcello (1686–1739). Included in Marcello's setting are melodies from Hebrew chanting of the psalms that he picked up from Venetian synagogues and others derived from the studies of the Renaissance musicologist Vincenzo Galilei, who thought that these melodies were the ones to which the "Homeric" *Hymn to Demeter* had been sung in ancient times. This explains Stephen's disjointed comments on u411. See E. L. Epstein, "King David and Benedetto Marcello in the Works of James Joyce," *James Joyce Quarterly,* VI (Fall, 1968), pp. 83–86. However, Stephen's comments (and Campbell's) on the musical metaphor can be understood either in the melodic or the harmonic sense.]

62  [*The Gospel According to Thomas,* Coptic text, established and translated by A. Guillaumont, H.-Ch. Puech, G. Quispel, W. Till, and Yassah 'Abd al Masih (Leiden: E. J. Brill; New York: Harper, 1969), pp. 55, 57.]

63  [Joyce was not content with Gnosticism. He often associated it with the type of woolly Platonism he encountered in his youth among the intellectuals of Dublin, and which he describes satirically in the library scene in *Ulysses*. In fact, Stephen sardonically intones a Gnostic version of the Credo on u152:

> Formless spiritual. Father, Word and Holy Breath. Allfather, the heavenly man. Hiesos Kristos, magician of the beautiful, the Logos who suffers in us at every moment. This verily is that. I am the fire upon the altar. I am the sacrificial butter.

The appearance in this selection of Campbell's favorite quotation from the Chāndogya Upaniṣad is not an accident; the association between Gnosticism and Eastern religion is close. On u153, Stephen returns to the attack:

> God: noise in the street: very peripatetic. Space: what you damn well have to see. Through spaces smaller than red globules of man's blood they creepycrawl after Blake's buttocks into eternity of which this vegetable world is but a shadow. Hold to the now, the here, through which all future plunges to the past.

Of course, it could be argued that Stephen, irritated at his being shunted aside by the intellectuals of Dublin, is unfair to them, and that Joyce himself really has greater respect for Gnosticism and Platonism in general than does Stephen. However, in *Finnegans Wake,* Joyce comments on Gnosticism in what seems to be his own voice. In the Shem the Penman chapter (I, vii), Joyce presents one answer to the question "When is a man not a man?" as "when he is a gnawstick and detarmined to" (170.5, 11–12); that is, a man is not a man when he is a Gnostic and a believer in Gnostic determinism.

At the most important point of the *Wake,* the sunrise section (Book IV), Joyce presents St. Patrick winning a debate with a Gnostic Eastern sage on the nature of human knowledge of reality. The sage defends inner knowledge—the creation of the inner spirit—as superior to the evidence of the senses.

St. Patrick argues that the actual world presented to the senses and lit by the actual sun represents a true picture of reality to fallen Man. In fact, St. Patrick presents his side of the debate with such power that the sage, shouting and sweating, falls with a thud on his bottom. This episode (611.4–613.4) hardly shows a totally respectful attitude towards Gnostic mysticism on the part of Joyce.]

64  [For an analysis of this section of *Ulysses,* see E. L. Epstein, *The Ordeal of Stephen Dedalus* (Carbondale: Southern Illinois University Press, 1971), pp. 156–173.]

65  For the full account of this adventure, see Heinrich Zimmer, *The King and the Corpse,* edited by Joseph Campbell, Bollingen Series XI (New York: Pantheon Books, 1948), pp. 239–316, translating and interpreting the narrative in Kālikā Purāṇa 1–19 and 42–44.

66  [It could be said that the drowned man in the sea and the god of the sea are both "drowned men." So are we when we go down into our own depths. In this section Joyce associates the inhabitants of the spiritual deep with Bloom.]

67  See Gershom G. Scholem, *On the Kabbalah and Its Symbolism* (New York: Schocken Books, 1965), pp. 104ff.

68  [It is here that Stephen recites the riddle from the "Nestor" chapter (U22):

The fox crew, the cocks flew,
The bells in heaven
Were striking eleven.
'Tis time for her poor soul
To get out of heaven. (U455)

In this rendition, however, Stephen's changes to the original words of the last two lines (" 'Tis time for this poor soul/To go to heaven") implicitly invite his mother's ghost to rise up and confront him, which happens eighteen pages later.]

69  [The reading of "Thursdaymornun" in the Corrected Edition is obviously a mistake. The phrase that the paralyzed Shakespeare is trying to say is "How my Othello ("Oldfellow") choked his Desdemona ("Thursdaymomum")." Here Stephen is suggesting that perhaps his father, Simon, his "old fellow" in Irish slang, may have been responsible for the death of Stephen's mother.]

70  ["And the horns of the righteous shall be exalted." From Psalm 75 (Vulgate 74). (See Gifford and Seidman, p. 513.) Horns in Biblical metaphor were symbols of great power. Stephen here seems to be defending Bloom, even while tacitly admitting that Bloom is a cuckold.]

71  [The scene in the Joyce family upon which this element in *Ulysses* is based was altered by Joyce for dramatic purposes. Ellmann makes it clear that it was not in reality Joyce's mother who ordered him to kneel down and pray at his mother's deathbed, but his uncle John Murray (136).]

72  ["*Transzcendente Spekulation über die anscheinende Absichtlichkeit im Schicksale des Einzelnen,*" in *Parerga und Paralipomena: Kleine philosophische Schriften,* Erster Band (1851), in Arthur Schopenhauer's *Sämtliche Werke,* Vierter Band, (Munich: R. Piper Verlag, 1913), pp. 223–250: especially pp. 242–248.]

73   [The source for the connection of urination to the dog theme is to be found in the "Proteus" chapter:

> [The dog] trotted forward and, lifting again his hindleg, pissed quick short at an unsmelt rock. The simple pleasures of the poor. (U39)]

74   [In fact, the only piece of furniture which has not been moved is the bed; this corresponds to the impossibility of moving Odysseus's bed in the *Odyssey*, Book XXIII, ll. 173–204.]

## CHAPTER IV

75   [*The Tempest*, IV.i., lines 156–157.]

76   [302.31–32.]

77   ["O'Lochlain (in Colm O'Lochlain's *Irish Street Ballads*) is vague about provenance, suggests that it may be the product of the nineteenth–century music hall in England, Ireland, or America." (See Adaline Glasheen, *Third Census of Finnegans Wake* (Berkeley: University of California Press, 1977), p. 93.) Glasheen also suggests that readers interested in the source of the Tim Finnegan ballad consult her article "Notes Towards a Supreme Understanding of the Use of 'Finnegan's Wake' in *Finnegans Wake*," in *A Wake Newslitter*, Volume I.]

78   [On "commodius," *A Skeleton Key* (p. 26) comments:

> "Commodius" sweeps the mind back to the Rome which showed its first severe symptoms of decay in the time of the emperor Commodus. It also suggests the broad and easy path that leads our present civilization to destruction.

On January 23, 1981 the veteran Joyce scholar Nathan Halper wrote to Campbell. Halper had promised Campbell at a meeting at the Century Club that he would "advise you about the possible mistakes that are in the *Key*." In this letter, Halper comments on the gloss for "commodius":

> ...The most serious mistake (here I'm goddamn sure) is in "commodius vicus." Your statement that this contains a reference to Commodus has been repeated by multitudes of writers since. I won't blame you; they would have thought of this all by themselves. None the less, he has nothing to do with the case. Life—the dream—the book—the river and anything it stands for—run in a "commodius vicus." What has this to do with poor little Commodus? (Except, of course, for some resemblance in the sound.) Vicus-Vico is a controlling principle. What has Commodus done to be a modifier? He died at 29. Surely, then, he is not a type of HCE. You say that "Rome showed its first severe symptoms of decay in the time of the emperor Commodus." Are you not forgetting the time, so loved by Suetonius, of the later Tiberius, Caligula, Claudius, and Nero?
> One may say that Joyce works in the name of the Roman emperors.

So he does. But, when he does, he uses the name without any distortion. What is more—if that is his purpose—he uses the name Commodus in its proper form on 157.26.

Why then is the word commodius used? What goes with Vico? What is the other controlling principle? Giordano (Jordan) Bruno. See 287.24 and a number of other places where they appear together. A jordan is a commode. River runs in a way that is described by Bruno and Vico. Also—a commode is used at night—the time of the dream. Also it is used for the excreta which are both an image and a fact in the pages of *Finnegans Wake*. . . .

Halper's suggestion—that commodius decodes as a jordan (Giordano Bruno), and that "commodius vicus" therefore equals Bruno-Vico—is ingenious, and it fits in with Campbell's idea that the Liffey, in its dying course through Dublin Bay, bears with it the filth of Dublin, "all the greedy gushes out through their small souls. And all the lazy leaks down over their brash bodies" (627.18–20).]

79 [The French word *violer* also means "to rape." Joyce again finds a word that suggests two opposing ideas: one, romantic love, and the other, aggressive violation.]

80 [*A Skeleton Key* (p. 26, n. 3) comments:

Note the curious implication of "rearrived." Joyce intends to indicate that in the courses of the Viconian cycle, all has happened before and is on the point of happening again.

81 [Isaac Butt, the original leader of the Irish Parliamentary party in Westminster, was superseded by Parnell, who intended the Irish group to have a much more active role in securing Irish Home Rule.]

82 [The two women in Thackeray's *Vanity Fair,* Amelia and Becky, the good girl and the bad girl, correspond to the two sides of Issy, the daughter in *Finnegans Wake.*]

83 [Susanna was wrongly accused by two old men who lusted after her (like the Four Old Men lust after Issy); Esther was favored over Vashti by King Ahasuerus, so there may be a good-woman, bad-woman theme here; Ruth was loved by Boaz, an older man, but there is no obvious *Wake* reference here.]

84 [It was only one of his sons who saw him exposed, Ham. The other two covered Noah up without looking at him.]

85 [Thomas Parr, nicknamed "Old Parr," was supposed to have lived from about 1483 to 1635, making him about 152 years old when he died.]

86 [It occurs in this form in the Old English battle poem "The Battle of Brunanburh."]

87 [There are also many Moslem references here.]

88 [*A Skeleton Key* (p. 39, n. 3) comments: "The key theme of the *Wake:* in a communion feast the substance of All-Father is served by All-Mother to the universal company."

89 [*A Skeleton Key,* p. 40.]

90 [*A Skeleton Key,* p. 97, n. 5.]

91 [*A Skeleton Key,* p. 107.]

92 [These two paragraphs are based on *A Skeleton Key,* pp. 110–111.]

93 [*A Skeleton Key* (p. 115, n. 12) comments:

> This colloquy between the Mookse and the Gripes sets forth obscurely the theological differences between the Roman (Mookse) and Irish (Gripes) churches. The Irish church was pre-Gothic in character, mystical in spirit, and resembled the Greek Orthodox.]

94 [Originally published in *Chimera: A Literary Quarterly,* Vol. IV, No. 3 (Spring, 1946), pp. 68–80.]

95 Sigmund Freud in *The Interpretation of Dreams* (Modern Library edition of *The Basic Writings of Sigmund Freud*), p. 422, says, "A dream frequently has the profoundest meaning in the places where it seems most absurd."

96 Frank Budgen, *James Joyce and the Making of Ulysses* (London: Grayson, 1935), p. 291.

97 "Divases": from the Sanskrit root *div,* "to shine, to be glad"; the noun *div* (*divas*) means "day"; *-vases* suggests the opening chalice of the bud. "Divases" is to be read as the present tense (third person singular) of the verb; its subject, "day." The Sanskrit word *padmā* means "lotus." The Sanskrit *ādya* is "today." "Umbrilla" suggests "umbilicus." "Parasoul" (from the Sanskrit *para,* "supreme") means "Oversoul": cf. Emerson.

Joyce has precedent for his Lotus-Umbrella correlation. The lotus stemming from Viṣṇu's navel is cognate with the Tree of Life atop the central mountain of the world (in Hindu iconography, the Jambu tree atop Mount Sumeru); this tree, in turn, is duplicated by the symbolical umbrella on the summit of the traditional Buddhist reliquary mound (e.g.: Stūpa I at Sāñcī; see Zimmer, *Myths and Symbols in Indian Art and Civilization,* Figure 63). A Christian counterpart of the World Lotus growing from Viṣṇu's navel will be recognized in the Tree of Jesse: the genealogical tree of Christ's descent, which is represented in Christian art as rooted in Jesse, the father of David (e.g.: Tree of Jesse Window, Chartres Cathedral). Jesus as the culminating blossom of the Tree of Jesse is a homologue of the Buddha seated on the lotus.

Mountain, Navel, Tree, and Lotus are variant representations of the mythological figure of the *axis mundi,* i.e., the point where the abundance of eternity flows into and becomes the abundance of time. This point is rediscovered by the striving individual in that center of intellection where the contraries of empirical experience are transcended and eternity is apprehended in a luminous instant (the young James Joyce's "luminous silent stasis of esthetic pleasure" [P213]). Buddha attained Illumination under the Bo-tree on the Immovable Spot (*axis mundi,* World Navel); Jesus won the victory of Holy Rood upon the hill (Golgotha, Calvary) which in medieval iconography is represented as the center of the world.

Joyce's use of such images is always consistent with their traditional connotations. His effects are achieved by surprising identifications (lotus with umbrella, umbrella with umbilicus, sleeping man with reliquary mound). Humphrey Chimpden Earwicker, Joyce's Cosmic Man (HCE = Here Comes Everybody) flourishes like a

> buaboabaybohm, litting flop a deadlop (aloose!) to lee but lifting a
> bennbranch a yardlong (ivoeh!) on the breezy side (for showm!), the
> height of Brewster's chimpney and as broad below as Phineas Barnum.
> (29.2–5)

A description of him as the Cosmic Tree-Man-Angel ("The form masculine. The gender feminine") appears on pages 503–506. His initials peer through the "Howth Castle and Environs" of the first sentence of the book: he is the Hill of Howth.

In conclusion, it should be noted that umbrellas were used first ceremonially and symbolically, not practically; the umbrella was a symbolic tree held over the head of a king. As the Anointed of God, the king was the Hero of the Tree, and where he stood, that was the *axis mundi.* Jonas Hanway (1712–1786), the first gentleman to carry an umbrella in London, was stoned in the street. "Saint Jamas Hanway, servant of Gamp, lapidated," we read at 449.14–15.

98    "Weapons cut It not; fire burns It not; water wets It not; the wind does not wither It. Eternal all-pervading, unchanging, immovable, the Self is the same for ever" (Bhagavad Gītā 2.23, 24). "The spirit wanders, comes now here, now there, and occupies whatever frame it pleases. From beasts it passes into human bodies, and from our bodies into beasts, but never perishes" (Ovid, *Metamorphoses* 15.165–168). "When we all sing, it is that One Man who sings in us" (St. Augustine, In. Ps. 122). "He is ee and no counter he who will be ultimendly respunchable for the hubbub caused in Edenborough" (29.34–36).

99    [*The Tempest*, IV.i., lines 156–157.]

100    See C. S. Boswell, *An Irish Precursor of Dante: A Study of the Vision of Heaven and Hell Ascribed to the Eighth-century Irish Saint Adamnan* (London, 1908).

101    Cited by Ananda K. Coomaraswamy, "Recollections, Indian and Platonic," in *Journal of the American Oriental Society,* Supplement 3 (April–June 1944), pp. 3–4. [Another translation of this passage is:

> And in dreams the mind beholds its own immensity. What has been
> seen is seen again, and what has been heard is heard again. What has
> been felt in different places or faraway regions returns to the mind
> again. Seen and unseen, heard and unheard, felt and not felt, the
> mind sees all, since the mind is all.—Juan Mascaro. *The Upanishads*
> (Baltimore, Maryland: Penguin Books, 1965), p.72.)]

102    Quotation from the mystical poet Rumi, *Mathnawi* 4.3067.

103    "In that which is night to all beings, the man of self-control is awake" (Bhagavad Gītā 2.69). The Gītā is the "Bhagafat gaiters" worn by HCE (35.10).

104 See. Zimmer, *Myths and Symbols in Indian Art and Civilization,* pp. 38–50.

105 *Finnegans Wake* corresponds to Dante's *Purgatorio,* as *Ulysses* to the *Inferno.* (See Thomas McGreevy, "The Catholic Element in Work in Progress," in *Our Exagmination Round His Factification for Incamination of Work in Progress* [Paris: Shakespeare & Company, 1929], pp. 119–127:

> Mr. Joyce never loses sight of the fact that the principality of hell and the state of purgatory are in life and by the law of nature not less within us than the kingdom of heaven. [p. 125])

The Christian image of Purgatory is cognate with the Oriental of Metempsychosis. These are two ways of symbolizing the mystery of the Progress of the Soul, i.e., the gradual purgation from consciousness of the delusory fears and desires that attach the ego to the ephemera of phenomenal existence and preclude the soul from that beatific experience of Being which is its proper state. "Not till the soul knows all that there is to be known can she pass over to the unknown good" (Meister Eckhart). The Christian mythology provides Purgatory, and the Oriental a series of additional lives, to allay the life lust and prepare the spirit for its perfect centeredness. In *Finnegans Wake* the Mount-of-Purgatory theme coalesces with the World Mountain, and the synthesis is immediately equated with the Wheel of Rebirth, which is identical with the Time-Cycle: "The untireties of livesliving being the one substance of a streamsbecoming" (597.7–8). The center of the Wheel (*axis mundi*) corresponds to the summit of the Mountain (Terrestrial Paradise). In *Finnegans Wake* that point of illumined repose is never quite attained. The crisis is approached but reneged at 608.33–36:

> Passing. One. We are passing. Two. From sleep we are passing.
> Three. Into the wikeawades warld from sleep we are passing. Four.
> Come, hours, be ours!
> But still; Ah diar, ah diar! And stay.

One page before the last in the book we read: "It's something fails us. First we feel. Then we fall." (627.11)

Had the transition been effected, the experience would have been transmuted from the purgatorial to the heavenly. But Joyce was reserving the beatitudes of Paradise for a final volume, which was to have treated of the timeless, boundless sea: that cosmic water of immortality on which reposes the Lord, the Cosmic Giant, dreaming his dream of the world.

106 The man or woman who had died was identified with, and called, Osiris. "N" here stands for the personal name of the deceased, which was added to the supernatural appellation (Osiris Anfankh, Osiris Ani, etc.). In *Finnegans Wake* "Here Comes Everybody," "Haveth Childers Everywhere," etc., are the supernatural "death-titles" of the man who in daily life is known as Mr. Humphrey Chimpden Earwicker.

107 Frank Budgen, "Joyce's Chapters of Going Forth by Day," in *Horizon* (September, 1941).

108 The strange name of Joyce's hero, "Earwicker" (scrambled above as "Ciwareke") becomes suddenly meaningful in this Egyptian context. The name is humorously accounted for in *Finnegans Wake* (30–31) as derived from "earwig" ("earbeetle"): the earwig is popularly supposed to creep into the ear of a person asleep and into his brain. This "dangerous" insect is Joyce's Irish counterpart and parody of the *scarabaeus* (the Mediterranean "dung beetle"), which in Egyptian iconography represents Khepera, the sun-god, and is a primary symbol of resurrection and immortality. (The scarabaeus rolls before it a large ball of dung, from which its young are brooded: the sun-disk was likened to such a life-productive dung-ball rolled before the god.) A little faïence, ivory, or stone representation of this beetle, bearing an inscription on the flat underside, was placed, with a prayer, over the heart of the mummy before the mummy-case was closed. This symbolized the presence of the vital solar principle, by virtue of which Osiris N. should awake immortal. Though symbolized in the beetle, the god was actually within, as the permanent actuator, forgotten during the dream of life. The prayer and symbol served to precipitate recollection. Comparably, Earwicker ("Awaker"): he is the earwig in the sleeper's (i.e. reader's) ear. And *Finnegans Wake* itself is the accompanying papyrus, The Book of the Dead.

109 Throughout *Ulysses,* Stephen is obsessed with the problem of the consubstantiality of the Father and the Son:

> A *lex eterna* stays about Him. Is that then the divine substance wherein Father and Son are consubstantial? (U32)

> Fatherhood, in the sense of conscious begetting, is unknown to man. It is a mystical estate, an apostolic succession, from only begetter to only begotten. On that mystery and not on the madonna which the cunning Italian intellect flung to the mob of Europe the church is founded and founded irremovably because founded, like the world, macro and microcosm, upon the void. Upon incertitude, upon unlikelihood. (U170)

> We walk through ourselves, meeting robbers, ghosts, giants, old men, young men, wives, widows, brothers-in-love, but always meeting ourselves. (U175)

The crisis of recognition occurs in the underworld scene of the brothel, where Stephen ("Son"), cogitating at the upright piano, turns and sees Leopold Bloom ("Father"):

#### STEPHEN

> (*Abruptly*) What went forth to the ends of the world to traverse not itself. God, the sun, Shakespeare, a commercial traveller, having itself traversed in reality itself becomes that self. . . . Self which it itself was ineluctably preconditioned to become. *Ecco!* . . .
> (*Stephen turns and sees Bloom*) (U412)

The shared meal in the Bloom kitchen (U547–573) is the sacramental union of "Son" and "Father," the pair of opposites, "poles apart" (U518, 524). Immediately thereafter, Stephen vanishes in the night (U578), and Bloom goes into the womb of sleep (U583–607). Molly, in her sleepful mind, compounds the two (U639–644) and the volume ends.

However, in the riverrun of *Finnegans Wake*, Anna Livia Plurabelle's "untitled mamafesta memorialising the Mosthighest" (104.4), Son and Father reappear, reborn, but now indissolubly synthesized. For the differentiated egos of the normal day world (*Ulysses* is *all* egos) "by the coincidence of their contraries reamalgamerge" (49.37–38) in

> this harmonic condenser enginium..., so as to serve him up a melegoturny marygoraumd, eclectrically filtered for allirish earths and ohmes. (310.1; 309.23–24)

> ...under the closed eyes of the inspectors the traits featuring the chiaroscuro coalesce, their contrarieties eliminated, in one stable somebody... (107.28–30)

[For an extended treatment of the father-son theme in *A Portrait, Ulysses,* and *Finnegans Wake,* see E. L. Epstein, *The Ordeal of Stephen Dedalus.*]

110   Last verse and chorus of the song "Finnegan's Wake."

The whiskey works two ways: on the one hand it precipitates the Fall ("The Cup of Bitterness"), but on the other brings about the Resurrection ("The Living Waters"). In this connection it should be noted that Finnegan's hod may be likened to a great cup which he carries up to God filled with Matter (bricks), and down to man, filled with Spirit (air: *pneuma*). Compare the words of Hermes Trismegistos:

> He filled a mighty Cup with it [with Mind], and sent it down, joining a Herald to it, to whom He gave command to make this proclamation to the hearts of men: "Baptize thyself with this Cup's baptism... Thou that hast faith, thou canst ascend to Him that hath sent down the Cup." (Hermes, *Lib.* 5, the book called "The Cup, or Monad," par. 4.)

And now the words of Macrobius:

> ...the soul is dragged back into body, hurried on by new intoxication, desiring to taste a fresh draught of the superfluity of naughtiness [the overflow of "matter"], whereby it is weighed down and brought back to earth. The Cup of Father Liber [Dionysos, Bacchus] is a symbol of this mystery; and this is what the Ancients called the River of Lethe. (Comment, in *Somn. Scip.* XI. ii. 66).

The River of Lethe is Joyce's River Liffey (riverrun), which is personified as Anna Livia Plurabelle (ALP), the mother of life: "Our callback mother...over her possetpot" (294.28–29, 31); "old missness wipethemdry...happy tea area, naughtygay frew" (578.19, 22–23). Anna Livia's everlasting cup of tea, "the muttheringpot" (20.7), corresponds to the Cup in which the World Creator mixed the elements of the universe (Plato, *Timaeus,* 41 D). "Father Times and Mother Spacies boil their kettle with their crutch" (600.2–3). As such it is a miniature of the universe and a source of revelations. Compare Genesis 44:5: "(The cup)...in which my lord (Joseph) drinketh, and whereby indeed he divineth..." "Miss Rachel Lea Varian, she tells forkings for baschfellors, under purdah of card palmer teapot tosspot Madam d'Elta..." (221.12–13).

The motif of the Two Cups appears in *Finnegans Wake* under the images of (1) the evening drink that puts to sleep (Finnegan's fall, 5–6; Earwicker's collapse, 381–382); and (2) the breakfast cup of tea or coffee that awakens ("when cup, platter, and pot come piping hot" 615.9).

The two represent the counterplay of opposites (death and birth, spirit and matter, fall and redemption, evil and good, etc.) within the field of creation. Tea as "The Cup of Bitterness" (Christ's taste of gall on the Cross) is suggested in the phrase "With a capital Tea for Thirst!" (302.9), capital Tea having already been presented as the Cross at 235.28: "T will be waiting for uns as I sold U at the first antries." Tea as "The Living Waters" we find at 406.28: "Tea is the Highest! For auld lang Ayternitay!" Finally, a certain dubiousness as to which is which of the pair of opposites is suggested by the revelation (492) that the fluid in the bottle carried on a certain occasion by ALP was not beer but urine. (Compare U11).

III    That is, Mr. H. C. Earwicker (the new tavern keeper in Chapelizod), Annie or Anna his wife, Shem and Shaun his sons, and Isobel his daughter. See *A Skeleton Key to Finnegans Wake,* pp. 3–23.

Edmund Wilson's early articles, "H. C. Earwicker and Family," and "The Dream of H. C. Earwicker," in *New Republic* (June 28 and July 12, 1939; later united in his volume *The Wound and the Bow*), are still among the best discussions of the domestic circumstances of the Earwicker household. Mr. Wilson made the mistake, however, of assigning to Annie, Earwicker's wife, the name Maggie, by which Joyce designates one of her rivals. (The Maggies, 7, 142, etc., are the servant-girl temptresses in the park.) This error was inherited by several subsequent American elucidators (e.g., Harry Levin, *James Joyce* [New Directions Books, 1941], pp. 150, 200). [See *The Wound and the Bow,* new printing with corrections, 1947. (Editorial comment from *Chimera*)]. Mr. Wilson also made the mistake of describing the encyclopedic text as the stream of consciousness, or rather unconsciousness (the dream), of the moderately educated Mr. Earwicker, whereas from the first sentence the explicatory language is that of a universally informed and alert observer and interpreter—not the dreamer. Following Wilson, it has become standard practice in Joyce criticism to observe that one is hard put to account for the range of the unlearned tavern keeper's stream of fantasies (viz. Levin, p. 175).

But James Joyce has, in fact, so little confined us to Mr. Earwicker's stream of unconsciousness that for the final monologue (619–628) we have entered the mind of Anna, and in the bedroom scenes of Book II, Chapter 4, we are studying, externally, both the husband and the wife ("Man with nightcap, in bed, fore. Woman, with curlpins, hind. Discovered." 559.20–21). On 556–557 we see the so-called dreamer walking up a flight of stairs; on 576–580 he is coming down a flight together with his wife. On 228–230 we are within the mind of one of his sons. *Finnegans Wake* is not by any means the literal reproduction of this simple citizen's stream of night-thoughts (hardly a sentence of the work submits to such interpretation), but a view of his whole world, micro- and macrocosmic, through the eye of clairvoyant-sleep, instead of the eye that we are used to in the modern novel, namely that of day.

112 The Book of the Dead, Chapter of the Coming Forth by Day in the Underworld.

113 "Now by memory inspired, turn wheel again to the whole of the wall" (69.5–6). Compare Nicholas of Cusa, *De vis. Dei* 9, 11; also Coomaraswamy [see note 102 above], pp. 2, 25.

114 St. Augustine, In. Ps. 122; compare Bhagavad Gītā 2.18.22.

115 The "rising germinal" (354.34–35): HCE as the "Russian General" whose energetic presence haunts the whole night-world of *Finnegans Wake* (see especially 338–355).

The principal historical prototype of Joyce's ubiquitous Russian is the celebrated defender of Sebastopol in the Crimean War, General Franz Eduard Ivanovitch Todleben (1818–84).

> He was enmivallupped. Chromean fastion. With all his cannonball wappents. In his raglanrock and his malakoiffed bulbsbyg and his varnashed roscians and his cardigans blousejagged and his scarlet manchokuffs and his treecoloured camiflag and his perikopendolous gaelstorms ... Toadlebens! Some garmentguy! (339.9–13, 21–22).

Note the names of the general's English opponents, Lord Raglan and the Earl of Cardigan (leader of the Light Brigade), as well as those of his inept superior, Prince Menshikov, and the Malakoff fortification. (Perikopendolous refers to the Crimea, which is, as it were, pendulous from Perekop—Perekop being the medieval name of the land between the mouths of the Dnieper and Dniester.) A. W. Kinglake's description of the figure of General Todleben directing his forces will be recognized by every student of the numerous battlescenes of *Finnegans Wake*: "It was not at table or desk, but on that black charger of his which our people used to watch with their glasses that he mainly defended Sebastopol" (A. W. Kinglake, *The Invasion of the Crimea*, VIII, 218). Todleben's amazing defense of his position against odds (throwing up earthworks, etc., overnight) serves Joyce as a symbol of the dogged struggle for existence, while the name itself (*Todleben,* German: "Death-Life") suggests the god Māra-Kāma, "Death and Desire," the Hindu divine weaver of the illusion of the world—the world itself being the vortex of death and life.

Just when success seemed assured, Todleben was wounded by a ball in the calf of his right leg and compelled to retire from the field (Kinglake, p. 217), whereupon the victory passed to the besiegers. This event supplies Joyce with his persistent fate-probing question, "Who shot the Russian General?" which is a variant of the problem and theme of the Fall. Joyce describes the shot as fired while the great man was relieving himself in the latrine or afield (343.34–353.32), which permits an association with Earwicker's indescretion in the bushes (31), encounter with the cad in the park (35–36, 50–51), and arrest (62–73).

Joyce attributes the shot to a popular Anglo-Irish hero, Buckley, modeled apparently on a young British naval lieutenant Cecil Buckley, who is credited by Kinglake (pp. 67, 71, 74) with the leadership of a number of dangerous secret landing missions against the Russians; but since Buckley represents the same life force as the general (the "rising germinal!") he becomes confounded in *Finnegans Wake* with the man he shot (viz., 101).

The fact is, in so far as Todleben represents the life force that lives in all beings, he must be regarded as having shot himself through the instrumentality of that other; for "Even as a person casts off worn out garments and puts on others that are new, so the embodied Self casts off worn out bodies and enters into others that are new" (Bhagavad Gītā 2.22). The battlescenes of history can be regarded as events in the dressing room of an indestructible hero forever changing clothes: Joyce's Here Comes Everybody ("some garment guy!") in his Cardigan blouse, Raglan coat, and Menshikov scarlet cuffs. He is the life dwelling also in the toad—Toad-lebens. All living things both conceal and show him forth.

116 Compare C. G. Jung, *Modern Man in Search of a Soul* (New York, 1936), p. 215:

> If it were permissible to personify the unconscious, we might call it a collective human being combining the characteristics of both sexes, transcending youth and age, birth and death, and, from having at his command a human experience of one or two million years, almost immortal. If such a being existed, he would be exalted above all temporal change; the present would mean neither more nor less to him than any year in the one-hundredth century before Christ; he would be a dreamer of age-old dreams, and owing to his immeasurable experience, he would be an incomparable prognosticator. He would have lived countless times over the life of the individual, of the family, tribe, and people, and he would possess the living sense of the rhythm of growth, flowering and decay.

### CHAPTER V

117 [Joseph Campbell and Henry Morton Robinson in *The Saturday Review of Literature;* Part I: Vol. 25 (December 19, 1942), pp. 3–4; Part II: Vol. 26 (February 13, 1943), pp. 16–19.]

118 [The reference to "Sabrine asthore" in the *Wake* is not to Kate, the housekeeper of the Earwicker family, but to Anna Livia, the wife and mother of the family.]
119 Thornton Wilder, *The Skin of Our Teeth: A Play in Three Acts* (New York: Harper and Brothers, 1942), 142 pp.
120 [MRS. ANTROBUS: (*she flings something—invisible to us—far over the heads of the audience to the back of the auditorium.*) It's a bottle. And in the bottle's a letter. And in the letter is written all the things a woman knows. It's never been told to any man and it's never been told to any woman, and if it finds its destination, a new time will come. We're not what books and plays say we are. We're not in the movies and we're not on the radio. We're not what you're all told and what you think we are. We're ourselves. And if any man can find one of us he'll learn why the whole universe was set in motion. And if any man harm one of us, his soul—the only soul he's got—had better be at the bottom of that ocean—and that's the only way to put it.... (*The Skin of Our Teeth,* Act II.)]
121 [Gilbert A. Harrison, *The Enthusiast: A Life of Thornton Wilder* (New Haven/New York: Ticknor & Fields, 1983), pp. 231–232.]
122 [See Harrison, pp. 256–257, for the date of the London production.]
123 [Written at Durham Cottage, 4 Christchurch Street, Chelsea, London SW3, probably during January of 1948. From unpublished materials in the Thornton Wilder Collection, Beinecke Library, Yale University, Beinecke Uncat ZA Wilder Box 25.]
124 [Robert Van Gelder, "Interview with a Best-Selling Author: Thornton Wilder," *Cosmopolitan,* CXXIV (April, 1948), p. 120; quoted in Donald Haberman, *The Plays of Thornton Wilder: A Critical Study* (Middletown, Connecticut: Wesleyan University Press, 1967), p. 118.]
125 Harrison, p. 233.
126 [Thornton Wilder, *Three Plays* (New York: Harper, 1957); quoted in Malcolm Goldstein, *The Art of Thornton Wilder* (Lincoln, Nebraska: University of Nebraska Press, 1965), p. 129.]

## CHAPTER VI

127 [These dialogues are reproduced from discussions with the audience at a reading of Joyce by Campbell at the New York YMHA in 1956 entitled "Symbolism in *Finnegans Wake*" (L26), and from question-and-answer sessions during his seminar "James Joyce and Pablo Picasso: Mythology in 20th Century Literature and Art" (L820).]
128 [On the other hand, Aristotle's father was a physician, so the term may bear a primarily medical significance.]
129 [See Ellmann, *James Joyce,* pp. 422, 466, 467, 628–629, 659, 676–681.]
130 [Campbell made this remark in 1968. Schopenhauer's essay has since been translated. See Arthur Schopenhauer, *Parerga and Paralipomena: Short Philosophical Essays,* translated from the German by E. F. J. Payne. (Oxford: Clarendon Press, 1974), Vol. I, pp. 199–223.]

131  [In "*Parerga und Paralipomena: Kleine philosophische Schriften,*" Erster Band, in Arthur Schopenhauer's *Sämtliche Werke,* Vierter Band (Munich: R. Piper Verlag, 1913), pp. 223–250, especially pp. 242–248.]

132  [William Wordsworth, "Lines Composed a Few Miles above Tintern Abbey, on Revisiting the Banks of Wye during a Tour. July 13, 1789," lines 88–93.]

133  [*Versuch über das Geistersehn und was damit Zusammenhängt,* "Inquiry into Phantom Sightings and What Follows from Them," in *Parerga und Paralipomena,* op. cit., pp. 251–344.]

134  [Or "everything transient is just a metaphor."]

135  [After the *Wake* was published Joyce was weary, and the reception of the *Wake* sometimes annoyed him. At one point, he declared that he was now just resting:

> When [his friend Jacques Mercanton] alluded to the possibility of another project in a still distant future, he answered: "For the moment I am taking a rest. Now it is time for the others to do a bit of work."— See "The Living Joyce," in Willard Potts, editor, *Portraits of the Artist in Exile: Recollections of James Joyce by Europeans* (Seattle: University of Washington Press, 1979), p. 249.)

It is not clear whether the "others" were other writers, or critics at work interpreting the *Wake.*

However, there is some evidence that Joyce was at least considering another work. All the hints add up to suggestions that the work would be short, simple, about awakening, and about the sea. "When [his brother] Stanislaus rebuked him for writing an incomprehensible nightbook, James replied that there would be a sequel, an awakening" (see Ellmann, *James Joyce,* p. 603.) According to his friend Louis Gillet, in September 1939, Joyce was in Brittany accompanying Lucia for treatment at a clinic at La Baule:

> The rest of the day [after he had seen Lucia] wore away in walks on the beach. They reminded him of the time when on the seashore of Ireland, in the customs tower, he had spoken about matters of heaven and earth with his friends Haines and Mulligan, and where the waves had brought him the smile of Nausicaa. He remembered also the quays of Trieste and the sails on Ulysses' sea. Now his work was done. He was on vacation. But the waves roared as ever; another war had started, the Ocean continued beating the shore and chafing on its edges. Genesis pursued its course. And in his mind was rising the idea for a new poem whose fundamental theme would be the murmur of the sea. (See Potts, p. 203.)

For other accounts of Joyce's fascination with flowing water, see Potts, 279–280 and n., 289–290. For some other comments on what Joyce's post-*Wake* book would have been, see Ellmann, *James Joyce,* pp. 731, 740; see also E. L. Epstein, "James Augustine Aloysius Joyce," in Zack Bowen and James F. Carens, editors, *A Companion to Joyce Studies* (Westport, Connecticut/London: Greenwood Press, 1984), pp.34–36.]

# A JOSEPH CAMPBELL BIBLIOGRAPHY

*Following are the major books authored and edited by Joseph Campbell. Each entry gives bibliographic data concerning the first edition. For information concerning all other editions, please refer to the mediagraphy on the Joseph Campbell Foundation Web site (www.jcf.org).*

## AUTHOR

*Where the Two Came to Their Father: A Navaho War Ceremonial Given by Jeff King.* Bollingen Series I. With Maud Oakes and Jeff King. Richmond, Va.: Old Dominion Foundation, 1943.

*A Skeleton Key to Finnegans Wake.* With Henry Morton Robinson. New York: Harcourt, Brace & Co., 1944.

*The Hero with a Thousand Faces.* Bollingen Series XVII. New York: Pantheon Books, 1949.

*The Flight of the Wild Gander: Explorations in the Mythological Dimension.* New York: Viking Press, 1969.*

*The Masks of God,* 4 vols. New York: Viking Press, 1959–1968. Vol. 1, *Primitive Mythology,* 1959. Vol. 2, *Oriental Mythology,* 1962. Vol. 3, *Occidental Mythology,* 1964. Vol. 4, *Creative Mythology,* 1968.

*Myths to Live By.* New York: Viking Press, 1972.

*The Mythic Image.* Bollingen Series C. Princeton: Princeton University Press, 1974.

*The Inner Reaches of Outer Space: Metaphor As Myth and As Religion.* New York: Alfred van der Marck Editions, 1986.*

*The Historical Atlas of World Mythology:*

Vol. 1, *The Way of the Animal Powers.* New York: Alfred van der Marck Editions, 1983. Reprint in 2 pts. Part 1, *Mythologies of the Primitive Hunters and Gatherers.* New York: Alfred van der Marck Editions, 1988. Part 2, *Mythologies of the Great Hunt.* New York: Alfred van der Marck Editions, 1988.

Vol. 2, *The Way of the Seeded Earth,* 3 pts. Part 1, *The Sacrifice.* New York: Alfred van der Marck Editions, 1988. Part 2, *Mythologies of the Primitive Planters: The Northern Americas.* New York: Harper & Row Perennial Library, 1989. Part 3, *Mythologies of the Primitive Planters: The Middle and Southern Americas.* New York: Harper & Row Perennial Library, 1989.

*The Power of Myth with Bill Moyers.* With Bill Moyers. Ed. Betty Sue Flowers. New York: Doubleday, 1988.

*Transformations of Myth through Time.* New York: Harper & Row, 1990.

*The Hero's Journey: Joseph Campbell on His Life and Work.* Ed. Phil Cousineau. New York: Harper & Row, 1990.*

*Reflections on the Art of Living: A Joseph Campbell Companion.* Ed. Diane K. Osbon. New York: HarperCollins, 1991.

*Mythic Worlds, Modern Words: On the Art of James Joyce.* Ed. Edmund L. Epstein. New York: HarperCollins, 1993.

*Baksheesh & Brahman: Asian Journal—India.* Eds. Robin and Stephen Larsen and Antony Van Couvering. New York: HarperCollins, 1995.*

*The Mythic Dimension: Selected Essays 1959–1987.* Ed. Antony Van Couvering. New York: HarperCollins, 1997.

*Thou Art That.* Ed. Eugene Kennedy. Novato, Calif.: New World Library, 2001.*

*Sake & Satori: Asian Journals—Japan.* Ed. David Kudler. Novato, Calif.: New World Library, 2002.*

*Myths of Light: Eastern Metaphors of the Eternal.* Ed. David Kudler. Novato, Calif.: New World Library, 2003.*

---

* Published by New World Library as part of The Collected Works of Joseph Campbell.

## EDITOR

*Books Edited and Completed from the Posthuma of Heinrich Zimmer:*

*Myths and Symbols in Indian Art and Civilization.* Bollingen Series VI. New York: Pantheon, 1946.

*The King and the Corpse.* Bollingen Series XI. New York: Pantheon, 1948.

*Philosophies of India.* Bollingen Series XXVI. New York: Pantheon, 1951.

*The Art of Indian Asia.* Bollingen Series XXXIX, 2 vols. New York: Pantheon, 1955.

*The Portable Arabian Nights.* New York: Viking Press, 1951.

*Papers from the Eranos Yearbooks.* Bollingen Series XXX, 6 vols. Edited with R. F. C. Hull and Olga Froebe-Kapteyn, translated by Ralph Manheim. Princeton: Princeton University Press, 1954–1969.

*Myth, Dreams and Religion: Eleven Visions of Connection.* New York: E. P. Dutton, 1970.

*The Portable Jung.* By C. G. Jung. Translated by R. F. C. Hull. New York: Viking Press, 1971.

*My Life and Lives.* By Rato Khyongla Nawang Losang. New York: E. P. Dutton, 1977.

# INDEX

## A

"About the Theatre" (Mann), 294n. 11
abyss (biological force), 53; archetype lord
of the abyss, Mananaan MacLir-
Neptune (Poseidon)-Śiva, 151, 154, 195,
299n. 40; disintegration into, of opposites, to become one, 199; fulfillment
motif, 194; imagery of death and
sacrifice, 194
Adam and Eve: androgyny of Adam before
Eve, 204; church in Dublin, 203; expulsion from the Garden, 25; fall, 208, 214,
262 (*see also* fall); "in his own
image...male and female" (Genesis
1:27), 154; Pelagian heresy and Original
Sin, 42; sin of, 202; Tree of Knowledge,
Tree of Life, and, 25–26
Adrian IV, 224
AE (George William Russell), 141
Aelous, 53, 93
"Aeolus" (chapter), 93–95
affect images, 3–8; modern world and loss
of, 4; in *Portrait,* 27–28, 30, 193
Ajanta, cave of, 25

Amenti, 247, 248–49
Ananta, 196, 245
*Anatomy of Criticism* (Frye), 152
androgyny, 54–55, 144–45, 185, 204, 294n.
8, 301n. 57
animality motif, 78
anti-Semitism, 61–62
Aphrodite, 51
apotheosis, 8, 194
Aquinas, St. Thomas, 21–25, 295n. 14
archetypes: duads, 218; father/mother
(HCE/ALP) in *Finnegans Wake,* 195,
218, 237, 242; female, in *Ulysses,* 56, 190;
Joyce amalgamation of system, 195;
Joyce's unwritten book and, 290; male,
in *Finnegans Wake,* 190; opposites (mutually supplementary antagonisms), 195,
241–42, 251, 271, 311n. 110; transition
from the provincial to, 28. *See also*
*specific images*
Aristotle, 23, 67, 298n. 32; *catharsis,*
275–76, 315n. 128; pity and terror, 23,
275–76
Arius, 71
Armorica, 205

# G

## Q

## R

# Y

# Z

# ABOUT THE AUTHOR

JOSEPH CAMPBELL was an American author and teacher best known for his work in the field of comparative mythology. He was born in New York City in 1904, and from early childhood he became interested in mythology. He loved to read books about American Indian cultures, and frequently visited the American Museum of Natural History in New York, where he was fascinated by the museum's collection of totem poles. Campbell was educated at Columbia University, where he specialized in medieval literature and, after earning a master's degree, continued his studies at universities in Paris and Munich. While abroad he was influenced by the art of Pablo Picasso and Henri Matisse, the novels of James Joyce and Thomas Mann, and the psychological studies of Sigmund Freud and Carl Jung. These encounters led to Campbell's theory that all myths and epics are linked in the human psyche, and that they are cultural manifestations of the universal need to explain social, cosmological, and spiritual realities.

After a period in California, where he encountered John Steinbeck and the biologist Ed Ricketts, he taught at the Canterbury School, and then, in 1934, joined the literature department at Sarah Lawrence College, a post he retained for many years. During the 1940s and '50s, he helped Swami

Nikhilananda to translate the *Upanishads* and *The Gospel of Sri Ramakrishna.* He also edited works by the German scholar Heinrich Zimmer on Indian art, myths, and philosophy. In 1944, with Henry Morton Robinson, Campbell published *A Skeleton Key to Finnegans Wake.* His first original work, *The Hero with a Thousand Faces,* came out in 1949 and was immediately well received; in time, it became acclaimed as a classic. In this study of the "myth of the hero," Campbell asserted that there is a single pattern of heroic journey and that all cultures share this essential pattern in their various heroic myths. In his book he also outlined the basic conditions, stages, and results of the archetypal hero's journey.

Joseph Campbell died in 1987. In 1988, a series of television interviews with Bill Moyers, *The Power of Myth,* introduced Campbell's views to millions of people.

# ABOUT THE
# JOSEPH CAMPBELL FOUNDATION

THE JOSEPH CAMPBELL FOUNDATION (JCF) is a nonprofit corporation that continues the work of Joseph Campbell, exploring the fields of mythology and comparative religion. The Foundation is guided by three principal goals:

First, the Foundation preserves, protects, and perpetuates Campbell's pioneering work. This includes cataloging and archiving his works, developing new publications based on his works, directing the sale and distribution of his published works, protecting copyrights to his works, and increasing awareness of his works by making them available in digital formats on JCF's Web site.

Second, the Foundation promotes the study of mythology and comparative religion. This involves implementing and/or supporting diverse mythological education programs, supporting and/or sponsoring events designed to increase public awareness, donating Campbell's archived works (principally to the Joseph Campbell and Marija Gimbutas Archive and Library), and utilizing JCF's Web site as a forum for relevant cross-cultural dialogue.

Third, the Foundation helps individuals enrich their lives by participating in a series of programs, including our global, Internet-based Associates program, our local international network of Mythological Roundtables, and our periodic Joseph Campbell related events and activities.

For more information on Joseph Campbell
and the Joseph Campbell Foundation, contact:

JOSEPH CAMPBELL FOUNDATION
www.jcf.org
Post Office Box 36
San Anselmo, CA 94979-0036
Toll free: (800) 330-MYTH
E-mail: info@jcf.org

New World Library is dedicated to
publishing books and audio products
that inspire and challenge us to improve
the quality of our lives and our world.

Our products are available
in bookstores everywhere.
For our catalog, please contact:

New World Library
14 Pamaron Way
Novato, California 94949

Phone: (415) 884-2100 or (800) 972-6657
Catalog requests: Ext. 50
Orders: Ext. 52
Fax: (415) 884-2199

Email: escort@newworldlibrary.com
Website: www.newworldlibrary.com